The Handbook of
LEASING:

TECHNIQUES & ANALYSIS

Terry A. Isom
Sudhir P. Amembal

PBI
a petrocelli book
new york / princeton

Designed by Diane L. Backes
Typesetting by Backes Graphics

Printed in the United States of America
1 2 3 4 5 6 7 8 9 10

Library of Congress Cataloging in Publication Data

Isom, Terry A.
  The handbook of leasing.

  Bibliography: p.
  Includes index.
  1. Leases—United States. 2. Leases. I. Amembal, Sudhir P. II. Title.
KF946.I8   346.7304'346   81-23381
ISBN 0-89433-157-4   347.3064346   AACR2

The Handbook of
LEASING

FOR JANET AND VALERIE

*without whose moral support, patience, love, and
understanding this book could never have been written.*

Contents

Preface

During our years of teaching lease seminars and consulting throughout the United States and Europe, we have been able to isolate numerous problems that occur in the leasing industry which have not been adequately addressed in current texts on the subject of leasing. The few existing books on leasing tend to concentrate on either the Lease versus Buy decision, or on the legal aspects of structuring leases. The purpose of *HANDBOOK ON LEASING: Techniques and Analysis* is to provide a general overview of the many problems encountered in the leasing industry without undue concentration on one aspect of leasing. The book is evenly balanced between the needs of the lessor and those of the lessee.

Lessors or potential lessors are confronted with numerous problems such as:

1. *How to Compute Lease Yields.* Yield analysis is fully explained using both the advanced financial calculator and lease tables for leveraged and nonleveraged leases. Over twenty-three basic lease yields commonly used in the leasing industry are explained.
2. *Understanding of State of the Art Analytical Techniques.* Adjusted Internal Rate of Return, Modified Return on Equity, Adjusted Net Present Value, Standard Sinking Fund, and the Multiple Investment Methods are discussed in depth.
3. *Structuring Leases.* Twenty three major groups of lease-structuring variables are discussed in context of lessor requirements, lessee needs, and risk considerations. Risk assessment deals with the ten "C"s of lease creditworthiness.
4. *IRS Definition of a Lease.* Only under true IRS operating leases does the lessor receive the full tax benefits. Therefore, Revenue Ruling 55–540 and Revenue Procedure 75–21 along with an IRS Equipment Leasing Guide are examined so that the lessor may properly structure a lease to gain such tax benefits. Additionally, the new safe harbor IRS rulings affecting leasing are reviewed in depth, section 168(f)8.
5. *Management and Analysis of Leasing Companies.* Specialized financial statements are presented which are helpful in managing a lease company. Additionally, a fourteen–variable sensitivity model is described which pinpoints the critical variables that determine the profitability of a leasing company.

6. *Accounting for Capital Leases.* This subject is explained in depth using journal entries and "T" Accounts. Sales-Type, Direct Financing, and Leveraged Leases are individually analyzed in terms of their accounting and disclosure requirements.

7. *Legal Issues in Lease Transactions.* Nine areas of legal concern are examined to better inform lessors of their potential legal liability. The new federal bankruptcy act is discussed along with the Uniform Consumer Credit Code and other topics of interest to lessors. Additionally, a lease agreement is broken down into twenty-two topical areas and the legal implications of each is discussed.

8. *Income Tax Considerations.* Investment tax credit, depreciation (ACRs), and interest deductions are discussed from the lessor's viewpoint. Methods of enhancing lease yields through the proper use of these variables are discussed.

Lessees or potential lessees are also confronted with unique problems encountered in the leasing environment such as the following:

1. *The Effects of the Capital Lease on Financial Statements.* Capital lease accounting requirements, according to FASB statement Number 13, can adversely affect the financial statements and financial ratios of the lessee. The complete effect of the capital lease versus the operating lease is examined.

2. *Factors Influencing Leasing's Popularity.* Twenty major reasons on leasing's popularity as a form of equipment financing are discussed in depth.

3. *The Lease versus Buy Decision.* The seven essential steps of the Lease versus Buy decision are examined in depth. Most authors discuss only the first step—the financial decision—but the other six steps are the elements of the decision process that often make leasing preferable to buying. Liquidity preference, nonfinancial considerations and other steps are included in the process.

4. *Qualitative Reasons to Lease.* Thirty-six difficult to quantify, qualitative reasons why leasing might be preferable to buying are discussed.

5. *Accounting and Reporting for Leases.* How a lessee accounts for both operating and capital leases is explained along with disclosure requirements.

Throughout the book, problems confronting lessors are also discussed in terms of their impact on the lessee. For example, lease yields are generally considered a concern of the lessor—but what is an income yield to a lessor is also an interest expense to the lessee.

HANDBOOK ON LEASING: Techniques and Analysis is intended to be a reference source for both uninitiated and experienced leasing company personnel. Heavy emphasis is placed on understanding lease structuring and its impact on lease yields. Lease sales personnel will find the book an extremely useful reference when creating sales brochures and programs. In fact, much of the book's content was derived from in-house seminars delivered to banks and leasing companies' management and sales personnel.

In summary, the book provides the reader with a comprehensive understanding of the financial, accounting, structuring, and legal considerations required for the proper structuring of leases from both the lessee's and lessor's viewpoint.

Numerous legal, tax, and industry specialists were consulted during the preparation of HANDBOOK ON LEASING: Techniques and Analysis. The authors would like to express their appreciation to them and especially to Jonathan M. Ruga, MBA, CPA, J.D., who wrote the majority of Chapters 11, 12, and 13.

Terry A. Isom

Sudhir P. Amembal

1

Factors Influencing Leasing's Popularity in Today's Economy

In view of an estimated $160 billion dollars invested in leased equipment in the United States, businessmen must look to leasing during the 1980s as a viable alternative to the more conventional forms of equipment financing. Today the use of equipment from satellites to hospital beds is obtained through leasing. Modern management is becoming increasingly aware of the flexible options and advantages this emerging form of financing offers. Leasing companies have grown nationally from a handful of lessors twenty years ago to thousands of public, private, and bank subsidiary leasing companies today.

Although leasing has become extremely popular during the last two decades, it is certainly not a novel concept to the world of business. Leasing finds its origin in antiquity. Leasing of farmland and ships occurred in Phoenician times. In medieval times, real estate was leased to feudal tenants who paid their rent with commodities grown on the land their masters owned. However, the leasing of factory machinery, office equipment. machine tools, railroad cars, and computers is a relatively new concept in leasing. An industrial equipment leasing boom began in the mid 1950s and experienced its most rapid growth in the 1960s, when leasing expanded into nine major areas:

1. *Aircraft*—jets and allied service equipment
2. *Autos*—for personal and business use
3. *Computers*—including central processing units and peripheral equipment
4. *Furnishings*—for hotels, motels, and office buildings
5. *Industrial Machinery and Equipment*—including machine tools and heavy equipment used in construction, mining, and oil exploration
6. *Medical Equipment*—leased primarily to hospitals and medical clinics

7. *Office Equipment*—including typewriters, calculators and copying equipment
8. *Railroad Cars*—flat cars, hoppers, and refrigerated cars
9. *Trucks*—frequently including complete truck maintenance and other services

Insight into the numerous and complex factors that have led to an expansion of leasing into these previously unexploited areas is essential to an understanding of leasing. Understanding the underlying causes of leasing's popularity will better prepare lessees in negotiating and structuring leases. Then, too, lessors can predict profitable new opportunities within the industry through an improved awareness of past trends.

The popularity of leasing is primarily the result of the following factors:

1. PSYCHOLOGY OF USE PREFERENCE OVER OWNERSHIP
2. OBSOLESCENCE HEDGE
3. AFFORDABILITY TO LESSEES
4. ADDITIONAL SOURCE OF DEBT FINANCING CAUSED BY THE DRYING UP OF CONVENTIONAL CAPITAL FINANCING SOURCES: STOCKS AND BONDS, AND COMMERCIAL BANK LOANS
5. INFLATION HEDGE
6. TAX ADVANTAGES TO LESSORS AND LESSEES
7. LACK OF TAX ADVANTAGES & BUDGET RESTRAINTS OF NON-PROFIT ORGANIZATIONS
8. INDIVIDUAL TAX SHELTERS
9. DIVERSIFICATION OF FINANCING SOURCES
10. RISK-TAKING LESSORS
11. RESTRICTED OWNERSHIP
12. CONSERVATION OF WORKING CAPITAL
13. VERTICAL, HORIZONTAL, AND CONGLOMERATE INTEGRATION
14. LOWER AFTER-TAX PRESENT VALUE OF COSTS
15. OFF-BALANCE SHEET FINANCING
16. ECONOMIES OF SCALE IN LESSOR PURCHASING AND SERVICING
17. PROFITABLE EXPERIENCE OF THE LEASING INDUSTRY
18. INTERNATIONAL LEASING TO MULTINATIONAL AND FOREIGN BUSINESS
19. CONVENIENCE TO THE LESSEE
20. FLEXIBILITY IN LEASE STRUCTURING
21. NONFINANCIAL SERVICES

ANALYSIS OF CAUSAL FACTORS

Psychology of Use Preference Over Ownership

Enlightened businessmen realize that the use of a piece of equipment is far more important to the production of income than a piece of paper conveying title to the equipment. It is the use of equipment that produces profit, not ownership. In fact, if equipment can be used for most of its economic life without its user having the full legal responsibilities, risk, and burdens of ownership, then why should that user ever desire to own it? Even farmers, who may have traditionally valued land ownership, now readily acknowledge that the USE of land is more important than the OWNERSHIP of it. Numerous farmers and ranchers lease tracts of land in order to increase production of cattle or crops. Psychologically, however, many people are unwilling to separate the concept of asset use from asset ownership. We have spoken to owners of businesses in developing countries where we have heard the remark, "I don't want to lease because there is no prestige or recognition without ownership of the equipment." Success, to many people, is still measured by ownership rather than by use of assets. Until a nation is psychologically prepared for the self-assumed loss of prestige and success that purportedly occurs when an asset's use is obtained with a lease rather than with conventional ownership methods, leasing will not gain in popularity as rapidly as it has in countries where a change in emphasis of USE over OWNERSHIP has occurred.

A similar change in emphasis has occurred in the accounting field. Until World War II, the accounting profession tended to judge a company's success by its balance sheet—what it OWNED. Net worth was the all-important yardstick. As companies continued into the post-war expansionary period, they financed much of their growth with borrowed funds. The lenders of these funds were more interested in having their interest paid when due than in the net worth of the company. Net worth has value only in bankruptcy liquidation which is a more remote occurrence than lack of profit or liquidity problems. Thus, a shift in accounting emphasis occurred in which the income statement came into prominence. The income statement measures the results of the USE of what is owned. It is from the cash results of net income that interest to creditors is paid. The balance sheet, therefore, began to take a secondary position. For example, the LIFO inventory method better matches inflationary rises in costs with inflated revenue shown on the income statement. But this method is detrimental to the balance sheet which carries inventory at costs far below market prices. Consequently, LIFO balance sheets understate costs in order to make the income statement more accurate. Thus, measuring the results of the USE of assets on the income statement has become more important than measuring the OWNERSHIP of assets on the balance sheet.

Since many leases are a form of off-balance sheet financing (certain operating leases do not appear on the face of the balance sheet), a company's return on assets appears higher than if the lease were capitalized as an asset and corresponding liability. Such improvement in return on investment is apparent because net income is divided by a smaller asset base. Since operating results are frequently judged by return on assets, leasing an asset without obtaining ownership or the resultant capitalization and inclusion in the balance sheet is helpful to many lessees.

Obsolescence Hedge

Another reason why emphasis of USE over OWNERSHIP has occurred is because of the penalties attached to the ownership of certain equipment, such as computers, which have been developed by rapidly growing, high-technology industries. Some computers have become obsolete between the order date and the delivery date. Who wants to own an outmoded piece of equipment? Short-term, cancelable leases permit firms to avoid the pitfalls of owning obsolete equipment. If a piece of equipment is outdated, the lessee cancels the lease and orders updated equipment. Usually, however, leases are only cancelable after a short noncancelable period such as six months to one year.

A new lease type known as the "upgrade lease" has recently been developed where automatic replacement of obsolete equipment is written into the lease agreement. These leases are usually provided by lessors who manufacture the leased equipment and are in a position to provide updated models to their lessees. As long as technological advances continue in certain industries, the short-term cancelable lease and the upgrade lease will be a popular means of hedging against economic and physical obsolescence.

Affordability to Lessees

The preferable use of assets obtained through LEASING compared to use obtained through OWNERSHIP is further enhanced by inflation. Inflationary price increases have priced certain assets virtually beyond ownership possibilities. Much farm and ranchland could never be profitably utilized if the farmer had to purchase the land at today's prices. This explains why many tracts of land are leased today. Land is becoming prohibitively expensive. Certain types of medical equipment are also extremely costly. Doctors in medical clinics often enter into joint venture leases. These leases allow them the use of expensive equipment well beyond the purchase capability of an individual member of the group. New home starts are constantly being overshadowed by multiple-unit starts (apartments) which will be leased—few can now afford homes or condominiums. By the 1990s few young couples will be able to afford a new home. Leasing will be their only alternative. The same trend, of course, is pervading the equipment industry. As equipment is priced beyond a company's purchasing ability, no alternatives remain but to lease.

Additional Source of Debt Financing Caused by the Drying Up of Conventional Capital Financing Sources: Stocks and Bonds, and Commercial Bank Loans

Adding to the rapid growth in the volume of leasing since the 1960s have been continued capital needs for business expansion and modernization combined with a limited availability of capital funds from the usual channels of equity stock issued and bond financing. Fewer stock and bond issues during the 1970s resulted in a shortage of new investment capital for many small- and intermediate-sized firms. Many economic factors led to the drying up of conventional capital financing sources. Notable among them are: (1) the use of loanable funds for government spending and consumer credit and (2) shifting of equity investors away from the stock market to higher yielding investments in the money market, real estate, etc.

The net result of this dearth of conventional capital forced many companies to seek installment loans from banks for equipment financing. Yet banks had been suffering from their own capital shortages during the same period and could not totally or effectively solve the problem. In order to sell their products, many manufacturing companies turned to leasing to make their equipment available to needy clients who otherwise could not obtain the use of the equipment. Thus, leasing's popularity was enhanced by necessity stemming from numerous underlying economic factors and by providing an additional source of debt not otherwise available.

Inflation Hedge

When compared to conventional equipment financing with its large down payments, short-term payouts, and de-emphasis of residual values (balloon payments), leasing offered a hedge against inflation. The longer terms, lower down payments, and emphasis of residual value at the end of the contract generally available in leases allow the lessee to pay future lease payments with inflated dollars. The lessor can obtain protection from inflation by borrowing long-term and passing this protection to the lessee in the form of equal lease payments over a long term. Generally speaking, it is always better to borrow long in a period of inflation assuming one's revenue sources are also expected to inflate correspondingly. Leasing, of course, is an effective way of borrowing long.

Tax Advantages to Lessors and Lessees

With the advent of accelerated depreciation in the 1950s and investment tax credit in the 1960s, leasing's popularity was given an additional boost. The lessor-owners of equipment could now obtain, as a result of these changes in the Internal Revenue Code, meaningful tax savings which enhanced their lease yields. So significant were the savings that lessors could pass on to lessees part of the savings in the form of lower lease payments. Note that the traditional bank loan offers no additional tax savings to the lender. However, restructuring a loan in the form of a lease might provide the lender tax savings that, in part, could lower the lease payment below the corresponding bank loan payment (assuming the loan and lease interest yields are comparable with similar payback periods).

In addition to the tax savings derived from accelerated depreciation and the investment tax credit, tax benefits are obtained from the use of financial leverage. In a leveraged lease the owner-lessor of the equipment provides ten to forty percent of the necessary capital to acquire the equipment, whereas the remainder of the capital is borrowed on a nonrecourse basis from institutional creditors. The nonrecourse loan is secured by an assignment of the lease payments, an assignment of the lease, and a collateral lien on the equipment itself. The advantage to the lessor in the leveraged lease is that all tax benefits incidental to ownership of the equipment pass through to the lessor even though the lessor's equity interest is only ten to forty percent in the lease. This "financial leverage" creates greater than proportionate tax savings to the lessor. For example, an investment tax credit of ten percent received in the first year of a lease represents a fifty percent return of investment in the case where the lessor has only a twenty percent equity involvement in the leveraged lease (ten percent is fifty percent of twenty percent equity investment).

It should be noted that according to current tax law the investment tax credit may, under certain conditions, be passed on to the lessee. Moreover, there are other direct tax benefits that a lessee might obtain. For example, under a properly structured sale—leaseback of improved real estate—the lessee can virtually depreciate the land portion of the real estate (normally nondepreciable) and depreciate the new fair market value of the building which has increased due to the sale. Of course, capital gains taxes must be paid by the seller-lessee if his basis in the property was low prior to the sale. Nevertheless, the depreciation benefits implicit in each lease payment are frequently worth entering into the sale-leaseback arrangement. Note that the lessee does not actually depreciate the real estate, it is just that the new lease payment is the fully tax deductible equivalent of depreciation on the land and improvements thereon. Note too, that another motive for sale-leaseback arrangements is to minimize the risk of ownership of real estate that might become obsolete for the lessee's purposes. For example, Safeway leases back stores so that where grocery sales are insufficient it can move to a new location without the risk and burden of leasing or selling the unproductive facility.

The Economic Recovery Tax Act of 1981 also increased the tax advantages of leasing by more clearly defining what a lease is from an IRS viewpoint thus facilitating lease structuring. Furthermore, the new tax act permits the selling of tax benefits through the mechanism of a "wash lease" designed to allow a lessor to purchase Investment Tax Credit and Accelerated Depreciation from a lessee-user of the equipment.

Lack of Tax Advantages and Budget Restraints of Nonprofit Organizations

Equipment leasing will continue to be increasingly used by nonprofit organizations such as hospitals and state and local governments which are confronted with budget limitations and cannot take advantage of tax benefits on equipment purchases.

To acquire equipment through purchasing, many state and local governments are required to have special capital appropriations made by their legislatures or decision-making bodies. These capital appropriations are generally made once a year, thus prohibiting mid-year acquisition of equipment required for unanticipated needs or emergencies. In these cases leasing can solve the problem. Lease payments can be paid out of operating budgets rather than the already depleted capital acquisition budget. Operating expenses generally require only days or weeks for approval as compared to the annual capital appropriations approval.

Since tax advantages are not available to nonprofit organizations, these benefits can be retained by the lessor and partially passed on to the nonprofit company in the form of reduced lease rental payments. Also, properly structured leases to certain government agencies result in the implicit interest in the leases becoming tax-exempt like interest on municipal bonds. Giving the interest tax-exempt status is required since the lessor must be compensated for his loss of the Investment Tax Credit which is not available to lessors leasing to certain governmental units.

Individual Tax Shelters

The fact that an individual can operate a leasing company as a sole proprietor and receive personally all the tax benefits from it has given an additional impetus to the popularity of leasing. In effect, tax losses derived from interest and depreciation deductions, investment tax credits, and energy credits can pass through to an individual. This offsets his other income which results in fewer taxes being paid.

It should be noted that recent tax reform acts have attempted to limit lease tax shelters; however, with proper structuring, such tax shelters are still available.

Some syndications of lease tax shelters allow individuals to become part owner-lessors in large leveraged lease transactions. In effect, the owner-lessors are general partners or limited partners with other partnership members who have provided the capital for the lessor, ten percent equity portion of the leveraged lease. These and other innovative means of involving individuals have stimulated the leasing business by making more capital available to lessees.

Diversification of Financing Sources

Recent drying-up of bank funds due to the 1980 credit crunch has made many businesses acutely aware of the dangers of depending solely upon banks as sources of equipment financing. Diversification of equipment financing sources makes good business sense whether credit is in short supply or not. It is important to note that federally chartered banks have, by regulatory law, built-in limits on the availability of loanable funds.

For example, national banks have legal lending limits—currently no more than ten percent of their legal capital can be lent to any single customer. Also, a 1979 ruling by the comptroller of the currency has forced banks to treat leases exactly like commercial loans for purposes of determining legal lending limits for a particular customer. So, banks that provide leasing, in addition to conventional bank loan financing, have inherent lending limitations which promote diversification on the part of the lessee-borrower.

Risk-Taking Lessors

When compared to the relatively risk-averse banking community, leasing companies appear to be risk-takers. The reason for this different viewpoint about risk is partly traditional and partly the nature of the market. Traditionally, banks look more to the general credit worthiness of the person requesting the loan than to the equipment itself as collateral, whereas two party leasing companies and specializing third party lessors look mostly to the equipment as collateral. Hence, a leasing company would be more likely to lease to a newly-formed company lacking a financial track record or to a company in financial trouble. The nature of the leasing market emphasizes equipment's collateral value since many leasing companies specialize in leasing only certain types of equipment. Such specialization gives them access to and understanding of resale markets. Being able to resell quickly repossessed equipment minimizes the risk to the lessor and allows him to depend more upon the equipment value than upon the general credit of the lessee.

Traditionally, the first leasing companies were two-party, lessor-manufacturers who employed leasing to expand sales. These lessors also knew resale values and markets for the equipment they had produced and were acquainted with equipment marketing techniques. Therefore, leasing was a natural extension of the manufacturers' normal business.

Perhaps banks should not serve the higher risk niche of the economy anyway since banks are guardians of public funds. Fortunately, however, for economically disadvantaged firms there are leasing companies that serve this high risk niche within the economy. Recent inflationary price increases have somewhat vindicated leasing companies' heavy dependence upon equipment for residual value since many types of used equipment have become quite valuable lately, especially heavy equipment like jets, railroad cars, etc. A strong resale market for equipment removes much of the risk from leases that depend heavily on unguaranteed residuals for their overall yields.

Restricted Ownership

In certain situations ownership is not available to the user of land or equipment. Leasing in this situation represents the only available means of obtaining use of the land or equipment. This occurs when ownership has been restricted, for example, when the government owns land but still intends private citizens to use it. Large tracts of Forest Service and Bureau of Land Management lands are leased to private individuals for sheep- and cattle-raising, mining, and oil exploration purposes. Although most cases of restricted ownership have applied to land, there are situations emerging where the government owns certain machinery or equipment and will not sell it, but will lease it. Communication satellites and other forms of high cost, extremely sophisticated scientific equipment are frequently leased to private users. To the degree that land and other types of equipment are developed which require governmental control or where the nature of the equipment is such that it cannot be sold (certain telephone equipment), leasing will continue to grow in popularity.

Conservation of Working Capital

As a general rule leasing companies require lower down payments than other financial institutions. For example, the typical lease requires the first and last rental payments paid in advance (representing two to four percent down) whereas many banks require a ten to twenty percent down payment. Then, too, other incidental costs of acquiring the asset such as sales tax and installation charges can be included as part of the lease payment rather than being paid in advance in addition to a large down payment. Obviously, in this credit-tight economy, not tying up cash in large down payments and other incidental costs allows a company to employ cash savings for other more profitable working capital requirements. Frequently, the opportunity cost of tying up cash in equipment acquisitions almost necessitates leasing as an alternative, especially for rapidly growing companies whose available cash is invested in highly profitable inventory and receivables.

Vertical, Horizontal, and Conglomerate Integration

Integration refers to ways in which a company can expand operations. *Vertical integration* refers to acquisition of the means of producing a product from the raw material sources, through production and transportation to the final wholesale and retail outlets. *Horizontal integration* refers to expansion into the sales and production of related products (like wax production for an oil company). *Conglomerate integration* is where a company enters into a wholly unrelated business venture.

Manufacturing firms use leasing as an additional way to sell goods. These leases are known as sales-type capital leases. Sales proceeds include not only lease interest but gross profit on sales which normally would have been recognized under an outright sale. Sales-type leases are becoming widespread among manufacturers as they learn from third-party leasing companies who have already proven their utility and profitability. Thus, establishing a captive lease company to further promote sales is an important step in vertically integrating one's company. An additional advantage of such integration is that the leasing company can better serve the client due to its extensive knowledge of the product. For example, knowledge of the product permits the lessor to predict with greater accuracy residual values which remove some risk from leasing. The better the estimate of residual value, the lower the lease payment charged the lessee. Also, control over residuals allows the lessor-manufacturer to sell new equipment at the termination of the lease to a somewhat captive clientele.

Many captive lease companies find leasing so profitable that they begin leasing equipment other than that manufactured by the parent company. This expansion into new, unrelated product leasing is a form of *horizontal integration* that is becoming popular among manufacturer-lessors.

Some companies enter into the lease business as a totally unrelated business opportunity compared to their normal operations. Totally new business ventures involved with leasing would represent a form of *conglomerate integration.* An airline acquiring a lease company would be an example of conglomerate integration. However, a bank acquiring a leasing company would be a form of horizontal integration since the leasing service is closely related to the bank's loan service.

Thus, the natural path of expansion from a vertically integrated manufacturing company beginning to lease others' products (horizontal integration) to other companies conglomerately acquiring lease companies as new investment opportunities has led to an increase in leasing's popularity.

After-Tax Present-Value of Costs

In terms of total after-tax present value of costs, leasing may provide a lower cost to the lessee than conventional financing. However, it is important to note that this situation only occurs when the lessee is in a high income tax bracket coupled with a high cost of capital. Additionally, the lease term must generally be in excess of that provided by conventional financing. As previously explained, leasing companies will frequently offer longer terms than those available at banks. The combination of a high cost-of-capital discount rate which exceeds the cost of debt, a high income tax bracket providing the maximum tax benefits and a long lease term will frequently result in a lease having a lower after-tax cost. Note, however, that use of a high discount rate, such as cost of capital, is subject to some controversy. This will be explained in more depth in chapter seven. On the other hand, when a lessee is in a low tax bracket or cannot use tax benefits at all due to a loss carryforward, then a lower cost lease might also be available if the lease company retains all the tax benefits and will also pass some of these savings on to the lessee.

Another situation which frequently results in lower after-tax present value of costs is where the lessee acquires an asset under a short-term, full-payout lease that still qualifies as a true lease under IRS rulings. In this case, most of the cost of the equipment has been paid in tax-deductible lease payments over a shorter period of time than that required to depreciate the asset under an outright purchase financed conventionally. Thus, the tax benefits accrue to the lessee over a shorter period of time than the purchase alternative, which lowers the present value of leasing costs. It is quite difficult, however, to find a short-term full-payout lease that qualifies as a true lease from an IRS point of view. This characteristic will be explained in chapter two. A full-payout lease has cash returns to the lessor that are sufficient to cover the asset's cost, overhead, debt service, and reasonable rate of return without dependence upon any residual salvage value or purchase option. In other words, it is closely akin to a conditional sales contract.

To determine properly whether a lease will cost less than an outright purchase of equipment, a formal analysis should be made. The techniques used in the Lease versus Buy decision are the subjects of chapters seven and eight.

Off-Balance Sheet Financing

Leases structured as operating leases in accordance with the requirements of FASB statement No. 13 do not appear on the balance sheet of the lessee and therefore improve the company's ostensible appearance of being liquid, profitable, and solvent. This "off-balance sheet" effect of an operating lease is the subject of chapter three. Capital leases however do appear on the lessee's balance sheet and should not be confused with operating leases. The difference between these two types of leases is the subject of chapter two.

Economies of Scale in Lessor Purchasing and Servicing

Certain lease companies, due to their large size, can generate savings in the form of quantity discounts received from volume purchasing. Such savings might be partially passed on to the lessee. Additional savings from economies of scale might be obtained through the "full service lease" where the cost of maintaining the leased equipment is included as part of each rental payment. In this case, if the leasing company is proficient in maintaining equipment because of its large size, then savings can be passed on to the lessee. However, it does not always follow that large size and efficiency go hand-in-hand. Therefore, savings must be ascertained by comparison with lease rates charged by competing companies.

As previously mentioned, large leasing companies have access to secondary markets in which returned equipment may be resold. Rapid disposal and high resale value on returned equipment permit a higher reliance on residual value. Such reliance permits the lessor to charge a lower lease payment to the lessee. Though large scale operations do not guarantee savings to lessees, at least they present the possibility of savings. With proper negotiation, the lessee should be able to receive some of the savings of economies of scale in cases where the lessor is receiving such efficiency benefits.

Profitable Experience of the Leasing Industry

What greater motive underlying the proliferation of leasing could there be than years of profitable experience? Leasing is not a dying industry; it is a growing industry, its impetus maintained by earnings sufficient to justify any risks assumed by its members. "The rapid growth of the equipment leasing industry since the mid-1960s is evidence that leasing is a viable business method of acquiring new equipment. Future industry prospects are promising both in the United States and overseas. As the nation's economic recovery accelerates, rising corporate earnings will provide additional income to finance lease transactions. The value of new equipment on lease (at original cost) is expected to increase about twelve to fifteen percent annually for several years, reflecting a steadily growing acceptance of the leasing concept as a workable, financial tool."[1] The American Association of Equipment Lessors (AAEL), with headquarters in Arlington, Virginia,[2] has grown from a handful of members fifteen years ago to over 730 lessor members in 1980, which attests to the profitable

---

[1]*Equipment Leasing & Rental Industries: Trends and Prospects,* U.S. Department of Commerce, December 1976, Document No. 0003-008-00175-1, U.S. Government Printing Office, Page 16.

[2]Full address: 1700 North Moore Street, 19th floor, Arlington, VA 22209. Phone number: (703) 527-8655.

experience of its members. Also, the Western and Eastern Associations of Equipment Lessors have many local members.

International Leasing to Multinational and Foreign Businesses

Overseas leasing is expected to expand significantly in order to serve large multinational companies abroad as well as foreign companies who are also seeking new forms of asset financing. "Although equipment leasing abroad by U.S. companies only started in the late 1960s, equipment on lease (at original cost) in Western Europe and Great Britain was estimated at $30 billion by 1975. One of the reasons for the growing popularity of leasing as a form of financing new equipment abroad is that European banks generally offer loans for about three years and equipment buyers are therefore required to negotiate two or three loans during the life of a particular piece of equipment. About seventy-five American leasing companies—independent companies, members of joint ventures, and leasing subsidiaries of American banks— are engaged in leasing activity abroad. In addition, there are about 200 European companies in the leasing business, many belonging to the Leaseurope Trade Association. Leasing companies offer three types of financing to European clients—true leases, conditional-sale agreements, and secured loans and chattel mortgages for larger equipment purchases.

As in the United States, all types of equipment are being leased abroad—tankers, railroad cars, computers, machine tools, printing presses, restaurant equipment, mining equipment, and oil-drilling rigs. In contrast to the equipment leasing industry in this country, leveraged leases are not used internationally. Since foreign tax laws differ from U.S. tax laws, international leases do not offer the benefits of depreciation or the possibility of residual value.

While a large portion of overseas equipment leasing serves multinational companies abroad, the bulk of leasing activity for independent companies consists of 'cross-border financing'—where financing is provided in one country and the leased equipment is used in another. These types of lease transactions across international borders are generally not true leases, but conditional sales contracts since the contracts provide for the purchase of equipment at lease termination.[3]

Despite restrictive foreign government regulations concerning percent local ownership requirements, varying tax laws, foreign exchange fluctuations, and export laws, many equipment-leasing companies are still interested in expanding leasing markets abroad. The same reasons that led to an expansion of leasing in this country have also stimulated leasing abroad. For example, many U.S. based multinationals use leasing to promote foreign sales. Thus, international markets have created another factor leading to the popularity of leasing. An interesting stimulus to international leasing

---

[3]ibid, pages 7 and 8.

is the advantage to a foreign firm of using equipment through a lease and thereby avoiding import tariffs which can be as high as twenty percent of the asset's cost. There are numerous tax, import, and investment tax credit benefits available to the experienced international lessor.

Convenience To The Lessee

Although leasing is losing some of its time-saving convenience due to encroaching red tape it nevertheless offers many advantages over conventional forms of financing. Generally, acquiring the use of an asset through a lease involves less red tape and time than is required for conventional financing where it must be proved that 'you are rich enough not to need the equipment loan in the first place.'

Additional convenience and cost savings are obtained with operating leases. These require much less bookkeeping than outright purchases.Purchased assets must be capitalized and depreciated. Loan payments must be separated into principal and interest—all of this requires time and effort.

Cash flow projections are made easy since most leases have fixed equal periodic payments. Commercial loan financing of equipment requires payments that fluctuate with the prime rate. Financing equipment with internal funds is also subject to the vagaries of changing costs of capital.

Prior to equipment purchasing, most firms require a rigorous capital budgeting analysis. At the same time, these companies do not require the same lengthy analysis for leasing a piece of equipment. Government agencies frequently can acquire assets through leasing rather than waiting for time-consuming appropriations for purchases.

The fact that equipment can be obtained without undergoing lengthy capital budgeting procedures should not be a factor influencing leasing's popularity. When a company signs a lease contract it becomes more encumbered legally than if it had acquired the asset under a bank installment loan. Upon default under a lease, all remaining lease payments can be sued for, including principal and unearned interest. A bank under default can only collect the principal balance of the loan. It seems a mistake for any company not to perform the same capital budgeting analysis for a lease as it would for an outright purchase. If capital budgeting procedures take too long, financial analysts should be required to speed up the decision-making process rather than to lease simply because it is more expedient!

Flexibility In Lease Structuring

Leases are quite flexible in meeting the various needs of lessees. A brief description of several unique types of leases best illustrates the flexibility of leasing:

   a. *Swap Lease*—allows the lessee to exchange equipment in need of major repair with properly working replacement equipment to avoid costly maintenance and repair delays. Conventional equipment financiers seldom allow such replacements due to the legal complexities involved in exchanging collateral.

   b. *Upgrade Lease*—automatic exchange during the lease of outmoded equipment with newer model upgraded equipment, generally made available by manufacturer-lessors.

   c. *Master Lease*—a blanket lease covering numerous articles of equipment that arrive over a period of time. This avoids expensive duplication of leasing documents.

   d. *Joint Venture Leases*—several lessees join together to lease an otherwise prohibitively expensive piece of equipment. This technique is seldom allowed by banks who prefer one or two primary borrowers to assume full responsibility.

   e. *Skipped Payment Leases*—in the situation where equipment might remain idle during a portion of a company's fiscal year due to adverse weather conditions, a lease can be designed to omit payments during this period each year.

   f. *Trial Period Leases*—certain leases provide trial use periods of up to six months. During this time the lessee decides whether the machinery will accomplish the required task, and more importantly, generate revenue. This removes a good deal of the speculative risk from the lessee's acquisition of an asset.

   g. *Variable Term Lease with Constant Payments*—this lease allows a lessor to be compensated for changes in underlying costs of debt. When cost of debt goes up, the lease term is increased in order to compensate the lessor for underlying costs of capital. Lengthening the lease term is preferable to increasing the monthly payment to the lessee. Increased payment leases have become popular recently as leasing companies started employing "floating payment" or "variable payment" leases to pass on to the lessee the lessor's increased debt cost.

In addition to the above-mentioned flexible lease provisions, leases seldom contain many of the restrictive covenants found in loan agreements. For example, some loan restrictions prohibit future financing of equipment until the loan is paid down significantly. Leasing allows additional expansion without the burden of restrictions. In general, due to the lack of government restrictions, lease companies are in a better position to adapt to the needs of the lessee.

Nonfinancial Services

Nonfinancial services such as those offered under electronic data-processing and computer-operating leases often include the right to add core memory units or other peripheral equipment and services of data processing experts (programmers and systems analysts) to assist in solving application problems. Often the existence of such nonfinancial services makes leasing extremely attractive from the point of view of convenience and efficiency, even though the costs of such services are implicit in the lease payments.

COMPOSITION OF THE LEASING INDUSTRY

The leasing industry is composed of five basic types of lessors which are listed below with their approximate share of the leasing market in terms of leasing companies.

1. *Two-Party*, Vendor-Lessors or Manufacturer Lessors   50%
    a. Captive leasing companies of manufacturing firms.
    b. Dealer or retail-outlet-owned leasing companies.

2. *Three-Party*, Private and Public Corporations   25%
    a. Direct financing type of net leases.
    b. Service type leases for specialized lessors.

3. *Three-Party*, Financial Institutions   20%
    a. Bank divisions or captive leasing companies.
    b. Finance and industrial loan companies.
    c. Miscellaneous insurance companies and investment bankers.

4. *Three-Party*, Individual Tax Shelters   5%
5. *Four-Party*, Lease Brokers   NA

        100%

The largest component of the leasing industry is represented by two-party vendor-lessors or manufacturer-lessors. These leasing firms are generally captive leasing subsidiaries or divisions of manufacturing firms that employ leasing as a means of promoting sales. Also, many dealers or franchised retail outlets own leasing companies which serve to facilitate product sales. The two parties involved in the lease are described below:

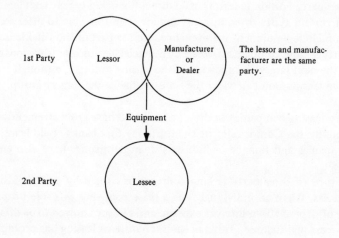

Two-Party leasing companies offer either operating leases or capital leases, entitled Sales-type Capital Leases, which will be described in chapter two.

Three-Party, Private and Public Corporate Lessors form the next largest component of the leasing industry. Most three-party leasing corporations are privately owned, although there are several large publicly owned leasing companies, such as United States Leasing International, Inc. (USLI). This company is the largest independent corporate third-party lessor in the United States, with more than $2 billion outstanding in equipment leases. Third-party leasing companies take their name from the fact that three parties are involved in the lease: the lessor, the lessee, and the manufacturer of the equipment, as shown below:

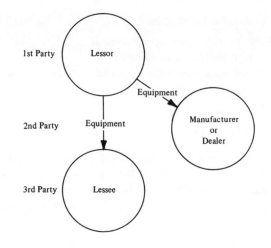

Most three-party corporate lessors offer direct financing-types of net leases. Others specialize in certain types of equipment and are therefore able to offer service-type leases which include equipment maintenance, etc., as part of the total lease package.

Three-party leasing companies owned by financial institutions (divisions or subsidiaries) form the next largest component of the leasing industry, although from a dollar-invested-in-leasing point of view they are probably the largest group within the industry.

Subsidiary leasing companies or divisions of banks have grown tremendously since a 1963 ruling by the Comptroller of the Currency that banks could lease. Some insurance companies and finance or industrial loan companies have also entered the leasing market.

Another type of three-party leasing company is owned by an individual for tax shelter purposes. When an individual runs a lease company as a sole proprietor the tax benefits of depreciation, interest expense and ITC are allowed to be offset against the owner's personal income. This tax shelter nature of leasing has prompted many individuals to establish their own leasing companies or to invest in large, leveraged leases as partners with others acting as joint-venturing lessors.

The last group of lessors are the Lease Brokers who are not actually lessors but finders of lessors, and who bring together all the parties necessary in a lease transaction. These quasi-lessors actually form four-party transactions, described below:

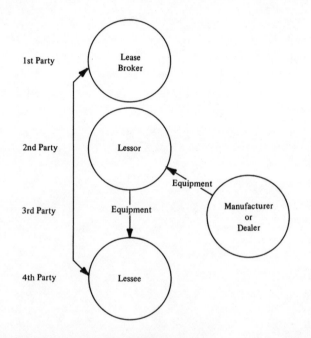

Although lease brokers seldom actually take part in a lease once all parties have been brought together and the lease structured, there are occasions where the broker joint ventures the lease with the lessor in lieu of receiving a brokerage commission.

Although the leasing industry is almost certain to continue growing in the future, its exact nature and composition are difficult to predict. Recent all time highs in the prime rate will have a definite effect on the leasing industry. Especially affected will be third-party leasing companies that depended upon banks as their source of leasable funds.

2

Types of Leases: Accounting, IRS, and ——— Industry Viewpoints ———

What is a lease? What is the difference between an operating lease and a capital lease? The answers to these basic questions can be given from an economic, legal, SEC, accounting, financial, IRS, or industry point of view. Which is right? The answer depends upon the needs of the person asking the question. For the sake of this chapter we will rely heavily upon the accounting definitions given by the Financial Accounting Standards Board (FASB), since the Board governs the accounting practices of virtually all public corporations. Then too, reliance will be placed upon IRS terminology and classification since taxes are such a crucial element in any decision concerning leases.

Almost twenty percent of all FASB statements and interpretations promulgated by the Financial Accounting Standards Board have been on the subject of leasing. The Securities and Exchange Commission (SEC) adopted on September 7, 1977, the FASB Lease Accounting Requirements for all public companies which must report annually to the SEC. Following is a list of the FASB statement, interpretations, and technical bulletins that relate to leasing as of January 1, 1982.

1) FASB Statements: (8)

   FASB 13, Accounting For Leases
   FASB 17, Initial Direct Costs
   FASB 22, Leases and Tax Exempt Debt
   FASB 23, Inception of the Lease
   FASB 26, Profit Recognition on Sales-Type Leases of Real Estate
   FASB 27, Classifications of Renewals or Extensions

FASB 28, Accounting for Sales with Leasebacks
FASB 29, Determining Contingent Rentals

2) FASB Interpretations: (6)

FASB INT 19, Lessee Guarantee of Residual Value
FASB INT 21, Leases in Business Combinations
FASB INT 23, Leases of Government Property
FASB INT 24, Leases on Part of a Building
FASB INT 26, Purchase of Leased Asset by Lessee
FASB INT 27, Loss on a Sublease

3) FASB Technical Bulletins: (9)

No. 79-10, Fiscal Funding Clauses
No. 79-11, Effect of a penalty on the term of a lease
No. 79-12, Interest Rate used in Calculating Present Values
No. 79-13, Current Value Financial Statements
No. 79-14, Upward Adjustment of Guaranteed Residual Values
No. 79-15, Sublease losses
No. 79-16, Income Tax Rate Changes and leveraged lease Accounting
No. 79-17, Cumulative Effect Adjustments
No. 79-18, Transition Requirements

In general, a lease is viewed as a contract between a lessor (owner of an asset) and a lessee (user of an asset) where the lessor grants the temporary possession and use of an asset to the lessee, usually for a specified period less than the asset's economic life at a fixed periodic charge (rental charge). However, even though a contract labeled as a "Lease" might contain these characteristics it will not necessarily be considered a lease from an accounting or IRS point of view. To understand why this situation might occur, it is necessary to understand the accounting and IRS criteria that distinguish true leases from installment sales contracts or other forms of pseudo-leases.

FASB ACCOUNTING DEFINITION OF A LEASE

The Financial Accounting Standards Board in its Statement Number 13 on Accounting for Leases divides all leases into two basic groups. A lease is either a capital lease or an operating lease. A *capital lease* is not really considered a true lease at all—but rather a SALE of equipment from the lessor's viewpoint and as a PURCHASE to the lessee. An *operating lease* is a true lease from both the lessor's and lessee's viewpoint.

Capital leases from the lessor's viewpoint can be further subdivided into three types of leases as described on the following page (defined later in the chapter).

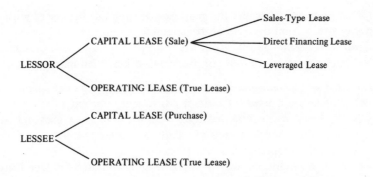

According to *FASB statement No. 13:* If at its *inception* a lease meets one or more of the following four criteria, the lease shall be classified as a capital lease by the *LESSEE*. Otherwise, it shall be classified as an operating lease.

1. The lease transfers ownership of the property to the lessee by the end of the *lease term.*
2. The lease contains a *bargain purchase option.*
3. The lease term is equal to seventy-five percent or more of the *estimated economic life* of the leased property.
4. The present value at the beginning of the lease term of the minimum lease payments, equals or exceeds ninety percent of the *fair market value* (FMV) of the property to be reduced by any investment tax credit retained by the lessor and expected to be realized by him prior to determining the ninety percent base.

    a. The lessor's discount rate shall be the *implicit rate* in the lease.

    b. The lessee's discount rate shall be his *incremental borrowing rate* unless he can determine the implicit rate in the lease and that rate is lower.[1]

Criteria three and four are ignored when the beginning of the lease term is within the remaining twenty-five percent of an asset's economic life. This situation occurs when used assets are leased during the last twenty-five percent of their economic lives.

Based on these accounting criteria, a lessee will account for leased equipment as though he had purchased it when any one of four events occurs:

1. *Actual ownership* will be obtained outright during the lease term.
2. *Potential Actual ownership* will be available through the exercising of a bargain purchase option.

---

[1] The capital lease criteria are an excerpt from paragraph 7, statement of Financial Accounting Standards Board, High Ridge Park, Stanford, Connecticut, 06905, USA.

3. *Effective ownership* occurs through use—wearing out the asset by using it for seventy-five percent or more of its economic life.
4. *Effective ownership* results from the price paid for use when present value of cost is ninety percent or more of property's original fair market value.

Thus, a lessee will be considered as having purchased equipment when he *owns* it, has *potential ownership, wears* it out, or *pays* ninety percent of its worth. When property is purchased it is capitalized; i.e., recorded both as an asset and an obligation. Hence, leases that are in effect, purchases are called "capital leases" since the acquired asset must be capitalized.

If none of these criteria are met then the lease is considered a true lease and is referred to as an OPERATING LEASE.

From the standpoint of the LESSOR, if at inception a lease meets any one of the preceding four criteria and in addition meet both of the following criteria, it shall be classified as a *sales-type capital lease* or a *direct financing capital lease,* whichever is appropriate. Otherwise, it shall be classified as an operating lease.

a. *Collectibility of the minimum lease payments* is reasonably predictable. A lessor shall not be precluded from classifying a lease as a sales-type lease or as a direct financing lease simply because the receivable is subject to an estimate of uncollectibility based on experience with groups of similar receivables.
b. *No important uncertainties* surround the amount of unreimbursable costs yet to be incurred by the lessor under the lease. Important uncertainties might include commitments by the lessor to guarantee performance of the leased property in a manner more extensive than the typical product warranty or to effectively protect the lessee from obsolescence of the leased property.

The preceding accounting criteria include certain italicized leasing terms that have specific accounting definitions and interpretations. For the sake of clarity and full understanding of the lease classification criteria the lease terms and other important terms are defined below:[2]

Inception of the Lease—the date of the lease agreement or commitment, if earlier. For purposes of this definition, a commitment shall be in writing, signed by the interested parties and shall specifically set forth the principal provisions of the transaction. If any of the principal provisions are yet to be negotiated, such a preliminary agreement or commitment does not qualify for purposes of this definition. (As amended, effective December 1, 1978 by *FASB Statement No. 23.*)

---

[2]Copyright© by Financial Accounting Standards Board, High Ridge Park, Stamford, Connecticut, 06905, U.S.A. Reprinted with permission. Copies of the complete document are available from the FASB. Most definitions are found in paragraph 5, statement of Financial Accounting Standards No. 13, Accounting for Leases, as amended by subsequent statements and interpretations. Parentheses added by authors.

"If the property covered by the lease is yet to be constructed or has not been acquired by the lessor at the inception of the lease, the *lessor* classification criterion concerning no important uncertainties mentioned above shall be applied at the date that construction of the property is completed or the property is acquired by the lessor."[3]

"If the lease agreement or commitment, if earlier, includes a provision to escalate minimum lease payments for increases in construction or acquisition cost of the leased property or for increases in some other measure of cost or value, such as general price levels, during the construction or pre-acquisition period, the effect of any increases that have occurred shall be considered in the determination of 'fair value of the leased property at the inception of the lease' for purposes of capitalizing leased equipment and in the determination of 'the estimated residual value of the leased property at the inception of the lease' for purposes of this paragraph."[4]

Fair Market Value of the Leased Property. The price for which the property could be sold in an arm's-length transaction between unrelated parties. The following are examples of the determination of fair value:

a. When the lessor is a manufacturer or dealer, the fair market value of the property at the inception of the lease will ordinarily be its normal selling price, reflecting any volume or trade discounts that may be applicable. However, the determination of fair value shall be made in light of market conditions prevailing at the time, which may indicate that the fair value of the property is less than the normal selling price and, in some instances, less than the cost of the property.

b. When the lessor is not a manufacturer or dealer, the fair market value of the property at the *inception of the lease* will ordinarily be its cost, reflecting any volume or trade discounts that may be applicable. However, when there has been a significant lapse of time between the acquisition of the property by the lessor and the *inception of the lease*, the determination of fair value shall be made in light of market conditions prevailing at the *inception of the lease*, which may indicate that the fair value of the property is greater or less than its cost or carrying amount.

Bargain purchase option. A provision allowing the lessee, at his option, to purchase the leased property for a price which is sufficiently lower than the expected *fair value* of the property at the date the option becomes exercisable that exercise of the option appears, at the *inception of the lease*, to be reasonably assured.

Bargain renewal option. A provision allowing the lessee, at his option , to renew the lease for a rental sufficiently lower than the fair rental of the property at the date

---

[3]*FASB Statement Number 23,* inception of the lease, Paragraph 7
[4]IBID, Paragraph 8

the option becomes exercisable that exercise of the option appears, at the *inception of the lease,* to be reasonably assured. "Fair rental" in this context shall mean the expected rental for equivalent property under similar terms and conditions.

Lease term. The fixed noncancelable term of the lease plus (i) all periods, if any, covered by *bargain renewal options* (as defined in definition 4.); (ii) all periods, if any, for which failure to renew the lease imposes a penalty on the lessee in an amount such that renewal appears, *at the inception of the lease,* to be reasonably assured; . . . (iii) all periods, if any, covered by ordinary renewal options during which a guarantee by the lessee of the lessor's debt related to the leased property is expected to be in effect; (iv) all periods, if any, covered by ordinary renewal options preceding the date as of which a *bargain purchase option* (as defined in definition 3) is exercisable; and (v) all periods, if any, representing *renewals or extensions* of the lease at the lessor's option; however, in no case shall the lease term extend beyond the date a *bargain purchase option becomes* exercisable. A lease which is cancelable (i) only upon the occurrence of some remote contingency; (ii) only with the permission of the lessor; (iii) only if the lessee enters into a new lease with the same lessor; or (iv) only upon payment by the lessee of a penalty in an amount such that continuation of the lease appears, at *inception, reasonably assured* shall be considered "noncancelable" for purposes of this definition.

To summarize, a lease term includes any of the following items:

(1) The fixed noncancelable term.
(2) Bargain renewal option periods.
(3) Nonrenewal penalty that reasonably assures extension.
(4) Ordinary renewal periods preceding a bargain purchase option.
(5) Lessor forced renewal (put options).
(6) Ordinary renewal periods during which the lessee co-guarantees the lessor's debt.

Estimated Economic Life of Leased Property. The estimated remaining period during which the property is expected to be economically usable by one or more users, with normal repairs and maintenance, for the purpose for which it was intended at the *inception of the lease,* without limitation by the lease term.

Estimated Residual Value of Lease Property. The estimated *fair value of the leased property* at the end of the lease term (as defined above).

Unfortunately, the term "residual value" has numerous meanings. It is frequently used in reference to any one of about *thirty three* occurrences at the termination of a lease. The following flow chart describes how the term "residual value," without any qualifying language can become extremely vague and ambiguous. Each item on the flow chart represents a residual value inuring to the benefit of the lessor at the end of the lease.

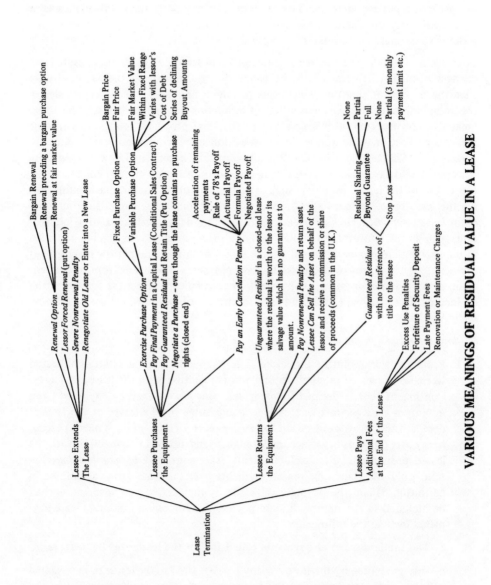

VARIOUS MEANINGS OF RESIDUAL VALUE IN A LEASE

Lease Termination

Lessee Extends The Lease
- *Renewal Option*
  - Bargain Renewal
  - Renewal preceding a bargain purchase option
  - Renewal at fair market value
- *Lessor Forced Renewal* (put option)
- *Severe Nonrenewal Penalty*
- *Renegotiate Old Lease* or Enter into a New Lease

Lessee Purchases the Equipment
- *Exercise Purchase Option*
  - Fixed Purchase Option
    - Bargain Price
    - Fair Price
  - Variable Purchase Option
    - Fair Market Value
    - Within Fixed Range
    - Varies with lessor's Cost of Debt
    - Series of declining Buyout Amounts
- *Pay Final Payment* in a Capital Lease (Conditional Sales Contract)
- *Pay Guaranteed Residual* and Retain Title (Put Option)
- *Negotiate a Purchase* – even though the lease contains no purchase rights (closed end)

Lessee Returns the Equipment
- *Pay an Early Cancelation Penalty*
  - Acceleration of remaining payments
  - **Rule of 78's Payoff**
  - **Actuarial Payoff**
  - **Formula Payoff**
  - **Negotiated Payoff**
- *Unguaranteed Residual* in a closed-end lease where the residual is worth to the lessor its salvage value which has no guarantee as to amount.
- *Pay Nonrenewal Penalty* and return asset
- *Lessee Can Sell the Asset* on behalf of the lessor and receive a commission or share of proceeds (common in the U.K.)
- *Guaranteed Residual* with no transference of title to the lessee
  - Residual Sharing
  - Beyond Guarantee
    - None
    - Partial
    - Full
  - Stop Loss
    - None
    - Partial (3 monthly payment limit etc.)

Lessee Pays Additional Fees at the End of the Lease
- Excess Use Penalties
- Forfeiture of Security Deposit
- Late Payment Fees
- Renovation or Maintenance Charges

Unguaranteed Residual Value. The *estimated residual value of the leased property* exclusive of a portion guaranteed by the lessee, by any party related to the lessee or by a third party unrelated to the lessor. If the guarantor is *related* to the lessor, the residual value shall be considered as unguaranteed.

Contingent Rentals. The increases or decreases in lease payments that result from changes occurring subsequent to the *inception of the lease* in the factors (other than the passage of time) on which lease payments are based, except as provided in the following sentence. Any escalation of *minimum lease payments* relating to increases in construction, acquisition cost of the lease property, or increases in some measure of cost or value during the construction or preconstruction period, as discussed in *FASB Statement No. 23* "Inception of the Lease," shall be excluded from contingent rentals. Lease payments that depend on a factor directly related to the future use of the leased property, such as machine hours of use or sales volume during the lease term, are contingent rentals and, accordingly, are excluded from *minimum lease payments.* However, lease payments that depend on an existing index or rate, such as the consumer price index or the prime interest rate, shall be included in *minimum lease payments* based on the index or rate existing at the *inception of the lease;* any increases or decreases in lease payments that result from subsequent changes in the index or rate are contingent rentals and thus affect the determination of income as accruable. (As amended, effective October 1, 1979, by *FASB Statement No. 29*)

Minimum Lease Payments.

1. From the standpoint of the lessee: The payments that the lessee is obligated to make or can be required to make in connection with the leased property. Contingent rentals defined in paragraph nine above shall be excluded from minimum lease payments. However, a guarantee by the lessee of the lessor's debt and the lessee's obligation to pay (apart from the rental payments) *executory costs* (such as insurance, maintenance, and taxes) in connection with the leased property shall be excluded. If the lease contains a *bargain purchase option,* only the minimum rental payments over the lease term (as defined in definition 5) and the payment called for by the *bargain purchase option* shall be included in the minimum lease payments. Otherwise, minimum lease payments include the following:

    a. The minimum rental payments called for by the lease over the *lease term.*

    b. Any guarantee by the lessee or any party *related* to the lessee of the residual value at the expiration of the *lease term,* whether or not payment of the guarantee constitutes a purchase of the leased property. When the lessor has the right to require the lessee to purchase the property at termination of the lease for a certain or determinable amount, that amount shall be considered a lessee guarantee. When the lessee agrees to make up any deficiency below a stated amount in the lessor's realization of the residual value, the guarantee to be included in the minimum lease payments shall be the stated amount, rather than an estimate of the deficiency to be made up.

i.   A guarantee of the residual value obtained by the lessee from an *unrelated* third party for the benefit of the lessor shall not be used to reduce the amount of the lessee's minimum lease payments except to the extent that the lessor explicitly releases the lessee from obligation, including secondary obligation if the guarantor defaults, to make up a residual value deficiency. Amounts paid in consideration for a guarantee by an *unrelated* third party are *executory costs* and are not included in the lessee's minimum lease payments.

ii. A lease provision requiring the lessee to make up a residual value deficiency that is attributable to damage, extraordinary wear and tear, or excessive usage is similar to a *contingent rental* in that the amount is not determinable at the *inception of the lease*. Such a provision does not constitute a lessee guarantee of the residual value.

iii. If a lease limits the amount of the lessee's obligation to make up a residual value deficiency in an amount less than the stipulated residual value of the leased property at the end of the *lease term*, the amount of the lessee's guarantee to be included in minimum lease payments shall be limited to the specified maximum deficiency the lessee can be required to make up. The "stated amount" is the specified maximum deficiency that the lessee is obligated to make up. If that maximum deficiency clearly exceeds any reasonable estimate of a deficiency that might be expected to arise in normal circumstances, the lessor's risk associated with the portion of the residual in excess of the maximum may appear to be negligible. However, the fact remains that the lessor must look to the resale market or elsewhere rather than to the lessee to recover the unguaranteed portion of the stipulated residual value of the leased property. The lessee has not guaranteed full recovery of the residual value, and the parties should not base their accounting on the assumption that the lessee has guaranteed it.

c.   Any payment that the lessee must make or can be required to make upon failure to renew or extend the lease at the expiration of the *lease term*, whether or not the payment would constitute a purchase of the leased property. In this connection, it should be noted that the definition of *lease term* includes "all periods, if any, for which failure to renew the lease imposes a penalty on the lessee in an amount such that renewal appears, at the *inception of the lease,* to be reasonably assured." If the *lease term* has been extended because of that provision, the related penalty shall not be included in minimum lease payments.

2. From the standpoint of the lessor: The payments described in (i) above plus any guarantee of the residual value or of rental payments beyond the *lease term* by a third party *unrelated* to either the lessee or the lessor, provided the third

party is financially capable of discharging the obligations that may arise from the guarantee. If the guarantor is *related* to the lessor, the residual value shall be considered as unguaranteed.

To summarize, minimum lease payments include any of the following items:

1. Basic lease rental payments due during the lease term. Executory costs and contingent rentals are excluded.
2. Bargain renewal rental payments.
3. Ordinary renewal rental payments preceding a bargain purchase option.
4. Guaranteed residual value by the lessee or lessee related party (whether or not title passes to lessee).

   a. Lessor Viewpoint – total value of the guaranteed residual.

   b. Lessee Viewpoint – total maximum deficiency required to be paid by the lessee which might be less than the full guarantee due to a stop-loss provision in the lease. Furthermore, a guarantee by an unrelated third party would reduce the lessee's guarantee if so permitted by the lessor.

5. Guaranteed residual value by unrelated third party guarantors – included only from the lessor's viewpoint unless the lessee remains co-liable. If the guarantor is related to the lessor or not financially strong then the residual value is considered to be unguaranteed.
6. Nonrenewal penalties that are insufficiently severe to cause renewal.

Interest Rate Implicit in the Lease. The discount rate that, when applied to (i) the *minimum lease payments* (as defined above), excluding that portion of the payments representing *executory costs* to be paid by the lessor, together with any profit thereon, and (ii) the *unguaranteed residual value* (as defined above) accruing to the benefit of the lessor, causes the aggregate present value at the beginning of the *lease term* to be equal to the *fair value of the leased property* (as defined in definition 2) to the lessor at the *inception of the lease,* minus any investment tax credit retained by the lessor and expected to be realized by him . . .

If the lessor is not entitled to any of the amount realized on disposition of the property over a guaranteed amount, no unguaranteed residual value would accrue to his benefit.

In the case of a direct financing lease, initial direct costs as defined below, should be added to the fair value of the leased property prior to computing the implicit interest rate in the lease. Furthermore, it should be understood that the implicit rate in a lease is simply a pre-tax internal rate of return yield whose use in economic or financial analysis is limited due to several defects in its calculation as explained in chapter 4.

Lessee's Incremental Borrowing Rate. The rate that, at the *inception of the lease,* the lessee would have incurred to borrow over a similar term the funds necessary to purchase the leased asset.

Initial Direct Costs. Those costs incurred by the lessor that are directly associated with negotiating and consummating completed leasing transactions. Costs include, but are not necessarily limited to commissions, legal fees, credit investigations, and preparing and processing documents for newly acquired leases. In addition, that portion of salespersons' compensation, other than commissions, and the compensation of other employees that is applicable to the time spent in the activities described above with respect to completed leasing transactions shall also be included in initial direct costs. The portion of salespersons' compensation and the compensation of other employees that is applicable to the time spent in negotiating leases that are not consummated shall not be included in initial direct costs. No portion of supervisory and administrative expenses or other indirect expenses such as rent and facilities costs, shall be included in initial direct costs. (As amended, effective for leasing transactions and lease agreement revisions entered into on or after January 1, 1978 by *FASB Statement No. 17.*)

Sales-type Capital Leases. Leases that give rise to manufacturer's or dealer's profit (or loss) to the lessor (i.e., the *fair value of the leased property* at the *inception of the lease* is greater or less than its cost or carrying amount if different) and that meet one or more of the . . . [capital lease] . . . criteria for lessees and both of the criteria . . . [for lessors] . . . Normally, sales-type leases will arise when manufacturers or dealers use leasing as a means of marketing their products. Leases involving lessors that are primarily engaged in financing operations normally will not be sales-type leases if they qualify under the lessor capital lease criteria, but will most often be direct financing leases, described below. However, a lessor need not be a dealer to realize dealer's profit (or loss) on a transaction, e.g., if a lessor, not a dealer, leases an asset that at the *inception of the lease* has a *fair value* that is greater or less than its cost or carrying amount, such a transaction is a sales-type lease, assuming the criteria referred to are met. *A renewal or extension* of an existing sales-type or direct financing lease that otherwise qualifies as a sales-type lease shall be classified as a direct financing lease unless the renewal or extension occurs at or near the end of the original term specified in the existing lease, in which case it shall be classified as a sales-type lease. (As amended effective September 1, 1979, by *FASB Statement No. 27.*)

Direct Financing Leases. Leases other than leveraged leases that do not give rise to manufacturer's or dealer's profit (or loss) to the lessor but that meet one or more of the [lessee capital lease] criteria . . . and both of the criteria [for a lessor capital lease] . In such leases, the cost or carrying amount, if different, and *fair value of the leased property* are the same at the *inception of the lease.* An exception arises when the *(renewal or extension)* of a sales-type or direct financing lease occurs during the term of the existing lease. In such cases, the fact that the carrying amount of the property at the end of the original lease term is different from its fair value at the date shall not preclude the classification of the renewal or extension as a direct financing lease. (As amended, effective September 1, 1979, *FASB Statement No. 27.*)

Leveraged Leases. A leveraged lease is defined as one having *all* of the following characteristics:

1. Except for the exclusion of leveraged leases from the definition of a direct financing lease as set forth above it otherwise meets that definition. Leases that meet the definition of sales-type leases set forth above shall not be accounted for as leveraged leases but shall be accounted for as... [sales-type capital leases].
2. It involves at least three parties: a lessee, a long-term creditor, and a lessor (commonly called the equity participant).
3. The financing provided by the long-term creditor is nonrecourse as to the general credit of the lessor (although the creditor may have recourse to the specific property leased and the unremitted rentals relating to it). The amount of the financing is sufficient to provide the lessor with substantial "leverage" in the transaction. (10 percent equity with 90 percent debt under the new tax act).
4. The lessor's net investment, as defined in ... [definition 17 below] declines during the early years once the investment has been completed and rises during the later years of the lease before its final elimination. Such decreases and increases in the net investment balance may occur more than once.
5. The investment tax credit must be deferred and taken into income over the life of the lease; otherwise, the lease must be considered a direct financing lease and not a leveraged lease.[5]

Leveraged Lease Net Investment. The lessor shall record his investment in a leveraged lease net of the nonrecourse debt. The net of the balances of the following accounts shall represent the initial and continuing investment in leveraged leases:

1. Rentals receivable, net of that portion of the rental applicable to principal and interest on the nonrecourse debt.
2. A receivable for the amount of the investment tax credit to be realized on the transaction.
3. The *estimated residual value* of the leased asset. The estimated residual value shall not exceed the amount estimated at the inception of the lease.
4. Unearned and deferred income consisting of (i) the estimated pretax lease income (or loss), after deducting initial direct costs, remaining to be allocated to income over the lease term and (ii) the investment tax credit remaining to be allocated to income over the lease term.[6]

---

[5]IBID, Paragraph 42
[6]IBID, Paragraph 43

IRS DEFINITION OF A LEASE

The Internal Revenue Service (IRS) also is concerned whether a lease is a CAPITAL LEASE (conditional sales contract or other form of a sale) or an OPERATING LEASE (true lease). In the case of the capital lease the IRS permits the lessee to obtain the tax benefits of investment tax credit, accelerated depreciation, and interest included in the lease payments. On the other hand, in the case of an operating lease, the IRS allows the lessor rather than the lessee to retain the investment tax credit and accelerated depreciation (the ITC, however, may be passed to the lessee at the lessor's option). Moreover, with an operating lease the lessee may not claim a separate interest deduction for interest contained in each lease payment since the total lease payment is already fully tax deductible to the lessee. Therefore, it is essential to know whether a lease is CAPITAL or OPERATING in order to ascertain who will receive the tax benefits—the lessee or the lessor.

Recently, Congress passed the "1981 Economic Recovery Tax Act" in which a lease has been defined for tax purposes. Such a definition has been overdue since prior to the new law there was little information available from the IRS which clearly defined a lease.

The new tax law establishes a "safe harbor" election which virtually guarantees the lessor and lessee that their lease agreement will be considered an operating lease from a tax viewpoint if the "safe harbor" requirements are met.

To be within the confines of the "safe harbor" the following conditions must be met according to section 168(f) 8 of the IRS code:

1. CORPORATION STATUS

   The lessor must be a corporation, Sub-Chapter S-Corporations and personal holding corporations do not qualify for "safe harbor" status. However, partnerships, all the partners of which are corporations, do qualify along with grantor trusts wherein the grantor and beneficiaries are corporations. Therefore, individuals, regular general partnerships (with noncorporate members), limited partnerships, sole-proprietors, sub-chapter S corporations, personal holding companies, and regular grantor trusts cannot avail themselves of the new "safe harbor" lease requirements. These nonqualifying entities will still be affected by the old ambiguous lease definitions promulgated by the IRS. Also, certain closely held corporations (Code Section 465) have limits on tax benefits obtainable under leveraged leases containing nonrecourse debt.

2. MINIMUM "AT RISK" INVESTMENT

   At the time the leased property is first placed in service and at all other times during the lease term, the lessor must maintain a minimum "at risk" investment of at least ten percent of the cost (adjusted basis) of such property. Recourse debt incurred by the lessor is considered part of the "at risk" minimum investment as long as such debt is not also provided or co-signed by the lessee or any party related to the lessee. The lessors minimum investment *will not* be affected by any fixed purchase options (whether at a bargain or fair market value) or guaranteed residuals (put options) that have been structured into the lease.

3. LEASE TERM

The maximum term of the lease including any extensions does not exceed the greater of:

a. Ninety percent of the useful life of such property according to Section 167 of the IRS code (Facts and Circumstances life as established by the past history of the leasing company).

b. One hundred fifty percent of the ADR class life midpoint of the property as determined by the January 1, 1981 asset depreciation range (ADR) guidelines published by the IRS. The minimum term of the lease must be at least equal to the new ACRS depreciation life, code section 168(c)2, which will be three years or five for most leased equipment.

4. QUALIFIED LEASE PROPERTY

The "safe harbor" rule applies only to certain types of property which conform to the following rules:

a. Must have been placed in service after January 1, 1981.

b. Must be "recovery property" which is property eligible for the new ACRS (Accelerated Cost Recovery System explained in chapter 13).

c. New Section 38 property in the hands of the lessor which generally means any property that qualifies for the Investment Tax Credit. There are additional rules making the "safe harbor" extend to transactions already completed prior to the enactment of the new law which will not be explained here since they will not be applicable after November 13, 1981. These qualifing transactions must have been entered into between January 1, 1981 and August 13, 1981 to qualify for conversion into qualifying leases. Certain qualifying mass commuting vehicles also are considered as qualified lease property.

5. CHARACTERIZATION BY PARTIES

Both the lessor and the lessee must agree in a provision of the lease document that the contract agreement is to be characterized as a lease for purposes of the IRS tax treatment. This implies that the lessor will be designated the owner of the equipment which automatically entitles the lessor to the tax benefits of accelerated cost recovery, interest, and investment tax credit. Note, however, the investment tax credit may still be passed on to the lessee.

6. ELECTION TO HAVE "SAFE HARBOR" REQUIREMENTS APPLY
TO THE TRANSACTION

The agreement must be in writing and must state that all parties to the agreement elect to have the provisions of the safe harbor (Section 168(f)8 of the IRS code) apply to the transaction. The lessor and lessee must also file an IRS information return concerning the safe harbor lease. This return is explained in Appendix A at the end of the book which includes the new leasing regulations.

It is important to note that the Economic Recovery Tax Act of 1981 (P.L. 97-34) clearly indicates that if the "safe harbor" rules stated above are met then no other factors will be taken into account by the IRS in determining whether the lease is truly a lease rather than a conditional sales contract. Futhermore, "an agreement between the lessor and lessee requiring either or both parties to purchase (put option or guaranteed residual) or sell (call option) the qualified leased property at some price (whether or not fixed in the agreement) at the end of the lease term shall not affect the amount the lessor is treated as having at risk with respect to the property. Thus, inclusion of any of the following items in a lease will not alter its IRS classification as an operating lease:

1. Bargain purchase option (call option at less than the leased asset's expected future fair market value).
2. Fixed purchase options whether at a bargain or not, or for a nominal sum or not.
3. Fair market value purchase options.
4. Guaranteed residual where title may pass to the lessee (put option).
5. Guaranteed residual where title is not allowed to pass to the lessee which may contain residual proceeds sharing with the lessee or residual stop loss agreements.
6. Bargain renewal options as long as the extended lease term is still within the "safe harbor" time limit.
7. Lessee provided or co-guaranteed financing exclusive of the lessor's required ten percent at risk minimum investment.
8. Limited use property that can only be used by the lessee at the termination of the lease.

The impact of the new tax legislation on the leasing industry is expected to be significant. Companies unable to use their tax benefits due to prior operating losses are now able to exchange these tax benefits with lessors who will reciprocate by offering the lessee lower lease payments. Such exchanging of tax benefits has been facilitated by the new tax law. The more liberal lease definition guarantees both lessor and lessee that the lease agreement will be considered a lease for purposes of allowing the lessor to avail himself of the new accelerated depreciation (ACRS) and the increased investment tax credit which is now ten percent for ACRS five year depreciation life property (heretofor such five year life property would have qualified only for a 6.67 percent ITC).

Although, the new legislation will affect the majority of lease transactions entered into after January 1, 1981 there still remains a significant number of leases whose tax status will not be affected. These nonconforming leases will be defined according to the somewhat ambiguous guidelines established by various IRS sources. Most lease classifications made by the IRS, tax attorneys, and certified public accountants have been primarily based upon five sources: (1) Revenue Rulings, (2) Revenue Procedures, (3) Tax Court Cases, (4) Technical Advice Memoranda (TAMS), and (5) IRS Audit Guides.

It is important to keep in mind that these five sources of information only affect a lease wherein:

1. The lessor is an individual.
2. The lessor is a noncorporate partner of a general or limited partnership.
3. The lessor is a noncorporate grantor or beneficiary of a grantor trust.
4. The lessor is a corporate personal holding company.
5. The leased equipment is "used or old equipment."
6. The leased equipment is not considered Section 38 property since it does not qualify for the investment tax credit such as certain permanent attachments to real-estate (fixtures). Refer to chapter 13 for a more in depth description of Section 38 property.
7. The lease term violates the "safe harbor" requirements. Or there are other violations of the safe harbor rules.
8. The lease is a sale-leaseback of pre-1981 property.

From the five sources of tax information, I have selected the more important references which are listed below:

1. *Revenue Ruling 55-540,* Cumulative Bulletin 39, 1955-2.
2. *Revenue Procedure 75-21,* Cumulative Bulletin 715, 1976-1.
3. *Northwest Acceptance Corporation, Landmark Case,* 58 T.C. No. 80, 1972. Tried in Portland, Oregon, Docket No. 4846-70: and other similar court cases.
4. *Revenue Procedure 76-30,* Cumulative Bulletin 75). 1975-1.
5. Technical Advice Memoranda, (TAM) April 26, 1978, December 20, 1979, and February 15, 1980.
6. IRS Audit Guide Manual on Equipment Leasing and Equipment Leasing Tax Shelters, 8-7-1979.

REVENUE RULING 55-540

This ruling appeared in 1955 and cautioned users of the ruling that the intent of the lessor and lessee "read in the light of the facts and circumstances existing at the time the agreement was executed" would determine whether the agreement was a lease or a conditional sales contract. "No general rule, applicable to all cases can be established. However, it would appear, that in the absence of compelling persuasive arguments to the contrary, a sale and purchase rather than a lease may exist if any one or more of the following conditions exist:

1. "Portions of the periodic payments (rentals) are made specifically applicable to an equity to be acquired by the Lessee." For example, a lease allowing ten percent of each rental payment to build up an equity interest would indicate an installment sale.

2. "The lessee will acquire title upon the payment of a stated amount of rentals which under the contract he is required to make." This situation occurs two ways:

   a. Paying a stated number of rentals after which title transfers.

   b. Title transfers automatically at the end of the lease without a purchase option or guaranteed residual.

3. "The total amount which the lessee is required to pay for a relatively short period of use constitutes an inordinately large proportion of the total sum required to be paid to secure the transfer of title." This situation occurs when a lease contains a *purchase* option or a bargain *rental renewal* option as described below:

   a. "A lease will be denied when total rental payments and any purchase option price approximate the price at which the equipment could have been acquired by purchase at the time of entering into the agreement, plus interest and/or carrying charges." However, if the lease term is not unusually short then the sum of the lease payments and the purchase option may exceed the purchase cost and associated interest that would be paid under a deferred payment plan (conditional installment sales contract). The court ruling on the Northwest Acceptance Corporation Case held that under certain lease agreements the lessee in fact would pay one-half to one percent more under a lease than under a sales contract– since the lessor must be reimbursed for the contract costs: interest, overhead, risk factor, profit etc. Furthermore, it held that rental payments do not include interest per se– since interest is the cost charged for the use of money, not equipment. Then too, it explained that "financial leases" (examined later in the chapter) should have costs approximately equal to conditional sales contracts since they are hybrid leases wherein many but not all the risks of ownership have been passed to the lessee.

   b. "If the sum of the specified rentals over a relatively short part of the expected useful life of the equipment approximates the price at which the equipment could have been acquired by purchase at the time of entering into the agreement, plus interest and/or carrying charges on such amount, and the lessee may continue to use the equipment for an additional period or periods approximating its remaining estimated useful life for relatively *nominal* or token payments, it may be assumed that the parties have entered into a sales contract, even though a passage of title is not expressly provided in the agreement." Thus, the abnormally small renewal payment or the use of the equipment for its useful life will cause the lease to be considered a sale.

4. "The agreed rental payments materially exceed the current fair rental value. This may be indicative that the payments include an element other than compensation for the use of property." This criterion holds whether the lease contains a purchase option or not.

5. "The property may be acquired under a purchase option at a price which is nominal in relation to the value of the property at the time when the option may be exercised (bargain purchase option), as determined at the time of entering into the original agreement, or which is a relatively small amount when compared with the total payments which are required to be made."

    Although the Northwest Acceptance Corporation Case decision allowed ten percent purchase options, the trend nevertheless is towards twenty percent of original cost (IRS leveraged lease requirement), with most attorneys and CPA's stating that fifteen percent should be the *minimum* purchase option percentage under any lease. Leases nineteen years and longer generally require twenty percent purchase options which serves to refute the argument that the equipment has been leased for most of its useful life.

6. "Some portion of the periodic payments is specifically designated as interest or is otherwise readily recognizable as the equivalent of interest." This is the compliment to the first criterion which referred to payments including an equity interest. If a payment contains interest, the balance of the payment must be principal or equity.

Since Revenue Ruling 55-540 in 1955 there have been many court cases which have helped clear the muddy waters—yet total clarity has not been achieved. Some of the additional insight given by cases since 1955 regards the lease term other than the Economic Recovery Tax Act of 1981. Generally, if the total lease period including renewal periods is almost equal to the asset's useful life then the transaction might be considered a sale and not a lease. Most leases with terms of thirty years or more would be considered sales. In general, the lessor must demonstrate that leased equipment at the termination of a lease has a remaining useful life of longer than one year or twenty percent of the original useful life. This last guideline and the two that follow have been borrowed from Revenue Procedures 75-21 & 76-30 which set forth guidelines for determining whether certain transactions are in fact leases. It is important to note that the trend among attorneys and CPAs is to adopt the guidelines of Revenue Procedure 75-21 for all leases even though these guidelines were written specifically for leveraged leases. This approach is conservative; nevertheless, the guidelines of the revenue procedure cannot be wholly ignored even if the lease is nonleveraged.

Two additional guidelines borrowed from Revenue Procedures 75-21 and 76-30 regard the lessor's equity interest in the leased asset and the type of asset itself.

1. If the lessor has less than a twenty percent equity interest in the leased asset it might be considered a sale. Recourse debt counts as part of this required "at risk" twenty percent equity investment.

2. If the asset is a single purpose item having no alternate use at the end of the lease other than for the lessee (e.g. a concrete smokestack) then a sale will be considered to have taken place. Revenue Procedure 76-30 deals directly with this issue.

Of course the IRS may attack any agreement on the basis that it has been artificially contrived for tax avoidance motives. When this happens, the IRS must prove that tax avoidance was the sole motive and the transaction had no economic substance apart from tax avoidance. This proof is difficult to obtain. In cases where the lessor is controlled by the lessee, or where the lessor has no independent economic substance apart from the lessee, the lease arrangement might be collapsed by the IRS and be considered a sale.

Lessors must also assume some of the risk of loss from a lease transaction. If the total burden of loss is shifted entirely to the lessee the transaction might be considered a sale. "Hell or high water" clauses which force lessees to pay rent without any exceptions for lessor bankruptcy or destruction of the property might jeopardize a lease.

The question of risk assumption is somewhat vague since the IRS has not clarified the issue nor have court cases done so. Although the IRS on April 26, 1978 issued a Technical Advice Memorandum (TAM) that attempted to deal with this issue, the TAM dealt with the issue of guaranteed residual values on vehicle leases. Guaranteed residual values require lessees to make up the difference between the salvage sales price of the vehicle upon its return to the lessor at the termination of the lease and the guaranteed residual amount. If the vehicle is salvaged for more than the guaranteed residual, the proceeds frequently go to the lessee. In such cases, as the TAM pointed out, the leases will probably be considered sales since both the benefits (profit potential) and the burdens (risk) of ownership are vested in the lessee not the lessor. Reference to more recent TAMs emphasize that the IRS is placing great importance on situations where the burdens and benefits of ownership have been transferred to the lessee (see TAM 8019120 (12/20/79), TAM 8020014 (2/15/80), and TAM 8004141 (11/2/79)).

Recently the Internal Revenue Service prepared an Audit Guideline Manual on the subject of equipment leasing. This manual is to be used by IRS auditors when confronted with either equipment leasing tax shelters (noncorporate) or normal corporate lease companies. A complete copy of this Equipment Leasing Audit Guideline Manual appears in the Appendix to this book on page 301.

In this Audit Manual the IRS summarizes the criteria they will use in an audit situation to determine whether a transaction is a leasing arrangement or a mere financing arrangement. Basically, the items covered in the manual repeat the revenue ruling 55-540 guidelines but several newer items have been included concerning at risk investment, etc. as described below:

1. "The lessee's right to the leased asset is derived from the lease agreement. The agreement, although cast in the form of a lease, may in substance be a conditional sales contract. This determination is made based on the intent of the parties in light of the facts existing at the time of the execution of the agreement.

2. No one factor is controlling in determining the intent when the agreement is executed. However, if one or more of the following circumstances exists, the examiner should consider characterizing the transaction as a sale rather than a lease:

   a. Lessee acquires equity in the property through his/her "lease" payments. For example, after fifty percent of the lease payments have been made, the lessee may acquire a twenty-five percent ownership interest in the asset.

   b. Lessee acquires title to the asset after a required number of lease payments.

   c. Lessee's total lease payments are due in a relatively short period of time and substantially cover the total amount required to acquire the asset.

   d. Lease payments substantially exceed the fair rental value of the property. This may indicate that the asset is actually being purchased and that the financing is for a period less than the useful life of the asset.

   e. Provision may be made for the property to be acquired by the lessee at the end of the lease term for a nominal sum.

   f. Lessee participates in the investment with the lessor by providing loan guarantees or stop loss agreements to the lessor.

   g. Lessor has little or no "at risk" investment in the leased asset. Note: one of the requirements relating to leveraged leasing under *Rev. Proc. 75-21, 1975-1 C.B. 715,* modified by *Rev. Proc. 76-30, 1976-2 C.B. 647,* is that at all times during the lease term the lessor should have a minimum "at risk" investment of twenty percent.

3. Consider the following example: A lessor and lessee enter into an agreement whereby the lessee agrees to lease a computer for $31,000 per year that has an annual fair rental value of $15,000. The lease will run for eighty-four months (seven years) at which time the lessee will acquire title to the computer for $8,000. The lessor generally sells this type of computer for $155,000 which is equal to the present value of the seven lease payments at a ten percent rate of return ($150,900) plus the present value of the $8,000 payment to the lessor at the conclusion of the lease. The life of the computer is fourteen years. The lessee agrees to insure the equipment and keep it in good repair.

a. In this example it would appear that a sale and not a lease has taken place. The lessee is paying almost double the monthly fair rental value and will take title to the computer in a relatively short period of time. The total rental payments are equal to the cost of the computer plus a ten percent annual return on the unpaid balance of the cost. The lessee is accepting the burdens of ownership by insuring the property and agreeing to keep it in good repair.

b. By handling this transaction as a lease rather than a sale, the lessee is able to deduct the rental payments, which approximate the cost of the computer, over seven years rather than depreciating the asset over fourteen years if the transaction were properly treated as a sale. If the computer is acquired and sold in a subsequent year by the lessee, any gain would not be subject to IRC 1245 recapture, since depreciation was not claimed. In this type of arrangement the lessor generally passes the investment credit on to the lessee pursuant to IRC 48(d). It is clearly to the benefit of the "lessee" to treat this arrangement as a lease rather than a purchase.

4. Examiners should look to the substance of the transaction rather than the form to determine if an abusive tax shelter exists.

a. A determination should be made as to who has the burdens and benefits of ownership.

b. The substance of a transaction, rather than its legal form, is controlling for Federal Income tax purposes. If the burdens and benefits of ownership still inure to the lessee after a sale and leaseback transaction, it is indicative that the seller is still the owner of the property. Calling a transaction a sale and leaseback does not make it one, if in fact it is something else.

c. By using this approach the lessor would not be entitled to deductions related to the leased property since the lessee still retains ownership for Federal Income tax purposes. See *Rev. Rul. 68-590, 1978-2* C.B. 66, amplified by *Rev. Rul. 73-134, 1973-1 C.B. 60; Rev. Rul. 72-543, 1972-2 C.B. 87; Rev. Rul. 74-290, 1974-1 C.B. 41.*"[7]

An interesting section of the IRS Equipment Leasing Audit Guide dealt with certain Present Value Tests that the auditor should perform to establish whether or not the transaction is a sham. The section of the Audit Guide dealt with the following present value considerations:

1. The fair market value of a leased asset may be measured using the present value of the future income stream (rents) plus the present value of the salvage.

---

[7]IRS Audit Guidelines, *Equipment Leasing,* paragraph 852, 8-8-1979

If the present value of the future income stream does not exceed the present value of the total investment in the asset, then the examiner should question the lessor's motives for entering into the transaction.

2. The present value of future rents at a given rate of return should approximate the fair market value of the leased asset. The examiner can use this test to help determine if the asset was acquired by the purchaser-lessor at an inflated price.

3. The following example demonstrates the present value computation.

   a. Facts:

Purchase price of leased property	$2,500
Salvage value	$1,000
Annual rental income	$350
Annual expenses attributable to leased property	$150
Net annual income from leased property	$200
Length of lease	ten years

   b. Based on these facts, it appears that the taxpayer will have a total net profit on his/her investment of $500 since annual net income of $200 for a ten-year period plus salvage value of $1,000 equals $3,000, and the purchase price was $2,500. However, if the present value concept is applied to these facts, the results will show that the taxpayer incurred a loss on the investment.

   c. Exhibit 800-1 shows the present value of the future income stream and the salvage at the end of ten years assuming a six percent interest rate (the higher the assumed interest rate, the lower the present value).

   d. The $2,030 present value was obtained by multiplying the annual net income and the salvage value by the applicable factor for each period associated with the six percent rate of return. (See present value table at Exhibit 800-2.)

   e. The present value of the future income stream and salvage in the above example is $2,030. The investor would therefore lose $470 on his/her $2,500 investment which would indicate the transaction was not entered into for a profit.

4. Keep in mind that the true fair market value of a leased asset can generally be measured by the present value of the future income stream.

5. Depending on other factors involved in this type of issue, it could be argued that the taxpayer's basis should be reduced to an amount equal to the present value of the future income stream. This is especially true if a sophisticated taxpayer, such as a lending institution or insurance company, is involved, since many of their investment decisions are based on the present value concept.

6. Another approach would be to disallow the entire transaction as a sham if the cost of the property is artificially inflated. This approach should be considered if other key factors are present such as the guarantee of all or part of the pur-

chaser-lessor's loan by the seller-lessee, failure to show legitimate business purpose for the inflated purchase price, and/or the involvement of related parties.[8]

To summarize and contrast the new safe harbor criteria versus the old rules that affect nonleveraged operating lease definitions reference to the following list is helpful:

Items in leases that do not conform to the safe harbor requirements that might cause their disallowance as true operating leases:

1. Portions of the periodic rental payments are specified as equity.

2. An equity interest is transferred to the lessee by paying a stated number of rentals after which title transfers (during or at the end of the lease).

3. Lease payments over a relatively short period represent an unusually large proportion of the total amount needed to secure title (lease payments plus the purchase option). Payments without the purchase option usually exceed the original selling price of the asset plus an interest, overhead, and profit factor.

4. The lease contains a bargain renewal option that allows renewal of the lease at rates far below the base rentals after the original base rentals have exceeded the purchase price (full-payout lease followed by a bargain rental renewal).

Guidelines for operating leases conforming to the safe harbor rules:

1. The lease may specify portions of rentals as equity so long as the six safe harbor rules have been met.

2. The lease may transfer ownership, equity, or title at the inception, during, or at the termination of the lease so long as the six safe harbor requirements are met.

3. A lease may be structured on a full-payout basis where the lease payments alone are sufficient to cover the leased equipment's cost, plus underlying financing costs, leasing company overhead, and profit if the lease falls within the safe harbor.

4. The lease may contain a bargain renewal if the total lease term, including the bargain renewal extension, does not exceed the greater of 90 percent of the property's useful life or 150 percent of the property's ADR midpoint life as of January 1, 1981.

---

[8]IBID; Paragraph 872

5. Lease payments exceed the fair rental value whether a purchase option exists or not.

6. A bargain purchase option has been structured in the lease where the option's cost is less than the future expected fair market value of the leased asset. Generally, purchase options that are fixed in amount (non fair market value options) must be fifteen percent or more of the asset's original cost to the lessor to avoid IRS challenge or twenty percent on a leveraged lease.

7. A part of the periodic payments is specifically designated or recognized as interest. Note that TAM 8024066 (3/20/80) specifically allowed the lessor to reflect interest rate changes in the lease payment occasioned by increases in the lessor's underlying cost of debt. Such variable payment leases did not imply that interest was part of the payment. It is only when the lease specifically indicates a portion of each payment as interest that the lease's status is in jeopardy.

8. The total lease period, including renewal periods is almost equal to the asset's economic

5. Lease payments can materially exceed the fair rental value when all six safe harbor attributes have been met.

6. The following purchase options are acceptable under the new law:
   a. Nominal purchase options for a dollar.
   b. Bargain purchase options which are significantly below the asset's expected future value.
   c. Fair market value purchase options.
   d. Purchase options with "not to exceed" and "not below" ranges.
   e. Variable purchase options that change according to the lessor's cost of debt.

7. Lease payments can contain designated portions as interest under the new tax law. However, the lessee must treat lease payments as being fully tax deductible without separation into principal and interest.

8. Lease terms cannot exceed the greater of 90 percent of the property's useful life or 150

life. A lease term should always be less than 30 years.

percent of the property's ADR midpoint life. However, the minimum lease term must be equal to the asset's ACRs life (usually three to five years).

9. The remaining useful life at the termination of the lease is less than the longer of one year or twenty percent of its original useful life.

9. Same as number "8" above.

10. The lessor has less than a twenty percent at risk equity and recourse debt investment in the leased asset.

10. The lessor must be at risk ten percent at the inception and during the lease term. Lessee provided loans do not count towards this requirement.

11. The asset is single purpose and will have no alternate use at the end of the lease.

11. The asset does not have to be usable by any other person than the lessee at the termination of the lease.

12. Artificially contrived agreement for tax avoidance or receipt of tax benefits where the transaction has no economic substance or business purpose apart from tax avoidance. Phony lessor corporation fully controlled by the lessee with no economic substance apart from the lessee is a typical "sham."

12. The new tax law specifically allows leases to be constructed for no other purpose than the tax benefits contained therein. Thus, the "business purpose" test has been removed. The new law makes the point that "no other factors" will be "taken into account" beyond the six safe harbor rules in determining whether a transaction is a lease.

13. Total risk of loss (guaranteed residuals or put options with no downside stop loss protection for the lessee) and benefit of profit (residual proceeds sharing when the returned asset

13. In addition to all sorts of purchase options described in number "6" above the lease may contain any of these guaranteed residuals even though the burdens and benefits of

sells for more than the guaranteed residual) resides with the lessee. For example, leases containing guaranteed residuals (put options) without upside profit prohibitions or downside stop loss protections, or with "hell or high water clauses" might be considered conditional sales instead of leases.

ownership are passed to the lessee:

a. Guaranteed residual where title may pass to lessee at his option.

b. Guaranteed residual where title does not pass to lessee.

c. Guaranteed residuals with or without stop loss clauses for downside protection.

d. Guaranteed residual with upside profit sharing.

14. Lessee participates in the investment with the lessor by providing the loan, guaranteeing the loan, or investing part of the equity capital for the lease.

14. Both the lessee or any related party may provide or guarantee financing of the leased equipment.

15. Present value of the lease payments and the residual when discounted at the prevailing rate is less than the equipment's fair market value at the inception of the lease.

15. Phony, inflated equipment costs are not acceptable under any IRS provisions.

16. The 50/15 rule for noncorporate lessors is not met. This rule is explained in chapter 13 and if not adhered to might cause the lessor to lose the investment tax credit.

16. The lessor must be a corporation, or partnership with all corporate partners, or a grantor trust with corporate grantor and beneficiary and therefore the 50/15 rule is not applicable.

REVENUE PROCEDURE 75-21

As was previously mentioned, the trend in lease definition by the IRS and practitioners as well, is to adopt the guidelines set forth in Revenue Procedure 75-21. "The type of transaction covered by this Revenue Procedure is commonly called a 'Leveraged Lease'. "Such a lease transaction generally involves three parties: a lessor, a lessee and a lender to the lessor. In general, these leases are net leases where executory costs are paid by the lessee, the lease term covers a substantial part of the useful life of the leased property, and the lessee's payments to the lessor are sufficient to discharge the lessor's payments to the lender (ninety percent of the asset's cost plus interest)." Remember that these guidelines are starting to be applied to nonleveraged leases that do not conform to the new safe harbor requirements. Note too that Revenue Procedure 75-21 only applies to leveraged leases that do not conform to the safe harbor requirements of code section 168(f) 8.

"Unless other facts and circumstances indicate a contrary intent, for *advance ruling* purposes only," the IRS will consider an agreement to be a true operating lease if *all* the following conditions are met:

1. MINIMUM UNCONDITIONAL "AT RISK" INVESTMENT

a. *Initial Minimum Investment*

Equity including consideration paid in cash and personal liabilities assumed (recourse debt incurred) must represent twenty percent or more of asset's cost at the inception of the lease. The net worth of the lessor must be sufficient to satisfy such recourse debt. The twenty percent minimum investment must be "unconditional" which prohibits the lessee or related party from reimbursing the lessor for his initial investment.

b. *Maintenance of Minimum Investment*

The minimum investment must never fall below twenty percent throughout the entire lease term. This is determined by a complex formula that requires the difference between cumulative inflows and outflows to be always less than or equal to the sum of any equity investment greater than twenty percent of equipment cost and the cumulative pro rata portion of projected profit (exclusive of tax benefits). Thus, if a lessor has a thirty percent equity interest in a leveraged lease, cumulative net cash flow could never exceed ten percent of the asset's cost plus pro rata share of profit. Otherwise, such excess cash flow would imply that some equity is being returned placing the lessor in an equity position below twenty percent since any returns greater than ten percent plus profit would mean the remaining twenty percent position is being returned to the lessor.

c. *Residual Investment*

i. Must have a reasonably estimated residual value equal to twenty percent or more of the asset's original cost. The residual value cannot include the effects of inflation or deflation during the lease term nor removal and delivery costs incurred by the lessor.

ii. Must have a remaining life beyond the lease term of the longer of one year or twenty percent of the originally estimated depreciable life.

2. LEASE TERM AND RENEWAL OPTIONS

The lease term includes all renewal or extension periods except renewals or extensions at the option of the lessee.

3. PURCHASE AND SALE RIGHTS

No bargain purchase options are allowed. The lessee must pay fair market value for the leased asset which is required to be at least twenty percent of the asset's cost according to the *residual investment* requirement stated above. Note that this requirement states the residual must be twenty percent of the asset's cost in real dollars without the effect of inflation considered. Thus, leases which state twenty percent purchase options might be disallowed since they would allow the lessee to purchase the asset below its inflated fair market value. Also, the lessor is prohibited from abandoning the asset after the termination of the lease. Nor can the lessor force the lessee to purchase the asset since the lessor must have market risk.

4. NO INVESTMENT BY LESSEE

No part of the cost of the property may be furnished by the lessee. Improvements or additions to the property must be paid by the lessor unless they are owned by the lessee and are readily removable (nonfixtures) without causing damage and are not subject to bargain purchase options exercisable by the lessor.

a. Cost overruns and modifications can be passed on to the lessee in the form of increased rents.

b. *Normal* repair and maintenance paid by the lessee will not be considered improvements or additions.

5. NO LESSEE LOANS OR GUARANTEES

The lessee may not lend to the lessor any of the funds necessary to acquire the property or guarantee the indebtedness.

6. PROFIT REQUIREMENT

a. Lessor must make a profit beyond the tax benefits derived from ITC and depreciation tax shield. This test is met when the total rent paid by the lessee together with the estimated residual value are greater than disbursements for nonrecourse debt service and equity investment including interest for the recourse debt portion of the equity.

b. The lease must also generate a reasonable positive cash flow. In other words, the aggregate rents must exceed the aggregate disbursements (debt service and recourse debt service) at any time during the lease.

7. OTHER CONSIDERATIONS

a. *Uneven Rent Tests*

The IRS ordinarily will not raise any question about prepaid or deferred rent if the uneven rents meet either of two tests:

i. The annual rent does not vary more than ten percent above or below the average annual rent payable over the lease term.

ii. The annual rent during the first two-thirds is not more than ten percent above or below the average annual rent during the initial period and the annual rent during the remaining period is no greater than the highest annual rent during the initial phase and no less than one-half of the average annual rent during the initial period.

b. *Special Purpose Property*

Special purpose property without alternate use cannot be the subject of an operating lease from a tax viewpoint. This rule is explained in Revenue Procedure 76-30.

Since the enactment of the Economic Recovery Tax Act of 1981 the following changes have occurred in the leveraged lease requirements for lessors who meet all six safe harbor requirements.

Leveraged Lease Requirements for nonqualifying Lessors

1. *Minimum unconditional at risk investment.*
   a. *Twenty percent minimum investment.*
   b. *Minimum investment can never fall below twenty percent* throughout the entire lease term.
   c. *Residual value must be equal or greater than twenty percent of* the asset's original cost ignoring the effects of inflation and removal and delivery costs.
   d. Must have a remaining life beyond the lease term of the longer of one year or twenty

Leveraged Lease Requirements for Qualifying Lessors

1. *Minimum unconditional at risk investment.*
   a. *Ten percent minimum investment.*
   b. *Minimum investment can never fall below ten percent* during the full lease term.
   c. *Residual value may be nominal, at a bargain, at fair market value within a fixed range, or variable.* The amount may exceed or be less than twenty percent of the asset's cost. Inflation and removal costs are ignored.
   d. The lease term cannot exceed the greater of ninety percent of the property's useful life

percent of the originally estimated depreciation life.

or 150 percent of the property's January 1, 1981 ADR midpoint life.

2. *Lease Term* – includes all renewal or extension periods except those that are exercisable solely at the discretion of the lessee (call options). Put options-or lessor forced renewals are part of the lease term.

2. Same as the nonqualifying lessor requirements in terms of whether extensions are included. Leveraged Lease terms cannot be less than the minimum ACRs depreciation life.

3. *Purchases and Sale Rights* – No bargain purchase options are allowed. Fixed purchase options must be at least twenty percent of the asset's cost.

3. *Both nominal and bargain purchase can be used.* Both fixed and variable purchase options are permissable at, or below, or above the asset's expected fair market value.

4. *No investment by lessee* – No part of the cost of the property may be furnished by the lessee except for improvements or additions to the property that are readily removeable without causing damage and are not subject to lessor bargain purchase options.

4. *The lessee may pay part of the cost* of the cost of the equipment as long as all six safe harbor requirements are met.

5. *No lessee loans or guarantees.*

5. *The lessee or a related party may guarantee loans or provide financing for the acquisition of the equipment.*

6. *Profit requirement* – Lessor must make a profit beyond the tax benefits derived from the ITC and depreciation tax shield to give the lease an independent business purpose beyond tax reduction.

6. The "business purpose" test has been removed. A leveraged lease may be constructed soley for the purpose of obtaining tax benefits. Thus, no profit is required in the lease.

7. *The lease must generate a positive cash flow.*

7. *No cash flow requirements exist under the new act.*

8. *Uneven Rent Tests* – The IRS
ordinarily will not raise any question about prepaid or deferred
rent if either of the uneven rent
tests are met in a lease. Note,
however, that such an IRS challenge would not nullify the lease's
status as a lease. The lessor might
simply be forced to take some
additional revenue into income.

8. Although the *new tax act does
not discuss uneven rent*, it is assumed by many that the IRS may
still question deferred or prepaid
rent if there is much disparity between the high and low payments.

9. *Special Purpose Property* without alternate use cannot be the
subject of an operating lease.

9. *The new act allows special purpose property* that cannot be
used by anyone except the lessee
to be the subject of a lease.

10. *The leased property may be new
or used.*

10. *Only new Section 38 property
qualifies for the safe harbor.*

11. *The lessor may be an individual,
partnership, limited partnership,
or grantor trust.*

11. *The lessor must be a corporation*
or a partnership or grantor trust,
all the parties of which are
corporations.

Frequently, IRS definitions of a lease are confused with accounting FASB 13 definitions. It is essential to keep these concepts separate, since many lease compa- nies in the United States have capital leases on their books from an accounting point of view, but report the same leases to the IRS as operating in order to avail them- selves of the ITC and depreciation deductions. Note in this situation, the lease com- pany reports no depreciation on its accounting income statement – it is reported only on the company's tax return.

On the other hand, many lessees in the United States have capital leases on their books from an accounting viewpoint, which implies they must capitalize and, sub- sequently depreciate the asset. Such depreciation expense, however, does not ap- pear on the lessee's tax return since the lease is reported to the IRS as an operating lease.

There are situations where the lessor has an accounting operating lease, but has passed the ITC to the lessee from a tax viewpoint. Furthermore, the lessor could report the entire transaction to the IRS on a capital lease basis which would preclude the lessor from claiming a depreciation deduction. Nevertheless, the lessor would be obliged to depreciate the asset from an accounting point of view since an operating lease implies that the lessor is the owner of the asset and must therefore depreciate it.

Keep in mind that under the new tax legislation (and under previous rulings and procedures), the IRS cannot attack a lease's status solely because the lessor accounts for the lease in a manner inconsistent with its tax return treatment.

Such contradictory methods of reporting to shareholders versus the taxing authorities is not as prevalent in Europe where a corporation's taxes are determined as a percentage of the accountant's assessment of net income in conformity with the country's generally accepted accounting principles.

INDUSTRY LEASE DEFINITIONS

Within the leasing industry there are many leasing terms which unfortunately vary in meaning from locale to locale and from leasing company to leasing company. Even so, understanding of leasing jargon is essential to a working knowledge of leasing. The authors have attempted to use the most generally accepted definitions of industry terms to equip the reader with sufficient understanding to analyze leases.

FULL-PAYOUT AND NON-FULL-PAYOUT LEASES—

A lease in which the total of the lease rental payments alone (without dependence upon guaranteed or unguaranteed residuals or purchase options) pays back to the lessor enough to cover the entire cost of the leased asset together with the cost of financing, the lessor's overhead, and a remaining rate-of-return acceptable to the lessor.

As an example of how members of the leasing community use the same term but with different meaning notice how the Comptroller of the Currency, John G. Heimann, April 20, 1979 in Banking Circular No. 125 uses the term "full-payout" in a completely opposite way from the definition above (refer to paragraphs 4 & 7 through 10 in the circular reproduced below). Note, too, that the Comptroller's definition would include all leases. Most of the circular is reproduced in order to serve as a reference to the reader for other common lease terms that will be discussed in this section. Then, too, the circular points out how other branches of the government other than the IRS have influenced the leasing market. Notice how banks cannot structure leases with purchase options above twenty-five percent (paragraphs 9 & 10).

Comptroller of the Currency
Administrator of National Banks

Washington, D.C. 20219

April 20, 1979

Banking Circular No. 125

To: Presidents of all National Banks
Subject: Leasing of Personal Property— Interpretive Ruling 7.3400

This Office recently issued an amended version of Interpretive Ruling (I.R.) 7.3400, 12 C.F.R., 7.3400, dealing with the leasing of personal property by national banks. The ruling allows national banks to lease personal property to customers where the lease transaction is the functional equivalent of an extension of credit on the property to the lessee. Consistent with this concept of lease financing I.R. 7.3400 establishes the following guides that national banks should adhere to in their leasing activities.

1. National banks may purchase or acquire personal property in a direct lease situation only in response to a lessee's request for that specific property. Inventorying of property is not consistent with the concept of lease financing permissible for banks.
2. Banks may advertise their entrance into, or general participation in, the leasing business as long as their advertisements merely announce the availability of an alternative financing device rather than attempt to merchandise a particular piece of property.
3. All leases should be written on a "net" basis. Except as otherwise provided in paragraphs 4,5 and 6 below, under a net lease, a bank may not directly or indirectly provide or be obligated to provide for:

   a. servicing, repair or maintenance;

   b. the purchasing of parts and accessories;

   c. the loan of replacement property;

   d. the purchasing of insurance; or

   e. the renewal of licenses and registration.

4. National bank lessors may lease improvements or additions to the property upon a lessee's request if it is accomplished in accordance with the full-payout requirements of the ruling. In other words, the lease must be amended to include the specific improvement or addition, and the lease payments must be adjusted to amortize the bank's cost and maintain the character of a full-payout lease.
5. Insurance (liability or property) may only be purchased for the lessee if he has defaulted on his agreement to do so and the bank subsequently bills him for the premium. The ordinary purchase of insurance required under the lease is a service responsibility that should be assumed by the lessee to satisfy the requirements of a net lease.
6. Initial licensing and registration of property may be completed by the bank. Renewal licensing and registration may be handled by the bank where it is considered necessary to protect its interest as an owner or financer of the property, and that need is properly documented.
7. The economics of the lease should constitute a full-payout transaction. The bank should realize 100% of its investment in the property plus the cost of financing from:

   a. rentals;

   b. estimated tax benefits; and

   c. the estimated residual value.

8. A lease may be terminated prior to its stated expiration. However, the lessee must be obligated to ensure that the lease is a full-payout agreement with respect to the bank, notwithstanding its abbreviated duration.

9. The estimated residual value relied upon to yield a full-payout lease (not the actual residual value of the property) may not exceed 25% of the cost of the property.

10. Unguaranteed residual values up to 25% and guaranteed residual values may be combined for the purposes of structuring a full-payout lease as long as the total estimated residual value is realistic and reasonable.

11. A guarantee may be contractual and may take the form of an insurance policy insuring the residual value of the property.

12. National bank lessors must be able to document that a guarantor has the resources to meet the guarantee in order for that guarantee to be acceptable.

13. The estimate of residual values must be reasonable in light of all of the circumstances and the type of property leased. That estimate should be properly documented.

14. Concentrations of leases of one particular type of property and reliance on excessive aggregate residual values in any given future, fiscal year should be carefully monitored to detect unsafe and unsound situations.

15. All leases executed after the effective date of the ruling will be considered obligations of the lessee for the purposes of 12 U.S.C. SS84 and 371c.

16. The outstanding obligation of a lessee should be computed as the sum of the present value of both the lessee's payments and the residual value of the property. A lease obligation, whether evidenced by a leveraged or nonleveraged lease, should be reduced by that portion of each payment allocated to principal. . .

John G. Heimann
Comptroller of the Currency

NET, NET-NET, AND TRIPLE NET LEASES—

The term net lease and triple net lease generally refer to leases in which the lessee is obligated to pay the following typical executory costs in addition to and separate from the basic lease payments:

1. Sales tax
2. Property tax
3. Insurance
4. Maintenance & Servicing
5. Repair
6. Temporary Replacement Property
7. Parts & Accessories
8. Licenses and Registration

Notice in the Comptroller of the Currency's circular (Paragraph 3) that net-lease is defined in almost the same manner with the exception of property taxes and sales taxes which were omitted from the government's definition.

In the net-net lease the lessee is further obligated to guarantee a certain residual value to the lessor at the end of the lease. The lessor sells the returned asset and the lessee must make up any deficit between the salvage proceeds and the guaranteed residual amount.

FINANCIAL LEASE

Financial leases are generally net leases structured on a full-payout basis over a term close to the asset's economic life. From a tax and accounting point of view they are generally considered CAPITAL leases due to their full-payout nature, long-terms, and shifting of the burdens of ownership to the lessee. Under the new tax act financial leases will still be considered operating leases from a tax viewpoint.

CLOSED AND OPEN-ENDED LEASES

Closed-end leases or "walk away" leases are usually structured on a net-lease basis where at the end of the lease the property reverts back to the lessor. The full risk of residual value loss rests with the lessor. Ownership possibilities are "closed" to the lessee.

Open-end Leases are generally net-leases where the title to the asset passes to the lessee upon exercising of a purchase option or payment of a guaranteed residual. Frequently these leases are structured like financing leases on a full-payout basis. Part of the risk of residual value has been passed to the lessee. Ownership possibilities are "open" to the lessee.

PERCENTAGE LEASE

Percentage leases require the lessee to pay a fixed amount of rent each period plus a percentage of gross revenue received during the previous period. Usually the additional percentage rent is calculated as a percentage of revenue received above a minimum base amount. Such lease arrangements help compensate lessors in part for the effects of inflation since percentage leases are generally structured for the long term use of commercial real estate, e.g., shopping mall space.

MASTER LEASE

Master leases are structured for lessees who either will be leasing numerous pieces of equipment to be received over a period of time, or leasing equipment that requires frequent substitution. The master lease pre-establishes lease rates and terms for equipment received or substituted as needed. These leases eliminate much of the red tape that would be involved in renegotiating a separate lease for each new piece of equipment. Leasing of auto or truck fleets to a single lessee are frequently accomplished on a master lease basis.

WASH LEASE

The Economic Recovery Tax Act of 1981 created a lease that permits the transference of tax benefits (ITC & ACRs) from the owner-user of a piece of equipment to an investor. In effect, a hybrid leveraged sales-leaseback arrangement is created wherein the lessor-investor is considered the owner of the property for tax purposes but the lessee-user of the equipment is the legal owner. In most cases the owner-user of the equipment has provided his own financing which makes the "wash lease" leveraged since the debt obtained by the lessee-user is nonrecourse to the lessor-investor. The lease is called a "wash lease" since the subsequent *lease payments* to the lessor exactly equal or "wash out" the subsequent *loan payments* to the lessee. The lessor acts as if he has purchased the equipment from the lessee (sales-leaseback) and therefore must pay back to the lessee the balance of the purchase price after the down payment. The lease payments exactly equal the loan payments. Refer to the appendix at the end of the book for the numerous IRS guidelines affecting the wash lease.

CONCLUSION

Although accountants and CPA's have fairly well defined what a true lease (Operating) is in contrast to an installment sale (Capital Lease) the distinction is not as clear from an IRS point of view for the noncorporate lessor. Furthermore, nonleveraged leases have different IRS guidelines to follow than leveraged leases. Industry lease definitions vary in meaning from place to place but are nevertheless useful in understanding general industry jargon. The Economic Recovery Tax Act of 1981 has done much to define a lease for a corporate lessor but accomplished little for the noncorporate lessor.

3

A Comparison of
the Effects on Financial Statements
of the Capital Lease
___ Versus the Operating Lease ___

Chapter 2 contrasted the CAPITAL LEASE with the OPERATING LEASE in terms of FASB 13 accounting and Internal Revenue Service definitions. This chapter will compare an operating lease to an identically structured capital lease to demonstrate the effects upon a company's financial statements. The financial statement impact will be analyzed in terms of the adverse changes in a company's liquidity, solvency, financial leverage, profitability, and cash flow that result from capitalizing a lease rather than treating it as an off-balance sheet operating lease. Finally, the disclosure and reporting requirements of FASB 13 will be examined from a financial analyst's and banker's viewpoint.

FINANCIAL STATEMENT EFFECT

In the situation where a company acquires equipment with an operating lease (true lease), each monthly lease payment is treated as an operating expense which appears in the company's income statement. However, when equipment is financed with a capital lease (purchased), each monthly lease payment is divided into two portions: (1) a portion representing interest expense included in each lease payment; and (2) a portion representing a principal reduction of the current liability entitled lease payable. Also, a charge to depreciation expense must be made in addition to the interest expense portion of the lease payment since the company has capitalized the purchased asset in accordance with the requirements of FASB 13. Generally, in the early years of a capital lease, the combined total of the depreciation and interest expense will exceed the lease expense that would appear on the income statement of a company leasing equipment under a comparable operating lease, even if straight line depreciation were being used by the company. These excess expenses which appear in the financial statements in the early years of the capital lease have a definite effect both upon a company's financial statements and financial ratios. The balance sheet is most directly affected by the capital lease since the purchased equipment must appear as an asset along with a corresponding lease payable shown as a liability on the balance sheet.

In order to better describe the varying effects of the operating lease compared to the capital lease on a company's financial statements, a simplified Balance Sheet, Income Statement, and Statement of Changes in Financial Position-Cash Basis which appear on the next two pages will be analyzed.

The following financial statements of ALPHA COMPANY are based on the assumption that the operating lease and capital lease qualify as such under both accounting and Internal Revenue Service guidelines. This situation will not always be the case since a lease can be reported as a capital lease from an accounting viewpoint and as an operating lease from an Internal Revenue point of view. Furthermore, the adverse effects shown on ALPHA COMPANY's statements of the capital lease only occur during the early portion of a lease term. During the remaining latter portion of a capital lease the financial statement effects become favorable when compared to an operating lease. Additionally, many people feel that capital leases do not adversely affect financial statements. These people contend it is the other way around. Capital leases properly state a company's financial position and it is the improperly accounted for operating lease that affects the financial statements adversely by understating assets and liabilities and overstating income. Whichever viewpoint is correct is not the issue here, the point is there can be dramatic differences between the two methods of accounting.

Reference to the footnotes appearing in the following financial statements permits a succinct summary of the differing effects of the two opposite methods of accounting for leases.

BALANCE SHEET EFFECTS

Footnote 1   The capital lease requires the capitalization (inclusion as an asset in the amount of $57,000) of the leased equipment; whereas, the operating lease shows no dollar amount capitalized or referenced to the leased equipment on the balance sheet.

Footnote 2   Additional accumulated depreciation in the amount of $7,000 appears on the capital lease balance sheet since capitalized equipment must be depreciated according to generally accepted accounting principles. The other $10,000 of accumulated depreciation applies to the company's other nonleased assets. By the end of the leased asset's economic life the additional depreciation will completely offset the capitalized leased asset mentioned in Footnote 1 above. In other words, the capitalized asset's book value will be reduced to zero.

ALPHA COMPANY

BALANCE SHEET

ASSETS

	Operating Lease	Capital Lease
Current Assets:		
Cash	2,000	3,000
Accounts Receivable	6,000	6,000
Inventory	4,000	4,000
Fixed Assets:		
Property, Plant, Equipment	48,000	48,000
Capital Leased Equipment[1]	0	57,000
Less Accumulated Depreciation[2]	(10,000)	(17,000)
TOTAL ASSETS	$50,000	$101,000

LIABILITIES

	Operating Lease	Capital Lease
Current Liabilities:		
Accounts Payable	3,000	3,000
Current Portion Leases Payable[3]	0	6,000
Long-Term Liabilities:		
Bonds Payable	20,000	20,000
Long-Term Portion Leases Payable[4]	0	46,000
TOTAL LIABILITIES	$23,000	$75,000

STOCKHOLDER'S EQUITY

	Operating Lease	Capital Lease
Common Stock (5,000 shares):	7,000	7,000
Retained Earnings:		
Prior	10,000	10,000
Current Portion[5]	10,000	9,000
TOTAL EQUITY	$27,000	$26,000
TOTAL LIABILITY AND EQUITY	$50,000	$101,000

ALPHA COMPANY
INCOME STATEMENT

	Operating Lease	Capital Lease
Revenue:		
Sales	$150,000	$150,000
Costs of Goods Sold:	(80,000)	(80,000)
Gross Profit:	$70,000	$70,000
Operating Expenses:		
Selling	(2,000)	(2,000)
General & Administrative	(22,000)	(22,000)
Lease Expense[6]	(15,000)	0
Depreciation Expense[7]	(5,000)	(12,000)
Operating Income:	$26,000	$34,000
Other Income & Expenses:		
Interest Expense[8]	(6,000)	(16,000)
Income Before Taxes:	$20,000	$18,000
Income Taxes 50%[9]	(10,000)	(9,000)
Net Income:	$10,000	$9,000

STATEMENT OF CHANGES IN FINANCIAL POSITION – CASH BASIS

	Operating Lease	Capital Lease
Sources of Cash:		
Operations:		
Net Income	$10,000	$9,000
Add: Depreciation	5,000	12,000
TOTAL SOURCES	$15,000	$21,000
Uses of Cash:		
Dividends	(4,000)	(4,000)
Purchase of Equipment	(10,000)	(10,000)
Reduction of Lease Liabilities[10]	0	(5,000)
TOTAL USES	$(14,000)	$(19,000)
Net Cash Increase: [11]	$1,000	$2,000

Footnote 3   Capital leases are recorded in the accounting records of the company as assets along with an equal liability entitled lease payable. The lease payable is then separated into a current portion due and long-term portion due. The current portion due represents the principal portion of all lease payments due during the next twelve months. The current portion due does not include the interest portion of payments due; this will appear in the income statement as an interest expense as it is paid or accrued. After the first month of a lease the total lease liabilities, both current and long term (Footnote 4), will no longer equal the leased asset's carrying amount since part of the liability will have been paid off. Thus, the total of the current lease liability of $6,000 plus the long-term portion of $46,000 no longer equal the asset's original carrying amount of $57,000 (Footnote 1). These two liabilities total $52,000 which is $5,000 less than the original carrying value of $57,000. This $5,000 difference represents the amount that was paid as a principal reduction on the lease liability (see Footnote 10).

Footnote 4   The capital lease requires the remaining $46,000 long-term portion of the lease payable to be classified as a long-term liability.

Footnote 5   The current portion of retained earnings represents current year net income as reported on the income statement. The capital lease retained earnings are $1,000 lower than those of the operating lease due to the fact that the sum of interest and depreciation expense ($10,000 additional interest plus $7,000 extra depreciation equals $17,000) shown on the capital lease income statement exceeds the lease expense ($15,000) as shown on the operating lease income statement by $2,000 dollars pretax or $1,000 dollars after-tax.

INCOME STATEMENT EFFECTS

Footnote 6   The $15,000 lease expense is the only expense item shown under an operating lease.

Footnote 7   Depreciation expense for the capital lease is $7,000 higher than it would have been relative to the operating lease since the capitalized leased asset must be depreciated each accounting period. Five thousand of the total depreciation expense pertains to the nonleased equipment. The $7,000 extra depreciation represents straight line depreciation for an asset with an eight year life and a $1,000 anticipated salvage value.

Footnote 8   Interest expense for the capital lease is $10,000 higher than it would have been relative to the operating lease. Each capital lease payment is separated into principal and interest, whereas no portion of the operating lease payment is allocated to interest. The principal portion of the payment, $5,000, previously reduced the lease payable under current liabilities on the balance sheet. Six thousand of the total $16,000 interest expense pertains to the other long-term liabilities.

Footnote 9   Income taxes are $1,000 lower under the capital lease option since the depreciation and interest expense in excess of the operating lease payment form an additional tax shield of $2,000 which saves $1,000 in taxes, assuming a fifty percent tax bracket.

STATEMENT OF CHANGES IN FINANCIAL POSITION EFFECTS

Footnote 10   The difference between the capital lease payment of $15,000 and the $10,000 interest expense portion of the payment must be shown as an additional use of funds attributable to a reduction of the principal portion of the current lease payable. Such principal payments do not appear in the income statement since they are not expenses, they do, however, impact the cash flow statement.

Footnote 11   The depreciation and interest expense tax shield under the capital lease option results in an additional $1,000 in net cash flow under the capital lease alternative. This extra cash flow will always be equal to the tax rate times the capital lease's depreciation and interest expense which is in excess of the operating lease payment.

IMPACT ON FINANCIAL RATIOS

From the information contained in the ALPHA COMPANY's financial statements, one can readily calculate and evaluate selected ratios which indicate the company's position in regard to liquidity, solvency, financial leverage, profitability, and cash flow.

REVIEW OF ASSUMPTIONS

The ALPHA COMPANY example was based upon the assumption that in the early years of a capital lease it would provide tax deductible expenses (interest plus depreciation) in excess of the lease payment expense under the operating lease. This assumption does not always hold true since we could structure a shorter-term, full payout lease without a purchase option, then payments would exceed the combination of the capital lease depreciation and interest expense. It is important to note, however, that most short-term, full payout leases would not be classified as operating leases from an accounting viewpoint since the present value of their minimum lease payments usually exceeds ninety percent of the fair market value of the leased asset and must therefore be capitalized. Nevertheless, certain short-term, nonfull payout leases might still have payments in excess of the tax shield afforded by capital leases. Thus, it is important to check underlying assumptions and alternatives prior to making a general statement in regard to the net income and after-tax cash flow effect of an operating versus a capital lease. However, one may generalize that a capital lease lowers return on assets and increases financial leverage when compared to an operating lease.

DISCLOSURE REQUIREMENTS

The adverse effects on financial statements and selected financial ratios of the capital lease is mitigated by the disclosure requirements of FASB 13. Basically, the FASB statement requires companies with operating leases to disclose enough additional data so as to make them almost comparable to capital leases. Any knowledgeable financial analyst could find sufficient information in the required lease disclosure footnotes to make adjustments to the financial statements for the sake of direct comparison to the capital lease.

Bankers are fully aware of the fact that operating leases impact the financial leverage and risk of a company. In 1979, the Comptroller of the Currency determined in Interpretive Ruling 7.3400 that starting June 12, 1979, leases will be included as part of a bank's legal lending limit (National Banking Laws 12 U.S.C. 84).[1] "Legal lending limits" restrict banks from lending more than ten percent of their contributed capital (unimpaired capital stock) and retained earnings (unimpaired capital surplus) to any single individual, partnership, or corporation. Thus, a bank must combine a borrower's commercial loans (capital leases and other installment loans) and operating leases to ascertain whether it is within its legal lending limits. Whether a lease is classified as operating or capital, the banking community views them identically from a lending limit point of view. This ruling will tend to give companies the incentive to lease from third party lessors which are independent of their banks.

FASB 13 requires the following disclosure for an operating lease on the books of the lessee.[2]

1. Future minimum rental payments required as of the date of the latest balance sheet presented, in the aggregate and for each of the five succeeding fiscal years.
2. Total noncancelable sublease rentals to be received.
3. Total lease rental expenses for the period separated into:

    a. Standard minimum rental expense.

    b. Contingent rentals incurred.

    c. Sublease rentals incurred.

4. A general description of the lease:

    a. Basis for contingent rentals.

    b. Terms of renewal or purchase options and escalation clauses.

    c. Lease restrictions, e.g., additional debt or leasing.

    d. Miscellaneous

---

[1] Federal Register. Vol. 44, No. 73, Friday, April 13, 1979, Rules and Regulations.

[2] "Accounting for Leases," Statement of Financial Accounting Standards Board No. 13, Financial Standards Board, November 1976, pages 15-16.

		Operating Lease	Capital Lease
LIQUIDITY			
Current Ratio	$\dfrac{\text{Current Assets}}{\text{Current Liabilities}}$	$\dfrac{12,000}{3,000} = 4.00$	$\dfrac{13,000}{9,000} = 1.44$
Quick or Acid Test Ratio	$\dfrac{\text{Quick Assets}}{\text{Current Liabilities}}$	$\dfrac{8,000}{3,000} = 2.67$	$\dfrac{9,000}{9,000} = 1.00$
Net Working Capital	$\begin{array}{l}\text{Current Assets}\\-\ \text{Current Liabilities}\\=\text{Net Working Capital}\end{array}$	$\begin{array}{l}12,000\\-\ 3,000\\\hline 9,000\end{array}$	$\begin{array}{l}13,000\\-\ 9,000\\\hline 4,000\end{array}$
SOLVENCY			
Times Interest Earned	$\dfrac{\text{Interest} + \text{Taxes} + \text{Net Income}}{\text{Interest}}$	$\dfrac{26,000}{6,000} = 4.33$	$\dfrac{34,000}{16,000} = 2.13$
FINANCIAL LEVERAGE			
Debt to Equity	$\dfrac{\text{Debt}}{\text{Equity}}$	$\dfrac{23,000}{27,000} = .85$	$\dfrac{75,000}{26,000} = 2.88$
Percentage Debt	$\dfrac{\text{Debt}}{\text{Assets}}$	$\dfrac{23,000}{50,000} = .46$	$\dfrac{75,000}{101,000} = .74$
PROFITABILITY			
Net Profit Margin	$\dfrac{\text{Net Income}}{\text{Sales}}$	$\dfrac{10,000}{150,000} = .067$	$\dfrac{9,000}{150,000} = .060$
x Asset Turnover	$\dfrac{\text{Sales}}{\text{Assets}}$	$\dfrac{150,000}{50,000} = 3$	$\dfrac{150,000}{101,000} = 1.49$

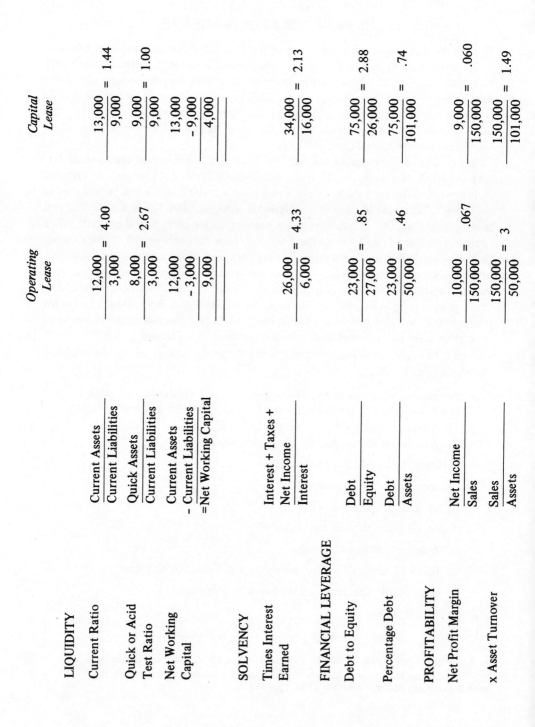

= Return on Assets	$\dfrac{\text{Net Income}}{\text{Assets}}$	$\dfrac{10{,}000}{50{,}000} = 20\%$	$\dfrac{9{,}000}{100{,}000} = 9\%$
x Leverage Factor	$\dfrac{\text{Assets}}{\text{Equity}}$	$\dfrac{50{,}000}{27{,}000} = 1.85$	$\dfrac{101{,}000}{26{,}000} = 3.8$
= Return on Equity	$\dfrac{\text{Net Income}}{\text{Equity}}$	$\dfrac{10{,}000}{27{,}000} = 37\%$	$\dfrac{9{,}000}{26{,}000} = 35\%$
x Retention Percentage	$\dfrac{\text{Net Income} - \text{Dividends}}{\text{Net Income}}$	$\dfrac{10{,}000 - 4{,}000}{10{,}000} = 60\%$	$\dfrac{9{,}000 - 4{,}000}{9{,}000} = 56\%$
= Potential Growth Rate	Return on Equity xRetention Percentage	$\begin{aligned}37.0\%\\ \underline{\text{x}60.0\%}\\ =22.2\%\end{aligned}$	$\begin{aligned}35.0\%\\ \underline{\text{x}56.0\%}\\ =19.6\%\end{aligned}$
Earnings Per Share	$\dfrac{\text{Net Income}}{\text{Total Shares}}$	$\dfrac{10{,}000}{5{,}000} = \$2$	$\dfrac{9{,}000}{5{,}000} = \$1.80$

EXCESS CASH FLOW COMPUTATION

Excess tax shield under the capital lease:

Capital lease interest expense	$10,000
Capital lease depreciation	7,000
Total capital lease deductions	17,000
Deduct operating lease payment	(15,000)
Equals excess tax shield	$ 2,000
Times Income Tax Rate	x .50
Equals Excess in Cash Flow[1]	$ 1,000

[1] Compare this to the same results found in the statement of changes in financial position – cash basis presented above.

FASB 13 requires the following disclosure for a capital lease on the books of the lessee[3] (note the similarity to the disclosure requirements of the operating lease):

1. The gross amount of assets recorded under capital leases as of the date of each balance sheet presented by major classes according to nature or function. This information may be combined with the comparable information for owned assets.

2. Future minimum lease payments as of the date of the latest balance sheet presented, in the aggregate and for each of the five succeeding fiscal years, with separate deductions from the total for the amount representing executory costs, including any profit thereon, included in the minimum lease payments and for the amount of the imputed interest necessary to reduce the net minimum lease payments to present value.

3. The total of minimum sublease rentals to be received in the future under noncancelable subleases as of the date of the latest balance sheet presented.

4. Total contingent rentals (rentals on which the amounts are dependent on some factor other than the passage of time) actually incurred for each period for which an income statement is presented.

IMPLICATIONS FOR FINANCIAL ANALYSIS

Now that we have discussed the basic differences between the capital lease and the operating lease, what are the implications for the analyst or any other user of the financial statements?

In the first place, it should be realized that during the noncancelable period of a capital or operating lease, a true obligation has been incurred by the company. Proper consideration of this obligation is required if the analyst is to fully understand the liquidity and financial leverage of the company. Overlooking lease debt under an operating lease is the same as ignoring any other commitment to creditors. In fact, leases sometimes represent very dangerous liabilities to the lessee.

In the common situation where the operating lease contract provides for acceleration of the remaining lease payments (which payments include principal and interest) in the event of lessee default, then the liability becomes greater than it would be under a loan agreement. When loan agreements are in default, the lender can only collect the unpaid remaining principal balance due, plus accrued interest. Whereas, if the same loan were structured as an operating lease, all of the following could be collected upon default: (1) principal; (2) accrued interest (past due lease payments); and (3) late charges; (4) remaining unpaid lease payments. So the nonconsideration of lease debt or lease obligations could represent a dangerous omission from the evaluation of liquidity and financial leverage.

---

[3]FASB No. 13, page 15.

In the second place, profitability percentages in terms of return on assets or return on equity are overstated when an operating lease is employed by a company rather than a capital lease. Profitability as a measure of a company's USE of assets should remain the same whether the USE of the asset is obtained under a capital lease or an operating lease. Unfortunately, traditional profitability analysis (without proper adjustment) is simply a measure of a company's OWNERSHIP of assets. When an asset is used without ownership, it does not show up on the balance sheet as an asset. Thus, return on assets is erroneously overstated.

To remedy this situation of an overstated return on assets and an understated liability, the balance sheet should be adjusted to reflect proper asset and liability amounts. This task can be accomplished through the use of information provided directly by the company or, if not available, then the information can be gleaned from the footnote disclosure describing the operating lease.

The footnote describing the operating lease, per FASB 13 guidelines, should disclose the future minimum rental payments required as of the date of the latest balance sheet, in the aggregate and for each of the five succeeding fiscal years. From this information, an approximation of the present value of the lease liability and leased asset value can be calculated by applying a discount rate of the company's incremental cost of debt to the average lease payments disclosed. The approximate cost of debt should be disclosed in other footnotes of the company; otherwise, use prime plus five percent as a discount rate. The average lease payment could be calculated by dividing the total of the next five years' lease payments by five. An approximation of the number of years remaining in the lease could be calculated by dividing the average lease payment just calculated into the total lease payments due as disclosed in the operating lease footnote. Given the average payment, discount rate, and number of payments, an approximation of the lease liability can be calculated using either a financial calculator or a table of present value factors.

The information referred to above should be used as follows to restate the balance sheet:

1. Add the total present value of lease payments to total assets.
2. Add the present value of the first year's payment to current liabilities.
3. Add the difference between number one above and number two above to long-term liabilities.

Once these adjustments have been made, recomputation of the following ratios will reflect the company's actual liquidity, financial leverage, and profitability status.

LIQUIDITY

1. Current Ratio
2. Quick Ratio

LEVERAGE

1. Debt to Equity
2. Percentage Debt

PROFITABILITY

1. Return on Assets
2. Return on Equity

An example of readjustment of financial statements for an operating lease based upon information contained in a footnote will now be explained.

Refer to exhibit *A* below describing a typical operating lease footnote. Follow these steps to determine the balance sheet adjustments:

1. Determine the average lease payment during the next five years.

    a. Total the lease payments from year one throught year five ($50,000 through the $35,000 figure). The resulting total will be $200,000.

    b. Divide the total from step *a* above by five, which results in an average lease payment of $40,000 ($200,000/5 = $40,000).

2. Determine the average term of the operating leases by dividing the total lease payment calculated in step *1a* above, $40,000. The resulting quotient is eight years— $320,000/$40,000 = eight years.

3. Determine or approximate the appropriate incremental cost of debt by finding a rate in the debt disclosure footnotes or by using the current prime rate plus five percent. Assume for this case that the appropriate cost of debt is fifteen percent.

4. Determine the present value of eight payments of $40,000 each discounted at fifteen percent, where the present value of an ordinary annuity factor for n = 8, i = 15% is 4.4873. To accomplish this step, simply multiply the present-value factor of 4.4873 times the $40,000 average lease payment. The resulting product of $179,492 represents the amount that should be added back to total assets.

5. Determine the amount of the current liability. Take the present value of the first year's lease payments due of $50,000 and discount one period at fifteen percent (present value of one for one period at fifteen percent is .8696). The present value is found by multiplying the lease payment of $50,000 by the present-value factor of .8696. The resulting product of $43,480 represents the amount that should be added to current liabilities (current portion of leases payable).

6. Determine the amount of the long-term liability. This amount is arrived at by deducting from the asset value ($179,492, step 4 above) the amount of the current liability ($43,480, step 5 above); the difference is $136,012. This difference should be added to long-term liabilities of the firm.

EXHIBIT A

OPERATING LEASE FOOTNOTE

Minimum Lease Payments

Year	1	$50,000
	2	40,000
	3	40,000
	4	35,000
	5	35,000
Thereafter		120,000
Total		$320,000
Incremental Cost of Debt		15%

CONCLUSION

Whether a lease is accounted for as a Capital Lease or an Operating Lease has been demonstrated to have a significant effect on the financial statements and financial ratios of a company. Also, the importance of restating a company's balance sheet to reflect an operating lease's true debt obligation to the company has been explained.

4

Yield Analysis, Internal Rate of Return, Net Present Value Techniques ___ From the Lessor Viewpoint ___

Chapter 3 examined the effect of a capital lease compared to an operating lease on the books of the lessee. This chapter examines nonleveraged leases from the lessor's point of view. It describes the techniques used in the leasing industry to determine whether a given nonleveraged lease is a good investment. Answers to questions such as how profitable is a lease, what is a lease's yield, what is its net present value, will be explained. Leveraged lease accounting and analysis will be discussed in chapter 10.

The most common analytical techniques employed in the industry are yield and internal rate of return analysis. Some firms use net present value analysis. Also, the less frequently used payback method and accounting yields will be examined. The standard sinking fund method used for yield analysis of leveraged leases will be discussed in chapter 10.

LEASE YIELD ANALYSIS

In order to operate a leasing company successfully, the lessor must be able to structure a lease with a sufficient yield to cover not only operating expenses but interest expense and profit as well. Therefore, it is essential to an understanding of leasing to be able to calculate or to establish the required yield of a lease. There are nineteen common yields that can be calculated in relation to any particular lease. Of the nineteen yields, sixteen are valid from a financial and mathematical point of view. The nineteen yields will be categorized into the following three groups to facilitate their explanation: (1) Gross Pretax Yields; (2) Capital Budgeting Internal Rate of Return Yields; and (3) Accounting Yields.

In determining any of the various lease yields it is essential to know how to use an advanced financial calculator. Such a calculator can calculate an internal rate of return for numerous uneven positive or negative cash inflows that occur frequently in leases. The most versatile, efficient, and inexpensive hand-held financial calculators we have found are the Hewlett Packard Model 38C or 12C, advanced financial calculators. These models can handle up to twenty groups of uneven cash inflows, each group containing ninety-nine or fewer payments. Texas Instruments and other companies make calculators capable of handling lease problems, too. Whichever brand of calculator is used is not as important as knowing how to use it. Anyone seriously interested in leasing must know how to use financial calculators which are now considered basic tools of the trade.

The explanations of the lease yield calculations throughout this chapter have been based on the assumption that the reader has access to a Hewlett Packard Model 38C or 12C. However, the explanations and notations are readily adaptable to any other brand of calculator.

The calculation of each yield will be based upon the following assumptions:

1. Lease term: forty-eight months with the first and last rental payments beginning at the inception of the lease (two advance payments with forty-six remaining). The lease can, but is not expected to, be renewed for an additional twelve months.
2. Lessor is in a forty-six percent tax bracket.
3. The monthly rental shall be $2,937.
4. Security deposit of $1,350 is required to be paid in advance to secure faithful performance of all the conditions of the lease. The deposit is refundable at the end of the lease if all conditions have been performed. The security deposit is worth a pretax equivalent of $2,500 ($1,350 ÷ one minus the tax rate of forty-six percent).
5. The fair market value (retail price) of the leased equipment is $100,000.
6. A $17,500 purchase option is exercisable at the end of the lease. The option is considered sufficiently close to the asset's expected fair market value to allow the lease to remain classified as an operating lease on the books of the lessor from a tax point of view both a revenue ruling 55-540 and safe harbor tax point of view.
7. The lessor will retain the full investment tax credit of $10,000 (ten percent of FMV $100,000). The ITC is worth $18,519 on a pretax equivalent basis ($10,000 ITC ÷ one minus the tax rate of forty-six percent).
8. The lessor is a third-party lessor who has no expected gross profit in this accounting classified direct financing capital lease.

GROSS PRETAX YIELDS AND THEIR USE

1. *Gross Pretax Yield* where the advance payments, deposit, purchase option, and ITC are NOT considered. The outflows, inflows, and time periods of this particular yield are indicated below. Also, the calculator keys utilized and proper sequence used in calculating the yields are indicated below. The lease

a. | *Outflow* | *Inflows* | *Time* | *Yield* |
|---|---|---|---|
| -100,000 | 2,937 | for 48 Periods | 17.9904% |

b. $100,000   [CHS] [g] [CF$_0$]   shows a negative outflow at time "0."

    $2,937   [g] [CF$_j$]   shows amount of each payment.

    48   [g] [N$_j$]   shows the number of payments.

    [f] [IRR] =1.5%   calculates monthly IRR yield.

    [g] [12x] [f] [4]   = 17.9904% converted to annual four decimal place percent.

c. Use of the Gross Pretax Yield is widespread notwithstanding the fact that it is invalid from a strict mathematical point of view. The yield calculation above does not consider that the stream of lease payments contains only forty-six remaining payments since two were paid at the inception of the lease. Thus, the yield or IRR should be calculated by deducting two payments from the initial outflow and reducing the number of payments "n" by two. The next yield calculation will properly consider the two payments in advance and will result in an accurate lease yield that is almost two percent higher.

      Unfortunately, the incorrect gross pretax yield unadjusted for the two advance payments is widely quoted by lessors to inquisitive lessees who want to know the implicit interest rate in a lease. The reason for the yield's popular use is obvious – it understates the true implicit interest rate of the lease which unwary lessees assume to be accurate.

2. *Gross Pretax Yield with Advance Payments* where the advance payments are included but the deposit, purchase option, and ITC are excluded from the

computation. This yield is mathematically correct although not totally complete due to the exclusion of the deposit, etc. The yield is calculated as follows:

a. | *Outflow* | *Inflows* | *Time* | *Yield* |
|---|---|---|---|
| −100,000 | 2,937 | for 46 | 19,8178% |
| + 5,874 | | Periods | |
| − 94,126 Net | | | |

b. $94,126 [CHS] [g] [CF$_0$]   shows negative outflow at time "0" adjusted for 2 advance payments

$ 2,937 [g] [CF$_j$]

46 [g] [N$_j$]

[f] [IRR] = 1.65

[g] [12x] [f] [4] = 19.8178%

c. Employment of the Gross Pretax Yield with Advance Payments is common although it is used less than the previously mentioned invalid yield. The gross yield with advance payments is quite similar to the interest rate a bank would quote for a similar installment loan and therefore is quite useful in the leasing industry. The limitations, of the yield are that the deposit, purchase option, and the ITC have been ignored. These omitted items affect the lease yield significantly.

3. *Discount Interest or Add-on Interest Yield* is a type of pretax yield that ignores advance payments, deposit, ITC, and sometimes the purchase option. The yield is calculated as follows:

a. Compute total payments made under the lease including a purchase option if it is expected to be exercised.

48 x $2,937 =	$140,976
Option	17,500
Total	$158,476

(48 [Enter] 2,937 [X] = $140,976)

b. Deduct FMV of the   − $100,000
   leased asset.   = $ 58,476   = total interest to be paid.

c. Divide remainder by
   the number of years $\dfrac{\$58,476}{4}$ = \$14,619 = Average annual interest.
   in the lease.

   (58,476 | Enter | 4 | ÷ | = \$14,619)

d. Divide the quotient
   from "c" by the FMV
   of the leased asset. $\dfrac{\$\ 14,619}{\$100,000}$ = 14.6190%   Add-on rate
   The new quotient is   per year.
   the add-on yield.

e. If the option were
   not expected to be
   exercised the Discount
   Rate would be:
   $40,976 ÷ 4 = $10,244 ÷ 100,000 = 10.2440%

f. Quoting of add-on or discount interest yields to lessees is frequent although highly unscrupulous. The discount or add-on yield obviously understates the real interest rate implicit in the lease. Furthermore, it is
   based on the false premise that the entire principal (FMV) of the lease receivable on the lessor's books never diminishes throughout the lease term.
   In reality, each lease rental payment to the lessor represents a return of
   investment (principal reduction) and a return on investment (interest income). Therefore, this yield is mathematically and financially incorrect.
   As long as unsuspecting lessees are gullible this yield will continue to be
   quoted by unprincipled lessors. Although such abuses might eventually
   prompt the Federal Government to expand the Uniform Consumer Credit
   Code (UCCC) to disallow such activities. The UCCC already requires an
   annual percentage rate (APR) to be calculated properly and be stipulated
   in consumer loan agreements.

4. *Gross Pretax Yield with Advance Payments and Deposit.* This yield is basically
   the same as number two above except the effect of the advance deposit will

now be taken into consideration. Since deposits are nontaxable they must be divided by one minus the tax rate to place them on a pretax equivalent basis. Thus, the $1,350 deposit is worth $2,500 in pretax value ($1,350 ÷ .54) to the lessor. If this adjustment is not made then the yield would not be truly pretax.

The ITC and purchase option are disregarded in computing this yield as shown below:

a.	*Outflow*	*Inflows*	*Time*	*Yield*
	– 100,000	2,937	for 46 periods	20.7066%
	+ 5,874	-0-	in the 47th period	
	+ 2,500	–2,500	in the 48th period	
	– 91,626			

b. $91,626 [CHS] [g] [CF$_0$]

$ 2,937 [g] [CF$_j$]

46 [g] [N$_j$]

0 [g] [CF$_j$] no payment in 47th period

$ 2,500 [CHS] [g] [CF$_j$] repayment of deposit in 48th period

[f] [IRR] = 1.73

[g] [12x] [f] [4] = 20.7066%

c. In the situation where the lessee does not expect to exercise a purchase option or to receive the investment tax credit then this yield is an excellent indicator of the implicit interest in the lease. However, from the lessor's viewpoint this yield is understated due to the retention of the ITC and the purchase option at the end of the lease which would make the lessor's yield higher were the option exercised. In any case this is perhaps the best yield to quote a lessee.

5. *Gross Pretax Yield with Advance Payments and Option* where the purchase option is considered at all. The purchase option is considered to be exercised at the end of the lease for $17,500.00 and the security deposit and investment tax credit are ignored. Calculation of this yield with a calculator and lease yield tables is described on the following page.

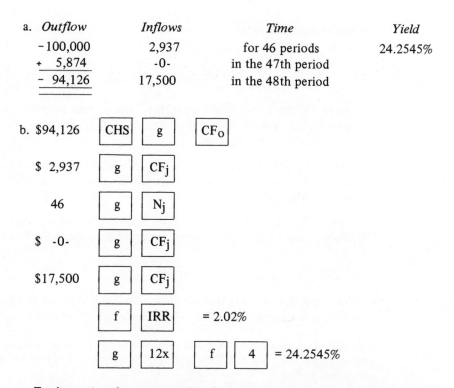

a. | Outflow | Inflows | Time | Yield |
    |---|---|---|---|
    | −100,000 | 2,937 | for 46 periods | 24.2545% |
    | + 5,874 | -0- | in the 47th period | |
    | − 94,126 | 17,500 | in the 48th period | |

b. $94,126   [CHS] [g]   [CF$_0$]

$ 2,937   [g] [CF$_j$]

46   [g] [N$_j$]

$ -0-   [g] [CF$_j$]

$17,500   [g] [CF$_j$]

[f] [IRR]   = 2.02%

[g] [12x]   [f] [4]   = 24.2545%

c. To determine the pretax yield of a lease using lease tables given a certain level periodic payment, the number of advance lease payments, and their percentage residual value, divide the monthly lease payment by the original cost of the leased asset. The resulting quotient will be the lease factor.

d. Refer to the tables of pretax lease yields (next three pages), and search for the lease rate factor calculated above under the column heading "Lease Rate Factor" and the row for the months in the lease. When you have located the closest lease rate factor, then read to the right in the row for the yield corresponding to the payments required in advance on your lease. If the lease also has a percentage residual value, then find the yield factor in the same row and *ADD* this yield factor to the one previously found for the number of advance payments.

e. *Example* – What pretax yield does the following lease offer the lessor?

   i. Forty-eight monthly payments of $2,937

   ii. Two payments required in advance

   iii. 17.5 percent residual value

   iv. FMV of asset leased $100,000.00

f. *Solution*

   i. Determine the Lease Rate Factor:

$$\frac{\$2,937.00}{\$100,000.00} = .02937$$

   ii. Search for the Lease Rate Factor under the column heading "Lease Rate Factor" and the forty-eight month row. This factor is found under the eighteen percent table.

   iii. Locate the proper yield factor for two (2) payments required in advance, which is 19.82 percent. This is the same yield calculated in yield number two above.

   iv. Add to 19.82 the residual value factor 4.29 which is an average of the fifteen percent and twenty percent residual value columns (3.74 + 4.84 ÷ 2).

   v. The pretax yield is, therefore, 24.11 percent (19.82 + 4.29).

   vi. For Lease Rate Factors that you have calculated which are not found in the tables, simply interpolate or use an advanced financial calculator.

g. Solution using a financial calculator where an IRR is found will give the answer as 24.2545 percent. This, of course, is the most accurate and easiest approach.

This yield is commonly used in the leasing industry since it gives the lessor a more comprehensive answer to the lease yield question. Certainly the exercising of a purchase option assumed in the calculation will significantly increase the lease yield. Unfortunately, this particular yield is deficient in that it ignores the ITC and the security deposit, both of which affect the yield to the lessor.

6. *Gross Pretax Yield with Advance Payments, Deposit, and Purchase Option* where the purchase option is assumed to be exercised at $15,000 since the deposit refund would offset the option cost ($17,500 – $2,500 deposit = $15,000). It is common to assume that the security deposit will in fact be refunded to the lessee at the end of the lease. Computation of this yield follows:

a.

Outflow	Inflows	Time	Yield
– 100,000	2,937	for 46 periods	25.1986%
+ 5,874	-0-	in 47th period	
+ 2,500	15,000	in 48th period	
– 91,626			

19% TABLE OF PRETAX LEASE YIELDS
(ITC Passed to Lessee)
BASE YIELD 19%

Lease Term In Months	Lease Rate Factor	PAYMENTS REQUIRED IN ADVANCE						RESIDUAL VALUE		
		0	1	2	3	4	5	10%	15%	20%
12	.09216	19.00	24.75	31.94	41.25	53.61	70.61	14.63	21.10	27.12
24	.05041	19.00	21.15	23.59	26.37	29.55	33.23	6.54	9.45	12.17
36	.03666	19.00	20.42	21.88	23.47	25.22	27.15	3.82	5.54	7.15
48	.02990	19.00	19.96	21.03	22.16	23.37	24.68	2.49	3.63	4.70
60	.02594	19.00	19.72	20.60	21.47	22.41	23.42	1.73	2.53	3.29
72	.02338	19.00	19.67	20.37	21.11	21.90	22.74	1.25	1.83	2.39
84	.02161	19.00	19.59	20.21	20.86	21.55	22.28	0.93	1.36	1.78
96	.02033	19.00	19.54	20.10	20.68	21.30	21.96	0.70	1.04	1.36

18% TABLE OF PRETAX LEASE YIELDS
(ITC Passed to Lessee)
BASE YIELD 18%

Lease Term In Months	Lease Rate Factor	PAYMENTS REQUIRED IN ADVANCE						RESIDUAL VALUE		
		0	1	2	3	4	5	10%	15%	20%
12	.09168	18.00	23.55	30.48	39.47	57.38	67.71	14.73	21.24	27.30
24	.04992	18.00	20.02	22.36	25.01	28.05	31.55	6.64	9.59	12.33
36	.03615	18.00	19.36	20.75	22.27	23.93	25.76	3.90	5.66	7.30
48	.02937	18.00	18.87	19.82	21.04	22.18	23.42	2.57	3.74	4.84
60	.02539	18.00	18.73	19.50	20.32	21.19	22.11	1.80	2.62	3.41
72	.02281	18.00	18.62	19.28	19.98	20.71	21.48	1.31	1.92	2.49
84	.02102	18.00	18.55	19.13	19.74	20.38	21.05	0.98	1.44	1.88
96	.01972	18.00	18.50	19.02	19.57	20.14	20.73	0.75	1.10	1.44

17% TABLE OF PRETAX LEASE YIELDS
(ITC Passed to Lessee)
BASE YIELD 17%

Lease Term In Months	Lease Rate Factor	PAYMENTS REQUIRED IN ADVANCE						RESIDUAL VALUE		
		0	1	2	3	4	5	10%	15%	20%
12	.09120	17.00	22.31	29.03	37.20	49.17	64.83	14.83	21.38	27.47
24	.04944	17.00	18.90	21.13	23.66	26.56	29.89	6.73	9.72	12.50
36	.03565	17.00	18.30	19.62	21.06	22.63	24.37	3.99	5.78	7.45
48	.02886	17.00	17.96	18.90	19.91	20.99	22.16	2.65	3.84	4.97
60	.02485	17.00	17.68	18.40	19.16	19.98	20.85	1.87	2.72	3.53
72	.02225	17.00	17.58	18.19	18.84	19.52	20.23	1.37	2.00	2.60
84	.02044	17.00	17.51	18.05	18.62	19.21	19.82	1.03	1.51	1.97
96	.01912	17.00	17.46	17.95	18.45	18.98	19.53	0.79	1.17	1.52

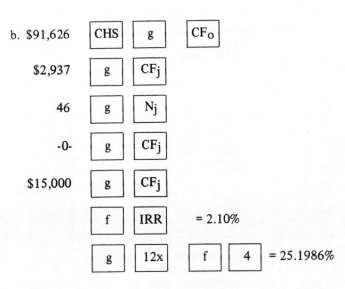

b. $91,626 CHS   g   CF₀

$2,937   g   CFⱼ

46   g   Nⱼ

-0-   g   CFⱼ

$15,000   g   CFⱼ

f   IRR   = 2.10%

g   12x   f   4   = 25.1986%

c. This is the most comprehensive yield covered thus far and is the most popular "accurate" gross pretax yield employed by lessors who desire an "overall" pretax lease yield which includes the exercising of a purchase option and the other structuring variables except the ITC. It is frequently used by lessors in the case where the ITC has been passed on to the lessee.

7. *Gross Pretax Yield with Advance Payments, Deposit, Purchase Option, and ITC* - this yield is based on the assumption that the ITC is retained by the lessor until the lessee exercises the purchase option when twenty percent of the original ITC must be recaptured. Assets sold prior to the end of their depreciation life cause ITC to be recaptured if the depreciation taken prior to the disposal date was less than five years. The investment tax credit of $10,000 must be adjusted to a pretax basis by dividing it by one minus the tax rate. The pretax value of the $10,000 ITC is worth $18,519 ($10,000 ÷ .54). If this adjustment is not made then the yield is not truly pretax since the value of ITC at $10,000 is aftertax rather than pretax because ITC is not a taxable item.

a.
Outflows	Inflows	Time	Yield
−100,000	+2,937	for 46 periods	38.0572%
+ 5,874	-0-	in 47th period	
+ 2,500	+17,500	Purchase Option	
+ 18,519ITC	−3,704	Recapture in 48th period (2,000 ÷ .54 = 3704)	
− 73,107	−2,500	Deposit refund	
	+11,296	Net inflow 48th period	

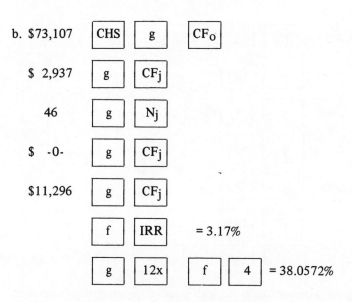

b. $73,107 [CHS] [g] [CF_0]

$ 2,937 [g] [CF_j]

46 [g] [N_j]

$ -0- [g] [CF_j]

$11,296 [g] [CF_j]

[f] [IRR] = 3.17%

[g] [12x] [f] [4] = 38.0572%

c. This yield is used frequently in the industry as a gross pretax indicator of profitability. The justification for considering the yield as pretax is that many analysts feel the investment tax credit is more a government incentive for capital investment than a type of tax. It is purely for the sake of convenience that the U.S. Treasury pays these investment incentives in the form of a tax reduction. Notice the ITC recapture at the end of the lease. The lessor will have earned only eight percent, thus two percent or $2,000 must be paid back to the IRS. Under the new tax act of 1981 lessors earn ITC at the rate of 2 percent a year.

8. *Gross Pretax Yield with Advance Payments, Deposit, ITC and an Unguaranteed Residual,* where the investment tax credit is not recaptured since with an unguaranteed residual the lessor, is assumed to still own and retain the asset and therefore is still entitled to the full ITC. This yield is calculated the same as number seven above except there is no recapture adjustment in the forty-eighth period.

a. *Outflows*	*Inflows*	*Time*	*Yield*
-100,000	2,937	for 46 periods	38.7730%
+ 5,874	-0-	in 47th period	
+ 2,500	15,000	in 48th period	(17,500-2,500)
+ 18,519			
- 73,107			

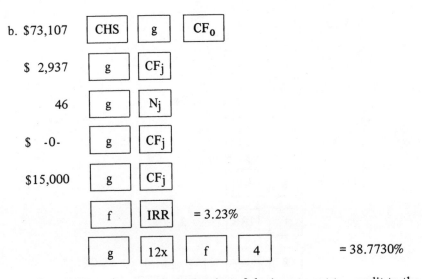

b. $73,107 [CHS] [g] [CF₀]

$ 2,937 [g] [CFj]

46 [g] [Nj]

$ -0- [g] [CFj]

$15,000 [g] [CFj]

[f] [IRR] = 3.23%

[g] [12x] [f] [4]   = 38.7730%

c. This yield demonstrates the high value of the investment tax credit to the lessor. Notice that when the lessor did not recapture the ITC the lease yield increased by 2.5 percent. This yield is also the most useful and comprehensive of all the gross, pretax yields calculated thus far.

9. *Gross After-Tax Yield with Advance Payments, Deposit, ITC, and a Purchase Option,* where the ITC is expected to be recaptured. The anticipated depreciation tax shield cash benefits are factored in as a source of lease revenue.

a. *Cash Flow Analysis:*

Lease Revenue	35,244	35,244	35,244	$29,370
ACRS Depreciation	−20,000	−32,000	−24,000	−16,000
Pretax Income	15,244	3,244	11,244	13,370
Taxes @ 46%	−7,012	−1,492	−5,172	−6,150
Gross After-Tax Income	8,232	1,752	6,072	7,220

Adjustments:

Tax Adjusted Purchase Option				13,130[1]
Depreciation	20,000	32,000	24,000	16,000
Deposit Refund				−1,350
ITC Recapture				−2,000
Total Cash Flow:	28,232	33,752	30,072	33,000

[1]17,500 − 8,000 Book Value=Taxable Gain; 9,500 gain x .46 = 4,370; 17,500 − 4,370 = 13,130.

b. *Net Investment Analysis:*

$$
\begin{array}{ll}
-100,000 & \text{Investment} \\
+\quad 3,172 & \text{After-Tax Advance Payments (5.874 x .54)} \\
+\quad 1,350 & \text{Deposit} \\
+\quad 10,000 & \text{Investment Tax Credit} \\
\hline
-\quad 85,478 &
\end{array}
$$

c. *Solution:*

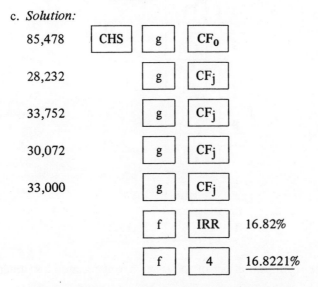

85,478	CHS	g	CF_0
28,232		g	CF_j
33,752		g	CF_j
30,072		g	CF_j
33,000		g	CF_j
		f	IRR 16.82%
		f	4 16.8221%

d. Although still considered a gross yield, this rate of return is figured on an after-tax basis. The yield can be compared directly with a company's after-tax cost of debt to ascertain the spread between return on assets and cost of debt. The drawback to this yield is that other tax deductible expenses should also be considered when arriving at a true after-tax yield. Also, the yield could be improved by computing the average monthly inflows each year and using these monthly figures in the yield computation.

10. Gross Pretax Yield with Advance Payments, Deposit, ITC pass-through, and a fixed purchase option (calculated from the lessee's point of view who is assumed also to be in a forty-six percent tax bracket).

a. *Inflows:*

$$
\begin{array}{ll}
+100,000 & \text{FMV Equipment} \\
-\quad 5,874 & \text{Advance Payments} \\
-\quad 2,500 & \text{Deposit (Pretax Equivalent)} \\
+\quad 18,519 & \text{ITC (Pretax Equivalent)} \\
\hline
+110,145 &
\end{array}
$$

Outflows:

Months 1-46	−$2,937
Month 47	$ 0
Month 48	−$17,500 + 2,500 = −$15,000

b. *Solution:*

110,145	CHS	g	CF$_0$
2,937		g	CF$_j$
46		g	N$_j$
0		g	CF$_j$
15,000		g	CF$_j$
		f	IRR	1.27%
g	12x	f	4	<u>15.1856%</u>

c. Notice the significant effect of the lessee having received investment tax credit.

11. *Quantification of Risk*

a. *Yields are* highly sensitive to the value placed on the unguaranteed residual. Determining unguaranteed residual values is a difficult subjective task. Lessors frequently use a combination of probability analysis, decision tree flowcharting, and standard deviation information to arrive at an expected value of the residual to be used in lease yield analysis.

This valuation technique can also be used in the situation where a lease contains a purchase option - since the lessor might not be certain that the purchase option will be exercised. If the option were not exercised, there would be doubt as to the expected value of the leased equipment reverting back to the lessor. The following six step residual valuation technique can be used to determine the expected value of the residual (EVR) whether the residual results from a purchase option, guaranteed residual, or unguaranteed residual.

b. Six Step Residual Valuation Technique

   i. *Step One*

Determine the alternative outcomes and the probability of their occurrence using decision-tree analysis. The lease contains a purchase option ($1,000) that may or may not be exercised.

		Expected *Outcome*	*Probability of* *Occurrence*
40% Purchase Option Exercised	—— $1,000		40%
	$ 900		10%
60%	$ 800		20%
Purchase Option Not Exercised	$ 700		40%
	$ 600		20%
	$ 500		10%

c. *Step Two*

Determine the joint probability of outcomes, which is the product of the branch probability where the option is not exercised, sixty percent, times the probability of each expected outcome.

$$.6 \times .1 = .06$$
$$.6 \times .2 = .12$$
$$.6 \times .4 = .24$$
$$.6 \times .2 = .12$$
$$.6 \times .1 = \underline{.06}$$
$$\underline{\underline{60\%}}$$

d. *Step Three*

Compute the expected value of the residual (EVR) assuming perfect information ($P_i R_1$ = EVR)

	Joint *Probabilities*		*Expected* *Outcomes*		*Expected* *Values*
Option Exercised	.40	X	$1,000	=	$400
Option Not Exercised	.06	X	$ 900	=	$ 54
	.12	X	$ 800	=	$ 96
	.24	X	$ 700	=	$168
	.12	X	$ 600	=	$ 82
	.06	X	$ 500	=	$ 30
	EVR			–	$820

e. *Step Four*

Compute the standard deviation of the EVR which indicates the degree of risk or variability in the EVR. σ is the symbol for the standard deviation.

$$EVR = \sqrt{\sum_{i=1} P_i(R_1 - EVR)^2}$$

.40	X	$(1,000-820)^2$	=	12,960
.06	X	$(900-820)^2$	=	384
.12	X	$(800-820)^2$	=	48
.24	X	$(700-820)^2$	=	3,456
.12	X	$(600-820)^2$	=	5,808
.06	X	$(500-820)^2$	=	6,144
				28,800

$$\sqrt{28,800} \quad = \quad 169.71 = \sigma \, EVR$$

f. *Step Five*

Compute the Expected Value of the Residual given a required probability that the residual will be equal or greater than. This required probability above which the residual value is expected is referred to as the EVR_C and is calculated from the following equation.

$$EVR_C = EVR - (\sigma \, EVR \times C)$$

Where:

EVR	=	Computed Above, 820.00
σ EVR	=	Computed Above, 169.71
C	=	Confidence Coefficients from Table Below

Frequently used confidence coefficients or required probabilities of occurrences:

		C Value
95%	=	1.65
90%	=	1.28
85%	=	1.04
80%	=	.84
75%	=	.67
70%	=	.52

Using a required probability of occurrence of ninety percent, the Expected Value of the Residual (EVR_C) would be calculated as follows:

$$EVR_C = EVR - (\sigma \, EVR \times C)$$
$$EVR_C = 820 - (169.71 \times 1.28) = 602.77$$

g. *Step Six*

We therefore conclude that we are ninety percent certain that the residual value will be equal or greater than $602.77. This amount could then be used to compute a lease yield that we would expect to receive on a lease with ninety percent confidence. Or the amount could be used in a lease versus buy decision.

CAPITAL BUDGETING YIELDS AND THEIR USE

Prior to computing the three commonly used capital budgeting yields several additional assumptions must be stated:

1. Lessor is leveraged 4:1 debt-equity; eighty percent debt-twenty percent equity. The debt costs twelve percent annual interest.
2. Lessor depreciates the leased asset over five years using new ACRs method.
3. General and Administrative cost have been allocated to lease expenses along with initial direct costs.
4. Investment tax credits and net operating loss tax benefits are assumed to result fully in tax savings.
5. The two advance payments, the security deposit, and the investment tax credit are not included in the following financial statements since these items are included as offsets against the initial cost of the lease at its inception.
6. Normally this analyʒis is performed on a monthly basis with proper tax allocation among quarters.

ACCOUNTING INCOME
(per IRS requirements)

Year:	1	2	3	4
Lease Revenue	+35,244	+35,244	+35,244	+29,370
Direct Costs	− 500			
ACRS Depreciation	−20,000	−32,000	−24,000	−16,000
General & Administration	− 1,500	− 1,500	− 1,500	− 1,500
Income Before Taxes	+13,244	+ 1,744	+ 9,744	+11,876
Income Taxes @ 46%	− 6,092	− 802	− 4,482	− 5,460
NET INCOME	+ 7,152	+ 942	+ 5,262	+ 6,410

CASH FLOW INCOME

Year:	1	2	3	4
Lease Revenue	+35,244	+35,244	+35,244	+29,370(4)
Direct Costs	− 500			
Option & Tax Gain (1)				+13,130
General & Administration	− 1,500	− 1,500	− 1,500	− 1,500
Taxes	− 6,092	− 802	− 4,482	− 5,460
Deposit Refund				− 1,350
ITC Recapture				− 2,000
Subtotal(2)	+27,152	+32,942	+29,262	+32,190
Loan Payments (12% Int.)	−26,339	−26,339	−26,339	−26,339
Less Interest Tax Savings	+ 4,416	+ 3,492	+ 2,457	+ 1,298
Net Cash Flow(3)	+ 5,229	+10,095	+ 5,380	+ 7,149

---

(1) Tax Gain = 100,000 − 92,000 Accumulated Depreciation = 8,000 − 17,500 option = 9,500
Tax Gain 9,500 X .46 = 4,370 − 17,500 = 13,130

(2) These cash flows are used in conventional Internal Rate of Return Analysis (IRR). Note the loan payments are not deducted from after-tax cash flow.

(3) These cash flows are used in Net After-Tax Return on Equity Analysis.

(4) Year four has less revenue due to the two advance payments paid at the lease's inception.

1. *Conventional Internal Rate of Return Yield (IRR)* − This method employs after-tax cash flows shown as the sub-total (2) on the cash flow statement. These cash flows represent the cash remaining after paying all cash expenses excepting loan payments. These cash flows represent the after-tax net cash available for creditors and equity holders. The calculation of the IRR is more complex than the previous yields because of the uneven cash flows occurring in each year.

a. *Outflow* *Inflow*   *IRR Yield*

	1	2	3	4	
− 100,000					
+ 3,172*	27,152	32,942	29,262	32,190	15.3880%
+ 1,350					
+ 10,000					
− 85,478					

*Advance payments $5,874 x .54

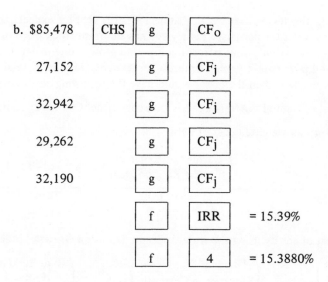

b. $85,478 [CHS] [g] [CF$_O$]

27,152 [g] [CF$_j$]

32,942 [g] [CF$_j$]

29,262 [g] [CF$_j$]

32,190 [g] [CF$_j$]

[f] [IRR] = 15.39%

[f] [4] = 15.3880%

c. Conventional Internal Rate of Return (IRR) analysis involves the comparison of a company's IRR, 15.3880% computed above, with the incremental, after-tax, weighted-average cost of capital of the company. If the IRR is equal or greater than the lease company's cost of capital, the lease investment should be made.

The question often arises; why should a lease be made if its IRR is equal to the firm's cost of capital? Does this situation not result in a simple break-even position that normally should be avoided? The answer is that if the firm's IRR equals its cost of capital then the leasing company is in an excellent position. To understand why this is true requires an understanding of the components making up the cost of capital.

Basically, cost of capital is an average cost of the two components of capital: namely, debt and equity. The cost of debt is the annual after-tax cost of interest paid creditors, whereas, the cost of equity is the cost of dividends paid shareholders and the implied cost of retaining some of each year's income in the company to maintain a constant growth in earnings per share. Thus, if creditors have received their interest, shareholders their dividends, and the company a sufficient addition in retained earnings to provide growth, then at break-even, where IRR equals these three elements, all costs have been taken care of.

Assuming the lessor used as the subject of this chapter expects to pay dividends of $2.04 per share next year, has a current stock price of $40, and requires a twenty-four percent compound growth rate in earnings per share, and pays twelve percent interest for its debt, is in the forty-six percent tax bracket, then the lessor would have the following cost of capital:

i.   Cost of Capital = After-tax weighted cost of debt + cost of equity

ii. After -tax weighted cost of debt =

$$\left(\begin{array}{c}\text{Debt Percentage}\\\text{Weighting Factor}\end{array}\right) \qquad \left(\begin{array}{c}\text{Current or Expected}\\\text{Interest Rate on Debt}\end{array}\right) \quad \text{X} \quad (1-\text{Tax Rate})$$

Weight	X	Debt Cost	X	Tax Adjustment
.80	X	.12	X	(1 - .46) = 5.18%

iii. Cost of equity using the widely accepted Gordon Growth Model:

$$\left(\begin{array}{c}\text{Equity Percentage}\\\text{Weighting Factor}\end{array}\right) \quad \text{X} \quad \left(\frac{\text{Dividend Next Year}}{\text{Stock Price Currently}}\right) \quad + \quad \left(\begin{array}{c}\text{Expected Growth}\\\text{Rate in EPS}\end{array}\right)$$

Weight	X	Dividend Yield + Growth Requirement		
.20	X	$\left(\frac{2.04}{40} + .24\right)$		
.2	X	$(.051 + .24)$	= 5.82%	

iv. Total combined after-tax average weighted cost of capital:

5.18% (Debt) plus 5.82% (Equity) equals 11.0%

v.   In this particular case the IRR was computed at 15.3880 percent which is in excess of the leasing company's eleven percent cost of capital. Therefore, we conclude the lease will make an excellent investment.

vi. The difficulty with the conventional IRR analytical technique is that it gives only a "go, no-go" answer and little information as to the actual return on equity investment after all expenses including interest have been considered. Thus, most knowledgeable financial analysts employ not only conventional IRR analysis but also the other yields previously described and the analytical techniques yet to be explained.

vii. Another difficulty with the conventional IRR method is the assumption inherent within the IRR calculations that all cash returns to the lessor can be reinvested at the IRR. Cash inflows frequently can only be invested at a lower reinvestment rate which is equal or less than the company's cost of capital. The next lease yield describes how to compensate for a reinvestment rate that differs from the IRR.

2. *Adjusted Internal Rate of Return (IRR adj.)* – This yield is based upon the same cash flows as the conventional IRR; however, the calculation is somewhat different as described below:

a. Assume a reinvestment rate of eleven percent which is equal to the firm's cost of capital. Determine the future value of each cash inflow assumed invested at the eleven percent reinvestment rate and total them. Then, find the IRR that relates this future value total to the present value of the lease costs (outflow at time zero). The reason a reinvestment rate is established is to overcome the difficulty of the implicit IRR assumption that all cash inflows are reinvested at the Internal Rate of Return which ofttimes is unrealistically high. Many firms assume a reinvestment rate equal to their cost of debt after-tax or their average pretax portfolio yield.

b.

Outflows	Inflows		11% Future Value Factor		Future Value
-100,000 1	27,152	X	1.368	=	37,144
+ 3,172 2	32,942	X	1.232	=	40,585
+ 1,350 3	29,262	X	1.110	=	32,481
+ 10,000 4	32,190	X	1.000	=	32,190
- 85,478					142,400

c.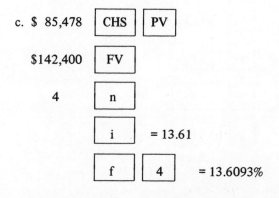

$ 85,478 [CHS] [PV]

$142,400 [FV]

4 [n]

[i] = 13.61

[f] [4] = 13.6093%

d. The adjusted IRR, therefore, gives a more realistic yield to compare with the firm's cost of capital. In this case, the 13.6093 percent adjusted IRR is still in excess of the company's eleven percent cost of capital even though the reinvestment rate of eleven percent was less than the 15.3880 percent IRR calculated in the previous yield. We therefore conclude the lease will be a good investment.

3. *Return on Equity Yield (ROE)*– this is an internal rate of return method that uses cash flows both after-tax and after loan payments. Also, the initial outflow includes only equity less advance payments, deposit, and ITC. This technique of ROE analysis may also be used to analyse leveraged leases. However, there are more advanced methods of analyzing leveraged leases such as the Standard Sinking Fund method (economic analysis) or the multiple investment or separate phases method (accounting reporting only). These two methods will be discussed in the chapter on accounting for leveraged and real estate leases, chapter 10.

The Return on Equity is determined as follows:

a. | *Outflows* | *Inflows* | | | | *IRR Yield* |
|---|---|---|---|---|---|
| −20,000 | *1* | *2* | *3* | *4* | |
| + 3,172* | 5,229 | 10,095 | 5,380 | 7,149 | 115.3065% |
| + 1,350 | | | | | |
| +10,000 | | | | | |
| − 5,478 | | | | | |

*After-tax advance payments.

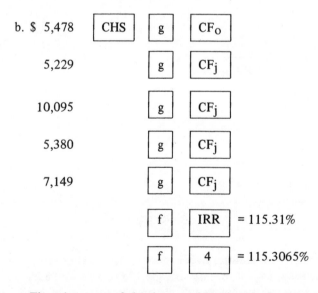

b. $ 5,478 [CHS] [g] [CF₀]

   5,229 [g] [CFⱼ]

   10,095 [g] [CFⱼ]

   5,380 [g] [CFⱼ]

   7,149 [g] [CFⱼ]

   [f] [IRR] = 115.31%

   [f] [4] = 115.3065%

c. The advantage of this lease yield is that the lessor can see the final, after-tax, after-loan payment net cash flow return on equity of a particular lease. This yield not only answers the capital budgeting question of whether to invest in a particular lease, it also tells how ultimately profitable the lease will be to the shareholders of the leasing company. The primary disadvantage of this yield is like that of the conventional IRR method which assumes that cash returns can be reinvested at the same high return on equity rate which is highly unlikely. The yield after next will include a lower reinvestment rate to avoid the high IRR reinvestment problem. An additional problem with this yield is that it assumes the company's debt to equity ratio is being systematically lowered, which generally is not the case for most lease companies. The yield is appropriate for a single investor lessor whose equity interest in a lease investment is increasing over time as the underlying debt is being paid off. Also, the initial tax benefits and advance payments should be allocated not only to equity, but to debt too, in the same ratio as the company's overall debt to equity ratio.

4. *Return on Equity* (Actuarial Cash Allocation) assuming a constant debt equity ratio. This ROE yield is the most applicable yield for a lease company that anticipates maintaining a constant debt to equity ratio.

a. *Step One*–Determine the company's after-tax cost of debt by multiplying the pretax interest rate times one minus the tax rate.

    12% X (1–.46) = 6.48%

b. *Step Two*–Convert the conventional Internal Rate of Return (yield "1" above) into its weighted average components. This is accomplished by multiplying the company's debt percentage times the after-tax cost of debt from step one above. The resulting product (weighted average debt component) is deducted from the conventional IRR which difference represents the weighted average equity component.

Debt Component	=	80% of 6.48%	= 5.184%
Equity Component	=	15.3880 – 5.1840	= 10.204%
		Total IRR, debt + equity =	15.388%

c. *Step Three*–Convert the weighted average equity component, 10.204%, into its nonweighted equivalent by dividing it by the company's equity percentage. This percentage represents the company's actuarial return on equity.

$$\frac{10.204\%}{.2} = 51.02\%$$

d. *Step Four*–To prove that the actuarial return on equity is 51.02% and to demonstrate the effect of actuarial allocation of cash flow in a manner to preserve the company's debt equity ratio proceed as follows. Allocate cash flow first to *RETURN ON INVESTMENT* (profit and interest) and second to *RETURN OF INVESTMENT* (principal).

	1	2	3	4
Cash Flow	27,152	32,942	29,262	32,190
Profit & Interest–				
15.388%	13,153	10,999	7,623	4,293
.05184 Debt (1)	4,431	3,705	2,568	1,446
.10204 Equity(2)	8,722	7,294	5,055	2,847
Principal Return	13,999	21,943	21,639	27,897
.2 Equity	2,800	4,389	4,328	5,579
Equity Sub-Total	**11,522**(3)	**11,683**	**9,383**	**8,426**
.8 Debt	11,199	17,554	17,311	22,318
Remaining Investment				
($85,478 Beg.)	71,479	49,536	27,897	-0-

(1)   .05184 X Remaining Investment ($85,478)

(2)   .10204 X Remaining Investment ($85,478)

(3)   8,722 + 2,800 = 11,522

e. *Step Five*–Compute the Actuarial Return on Equity using cash flows from the equity sub-total above. Note that the equity investment is assumed to be $17,096 which is twenty percent of $85,478 (the amount of the investment after the initial tax benefits, advance payments, and deposit are deducted).

17,096   [CHS]   [g]   [CF$_0$]

11,522   [g]   [CF$_j$]

11,683   [g]   [CF$_j$]

9,383   [g]   [CFj]

8,426   [g]   [CFj]

                     [f]   [IRR]   = 51.02 (ROE)%

                     [f]   [4]   = 51.0203%

f. *Discussion*—This return on equity (ROE) yield is a more realistic yield for the analytical purposes of a leasing company that expects to maintain a constant debt to equity ratio.

5. *Modified Return on Equity Yield*—This method is similar to Return on Equity, No. 4 above, except lease payments are here assumed to be reinvested at forty percent, the company's required return on equity.

a. *Outflow*   *Inflows*   *40% F. V. Factor*   *Future Value*

Outflow	Inflows		40% F. V. Factor		Future Value
$17,096	11,522	X	2.744	=	31,616
	11,683	X	1.960	=	22,899
	9,383	X	1.400		13,136
	8,426	X	1.000	=	8,426
			Total Future Value		76,077

b. $17,096 | CHS | | PV |

    $76,077 | FV |

       4 | N |

           | i | = 45.24%

           | f | | 4 | = 45.2412 Modified ROE%

c. This yield is very important from an analytical point of view because we know that a company's earnings per share can grow no faster than the product of its return on equity (ROE) times its retention rate. Retention rate means the percentage of net income remaining after dividends are paid. Thus, if the lessor in this case pays out forty percent of earnings in dividends then its retention factor is sixty percent. The product of the return on equity of 45.24 percent times the retention rate of sixty percent indicates a potential growth rate of 27.14 percent which is quite close to the firm's desired twenty-four percent (sixty percent of forty percent ROE = twenty-four percent) growth rate as discussed under the Cost of Capital topic. Note that this relationship between ROE and Retention only holds true if ROE is constant and there are no other sources of equity increase such as from anticipated common stock offerings.

ACCOUNTING YIELDS AND THEIR USE

There are two basic yields employed by accountants. Neither of these yields has wide acceptance in the leasing community for managerial analysis purposes. However, the implicit yield is used to account for leases in audited financial statements.

1. *Accountant's Rate of Return*—an erroneous method that employs average, after-tax net income divided by the lease total.

   a. Average Net Income as reported on the income statement, page 85.

   $$\begin{array}{r} 7,152 \\ +\ 942 \\ +5,262 \\ +6,410 \\ \hline \end{array}$$

   $$19,766 \div 4 = \frac{4,942}{100,000.00} = 4.94\%$$

   b. Another type of·Accountant's Rate of Return is the Average Rate of Return where the average net income is divided by the average lease investment (investment ÷ 2).

   $$\frac{4,942}{50,000.00} = 9.88\%$$

   c. Another modification would be to use Straight Line Depreciation in the above determination of after-tax accounting net income. But why bother, the methods are erroneous since they ignore the two most important facts:

   i. the time Value of Money

   ii. that depreciation represents a return of the original investment.

   These erroneous methods are used only on the CPA exam and by antiquated accountants.

2. *Implicit Yield - FASB 13 Method*—is a yield that quite closely resembles a Gross Pretax Yield with advance payments, purchase option, and ITC considered (similar to Gross Pretax Yield number eight described above). The implicit yield is computed as follows:

   a.

Outflow		Inflows	Time	Implicit Yield
-100,000	Initial FMV	2,937	for 46 periods	29.3024%
+ 5,874	Advance Pymt	-0-	in 47th period	
+ 8,000	ITC	17,500	in 48th period	
- 86,126				

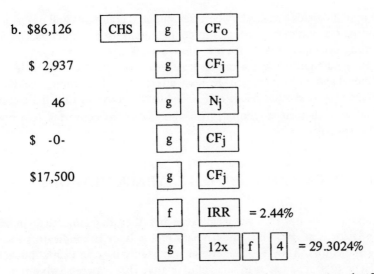

b. $86,126 | CHS | | g | | CF_O |

$ 2,937 | g | | CF_j |

46 | g | | N_j |

$ -0- | g | | CF_j |

$17,500 | g | | CF_j |

| f | | IRR | = 2.44%

| g | | 12x | | f | | 4 | = 29.3024%

c. A modification of the above would result from assuming the full ten percent ITC can be taken at the lease's inception since there is no purchase option but rather an unguaranteed residual or a guaranteed residual (title does not pass to the lessee as in a Closed-End Lease).

d.
Outflow	Inflows	Time	Implicit Yield
−100,000	2,937	for 46 periods	30.6754%
+ 5,874	-0-	in 47th period	
+ 10,000	17,500	in 48th period	
− 84,126			

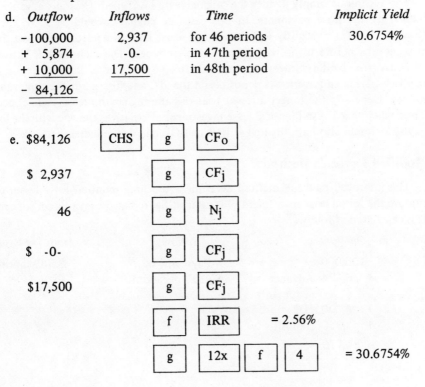

e. $84,126 | CHS | | g | | CF_O |

$ 2,937 | g | | CF_j |

46 | g | | N_j |

$ -0- | g | | CF_j |

$17,500 | g | | CF_j |

| f | | IRR | = 2.56%

| g | | 12x | | f | | 4 | = 30.6754%

Implicit yields are used by certified public accountants and others in accounting for nonleveraged leases in conformity with generally accepted accounting principals–FASB 13, etc. More specifically they are used to separate lease payments under a capital lease into principal (return OF lease investment) and interest (return ON lease investment). The implicit yield serves perhaps very few other needs and is slightly defective in that the effect of the advance deposit is ignored. Also, the ITC is not converted to a pretax equivalent basis.

PAYBACK AND MODIFIED PAYBACK METHODS

These two methods do not produce yields as such, rather they indicate the number of months a lessor is at risk. Thus, the payback methods are risk indicators and not profitability indicators. They are sometimes mistakenly used in capital budgeting decisions. Their preferred use is in analyzing relative risk between two alternative projects.

Payback Method

This technique simply divides the original lease investment (less any advance payments) by the lease payments. In this case the payback would be 32.05 months (94,126 ÷ 2937) or slightly less than three years. Thus, the lessor must wait thirty-two months before his initial investment is recouped. The technique is extremely defective for capital budgeting purposes. It ignores revenue inflows beyond the payback period and overlooks deposits and the ITC and disregards the time value of money. Generally the longer a lessor is at risk the higher the lease yield expected. Thus, when faced with identical lease investment alternatives the one with the longer payback should also have the higher IRR or ROE due to the increase in risk.

Modified Payback Method

This improved payback method determines the time required for a lessor to recapture the initial lease investment plus interest figured at the lessor's cost of capital. It is calculated as follows:

a. *Outflow*		*Inflow*	*Modified Payback*
− 100,000		Payments of	35.87 months
+ 5,874	Advance Payments	$2,937 per month	
+ 8,000	ITC		
+ 1,350	Deposit		
− 84,776			

b. $84,776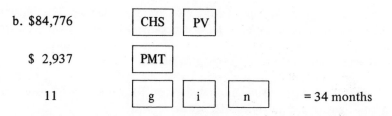

$ 2,937

11   = 34 months

c. Therefore, in this case the lessor will have recovered his entire investment plus interest at his eleven percent cost of capital rate within thirty-four months after the inception of the lease. The income earned during the remaining twelve months is pure excess profit. This technique is finding wider acceptance since it relates risk with return. Its only drawback is its lack of quantifiable information about the remaining lease payments beyond the modified payback period. Another method of computing either payback or modified payback is to use after-tax cash flows in place of pretax lease payments coupled with an after-tax discount rate.

NET PRESENT VALUE AND ITS USE

The net present value and adjusted net present value are two techniques used in lease analysis. These techniques are especially useful when ranking alternatives. Also, there are times when an IRR cannot be determined for a lease. This situation happens when there are multiple answers to an IRR problem caused by mixtures of positive and negative cash inflows in the lease. To overcome the negative cash flow problem the net present value technique is very helpful. The standard sinking fund method discussed in chapter 10 is another method used to cope with negative inflows.

Note that although we know the lease has an adequate net present value, we still cannot say much about its direct effect on the lease company, as do the other yields previously mentioned.

Adjusted Net Present Value Method.

This technique is similar to conventional net present value analysis except that cash inflows are assumed to be reinvested at lower rates than the conventional IRR percent. For example, future negative outflows require money to be set aside to cover the outflow. Generally, funds set aside for liquidity (negative outflows) purposes earn a rate lower than the IRR. Also, some leases have higher yields than the average lease in the company's portfolio. Thus, positive cash inflows from a particularly high yielding lease should be assumed to be reinvested at the average portfolio return. The method of adjusted net present value works as follows:

1. Find the present value of any negative cash inflows discounted at the "liquidity investment rate." Add this to the initial cash investment. Assume a six per-

cent after-tax liquidity investment rate for this example. Also, assume the third cash flow of the subject lease is negative instead of positive. Note: this method is closely related to the standard sinking fund method used in leveraged lease analysis discussed in chapter 10.

2. Find the future value of the positive cash inflows using an appreciation rate or "re-investment rate" equal to the average IRR earned on the lease portfolio. Assume an average portfolio IRR of twelve percent.

3. Find the present value of the future value total from "b" above discounted at the firm's eleven percent cost of capital.

4. Deduct the present value of the inflows from "c" above from the sum of the initial cash outflow plus the negative outflow found in "a" above. The difference is the adjusted net present value.

5. Calculations:

Outflows	Inflows		6% PV or 12% FV Factor		PV	FV
-100,000 1	35,524	x	1.4049	=		49,908
+ 3,172 2	31,107	x	1.2549	=		39,021
+ 1,350 3	(27,386)	x	.8396	= (22,993)		
+ 10,000 4	34,525	x	1.0000	=		34,525
- 85,478					22,993	123,454

- 22,993 P.V. negative inflow (Added algebraically to the outflow from above)

-108,471 Adjusted outflow

Adjusted inflow .6587, eleven percent PV Factor X 123,454 = $81,319

Thus, the adjusted cash inflows of $81,319 do not equal the adjusted outflow of $108,471, so we conclude the lease is not sufficiently profitable. In other words, we have an unacceptable negative net present value of $27,152 (-108,471 + 81,319).

LEASE PAYMENT COMPUTATION

This chapter has thus far been devoted to analyzing a lease with given payment, deposit, residual, and ITC assumptions. Frequently, a question arises as to the amount a lease payment should be given a desired yield, advance payment, deposit, ITC with recapture and purchase option. The Hewlett-Packard 38-C or 12C hand-held calculator makes this task easy as long as the lease company will not require more than one advance payment as part of the lease terms. The practice of requiring more than one advance payment should preferably be replaced with security deposits in most cases anyway, since such advance deposits are not taxable to the lessor.

An example will demonstrate the ease of solving for the lease payment. Using the assumptions for the lease used as the subject of the chapter, we would proceed as follows to compute a thirty-four percent yield equivalent to the Gross Pretax Yield Number seven previously explained:

Step One—Determine the net investment at the inception of the lease without the unknown advance lease payment.

-$100,000	Equipment Cost
+$ 2,500	Pretax Equivalent Deposit
+$ 18,519	Pretax Equivalent Investment Tax Credit
-$ 78,981	Net Outflow at Time "0"

Step Two—Determine the net residual interest of the lessor after return of deposit and investment tax recapture at the termination of the lease.

+$17,500	Purchase Option
-$ 2,500	Return of Deposit
-$ 3,704	Recapture of ITC (2% or $2,000 ÷ 54 = $3,704)
+$11,296	Net Residual Value for Lessor

Step Three—Compute the lease payment. Note in this case we will be solving for a thirty-four percent gross – pretax yield with only one advance payment. The calculator can easily solve for one advance payment as previously explained.

1. Set the upper right hand switch on the calculator to Beginning of Period so that an annuity in advance (annuity due) payment will be calculated (press g Peg on the 12C calculator).
2. Proceed as follows:

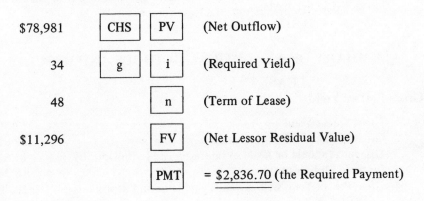

$78,981	CHS	PV	(Net Outflow)
34	g	i	(Required Yield)
48		n	(Term of Lease)
$11,296		FV	(Net Lessor Residual Value)
		PMT	= $2,836.70 (the Required Payment)

Step Four—Prove that the $2,836.70 payment does yield the lessor thirty-four percent by following the steps explained in yield seven previously explained.

Outflow

       $-100,000$
    $+$ 2,837   One Advance Payment
    $+$ 2,500   Pretax Equivalent Deposit
    $+$ 18,519   Pretax Equivalent ITC

    $-$ 76,144

| $ 76,144 | CHS | g | CF$_O$ |

| 2,836.40 | g | CF$_j$ |

| 47 | g | N |

| 11,296 | g | CF |

| f | IRR | = 2.83% |

| g | 12x | f | 4 | = 33.9940 or 34% |

Surprisingly, the hand-held calculator can solve even more difficult problems such as the required lease payment for a given yield where, in addition to the previous assumptions, the lessor must pay interest on the deposit and the lessee must pay credit life insurance as part of each lease payment.

The question of appropriateness of yield for a given lease will be the subject of chapter 6, which deals with analysis of a lease company.

SUMMARY OF ANALYTICAL METHODS AND RESULTS

Gross Pretax Yields

1. Gross Pretax Yield	17.9904%
2. Gross Pretax Yield with advance payments	19.8178%
3. Discount Interest or Add-On Interest Yield (with Option)	14.6190%
(without Option)	10.2440%
4. Gross Pretax Yield with advance payments and deposit	20.7066%

5. Gross Pretax with advance payments and option   24.2545%
6. Gross Pretax Yield with advance payments, option and deposit   25.1986%
7. Gross Pretax Yield with advance payments, option, deposit
   and ITC   38.0572%
8. Gross Pretax Yield with advance payments, residual, deposits   38.7730%
   and ITC and Unguaranteed Residual
9. Gross After-Tax Yield with advance payments, deposit, ITC,   16.8221%
   purchase option, and depreciation tax shield
10. Gross Pretax Yield with advance payments, deposit, ITC   15.1856%
   pass-through, and fixed purchase option from the lessee's point of view

Capital Budgeting Yields

1. Conventional Internal Rate of Return (IRR)   15.3880%
2. Adjusted Internal Rate of Return (IRR adj.)   13.6093%
3. Return on Equity Yield (ROE)   115.3065%
4. Return on Equity (Actuarial Allocation)   51.0203%
5. Modified Return on Equity Yield   45.2412%

Accounting Yields

1. Accountant's Rate of Return   4.94%
2. Accountant's Average Rate of Return   9.88%
3. Implicit Yield-FASB 13 Method (Reduced ITC)   29.3024%
4. Implicit Yield-FASB 13 Method (Full 10% ITC)   30.6754%

Payback Methods

1. Conventional Payback Method   32.05 months
2. Modified Payback Method   34.00 months

Net Present Value Techniques

1. Conventional Net Present Value $14,539
2. Adjusted Net Present Value Method   ($27,152)

Lease Payment Calculation

1. Payment $2,836.70

5

Structuring Leases:
Lessor and Lessee Needs,
_ Risk, and Structuring Variables _

A well structured lease results from the proper integration of four main groups of lease variables: (1) lessor's risk assessment variables; (2) lessor requirement variables; (3) lessee need variables; and (4) lease structuring variables.

RISK ASSESSMENT OF LESSEE

The first step in structuring a lease is for the lessor to evaluate and then quantify the risk inherent in the lease. Risk results from the degree of credit worthiness of the lessee combined with the collateral and residual value of the equipment to be leased. Then too, general business risk affects the transaction indirectly. Once risk has been assessed, it must be converted into a structuring variable.

In general, if a lease is deemed risky by the lessor, any of the following variables might be affected:

1. Lease yield increased with all other factors except payment amount remaining constant.
2. Additional advance payments required.
3. Security deposit required or increased.
4. Guaranteed residual required in lieu of a purchase option.
5. Lease term shortened.
6. Personal guarantee required.
7. Additional collateral beyond the leased equipment.

8. Increased late fees for delinquent rental payments (5% if ten days late plus 18% interest for example).
9. Security interest obtained to facilitate repossession (Filing of UCC forms).
10. All insurable risk insured.

Assignment of the risk inherent in a lease transaction is primarily a credit worthiness decision. Many lessors as well as bankers or other money lenders base their evaluation of risk on the ten "C"s of credit. The ten "C"s represent the first letter of each of the following credit components:

1. Character
2. Capacity
3. Capital
4. Credit
5. Conditions
6. Competition
7. Collateral
8. Cross-Border
9. Complexity
10. Currency

The first element, *character*, refers to the potential lessee's apparent or historically demonstrated integrity, honesty, and commitment to pay even during hard times. Short of previous experience with the lessee, this component is difficult to ascertain. Certainly, some degree of character assessment can be obtained from a personal interview or through checking with other lease companies or bankers with whom the potential lessee has obtained leases.

Capacity refers to the lessee's ability to pay as demonstrated by:

1. Adequate *liquidity*—good current and quick ratios.
2. Sufficient anticipated *cash flow* demonstrated by a cash budget or forecast for at least one-half of the lease term.
3. Growing net income in adequate amounts to indicate *solvency*.

Capital as demonstrated by a strong net worth coupled with limited financial leverage is important should a deficiency judgement arise after repossessing and selling the equipment. Capital represents the only value available to satisfy the judgement, in the event a lessee defaults.

Credit experience should be investigated by checking with Dunn & Bradstreet or any one of many other credit reporting services, such as merchants associations or local credit bureaus. Judgments, pending law suits and slow payment histories should be further investigated.

Conditions within the economy that might affect the lessor should be considered. For example, is the lessee in a cyclical industry that suffers more than other industries during a cyclical downturn in the economy (recession) or is the lessee in an industry that is being affected more than the average company by inflation? Perhaps the potential lessee's revenues cannot keep up with increasing costs due to an inelastic demand curve resulting in a price squeeze. Then, too, what effect will another "credit crunch" like those of 1974, 1979, and 1980 have on the lessee? These and other business economic conditions must be evaluated in terms of their potential impact on the lease transaction.

Competition might be reducing the market share of the lessee. A slowly diminishing market share might indicate excessive risk, whereas an increasing share of a growing market would indicate the optimum situation with the least risk. Alternatively, the most risk is found where a company has a diminishing share of a declining market which represents the worst possible competitive position. Those competitive positions indicating more than average risk should be identified and considered.

Collateral, too, is important since the lessor must first look to the equipment in case of default prior to obtaining any legal remedy directly from the lessee. Equipment that maintains value over time due to inflation and other causes is obviously superior to equipment that does not maintain resale value due to technological obsolescence. For example, heavy construction equipment, barges, etc., frequently are worth as much after being leased seven years as they were at the inception of the lease. In contrast, computers sometimes lose a significant amount of their value between the time they are ordered and the time they are delivered to the lessee. Collateral with questionable resale value requires the lessor to structure the lease in a manner to minimize the risk. For example, rather than offering the lessee a purchase option or no option at all (closed-end lease) a guaranteed residual can be required which minimizes the risk to the lessor.

Collateral subject to excessive wear and tear will require the lessor to enforce strict preventative maintenance clauses coupled with excess-use penalties in order to mitigate the effect of impaired collateral value.

Cross-Border political and economic conditions must be considered in risk analysis for leases to foreign countries. There are numerous tax and legal considerations that must also be considered in cross-border leases in addition to the foreign country's political climate and economic environment. Certainly, leasing to any of the mid-East, oil-producing, Arab nations entails some risk until their political unrest eases in terms of war between Iran and Iraq or political tension between Israel and its Arab neighbors. Not just political unrest must be considered, but also the basic laws governing tax benefits available from leasing in the foreign country must be understood and evaluated.

Complexity of the equipment increases risk since highly technological equipment loses value due to competition. Also, such technologically obsolete equipment is difficult to resell because of the limited market.

Currency—leases structured in foreign currencies are subject to the vagaries of international exchange rate fluctuations.

LESSOR REQUIREMENTS

Once the lessor has assessed the risk and credit worthiness of the lessee and converted that into structuring variables, the lessor must look to its remaining needs and then to the requirements of the lessee. Meeting the sometimes conflicting needs of the lessor and lessee represents the more difficult part of lease structuring. Sometimes a lessor will insist on structuring an operating lease in order to retain tax benefits while at the same time the lessee desires a capital lease so it too may avail itself of the ITC and depreciation tax benefits. Then, too, from an accounting point of view a lessee may request a lease to be structured as an operating lease which pressures the lessor to emphasize an unguaranteed residual value in order to avoid having the lease deemed capital, because of the "value of minimum lease payments criterion." Such residual reliance adds to the riskiness of the lease for the lessor.

Typical lessor requirements that might be at variance with lessee needs in lease structuring are enumerated below:

1. A yield sufficient to meet the lessor's after-tax, weighted cost of capital.
2. Floating or variable payment leases. Bank financing tied to prime rate might force the lessor to require variable payment leases.
3. Accounting for the lease on the lessor's books as a capital lease.
4. Tax structure of the agreement as an operating lease to obtain tax benefits.
5. Quantification and conversion of lessee risk into lease structuring variables.
6. A net lease rather than a full service lease.
7. Other tax requirements if the lessor(s) are noncorporate and are using leases as tax shelters.
8. Residual dependence—the lessor may want the equipment purchased by the lessee to avoid resale problems. On the other hand, the lessor may want the equipment returned at the end of the lease due to its increased value.
9. Whether to structure the lease as "leveraged" or otherwise.

LESSEE REQUIREMENTS

Lessee requirements would include the following items which frequently are at variance with the needs of the lessor mentioned above:

1. Few advance payments and no security deposit. Remember one of the primary motives for leasing is the minimization of the down payment to conserve working capital.
2. A lease that permits subsequent ownership through a fixed low percentage of cost purchase option or through a guaranteed residual permitting title transfer.

3. An extended lease term which directly affects the amount of each lease payment. The longer the lease term, the smaller the lease payment.

4. Sufficient lessor capacity to perform. Will the lessor be able to live up to the lease provisions or will he attempt to break the lease because of poor structuring? Will the lessor be able to deliver the equipment on time, in proper working condition, as ordered?

5. Avoidance of required renewals or severe penalties for nonrenewal, although renewals at the lessee's option might be desirable.

6. A capital lease from an IRS viewpoint might be needed so the lessee can obtain the tax benefits of ownership—depreciation and ITC.

7. An operating lease from an accounting viewpoint to obtain "off-balance sheet financing."

8. Obtaining the Investment Tax Credit (ITC) from the lessor even though the lease is considered "operating" from a tax viewpoint.

9. Obtaining variable payments or any other flexible lease structuring variable, like swap or upgrade clauses in the lease, required by the peculiarities of the lessee. At the same time the lessee wants to avoid variable lease payments tied to CPI or prime rate escalation clauses.

10. Avoidance of fair market value purchase options in lieu of fixed percentages or fixed amount purchase options.

11. Cancellation privileges early in the lease with a series of declining purchase options available during the cancellation period.

12. Fixed Payment Lease with variable term or variable residual guarantee in lieu of variable payments tied to prime rate. Such variable length or variable residual leases compensate the lessor for changing borrowing costs.

Given both the lessor needs and those of the lessee, the lessor must structure a lease compatible to both. Obviously, some compromise is in order. Frequently, though, lessees are not aware of the numerous structuring possibilities available and thus tend to be manipulated by better informed lessors. Lessees should therefore know about the many structuring variables and go prepared to negotiate.

A list of lease structuring variables would require a whole chapter; however, the following list of twenty-three groups of structuring variables highlights the significant structuring considerations:

1. Advance Payments.
2. Security Deposits.

   a. Interest Bearing

   b. Noninterest Bearing

3. Origination or Service Fees.
4. Duration of Lease.

5. Variability of Lease Payments to satisfy various lessee and lessor needs:

   a. Lessee Revenue Curve.

   b. Lessor's Borrowing Cost (Prime Rate Escalation Clause).

   c. Lessor's Other Underlying Costs (CPI Index Inflation Clause).

6. Penalties:

   a. Nonrenewal penalties.

   b. Cancellation penalties.

   c. Late payment penalties.

   d. Excess use penalties.

7. Residuals:

   a. Bargain Purchase Option(s).

   b. Fair Market Value Purchase Option(s).

   c. Guaranteed Residual—Title Transferable.

   d. Guaranteed Residual—Nontransferable Title.

      i. Stop Loss Clause.

      ii. Profit Sharing Clause.

   e. Unguaranteed Residual—Closed End Lease.

   f. None Required—Full Payout Direct Financing Lease.

8. Rental Renewal Options.

   a. Bargain Cost.

   b. Fair Market Value Cost.

9. Yield to Lessor sufficient to achieve the following objectives:

   a. Competitive Gross—Pretax Yield.

   b. Sufficient Return on Equity to maintain required growth rate.

   c. An Internal Rate of Return equal or greater than the lessor's Cost of Capital.

10. Accounting Capital or Operating Lease.

11. Sale-Leaseback Arrangement.

12. Leveraged or Not.

13. Debt to Equity Optimization in Leverage Lease to maximize reported accounting lease net income per FASB 13.

14. A True Lease or Conditional Sales Contract from Tax Viewpoint.

15. Net Lease or Not.

16. Contingent or Percentage Rentals based upon lessee's revenue.

17. Inclusion of flexible lease options:

   a. Upgrading with new models or added features for better efficiency.

   b. Swapping.

   c. Joint venturing.

   d. Including of delivery installation and licenses in a lease.

   e. Trial Periods.

   f. Nonfinancial services such as the assistance of a systems-analyst for a leased computer system.

18. Full-payout on nonfull-payout.

19. Fixed Payment Lease with compensating variables to cover changes in the lessor's cost of debt:

   a. Variable lease term.

   b. Variable residual guarantee.

20. Tax shelter for noncorporate lessor which requires conformity to certain IRS guidelines.

21. Passing on to lessee of certain lessor economies of scale obtained from quantity purchase discounts or efficient servicing of equipment.

22. Third party guarantees of residual value by insurance companies or manufacturers.

23. Tax Benefit Lease in the form of a "wash lease".

STRUCTURING EXAMPLES

Lease with Doubtful Future Resale Value

Suppose you are requested to provide a lease to a lessee for equipment you feel will have little future resale value at the end of the lease. Assuming the lessee has excellent credit, how might you structure the lease?

1. You might structure the lease on a full-payout basis so that your required yield is obtained without any dependence upon residual value. This method, however, has two serious drawbacks: (a) the lease might be considered a capital lease from a tax viewpoint, thus causing the lessor to lose tax benefits and (b) the resulting lease payments might be too large for the lessee.

2. In order to retain tax benefits and lower the monthly lease payments, a guaranteed residual could be structured into the lease. Then, if the equipment sells for less than the guaranteed residual at the end of the lease, the lessee will pay the difference. Too much emphasis on a guaranteed residual, however, has cer-

tain drawbacks: (a) should the lessee default, little collateral value might exist, and (b) total shifting of the "risk of loss" to the lessee might cause the IRS to deem the lease "capital" with the resulting loss of lessor tax benefits.

3. Although a fixed purchase option might allow the lease payments to be lowered for the lessee, such dependence upon an option that may or may not be exercised by the lessee would be risky, especially since the option could easily be in excess of the equipment's future value and, therefore, the lessee might not exercise the option. Nevertheless, a ten to fifteen percent purchase option might be the best approach to take in these circumstances. The new safe harbor rules for IRS purposes would allow full payout, guaranteed residual, or fixed percentage purchase options in leases.

Lease with High Expected Future Value:

Suppose you are requested to lease heavy equipement to a lessee and you anticipate the equipment will be worth eighty percent of today's value at the termination of the lease. Assuming excellent credit on the part of the lessee, in what ways could you structure the lease?

1. A fair market value purchase option structured into the lease would give the *lessor* the best return and protection. Knowledgeable lessees, however, prefer low (fifteen percent to twenty-five percent) fixed percentage purchase options so they might also take advantage of the increased value of the equipment.

2. A guaranteed residual value with title transferring to the lessee at his option might be an ideal solution. The guarantee allows the lessee to obtain low rentals during the lease and the value of the collateral protects the lessor against undue dependence upon the residual.

3. The lessor could simply depend upon an unguaranteed residual and offer neither a purchase option nor a title passing guaranteed residual to the lessee. Obviously, lessees would have to be sold on this approach, which might be a difficult task.

CONCLUSION

To structure a lease properly requires the simultaneous meeting of the diverse needs of the participants in the lease: Lessor, Lessee, Manufacturer, Lessor's Creditor, etc. Numerous lease structuring variables have evolved to meet the varying needs of the parties to the lease.

Analyzing a Lease Company: Specialized Financial Statements and ——————— Models ————

Financial analysts are frequently asked: How does one analyze a lease company? How do we know whether a lease company is maximizing profit? How does a particular lease company compare with others in the industry? The answers to these questions and others is the subject of this chapter.

It has been the authors' experience that three important informational sources are required to operate effectively or to analyze adequately a lease company. Two of the sources are financial statements and one is a sensitivity model, these are described below:

1. MANAGERIAL INCOME STATEMENT (modified from generally accepted accounting principles, GAAP, and placed on a modified cash basis).
2. CASH FLOW FROM OPERATIONS STATEMENT (showing relevant cash inflows and outflows depicting a company's net cash position).
3. SENSITIVITY MODEL (a summary statement indicating the results of the fourteen basic factors that determine profit in a lease company).

MANAGERIAL INCOME STATEMENT

A managerial income statement is different than a standard income statement presented in conformity with GAAP. The managerial statement is prepared in accordance with the needs of management, not those of the FASB. The basic difference is that the managerial statement begins with accrual revenue per GAAP which is then adjusted to a modified cash basis by deducting uncollected lease payments from lease payments reported on the accrual basis.

Conversion to a modified cash basis is essential to management. A lease company runs on cash flow, not ephemeral accrual dollars. Furthermore, lease yields are determined on a modified cash basis and, therefore, the determination and evaluation of net income must be based on similar cash information, not accrual. Then, too, most firms in the leasing industry evaluate current operating success on a modified cash basis not on accrual. Operating expenses, however, remain on an accrual basis. That is why the word "modified" is used with "cash basis" described above.

A *second difference* relates to the position of depreciation expense on the income statement and to the determination of depreciation. Depreciation is shown on the managerial statement as a deduction from Accrual Lease Revenue. Depreciation according to GAAP is considered an operating expense. When depreciation is properly computed (actuarial method) and deducted from accrual lease revenue the resulting difference is Expected Gross Profit. This gross profit is equal to the interest earned at the yield rate implicit in the portfolio of leases. If the leases in a portfolio were structured to yield eighteen percent over their lives it seems reasonable to assume that the gross profit shown in an income statement would reflect this fact. With properly computed depreciation, the gross profit will in fact represent the interest earned on the portfolio at eighteen percent.

To obtain a gross profit that reflects the lease interest earned at the portfolio yield rate, depreciation must be calculated according to the sinking fund or annuity method. This method results in a unique stream of depreciation charges which are small at first and then systematically increase towards the end of an asset's life. The method will be explained in more detail later in this chapter. GAAP does allow this method of depreciation since it is extremely systematic and rational and more representative of the true interest earnings that derive from the interest rate implicit in the lease portfolio. The sinking fund method is not as widely known as other methods of depreciation.

A *third difference* is that initial costs of setting up leases will not be deferred as required by FASB 13 for operating leases. Immediate write-off of initial direct costs is consistent both with cash basis lease accounting and the nature of lease yields. Lease yields are determined with initial direct costs being considered as part of the relevant cash inflows and outflows when they occur.

A *fourth difference* is that security deposits are listed as a source of other lease income. GAAP regards deposits as liabilities, deferred credits, rather than a source of income. If the deposits are subsequently returned to the lessee they would then be offset against the security deposits shown as income on the managerial statement in the period of return. Thus, deposits are shown net in the managerial income statement as sources of revenue which presentation is consistent with standard yield computation.

The *fifth difference* is that interperiod tax allocation is not used. Therefore, benefits derived from investment tax credits in excess of current tax liabilities will never-the-less be shown as a source of revenue (assuming ITC can be realized through carry-back) on the income statement. GAAP limits ITC inclusion in the income statement to the amount of tax liability, FASB Interpretation 25. Over and above showing excess ITC on the statement, benefits derived from accelerated depreciation will be shown as tax benefits in the period realized under IRS reporting. GAAP requires such benefits to be deferred and taken into income over the life of the asset, whereas management wants to know the total tax benefits obtained in any given period. In the authors' opinion, interperiod tax allocation is a busy work scheme of CPAs since ITC and accelerated depreciation were the results of laws established to give immediate tax benefits to businessmen. Why, therefore, do accountants want to defer them? Has the benefit not been realized? The answer commonly given is "deferral of these benefits more properly matches revenue and expense." We know, however, that proper matching of revenues and expenses occurs through the use of actuarial methods such as annuity depreciation, etc., which are based on cash flows implicit in leases and not on the arbitrary deferring or accruing of benefits.

The next page displays the recommended format for a managerial income statement for a lease company. The managerial statement can be used for a monthly or annual reporting period and is shown on a modified cash basis as described above. Note the numerous sources of other lease income and the treatment of investment tax credit as a revenue rather than an offset against income tax expense. The statement begins with accrual revenues but is converted to a modified cash basis by the inclusion of uncollected lease payments as an expense (accrual revenue reduction) listed under "Other Lease Costs."

XYZ LEASE COMPANY

MANAGERIAL INCOME STATEMENT

MODIFIED CASH BASIS

FOR THE YEAR ENDED 12-31-1990

Revenue:

Accrual Lease Revenue (ALR) $———

Less: Annuity Depreciation (D_aNR) (———)

   Gross Profit without Residual or ITC $———

Add: Residual Profit (D_aR-D_aNR) $———

Add: Investment Tax Credit Income $———

Expected Gross Profit: $———

Other Lease Income:

Sales-Type Lease Income (Net) ———

Insurance Income (Net) ———

Maintenance Income (Net)	———		
Contingent Rentals	———		
Service Fee Income	———		
Lease Underwriting (Brokerage)	———		
Interest on Short-Term Investments	———		
Late Payment Fees	———		
Security Deposits (Net)	———		
Gain on Disposal of Leased Equipment	———		
Total Other Income		$———	
Other Lease Costs:			
Initial Direct Costs	(———)		
Uncollected Lease Payments	(———)		
Loss on Disposal of Leased Equipment	(———)		
Total Other Costs		($———)	
Gross Profit on Lease Collections:			$———
Operating Expenses:			
Write-Offs (Bad Debt Expense)	(———)		
Operating Expenses (Gen. & Admn.)	(———)		
Total Operating Expense		($———)	
Income From Operations:			$———
Income Taxes and Debt Service:			
Interest on Debt	(———)		
Income Tax Benefits (Expenses)	———		
Total Income Taxes & Interest		($———)	
Net Income:			$———

If the lease company has primarily direct financing or sales-type capital leases then the first section of the Managerial Income Statement should be altered as follows:

Revenue:

Accrual Lease Payments	$———	
Less: Principal Portion	(———)	
Gross Profit without Residual or ITC		$———
Add: Residual Dependence Profit	$———	
Add: Investment Tax Credit Income	$———	
Expected Gross Profit:		$———

In order to separate direct financing lease interest into its three primary components it is necessary to compute three internal rates of return or portfolio yields: (1) yield without ITC or Residual, (2) yield with Residual, and (3) yield with ITC and Residual. With these separate portfolio yields it is possible to individually designate on the managerial income statement the three primary sources of lease gross profit. Note—many lease companies do not separate residual dependence or ITC dependence from total interest earned as we have done. Without proper understanding of the quality of interest earnings, a leasing company could go broke since the ITC or residual values may never be realized.

CASH FLOW FROM OPERATIONS STATEMENT

This statement, which appears on the next page, provides information about the total cash inflows and outflows generated from leasing operations. It is unlike the Managerial Income Statement in that the following additional SOURCES of cash appear:

1. Collection of heretofore past due lease payments is shown as an additional source of cash (such payments are not netted against uncollected lease payments in the Managerial Income Statement).
2. Noncash charges to income such as depreciation and amortization included in operating expenses are added back to net income as a source of cash.
3. Decrease in any other noncash or nonlease receivable current asset such as inventory or prepaid expenses would represent a source of cash.
4. Increases in current liabilities represent additional sources of cash caused by postponing payment of current expenses.

Furthermore, the cash flow statement contains the following additional USES of cash:

1. Repayment of long-term debt (principal portion only) used to finance leased equipment. Traditional cash flow statements do not regard this as an operational use of cash. But to a lease company cash borrowed to fund leases is an integral part of operations.
2. Reductions in current liabilities represent uses of cash from operations.
3. Uncollected lease payments must be deducted from accrual revenue. This subtraction has already been accomplished in the Managerial Income Statement previously discussed.

The next page presents a cash flow from operations statement that has been derived from the lease company managerial statement already discussed. It should be understood that other sources of cash inflow and outflow such as stock offerings, etc. could affect a leasing company's cash flow but these are considered nonoperation sources and would be shown in a separate section of a comprehensive cash flow statement.

XYZ LEASE COMPANY
CASH FLOW FROM OPERATIONS STATEMENT

FOR THE YEAR ENDED 12-31-1990

Sources of Cash from Operations:

Net Income per Managerial Statement	$————
Additions:	
1. Collections of past due rentals	————
2. Depreciation	————
3. Amortization of discounts, goodwill, etc.	————
4. Decrease in other current assets	————
5. Deposits[1]	————
6. Nonreported tax benefits[1]	————
Total Additions	$————
TOTAL OPERATIONAL SOURCES	$————

Uses of Cash from Operations:

1. Repayment of long-term debt used to finance leased equipment— principal portion only	————
2. Reductions in current liabilities	————
3. Uncollected lease payments[2]	————
TOTAL OPERATIONAL USES	$————

Net Cash Increase (Decrease): $————

---

[1] Already added in most cases to managerial income.

[2] Already deducted in most cases from managerial income.

Whereas the Managerial Income Statement informs management whether cash earnings are sufficient to cover operating expenses, the cash-flow-from-operations statement gives more insight into the lease company's liquidity position. For example, the cash flow statement indicates overall cash sources without reductions for non-cash charges such as depreciation, etc., and the statement also indicates whether the cash sources are adequate to cover repayment of principal on current and long-term borrowed funds. The information contained in the Managerial Income Statement does, however, have other uses since it becomes the input for the sensitivity model explained later in the chapter.

Following are examples of a Managerial Income Statement and a Cash-Flow-From-Operations Statement which will be completed using the following information:

1. XYZ Lease Company has $100,000 in assets of which $80,000 is debt (bearing interest at thirteen percent) and equity of $20,000.

2. The company's incremental, after-tax, weighted-average cost of capital is 10.541%.

3. Assume a forty-six percent corporate tax bracket.

4. Assume operating losses and investment tax credits result fully in tax savings due to the three year carryback rule.

5. Assume that $95,000 of the total assets are invested in leases as follows:

   a. Four-year leases (no advance payments) with gross pretax yields of 18.64 percent (IRR) including the effect of residual value and pretax yields of sixteen percent when residual values are not considered.

   b. Unguaranteed residuals of $9,500 on the total portfolio. The company has closed-end leases where the asset reverts to the lessor at the end of the lease and the lessee has no further ownership rights or financial obligations.

   c. Debt of $76,000 is used to leverage the $95,000 of leases (eighty percent leverage).

   d. Debt is amortized with annual payments of $25,551 which includes interest at thirteen percent APR.

   e. Leased assets are depreciated for tax purposes over seven years using DDB depreciation method. The full ten percent investment tax credit is retained by the lessor. Assume that $2,500 of the total ITC of $9,500 can be recognized in the first year due to carryback rule.

   f. Assume for accounting purposes "annuity type depreciation" is used to enhance meaningfulness of the statements.

6. Assume the following information concerning collections and operations:

		ANNUAL
a.	Uncollected Lease Payments	$ 885
b.	Sales-type lease revenue	4,000
c.	Sales-type lease costs	3,800
d.	DDB Depreciation	27,141
e.	Annuity Depreciation (without Residual) D_aNR	18,751
f.	Annuity Depreciation (with Residual) D_aR	16,243
g.	Write-offs	100
h.	Direct Costs	550
i.	Operating Expenses	900
j.	Interest	9,880
k.	Insurance Income	100
l.	Contingent Rentals	50
m.	Maintenance Income	50

7. The company pays out forty-five percent of all net income, in dividends to shareholders.
8. The tax benefit was derived as follows:

a.	Revenue	$ 33,951
b.	DDB Depreciation	(27,141)
	1) Gross Profit	6,810
c.	Other Lease Income	400
d.	Other Lease Costs	(1,435)
	1) Gross Profit on Lease Collections	5,775
e.	Write-offs	(100)
f.	G & A	(900)
g.	Income from Operations	4,775
h.	Interest	(9,880)
i.	Net Loss	$(5,105)

$5,105 X .46 = $2,348 Tax Benefit

XYZ LEASE COMPANY

MANAGERIAL INCOME STATEMENT

MODIFIED CASH BASIS

FOR THE YEAR ENDED 12–31–1990

Revenue:

Accrual Lease Revenue (ALR)	33,951		
Less: Annuity Depreciation (D_aNR)	(18,751)		
Gross Profit without Residual		$15,200	
Add: Residual Profit (D_aR-D_aNR)		$2,508	
Add: Investment Tax Credit Income		$2,500	
Expected Gross Profit:			$20,208

Other Lease Income:

Sales-Type Lease Income (Net)	200
Insurance Income (Net)	100

Maintenance Income (Net)	50	
Contingent Rentals	50	
Service Fee Income	-0-	
Lease Underwriting (Brokerage)	-0-	
Interest on Short-Term Investments	-0-	
Late Payment Fees	-0-	
Security Deposits (Net)	-0-	
Gain of Disposal of Leased Equipment	-0-	
Total Other Income		$ 400

Other Lease Costs:

Initial Direct Costs	(500)	
Uncollected Lease Payments	(885)	
Loss on Disposal of Leased Equipment	(-0-)	
Total Other Costs		($ 1,435)

Gross Profit on Lease Collections: $19,173

Operating Expenses:

Write-Offs (Bad Debt Expense)	(100)	
Operating Expenses (Gen. & Admn.)	(900)	
Total Operating Expense		($ 1,000)

Income From Operations: $18,173

Income Taxes and Debt Service:

Interest on Debt	(9,880)	
Income Tax Benefits (Expenses)	2,348	
Total Income Taxes & Interest		($ 7,532)

Net Income: $10,641

XYZ LEASE COMPANY

CASH FLOW FROM OPERATIONS STATEMENT

FOR THE YEAR ENDED 12-31-1990

Sources of Cash From Operations:

Net Income per Managerial Statement $10,641

Additions:

1. Collections of past due rentals	-0-	
2. Depreciation	16,243	
3. Amortization of discounts, goodwill, etc.	-0-	
4. Decrease in other current assets	-0-	
5. Deposits[1]	N/A	
6. Nonreported tax benefits[1]	N/A	
Total Additions	$16,243	
TOTAL OPERATIONAL SOURCES	$26,884	

Uses of Cash From Operations:

1. Repayment of long-term debt used to finance leased equipment- principal portion only	15,671	
2. Reductions in current liabilities	-0-	
3. Uncollected lease payments[2]	N/A	
TOTAL OPERATIONAL USES		$15,671

Net Cash Increase (Decrease): $11,213

---

[1] Already added in most cases to managerial income.

[2] Already deducted in most cases from managerial income.

SINKING FUND OR ANNUITY DEPRECIATION

If the purpose of depreciating assets is to allocate or match the expense of the asset's wearing out with revenues generated by the asset in a reasonable and systematic manner, then the sinking fund or annuity type method must be considered. These two methods separate cash inflows into return *of* principal (depreciation) and return *on* principal (interest) in such a manner that the interest represents a constant rate of return on the declining book value of the net investment in the lease. Any other method of depreciation, straightline or accelerated, will understate interest earned in a lease company.

The method works like this:

1. Compute the implicit Internal Rate of Return on the proposed lease project taking into consideration advance payments and residual value.

   a.

Time Period	0	1	2	3	4
Rental Payments		33,951	33,951	33,951	33,951
Initial Investment	(95,000)				
Advance Payment	–0–				
Residual					9,500
TOTALS	(95,000)	33,951	33,951	33,951	43,451

   b. IRR–18.64% or Gross Pretax Yield or 16.00% without the Residual.

2. Use the gross pretax yield (IRR) to split payments into principal and interest just as though you were amortizing a loan. Follow these steps:

   a. Charge to depreciation expense an amount equal to the advance payments (debit depreciation expense and credit accumulated depreciation). In this case, there were no advance payments.

   b. Multiply the IRR of .1864 times the remaining book value of the asset, $95,000 (.1864 x $95,000 = $17,708 earned lease income).

   c. Deduct the earned lease income from the total rental payment for the period. The difference is the amount of depreciation for the period.

   $33,951 – $17,708 = $16,243 depreciation

   d. Repeat steps c. and d. for each of the next three years.

   Year 2
   .1864 ($95,000 – $16,243) = $14,680 earnings
   $33,951 – $14,680 = $19,271 depreciation

   Year 3
   .1864 ($95,000 – $16,243 – $19,271) = $11,088 earnings
   $33,951 – $11,088 = $22,863 depreciation

   Year 4
   .1864 ($95,000 – $17,243 – $19,271 – $22,863) = $6,828 earnings
   $33,951 – $6,828 = $27,123 depreciation

3. Analysis:

	1	2	3	4
Lease Payments	33,951	33,951	33,951	33,951
Depreciation	(16,243)	(19,271)	(22,863)	(27,123)
Gross Lease Income	17,708	14,680	11,088	6,828
Remaining Book Value	95,000	78,757	59,486	36,623
Return on Investment*	18.64%	18.64%	18.64%	18.64%

*Gross lease income divided by remaining book value.

Note that the gross lease income or interest represents a constant 18.64 percent return on the declining book value of the lease investment. Use of other depreciation techniques tends to understate lease interest in the early years of the lease and overstate it in the remaining years.

SENSITIVITY MODEL

An extremely useful tool in managing and analyzing a lease company is a sensitivity model. A sensitivity model is basically an equation that shows the relative effect of a change in one of its variables on the remaining variables. Thus, the analyst can determine for example how sensitive return on equity is to a two percent decrease in collection activity. The models generally are made up of the critical variables that determine profitability. Also, the sensitivity equation uses the critical variables as *multipliers* in the equation. Each variable is multiplied by the other variables to arrive at various products which are important profitability yields.

Perhaps the most widely known and rudimentary sensitivity equation used for manufacturing companies is the following Du Pont model:

Du Pont Equation

$$\text{Net Profit Margin} = \frac{\text{Net Income}}{\text{Sales}}$$

$$\text{X Asset Turnover} = \frac{\text{Sales}}{\text{Assets}}$$

= Return on Assets

$$\text{X Financial Leverage Factor} = \frac{\text{Assets}}{\text{Equity}}$$

= Return on Equity

Note how one can determine the effect of a slight increase in net profit margin on both return on assets and return on equity simply by multiplying net profit margin times the remaining critical multipliers (critical variables).

The leasing sensitivity model created and used by the authors in analyzing and managing lease companies consists of fourteen separate variables. Each variable is a critical factor in determining the profitability of a leasing company. To properly manage and control a leasing company each of these critical elements must be constantly reviewed by management. Below is a list of these fourteen critical lease variables:

Fourteen Critical Lease Company Variables:

1. *Profitability Index*—Expected Gross Profit (Implicit Interest in Lease Payments without reliance on residual value).
2. *Residual Dependence*—Lease yield or interest derived from residual value.
3. *Time at Risk Factor*—Leased Asset Turnover (Reciprocal of Payback Period).
4. *Asset Utilization*—Total Asset Utilization, Percent of Assets Leased.
5. *Investment Tax Credit*—Revenue earned from realized investment tax credits.
6. *Other Income Factor*—Sales Type Lease Gross Profit, Insurance Income,etc.
7. *Initial Direct Cost Factor*—Direct Costs Including Commissions.
8. *Collections Factor*—Effect of Uncollected Lease Rentals.
9. *Write-Off Factor*—Bad Debt Write-Offs.
10. *Operational Expense Factor*—General and Administrative Expenses.
11. *Interest Expense Factor*—Cost of Debt.
12. *Income Taxes Factor*—Federal & State Income Taxes (Benefits or Expenses).
13. *Financial Leverage Factor*—Assets to Equity Ratio.
14. *Retention Factor*—Percentage of Net Income Retained.

In order to present the sensitivity equation on one page, the following symbols will be used:

1. ALR $=$ Accrual Lease Revenue
2. D_aR $=$ Annuity Depreciation computed with Residual Value.
3. D_aNR $=$ Annuity Depreciation computed with No Residual Value.
4. A_L $=$ Assets Leased (Leases Receivable)
5. A_T $=$ Total Assets (Includes Nonleased Assets)
6. ITC $=$ Investment Tax Credit
7. 0/I $=$ Other Income
8. U $=$ Uncollected Lease Payments
9. GP_1 $=$ ALR $-$ D_aR, Expected Gross Profit Including Residual Value
10. GP_2 $=$ GP_1 plus the Investment Tax Credit or $GP_1 + ITC$
11. GP_3 $=$ GP_2 plus Other Income (O/I) or $GP_1 + ITC$
12. GP_4 $=$ GP_3 less Direct Costs (D/C) or $GP_1 + O/I - D/C$
13. GP_5 $=$ GP_4 less Uncollected Rents (U) or $GP_1 + O/I - D/C - U$
14. GP_6 $=$ GP_5 less Write-Offs (W/O) or $GP_1 + O/I - D/C - U - W/O$
15. GP_7 $=$ GP_6 less Operating Expenses (O/E) or $GP_1 + O/I - D/C - U - W/O - O/E$

16. GP_8 = GP_7 less Interest Expense (I) or GP_1 + O/I - D/C - U - W/O - O/E - I
17. W/O = Bad Debt Write-Offs
18. D/C = Direct Costs (Direct Costs, Including Commissions)
19. O/E = Operating Expenses (G & A)
20. I = Interest on Debt
21. T = Taxes
22. E_T = Total Equity
23. NI = After Tax Net Income
24. D = Dividends

The next page presents the sensitivity equation. The variables have been labeled showing the critical factors governing the lease company's profitability. Starting from the left of the equation each variable is multiplied times the variable to its right and the resulting product is labeled below. The line to the right of the product indicates that all variables to the left of the left of the line have been multiplied together in order to arrive at that product. Each product's label depicts an important return on investment percentage. The seven most common return on investment percentages have been shown.

Using the information on the Managerial Income Statement and the other assumptions of XYZ Lease Company previously given, the sensitivity equation will be solved and each element's importance discussed variable by variable. The solution to the equation appears on page000. Following is an explanation of each variable in the sensitivity model.

EXPLANATION OF SENSITIVITY MODEL VARIABLES

1. PROFITABILITY INDEX $\dfrac{\text{ALR-D}_a\text{NR}}{\text{ALR}}$

a. $\dfrac{\$33,951 - \$18,751}{\$33,951}$ = $\underline{.4477}$

b. The profitability index indicates the percentage of each lease payment that is interest income. This interest income is also referred to as Lease Gross Profit when it appears on an income statement. Note that this interest percentage has been computed without any reliance on residual value. The particular lease in question has a sixteen percent gross yield when residual value is ignored. The sixteen percent figure is used to compute annuity type depreciation referred to in the model as D_aNR which stands for "Depreciation Annuity No Residual." The profitability index percentage increases as lease yields improve. Executory costs have previously been deducted from the gross lease revenue.

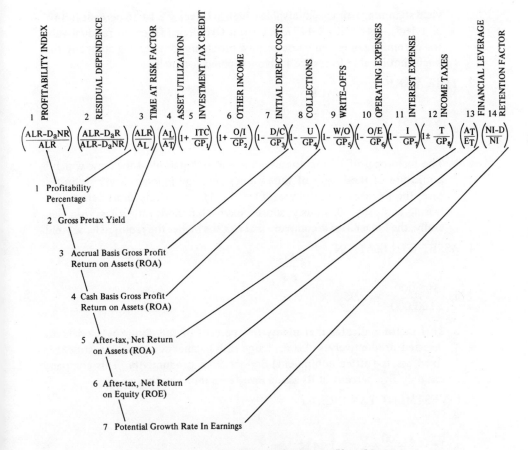

**Fourteen Critical Lease Company Variables
Sensitivity Model**

2. RESIDUAL DEPENDENCE

$$\frac{ALR-D_aR}{ALR-D_aNR}$$

a. $\dfrac{\$33,951 - \$16,243}{\$33,951 - \$18,751} = 1.165$

b. This factor demonstrates the degree to which the overall lease yield of the leasing company's portfolio is dependent upon residual value. In effect the profitability index in Number one above will increase by 16.5 percent due to the influence of anticipated residual value. The residual dependence factor shows the degree of overall yield dependence in relative terms by dividing the difference between factor one times factor two minus factor one by the product of factors one and two. The result shows the percentage of overall yield stemming from residual value which in this case is 14.16 percent [(.4477 X 1.165) - .4477] ÷ (.4477 X 1.165). Overdependence on residual value for current income can cause serious problems for a leasing company that might not be able to realize such anticipated residuals.

3. TIME AT RISK

$$\frac{ALR}{A_L}$$

a. $\frac{\$33,951}{\$95,000}$ = $\underline{.3573}$

b. The reciprocal of this factor gives the payback period of the lease which is a measure of the length of time money invested in leases is at *risk*. In this case, the payback is 2.798 years (1 ÷ .3574), a relatively short period for a leasing company. Obviously, shorter payback periods reflect less risk. Generally, the longer a lease company is at risk the higher the required lease yield.

4. ASSET UTILIZATION

$$\frac{A_L}{A_T}$$

a. $\frac{\$95,000}{\$100,000}$ = $\underline{.95}$

b. This factor indicates that ninety-five percent of the company's assets are invested productively in leases. Large cash balances or heavy investment in fixed assets (office equipment) detract from productivity. This company has only five percent of its assets invested nonproductively.

5. INVESTMENT TAX CREDIT

$$1 + \frac{ITC}{GP_1}$$

a. $1 + \frac{\$2500}{\$17,708}$ = 1.1412

b. This factor indicates that gross profit (product of factors one through four has increased by 14.12 percent because of investment tax credit income. Investment tax credits represent a major source of lease company revenue since this is one of the primary tax motivations behind leasing.

6. OTHER INCOME

$$1 + \frac{O/I}{GP_2}$$

a. $1 + \frac{\$400}{\$20,208}$ = $\underline{1.0198}$

b. This factor indicates that gross profit has increased by 1.98 percent because of gross profit earned on sales-type leases, insurance income, maintenance income, etc. Most successful lease companies are able to buy assets at lower prices than the lessee, thus enabling the lessor to earn sales-type profit on a lease in addition to implicit lease interest during the lease term.

Other lease income generally includes any or all of the following ten items:

1) Sales-Type Lease Income (Net)
2) Insurance Income (Net)
3) Maintenance Income (Net)
4) Contingent Rentals (Percentage Rentals)
5) Service Fee Income
6) Lease Underwriting (Brokerage Commissions)
7) Interest on Short Term Debt Investments
8) Late Payment Fees
9) Security Deposits (Net)
10) Gains on Disposals of Leased Equipment net of and disposal losses. The gain must exceed the amount already reported as residual income.

7. INITIAL DIRECT COSTS

$$1 - \frac{D/C}{GP_3}$$

a. $1 - \dfrac{\$550}{\$20,608} = \underline{.9733}$

b. Direct costs consist of variable costs such as commissions, legal fees, typing of leases, and other lease preparation costs. One minus the direct cost factor or 2.67 percent is the amount the gross profit margin (product of factors one through six) has been reduced due to direct costs.

8. COLLECTIONS

$$1 - \frac{U}{GP_4}$$

a. $1 - \dfrac{\$885}{\$20,058} = \underline{.9559}$

b. This factor indicates that only 95.59 percent of expected lease payments were collected during the period. Thus, a five percent delinquency factor exists. Uncollected rents should not be offset with any late fees collected since these were included in other income. Obviously, the lower the delinquency rate, the higher the earnings. Note that prior to this point in the lease model all yields (resulting product of factors one through six) have been on the accrual basis. Beyond this point all yields have been converted to a cash basis.

9. WRITE-OFFS

$$1 - \frac{W/O}{GP_5}$$

a. $1 - \dfrac{\$100}{\$19,173} = \underline{.9948}$

b. Less than one percent of gross profit has been written off the books as bad debt.

10. OPERATING EXPENSES

$$1- \frac{O/E}{GP_6}$$

a. $1- \dfrac{\$1,000}{\$19,073}$ = $\underline{.9476}$

b. Operating expenses caused about a five percent reduction in gross profit. Operating expenses are those general and administrative costs required to run a leasing operation (advertising, accounting, salaries, etc.) commonly known as overhead.

11. INTEREST EXPENSE

$$1- \frac{I}{GP_7}$$

a. $1- \dfrac{\$9,880}{\$18,073}$ = $\underline{.4533}$

b. 54.67 percent (1 - .4533) of actual gross profit has been spent on interest to service debt. Certainly, low cost servicing of debt financing can greatly enhance lease yields. Interest is generally the most costly single expense in operating a lease company.

12 INCOME TAXES

$$1- \frac{+T}{GP_8}$$

a. $1+ \dfrac{\$2,348}{\$8,193}$ = $\underline{1.2866}$

b. The Pretax Net Return on Assets has increased by 28.66 percent due to the tax benefits derived from the loss carryback totalling $2,348. Of course, tax expenses sometimes replace benefits in years where the lessor has used up his tax deductions.

13. FINANCIAL LEVERAGE

$$\frac{A_T}{E_T}$$

a. $\dfrac{\$100,000}{\$20,000}$ = $\underline{5}$

b. This factor shows the multiplying effect of financial leverage on earnings. Thus, whatever return on assets has been earned to this point in the equation will be multiplied by five to convert the yield to a return on equity (ROE) instead of a return on assets (ROA).

14. RETENTION RATIO

$$\frac{NI-D}{NI}$$

a. $\dfrac{\$10,641 - \$4,788}{\$10,641}$ = $\underline{.55}$

b. Fifty-five percent of net income is retained in the leasing company. This allows forty-five percent of net income to be paid out as dividends to shareholders. The more a company retains the faster its earnings can grow due to the expanded earnings base. In fact, an important rule in finance is that a company's earnings per share can grow no faster than the product of its Return on Equity (ROE) times Retention Ratio given no other sources of capital, whether debt or equity, are available. Growth rate in earnings is important since stock prices are heavily influenced by the company's ability to increase earnings each year at high compound growth rates. This company could expect to have its earnings grow by 28.98 percent next year which will, in fact, occur if the firm can maintain the same return on equity.

SENSITIVITY MODEL YIELDS

The results of the fourteen profitability factors are shown on the next page. Seven basic percentage yields result from these factors:

1. *Profitability Percentage*—the product of factors one and two, describes what percentage of total accrual basis revenue is interest; 52.16 percent in this case. The higher the portfolio yield the higher the percentage of interest contained in lease payments.

2. *Gross Pretax Yield*—the product of factors one through three describes profitability in terms of a portfolio yield which is equivalent to the expected pretax gross internal rate of return on the total portfolio. In this case the total yield including the effect of residual value is 18.64 percent.

3. *Accrual Basis Gross Profit Return on Assets*—the product of factors one through seven, indicates the total accrual basis gross profit return on assets including other income and initial direct costs. Thus, every dollar of the company's assets is able to earn on an accrual pretax gross basis 20.05 cents.

4. *Cash Basis Gross Profit Return on Assets*—the product of factors one through eight, describes *cash basis* pretax gross profit return on assets (ROA). This yield is the same as Number three above except it has been converted from accrual basis to cash basis by removing uncollected lease payments from accrual revenue. The yield indicates that every dollar of the company's assets is able to generate a cash of 19.17 cents on a gross pretax basis.

5. *After-tax Net Return on Assets (ROA)*—the product of factors one through twelve, indicates the NET after-tax cash return on assets. Thus, every dollar of the company's assets is able to generate 10.54 cents of net income after-tax.

6. *After-tax Net Return on Equity (ROE)*—the product of factors one through thirteen, indicates the NET after-tax cash return on equity (ROE). Thus, every dollar of equity capital is able to generate 52.69 cents of net income.

7. *Potential Growth Rate in Earnings*—the final product of all fourteen factors, indicates that the company's earnings can grow by 28.98 percent during the next year assuming all fourteen factors remain the same. It is further assumed that no other sources of equity capital are available such as common stock issues.

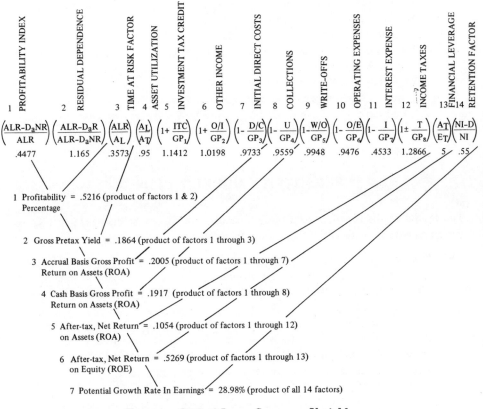

$$\left(\frac{ALR-D_aNR}{ALR}\right)\left(\frac{ALR-D_aR}{ALR-D_aNR}\right)\left(\frac{ALR}{AL}\right)\left(\frac{AL}{A_T}\right)\left(1+\frac{ITC}{GP_1}\right)\left(1+\frac{O/I}{GP_2}\right)\left(1-\frac{D/C}{GP_3}\right)\left(1-\frac{U}{GP_4}\right)\left(1-\frac{W/O}{GP_5}\right)\left(1-\frac{O/E}{GP_6}\right)\left(1-\frac{I}{GP_7}\right)\left(1\pm\frac{T}{GP_8}\right)\left(\frac{A_T}{E_T}\right)\left(\frac{NI-D}{NI}\right)$$

.4477	1.165	.3573	.95	1.1412	1.0198	.9733	.9559	.9948	.9476	.4533	1.2866	5	.55

Column headers (left to right): 1 PROFITABILITY INDEX, 2 RESIDUAL DEPENDENCE, 3 TIME AT RISK FACTOR, 4 ASSET UTILIZATION, 5 INVESTMENT TAX CREDIT, 6 OTHER INCOME, 7 INITIAL DIRECT COSTS, 8 COLLECTIONS, 9 WRITE-OFFS, 10 OPERATING EXPENSES, 11 INTEREST EXPENSE, 12 INCOME TAXES, 13 FINANCIAL LEVERAGE, 14 RETENTION FACTOR

1 Profitability = .5216 (product of factors 1 & 2)
  Percentage

2 Gross Pretax Yield = .1864 (product of factors 1 through 3)

3 Accrual Basis Gross Profit = .2005 (product of factors 1 through 7)
  Return on Assets (ROA)

4 Cash Basis Gross Profit = .1917 (product of factors 1 through 8)
  Return on Assets (ROA)

5 After-tax, Net Return = .1054 (product of factors 1 through 12)
  on Assets (ROA)

6 After-tax, Net Return = .5269 (product of factors 1 through 13)
  on Equity (ROE)

7 Potential Growth Rate In Earnings = 28.98% (product of all 14 factors)

Fourteen Critical Lease Company Variables
Sensitivity Model

The value of a sensitivity model can be seen by changing several of the variables to see the effect on the preceding seven yields. For example, change several of the variables in the previous equation as follows and determine how sensitive the resulting yields are to the changes:

1. Assume the company's asset utilization declines to ninety-one percent due to the purchase of a new office building.
2. Assume the collections percentage drops to ninety-two percent.
3. Assume the income tax factor becomes .98, implying that tax expenses are being incurred rather than benefits received.

The seven yields are altered as follows by the three changes in the lease profitability factors:

1. *Profitability Percentage* .4477 X 1.165 = .5216 No Change.
2. *Gross Pretax Yield* .5216 X .3573 = .1864 No Change.

3. *Accrual Basis Gross Profit Return on Assets (ROA)* .1864 X .91 X 1.1412 X 1.0198 X .9733 = .1921 which indicates a drop of almost one percent.

4. *Cash Basis Gross Profit Keturn on Assets (ROA)* .1921 X .92 = .1768 representing an almost two percent drop in ROA.

5. *After-tax Net Return on Assets (ROA)* .1768 X .9948 X .9476 X .4533 X .98 = .0740 which represents a drop of almost three percent.

6. *After-tax Net Return on Assets (ROE)* .0740 X 5 = .3700 which indicates a reduction of almost sixteen percent.

7. *Potential Growth Rate in Earnings* .3700 X .55 = 20.35% indicating that the company's potential growth rate in earnings has been reduced by almost one third.

As part of the American Association of Equipment Lessors' (AAEL) 1981 annual report, the following selected percentages were prepared by Deloitte, Haskins and Sells (DHS). The DHS survey results can be compared with the example just reviewed. However, in the authors' opinion the DHS survey is not necessarily descriptive of the industry due to survey limitations.

1980 DHS SURVEY*

PROFITABILITY AND FINANCING

	1976	1977	1978	1979	1980	1981
Return on total assets	1.0%	1.9%	2.4%	2.1%	1.6%	1.6%
Return on net worth	8.1%	14.6%	15.9%	14.6%	12.9%	12.5%
Aggregate total borrowings divided by aggregate owner's equity	5.0	5.2	4.6	5.0	6.0	5.4
Total borrowing as a percentage of total assets	70.0%	67.0%	70.0%	69.0%	70.0%	69.0%
Short-term borrowings as a percentage of total assets	39.0%	34.0%	34.0%	24.0%	34.0%	N/A
Long-term borrowings as a percentage of total assets	31.0%	33.0%	36.0%	45.0%	36.0%	N/A
Average bank prime interest rate	7.8%	6.8%	6.8%	9.1%	12.7%	15.2%
Interest expense as a percentage of total revenues	43.0%	39.0%	37.0%	42.0%	51.0%	53.0%
Times interest earned ratio	1.4	1.6	1.9	1.6	1.3	1.3

Net income as a percentage of total revenues has been more volatile than income before tax, but this is probably a function of different respondents and different tax practices, rather than a trend in effective tax rates.

	1976	1977	1978	1979	1980	1981
Income before tax on income as a percentage of total revenues	17%	24%	24%	21%	15%	15%
Net income as a percentage of total revenues	12	17	17	18	13	13

---

*SOURCE: American Association of Equipment Lessors' Annual Report. 1981

Although the sensitivity model's results can be compared with industry results it is preferable to make the comparison with the lessor's own past history in order to detect trends. Furthermore, the model is extremely amenable to forecasting future profitability and cash flow.

CONCLUSION

Use of specially designed management reports such as the Modified Cash Basis Managerial Income Statement and the Cash-Flow-from-Operations Statement coupled with a sensitivity model is very helpful to management in making economic decisions and in evaluating the results of past operations or in predicting future results. Sensitivity models not only indicate the key factors that influence a leasing company's success but they also show how sensitive the seven most important profitability yields are to changes in these factors.

7

Lease Versus
Buy Decision

Is it preferable to lease equipment or to purchase it? Leasing, as a viable alternative to conventional forms of equipment financing, can offer substantial economic savings to the lessee. Cost savings, however, represent only part of the overall reason why leasing might be preferable to conventional financing methods. A properly structured lease with a low down payment can assist in alleviating liquidity problems experienced by growing companies whose cash is tied up in accounts receivable and in inventory needed to meet the demands of a growing market for their products. Then, too, a lease might be preferable to the purchase because of certain flexible characteristics offered to the lessee in the lease agreement such as the privilege of canceling, upgrading, or swapping. Although the value of flexible lease terms is difficult to quantify, such flexibilities nevertheless influence the Lease versus Buy decision.

Since lower cost is only one of the reasons to lease rather than purchase, it follows that the Lease versus Buy decision will consist of several steps. In each step of the decision process we will analyze each of the reasons to lease or buy. The seven basic decision steps which lead to a final lease or buy conclusion are listed below:

1. Financial Decision
2. Indirect Cost Decision
3. Capital Budgeting Decision
4. Liquidity Preference Decision
5. Risk-Adjustment Decision
6. Qualitative Attributes Decision
7. Sensitivity Readjustment Decision

PRELIMINARY ASSUMPTIONS

Prior to an explanation of the steps used in the Lease versus Buy decision process, certain fundamental assumptions must be examined.

1. TYPES OF LEASES USED IN THE COMPARISON

It is fundamental to recognize that in general the decision confronting us is whether to purchase an asset with conventional installment financing or to lease the asset under a leasing arrangement which qualifies as an operating lease (true lease) from a tax point of view. The most common decision is not whether to finance conventionally or to enter into a capital lease (tax viewpoint) since these two alternatives are virtually identical. Both are forms of financing the purchase of an asset; neither are true forms of leasing. However, such a comparison is often made. The Lease versus Buy decision implies that from a tax perspective an operating lease will be compared to a purchase.

However, from an accounting standpoint, one could compare a capital lease with an operating lease since a capital lease is a disguised purchase arrangement. Additionally, a frequent comparison is made between an accounting capital lease and conventional financing where the capital lease is treated as an operating lease for tax purposes.

Later it will be shown that the decision format for the Lease versus Buy decision will allow for comparison between any of the following alternatives:

a. Installment Purchase versus an Accounting Capital Lease—an Operating Lease from a Tax Viewpoint.

b. Installment Purchase versus an Accounting Capital Lease—a Capital Lease from a Tax Viewpoint.

c. Installment Purchase versus an Accounting Operating Lease—an Operating Lease from a Tax Viewpoint.

d. Installment Purchase versus an Accounting Operating Lease—a Capital Lease from a Tax Viewpoint.

e. Tax Operating Lease versus an Accounting Operating Lease taxed as an Operating Lease.

f. Tax Operating Lease versus an Accounting Operating Lease taxed as a Capital Lease.

g. Tax Capital Lease versus an Accounting Capital Lease taxed as a Capital Lease.

h. Tax Capital Lease versus an Accounting Capital Lease taxed as an Operating Lease.

Item "c" is generally the comparison implied in the typical Lease versus Buy decision. Alternatives "a," "f," and "h" are also frequently analyzed as Lease versus Buy decisions. Note that in item "a" above, from an accounting view-point, we are merely comparing two alternative methods of purchasing; even so, from an after-tax viewpoint we are making a Lease versus Buy decision.

2. PRESENT VALUE COST MINIMIZATION TECHNIQUE

The overall decision methodology used in determining whether to lease or buy is based on the concept of present value. Present value analysis is a problem-solving technique that provides for the comparison of unlike investment ex-penses to be incurred during the economic life of a machine or other piece of equipment as compared with similar expenses of another machine or asset. The technique is also applied where two financing alternatives are available for the same asset. This situation is encountered when the Lease versus Buy decision is being made.

The present value technique discounts (reduces expenses in an amount equal to opportunity cost savings) each period's cash expense back to its present day value. The technique is based on the assumption that a dollar of expense post-poned until next year is worth less than a dollar spent today. Postponement of an expense for one year allows a company to earn an investment return (in-terest equivalent) on the money retained and invested during the one-year hold-ing period. These extra earnings on postponed cash expenses virtually lower today's effective cost of next year's expense.

The basic decision criterion employed in the Lease versus Buy decision will be the MINIMIZATION OF THE TOTAL PRESENT VALUE OF LEASING COSTS VERSUS PURCHASING COSTS. The task at hand is to determine the present cost of *leasing* an asset. Then we will determine the present cost of *buying* the same asset. Whichever total of present-value costs is lower will be the alternative to choose. In other words, we will attempt to MINIMIZE COSTS. Some firms use internal rate of return analysis (IRR) instead of present-value analysis. In my opinion, present-value analysis is a superior analytical tool in that it results in easy-to-understand comparative results because costs that en-ter into both the lease and buy alternatives can be listed side by side in a format that facilitates comparison as well as subsequent sensitivity analysis, examined later in the chapter. Another advantage of net present value over the IRR method is that IRR often results in multiple answers to the same problem. Multiple answers occur because of cash inflows experienced during the lease period rather than the normal cash outflows paid by the lessee.

A new technique known as terminal value analysis is frequently applied to the Lease versus Buy decision. This technique compares the future value of Leasing Costs versus buying costs. The future value appreciation rate is usually the les-sor's opportunity cost on funds invested in fixed assets or the lessor's incre-mental, after-tax, weighted average cost of capital. The proper decision in termi-nal value analysis is to choose the lower future cost total.

3. AFTER-TAX COSTS AND BENEFITS

All cash inflows and outflows will be adjusted for income taxes. Tax-deductible expenses will be reduced by the tax savings obtained from the deductibility of the expense. For example, since lease payments are fully deductible for tax purposes, they must be adjusted for the tax savings associated with each payment. A company in the forty percent tax bracket would save forty percent of each lease payment. Thus, the after-tax net effective cost would be sixty percent of each payment since forty percent of the total cost was offset with tax savings. All deductible expenses should be multiplied by one minus the company's effective incremental tax rate (1-t) to reduce the expenses to an after-tax basis. On the other hand, tax benefits which result from the tax shield created by interest included in loan payments and depreciation are determined by multiplying the tax rate (t) by the interest or depreciation expense in order to arrive at the net tax benefit.

The effect of taxation is so significant on revenues and expenses that their adjustment for taxes is an essential step in the Lease versus Buy decision. Of course, nontaxable entities such as government agencies or nonprofit organizations would not consider tax effects in a Lease versus Buy decision.

4. INCLUSION OF ALL PERTINENT COSTS

In order to fully account for costs relating to either the Lease or Buy alternative, include all costs, even those which are incurred under both alternatives, whether equal in amount or not. Although such a practice does not change the final decision, since equals added to unequals are unequal in the same order, it nevertheless serves three pragmatic purposes:

a. It forces one to consider systematically any and all pertinent costs which could easily be overlooked if one is in the habit of omitting costs that are assumed always to be equal.

b. Even though two expenses might be similar in nature, often they will cost different amounts. For example, maintenance frequently costs less when the expense is included in a lease as compared to the cost of maintenance when the asset is purchased.

c. The grand total of lease expenses and purchase costs gives more meaningful information to the analyst when all costs have been included. In addition to knowing which alternative is better, we also want to know the total cost of each option including all pertinent expenses for subsequent sensitivity analysis to be discussed later in this chapter.

5. DISCOUNT PERIODS USED IN PRESENT-VALUE ANALYSIS

Some authors suggest that the tax benefit derived from tax-deductible expenses be discounted quarterly rather than monthly. This approach is based on the IRS requirement that taxes be paid quarterly by corporations. Therefore, the tax benefit of a given deduction is not actually realized until one to three months hence. However, this approach unduly complicates the already complex Lease versus Buy decision. Furthermore, the difference between monthly compounding and quarterly compounding of lease expenses and related tax benefits is not appreciable.

6. PRESENT-VALUE DISCOUNT RATES

There will be three different present-value discount rates employed in the Lease versus Buy decision depending on which particular step in the decision model is being completed. The three different discount rates are defined as follows:

a. *After-tax Incremental Borrowing Rate* represents the interest rate a bank would charge currently or incrementally for a loan similar to a lease in amount, terms, and risk. If the company does not utilize bank borrowing, then the company's current cost of bonds, debentures, commercial paper or other forms of debt should be used. The borrowing rate which is used should be multiplied by one minus the firm's effective incremental tax rate (1-t) to adjust for the tax deductibility of interest expense incurred on debt used to acquire equipment.

This discount rate will be employed in the first step of the decision process, the financial decision. In this step we compare an installment loan directly to the lease alternative without considering other expenses incident to leasing or buying.

b. *Incremental, After-tax, Weighted-average Cost of Capital* is a weighted average of a company's cost of debt and of equity as discussed in chapter 4. This cost of capital is calculated by use of the following formula:

$$\text{Cost of Capital} = K_e \left(\frac{E}{D+E}\right) + K_d \left(\frac{D}{D+E}\right)$$

Where:

K_e = cost of equity = $\dfrac{D_1}{P_o}$ + G

D_1 = expected annual dividend next year

P_o = stock price at the present time "o"

G = expected growth rate in earnings per share

K_d = incremental after-tax cost of debt = i (1-t)

i = incremental cost of debt

t = incremental effective tax rate

E = current market value of the company's common stock

D = current market value of the company's debt

This discount rate will be used in steps two, three, four, and six in the decision model. There are other methods of computing a company's cost of capital, such as the "Capital Asset Pricing Model," which views a company's cost of capital as being determined by outside investors who determine the risk of the firm as compared to general stock market risk and then convert this to an interest rate cost. For purposes of the Lease versus Buy analysis, the preceding formula based on the widely known Gorden Growth Model is preferable because it can be readily calculated, whereas the others require difficult-to-obtain additional information.

c. *Risk-adjusted Cost of Capital* is calculated by adding to the Incremental, After-tax, Weighted-average Cost of Capital determined in "b" above, a risk premium. The risk premium will take the form of an additional percentage added to the cost of capital percentage discount rate to compensate for leases in which the risk of the asset acquisition is perceived to be above average.

When a risk premium is directly added to the cost of capital, there is an implicit assumption that the riskiness of the cost to be discounted is increasing exponentially with time. This assumption is implicit in the discounting process due to the effect of compounding of interest while using a higher discount rate.

If risk is not expected to increase over time but is expected to remain the same or decrease, then there are other techniques that can be used to adjust the cost-of-capital rate used for projects having average risk.

For example, suppose the risk penalty is estimated at five percent during the first year and is expected to decline by one percent each year of a five-year lease. The discount factors used during each year of the lease based upon the firm's cost of capital could be reduced directly by the declining risk penalties. This technique is demonstrated by the following table of adjusted fifteen percent cost of capital discount factors:

Year	15% Cost of Capital Discount Factor	−	Risk-adjustment	=	Risk-adjusted Discount Factor
1	.8696	−	.05	=	.8196
2	.7561	−	.04	=	.7161
3	.6575	−	.03	=	.6275
4	.5718	−	.02	=	.5518
5	.4972	−	.01	=	.4872
	Totals 3.3522				3.2022

Another method of adjusting for declining risk is to sequentially determine the appropriate discount factors starting in reverse order, last year to the first year, and multiplying each factor by the previous one as shown in the table below:

Years in Reverse Order	Required Discount Rate	PV Factor for 1 period	x	Multiply By Previous Factor	=	Risk-adjusted Discount Factor for each year
5	15 + 1 = 16	.8621	x	1	=	.8621 1
4	15 + 2 = 17	.8547	x	.8621	=	.7368 2
3	15 + 3 = 18	.8475	x	.7368	=	.6244 3
2	15 + 4 = 19	.8403	x	.6244	=	.5247 4
1	15 + 5 = 20	.8333	x	.5247	=	.4373 5
				TOTAL		3.1853

LEASE VERSUS BUY DECISION MODEL

Step One—Financial Decision

To facilitate identification of the pertinent lease costs to be included in the financial decision, refer to the format appearing below. These direct leasing costs have been categorized into the initial, subsequent, and terminal financial costs that form an integral part of the lease. Explanations of the more important components follow the format presentation (refer to footnotes).

PRESENT VALUE OF LEASING COSTS

Step One—Financial Analysis

ADD DIRECT LEASE COSTS:

	Amount	x	Tax Factor	x	PV Factor	=	Total Cost
Initial Costs:							
Closing, Origination, Service Fees[1]	$——	x	(1-t)	x	N/A	=	$——
Advance Rental Payments[2]	$——	x	(1-t)	x	N/A	=	$——
Security Deposits[2]	$——	x	N/A	x	N/A	=	$——

	Amount	x	Tax Factor	x	PV Factor	=	Total Cost
Subsequent Costs:							
Remaining Base Rental Payments	$——	x	(1-t)	x	PV_a	=	$——
Renewal Option Rental Payments[3]	$——	x	(1-t)	x	$PV_a + PV_1$	=	$——
Percentage Rentals (Est.)[4]	$——	x	(1-t)	x	PV_a	=	$——
Payment Increase due to prime rate or CPI Increases (Est.)[5]	$——	x	(1-t)		see Formula	=	$——
Terminal Costs:							
Residual Guarantee Deficiency	$——	x	(1-t)	x	PV_1	=	$——
Nonrenewal Penalty	$——	x	(1-t)	x	PV_1	=	$——
Purchase Option Plus Sales Tax	$——	x	N/A	x	PV_1	=	$——
SUB-TOTAL DIRECT LEASE COSTS							$==

DEDUCT DIRECT LEASE BENEFITS:

	Amount	x	Tax Factor	x	PV Factor	=	Total Cost
Investment Tax Credit[7]	$——	x	N/A	x	PV_1	=	($——)
Return of Security Deposit[8]	$——	x	N/A	x	PV_1	=	($——)
Loss of Security[8]	$——	x	(t)	x	PV_1	=	($——)
Depreciation Tax Shield Option Exercised[9]	$——	x	(t)	x	$PV_a + PV_1$	=	($——)
Residual Rebate (Est.)	$——	x	(1-t)	x	PV_1	=	($——)
NET FINANCIAL COST TO LEASE							$==

A similar format is used to calculate the financial cost of purchasing an asset with cash or through the use of an installment loan.

PRESENT-VALUE OF PURCHASING COSTS

Step One—Financial Analysis

ADD DIRECT PURCHASE COSTS:

	Amount	x	Tax Factor	x	PV Factor	=	Total
Initial Costs:							
Closing, Origination, Service Fees	$——	x	N/A	x	N/A	=	$——
Down Payment	$——	x	N/A	x	N/A	=	$——

	Amount	x	Tax Factor	x	PV Factor	=	Total
Security Deposit	$——	x	N/A	x	N/A	=	$——
Compensating Bank Balance[10]	$——	x	N/A	x	N/A	=	$——
Subsequent Costs:							
Periodic Installment Payments	$——	x	N/A	x	PV_a	=	$——
Payment Increase due to Prime Rate[11]	$——	x	N/A	see Formula		=	$——
Terminal Costs:							
Balloon Payment[12]	$——	x	N/A	x	PV_1	=	$——
ITC Recapture for Early Salvage[13]	$——	x	N/A	x	PV_1	=	$——
SUB-TOTAL COSTS							$——

DEDUCT PURCHASE BENEFITS:

	Amount	x	Tax Factor	x	PV Factor	=	Total
Investment Tax Credit[7]	$——	x	N/A	x	PV_1	=	$——
Return of Security Deposit[8]	$——	x	N/A	x	PV_1	=	$——
Loss of Security Deposit[8]	$——	x	(t)	x	PV_1	=	$——
Depreciation Tax Shield[14]	$——	x	(t)	x	PV_1	=	$——
Interest Tax Shield[15]	$——	x	(t)	x	PV_1	=	$——
Tax-adjusted Salvage Value[16]	$——	x	N/A	x	PV_1	=	$——
Return of Compensating Balance[10]	$——	x	N/A	x	PV_1	=	$——
TOTAL BENEFITS (Total of the above Benefits)							($——)
NET FINANCIAL COST TO PURCHASE (Deduct Benefits from Costs)							$——

Prior to an explanation of the footnoted components of the lease or the purchase format, it is important to remember that the present-value discount rate to be used in this step is the firm's *After-Tax Incremental Borrowing Rate*. The tax rate employed should be the incremental effective tax rate of the firm. When the symbol PV_a is used, it means that the present value of an annuity factor should be used. PV_1 means a present value of one factor is required. N/A means not applicable.

Use of the After-Tax Incremental Borrowing Rate at this step in the Lease-versus-Buy decision model serves several useful purposes. First, the present value of a loan with after-tax installment payments or a loan with small down payment, subsequent installment payments, and a large balloon payment at the end of the loan period, when discounted with the same after-tax interest rate implicit in the loan, will result in a present-value total exactly equal to the cash purchase price. When the present value of the loan payments plus down payment and balloon payments equal the cash purchase price, it is implied that the firm is indifferent between paying one hundred percent cash from company resources or financing the purchase of the asset with an installment loan. Thus, a company is assumed to have no liquidity problem or liquidity preference at this particular step in the model. In Step four we will deal with the concept of liquidity preference. Elimination of liquidity preference at this level in the decision model allows us to compare a cash purchase or an installment loan purchase directly with a lease from a purely financial viewpoint. If the present value of the lease payments exceeds the cash purchase price after completion of Step one, then from a purely financial viewpoint the lease is costing the firm more due to the higher implicit interest rate in the lease and because the purchase alternative offers greater tax benefits earlier in the asset's life.

We are not ignoring the fact that many firms are not indifferent concerning liquidity. Indeed many companies want to borrow or lease due to lack of funds to purchase the asset outright. Rather than ignoring the problem we are simply separating the liquidity problem from the financing problem and deferring treatment of liquidity preference until Step four.

Following are the footnote explanations of the various components of the lease format and the purchase format:

Footnote One   Frequently, loans and leases will require additional finance charges to be paid at the inception of the lease. Such finance charges are referred to as closing fees, origination fees, or service fees, and in most cases are simply disguised forms of interest required to be paid in advance. In the case of a lease these expenses are fully tax deductible and can usually be written off immediately. In the case of a loan, however, these fees must be added to the cost of the asset from a tax viewpoint and subsequently depreciated over the life of the asset.

Footnote Two   Advance rental payments are frequently required to be paid at the inception of the lease to compensate the lessor for additional risk that the lessor feels exists due to the lessee's lack of credit-worthiness. These payments are fully tax-deductible from the lessee's viewpoint. However, advance deposits are not tax-deductible and should not be confused with advance payments. Deposits are refundable at the termination of the lease—advance payments are not. Deposits secure performance under the lease in regards to proper maintenance, prompt payment, etc. Advance payments can serve the same purpose, but deposits are nevertheless treated differently for tax purposes than advance payments. This is true as long as the deposits are fully refundable at the end of a lease which assumes proper performance of lease obligations during the lease term.

Footnote Three   Renewal option rental payments are generally lower in amount than the payments required during the initial term of the lease. Therefore, a two-step procedure is required to determine the present value of the renewal payments. First, determine the present value of an annuity equal to the renewal payments for the renewal time period only. Second, take the present value of the amount determined in the first step by multiplying it by the present value of one factor for the number of periods during the initial lease term. For example, determine the present value of renewal payments of $2,000 each to be paid at the end of the fourth, fifth, and sixth year of a lease where the initial annual lease payments were $4,000 for each of the first three years. A ten percent discount rate has the following present-value factors: Present value of an ordinary annuity in arrears of one for three years equals 2.4869 and the present value of one discounted three years is .7513.

Step one:

$2,000 X 2.4869 = $4,973.80

Step two:

$4,973.80 X .7513 = $3,736.82

Footnote Four   Percentage or contingent rentals are generally based upon a fixed percentage of the lessee's gross revenue in excess of a base amount earned on the leased asset. The percentage rental is paid in addition to the normal periodic rental required under the lease agreement. If the lessee's revenue does not grow beyond the minimum base established in the lease, then percentage rentals may never be paid. However, when revenues are expected to grow, we are faced with the problem of estimating the present value of a growing stream of lease payments. In this situation it is common to expect that revenue will grow at a constant compound percentage rate each period during the lease term. In other situations, revenue might be expected to grow at a slower rate or by a constant amount each rental period. In either case, the following formulae can be employed to determine the present value of a growing stream of lease payments:

1. Present value of a stream of lease payments growing at a constant percentage rate each period (or decreasing at a constant rate); D = Discount Rate Percentage, G=Expected Percentage Growth Rate in lease rentals, PMT = Lease Payment at Present, n = number of payments.

$$PV = \left(\frac{PMT}{D-G}\right) \left[1 - \left(1 + \frac{D-G}{1+G}\right)^{-n}\right]$$

2. If a financial calculator is used, input the preceding information into the following keys and solve for present value.

$\boxed{i}$ $= \dfrac{D-G}{1+\dfrac{G}{100}}$

$\boxed{n}$ = Number of rental payments, the first being paid at the end of first period (ordinary annuity in arrears).

$\boxed{pmt}$ $= \dfrac{\text{Payment at the end of first period}}{1+\dfrac{G}{100}}$

3. Example of a constantly growing lease payment (percentage increase):
   Compute the present value of sixty monthly lease payments that are growing by one percent a month. The discount rate for present-value purposes is 1.5 percent a month and the monthly lease payment is $1,000.

$$\boxed{i} \;=\; \frac{D-G}{1+\frac{G}{100}} \;=\; \frac{1.5-1}{1+\frac{1}{100}} \;=\; \frac{.5}{1.01} \;=\; .49504 \;=\; \boxed{i}$$

$$\boxed{n} \;=\; 60 \;=\; n$$

$$\boxed{pmt} \;=\; \frac{pmt \text{ end of 1st period}}{1+\frac{G}{100}} \;=\; \frac{\$1,000}{1+\frac{1}{100}} \;=\; \frac{\$1,000}{1.01}$$

$$=\; \$990.10 \;=\; \boxed{pmt}$$

$$\boxed{pv} \;=\; \underline{\$51,286.87} \text{ (Note: disregard the fact that the calculator gives a negative answer)}$$

4. Present value of a stream of lease payments growing by a constant amount each period; CI = Constant Incremental Increase or decrease, D = Discount Rate, PMT = Payment at the end of the first period.

$$PV \;=\; \left(\frac{CI}{D}+PMT\right)\left[\frac{(1+D)^n-1}{D(1+D)^n}\right] - \left[\frac{CI \times n}{D(1+D)^n}\right]$$

If a financial calculator is used, input the preceding information into the following keys and solve for present value.

$$\boxed{i} \;=\; \text{Discount Rate ``D''}$$

$$\boxed{n} \;=\; \text{Number of rental payments, the first being paid at the end of the first period (ordinary annuity in arrears).}$$

$$\boxed{pmt} \;=\; pmt + \left(\frac{CI}{D/100}\right)$$

$$\boxed{fv} \;=\; -n\left(\frac{CI}{D/100}\right)$$

5. Example of a lease payment growing by a fixed increment each period.

Compute the present value of sixty monthly lease payments that are growing by $20 each month. The discount rate is 1.5 percent a month and the starting payment is $1,000.00.

$$\boxed{i} = 1.5$$

$$\boxed{n} = 60$$

$$\boxed{pmt} = pmt + \left(\frac{CI}{D/100}\right) = \$1000 + \left(\frac{\$20}{1.5/100}\right)$$
$$= \$1000 + 1,333.33 = 2,333.33 \text{ pmt}$$

$$\boxed{fv} = -n\left(\frac{CI}{D/100}\right) = -60\left(\frac{\$20}{1.5/100}\right) = -60 \times \$1,333.33$$
$$= -79,999.80$$

$$\boxed{pv} = \underline{\$59,143.57} \text{ (Note: disregard the fact that the calculator gives a negative answer)}$$

Footnote Five   Some lease payments are tied to increases in the prime rate or tied to increases in price indexes such as the Consumer Price Index (CPI), the Wholesale Price Index (WPI), or the Gross National Product Deflator. The previously described formulae can be used to determine lease payments that are expected to grow at a constant rate or by a constant amount. If neither of these two growth assumptions can be met, then each expected lease payment must be individually estimated and individually discounted—a laborious task at best.

Footnote Six   At the end of the lease term, after all renewal periods, one of several alternative courses of action will be taken depending upon the terms of the lease and the needs of the lessee. The flowchart shown on the following page describes the various alternatives available to the lessee.

The alternative chosen must be consistent with the anticipated disposal plans under the purchase alternative. For example, if the lessee purchases the asset and expects to hold it beyond the lease term, it should be assumed that either a lease purchase option will be exercised or a guaranteed residual will be paid where the title will pass to the lessee. If no option is available or title does pass with the payment of the guaranteed residual, it should be assumed under the purchase alternative that the asset will be salvaged the same date the lease terminates. Otherwise, the two alternatives will not be comparable.

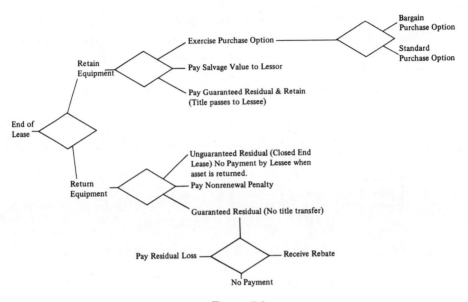

Figure 7.1

Footnote Seven   The Investment Tax Credit (ITC) at the lessor's option may be passed to the lessee under an operating lease. When the ITC is passed to the lessee it is calculated as a percentage of the cash equivalent cost (same as fair market value) of the leased equipment. The percentage, six percent, or ten percent is based upon the depreciation life assigned to the asset on the books of the lessor. In order to pass on the full ITC of ten percent, the equipment must be five year ACRs property.

A form should be filled out and signed by the lessor in order to properly pass the ITC to the lessee. The form should contain the following information:

1. Name, address, and federal identification number of both parties to the lease.
2. District IRS office of both lessor and lessee.
3. Description of the leased property.
4. Date of delivery of leased property to lessee.
5. Estimated useful life property (depreciation life) or ACRs life.
6. Basis of the leased property to the lessor.
7. Name, address, tax I.D. number of original lessor if the leasing company is also a lessee of the equipment and is simply sub-leasing the asset.
8. Fair market value of the asset (retail price).

Footnote Eight   In the event the lessee does not expect to receive a refund of the security deposit due to anticipated excess wear and tear of the equipment or other anticipated lease violations, such loss becomes a future noncash tax deduction. A tax benefit would therefore become available at the end of the lease in an amount equal to the tax rate times the unrefunded deposit. If the deposit is refunded it will not result in a taxable benefit since the deposit is merely the return of one's own funds.

Footnote Nine   If it is assumed that the lessee will exercise a purchase option at the end of the lease, then a tax benefit will be forthcoming in the form of a depreciation tax shield equal to the depreciation available in each quarter year of the asset's remaining depreciation life multiplied by the firm's incremental effective tax rate.

If the asset has a remaining life beyond one year, then a two-step discounting process similar to that explained in Footnote three must be used where Step one determines the present value of the depreciation in each quarter year of its remaining life and Step two discounts this amount to the present. Depreciation tax shelter is computed quarterly on the assumption that such tax savings only become cash benefits during the quarter in which taxes are paid.

Footnote Ten   Compensating bank balances are cash deposits required to be held in the borrower's checking account throughout the full length of the loan. This cash outlay is treated as any other cost of borrowing. Unfortunately, compensating balances are not tax-deductible, which further increases their net cost to the purchaser-borrower.

Footnote Eleven   Recently, some installment loan agreements have required installment payments that vary in unison with prime rate increases or decreases. Forecasting of future prime rates is therefore required—a formidable task. (Refer to Footnote four, which describes techniques to deal with constantly increasing payments.)

Footnote Twelve   In order to keep installment loan payments at a minimum and to compete with leasing companies, some banks allow the purchaser-borrower to pay a large balloon payment at the termination of the loan. This type of loan-structuring makes the installment loan very comparable to leases which require large guaranteed residuals to be paid at the end of the lease.

Remember, however, that such structuring of payments only helps a company's liquidity; it does not affect the financial cost of the loan because use of the firm's after-tax incremental borrowing rate as a discount factor always results in a present-value loan cost exactly equal to its equivalent cash cost no matter what the structure of the loan. (Liquidity preference will be covered in Step four of the decision model.)

Footnote Thirteen   If the purchaser of an asset anticipates salvaging the equipment before the time required to earn the full ten percent investment tax credit, a portion of the ITC must be recaptured. The amount to be recaptured and paid to the IRS is the difference between the ITC claimed and the amount earned at the date of salvaging the equipment. The new tax law allows equipment owners to earn ITC at the rate of 2% a year. Thus, an asset salvaged in its fourth year would require a 2% recapture.

Footnote Fourteen   Owned equipment qualifies to be depreciated under IRS rules. Depreciation results in tax savings which are equal to the incremental effective income tax rate times the annual or quarterly depreciation charge. Moreover, the IRS code allows accelerated depreciation for certain asset classes.

Footnote Fifteen   Interest is included as a cost in the installment loan payments listed on the purchase format. Since interest is tax-deductible, it results in a tax savings equal to the interest paid in each installment payment multiplied by the firm's incremental effective tax rate. Interest paid during any particular period can be easily calculated with the use of an advanced financial calculator or approximated through the use of the rule of 78's technique.

Some authors mistakenly conclude that deduction of interest tax savings from the installment payments represents double accounting for interest. They assert that since the discount rate being used is after-tax, deduction of interest savings once again from the installment payments is double accounting.

These authors fail to realize that one cannot use an after-tax discount rate on UNADJUSTED PRETAX INSTALLMENT payments. If the installment payments have been already adjusted for the tax consequence of tax-deductible interest therein then the after-tax discount rate is proper. But one cannot use after-tax discount rates with pretax installment payments.

To prove this point assume the following simple loan of $21,064.81 payable beginning one year hence in three annual installments of $10,000 with an implicit pretax interest rate of twenty percent. The firm's after-tax borrowing rate would be ten percent assuming a fifty percent tax bracket. Using the theory of the other authors, the present value of the three installment payments of $10,000 should be $21,064.81 when discounted using the after-tax cost of debt. However, this results in a present value of $24,868.52—overstated by $3,803.71. When we compute the interest included on an after-tax basis in each payment and discount these to the present, we arrive at a tax savings of $3,803.71—exactly equal to the overstatement. The point is: After-tax discount rates can only be used to discount after-tax cash flows. Deducting interest tax shield benefits is not DOUBLE ACCOUNTING; rather, it is PROPER ADJUSTING of pretax cash costs to after-tax cash costs.

Computation of the present value of the interest tax savings was completed as follows:

Year	Interest	Interest After-Tax	x	P.V. Factor 10%	=	P.V.
1	4,212.96	2,106.48	x	.9091	=	1,915.07
2	3,055.55	1,527.78	x	.8264	=	1.262.56
3	1,666.66	833.33	x	.7513	=	626.08
				TOTAL		$3,803.71

Another concluding point on this matter: Why should implicit interest included in lease payments be placed on an after-tax basis (which is accomplished when the whole lease payment is considered tax deductible) if we are not going to allow the same interest included in a loan payment to be placed on an after-tax basis? Consistency demands that the tax benefit of interest be deducted from the pretax installment payments.

Footnote Sixteen   If the equipment is assumed to be salvaged prior to the end of its economic life in order to make the purchase alternative equivalent to a shorter term lease, the resulting salvage proceeds represent a savings benefit. However, such proceeds must be adjusted for anticipated tax consequences. If the equipment is salvaged for more than its book value (tax basis or undepreciated cost at the salvage date) a gain follows and results in a tax equal to the tax rate times the gain. Depending upon the type of asset, the resulting tax might be computed differently, as is the case for assets qualifying for capital gains tax treatment in lieu of ordinary income tax treatment.

Should the salvage proceeds be less than the book value of the asset, a tax benefit would be earned in an amount equal to the loss times the tax rate. In either case, the salvage proceeds must have the tax benefit added to proceeds or tax expense deducted from proceeds before the net savings can be discounted as a purchase benefit.

FINANCIAL CONCLUSION FOR STEP ONE

Once the costs and offsetting benefits have been established for each alternative, the final financial cost comparison can be made. The alternative with the lower cost total would be the preferable choice if there were not numerous other considerations remaining in the Lease versus Buy decision. In effect, Step one will have demonstrated that from a purely financial funding point of view, either leasing or borrowing costs less. The next step in the decision process considers numerous other indirect costs that impact the Lease versus Buy decision.

Step Two—Indirect Cost Decision

A format helpful in analyzing indirect costs that affect the Lease versus Buy decision will be presented in this step along with explanatory footnotes beginning with Indirect Lease Costs followed by Indirect Purchase Costs. The present value factor used to discount cash flows will be the firm's incremental, after-tax, weighted cost of capital. The cost-of-capital discount rate is consistent with the uncertainty or variability associated with indirect costs. The company is obligated to pay financial-type payments (Step one, lease and loan payments) by contractual agreement, which implies that little uncertainty exists about the variability in the payments. Thus, the lower after-tax incremental borrowing rate is used in discounting, whereas costs and benefits incidental to the operating of the equipment (indirect costs) are subject to much greater variability. Therefore, a higher cost of capital discount rate is appropriate for these more uncertain costs. If risk beyond normal is anticipated with the particular equipment lease, then a risk adjustment to the cost-of-capital discount rate will be in order. However, such additional risk consideration will be dealt with in Step five of the decision model.

Discount rates reflect not only risk but also opportunity cost, which is another reason cost of capital is used as the discount rate in Step two. Although opportunity cost and risk are interrelated, a discount rate, in my opinion, should represent an interest equivalent (opportunity cost) of the additional income earned on money available for investment today because of a firm's ability to postpone an expense until a future date. Thus, if money can be invested at ten percent, then a $100 expense postponed one year really costs only $90.91 in today's dollars because it is possible to earn ten percent of $90.91 (which is $9.09) during the postponement period. When the savings of postponing the expense are deducted from $100.00, the cost today is $90.91 ($100.00-$9.09). It is therefore assumed that any funds available now for investment resulting from the postponement of expenses should earn an amount equal to the company's incremental, after-tax, weighted-average cost of capital. Generally, a company must be able to earn on its investments an amount equal to its cost of capital; otherwise, the market price of its stock will begin to fall. Faltering stock prices result from declining growth rates in earnings. Growth rates decline because net income is insufficient to meet the firm's reinvestment needs. The after-tax cost of a firm's debt is usually less than the firm's overall after-tax, weighted cost-of-capital. Therefore, it is theoretically sound to conclude that a company can earn more (in fact must earn more) than the cost of debt, and that employment of a firm's after-tax incremental cost of debt in discounting relatively uncertain indirect cost cash outflows in a Lease versus Buy decision would not properly reflect the real *opportunity cost nor the additional risk* associated with paying expenses now rather than postponing them to future periods.

Following are the formats for the analysis of indirect lease and purchase costs:

PRESENT VALUE OF LEASING COSTS

Step Two—Indirect Lease Cost Decision

ADD INDIRECT LEASE COSTS:

	Amount	x	Tax Factor	x	PV Factor	=	Total
Sales Tax in Advance[18]	$——	x	(1–t)	x	N/A	=	$——
Sales Tax[18]	$——	x	(1–t)	x	PV_a	=	$——
Property Tax[17]	$——	x	(1–t)	x	PV_a	=	$——
Insurance[17]	$——	x	(1–t)	x	PV_a	=	$——
Maintenance[17]	$——	x	(1–t)	x	PV_a	=	$——
Replacement Costs[19]	$——	x	(1–t)	x	PV_1	=	$——

	Amount	x	Tax Factor	x	PV Factor	=	Total
Fuel Costs (EST)[20]	$——	x	(1-t)	x	PV_a	=	$——
Variable Accounting Costs[21]	$——	x	(1-t)	x	PV_a	=	$——
Miscellaneous Costs Unique to Industry	$——	x	(1-t)	x	PV_a	=	$——
Delivery Charges	$——	x	(1-t)	x	N/A	=	$——
Installation Expenses	$——	x	(1-t)	x	N/A	=	$——
Excess use or Maintenance Charges[22]	$——	x	(1-t)	x	PV_1	=	$——
SUB-TOTAL INDIRECT LEASE COSTS							$——

DEDUCT INDIRECT LEASE BENEFITS:

	Amount	x	Tax Factor	x	PV Factor	=	Total
Sub-lease Income	$——	x	(1-t)	x	PV_a	=	($——)

NET INDIRECT COST TO LEASE (Deduct Benefits from Costs) $——

CUMULATIVE COST TO LEASE (Step 1 + Step 2) $——

PRESENT VALUE OF PURCHASE COSTS

Step Two—Indirect Cost Decision

ADD INDIRECT PURCHASE COSTS:

	Amount	x	Tax Factor	x	PV Factor	=	Total
Property Tax	$——	x	(1-t)	x	PV_a	=	$——
Insurance	$——	x	(1-t)	x	PV_a	=	$——
Maintenance	$——	x	(1-t)	x	PV_a	=	$——
Replacement Costs[19]	$——	x	(1-t)	x	PV_1	=	$——
Down-time Losses including lost goodwill[9]	$——	x	(1-t)	x	PV_1	=	$——
Fuel Costs[20]	$——	x	(1-t)	x	PV_a	=	$——
Variable Accounting Costs	$——	x	(1-t)	x	PV_a	=	$——
Spare Parts Inventory[23]	$——	x	(1-t)	x	PV_a	=	$——
Additional Facilities Costs[23]	$——	x	(1-t)	x	PV_a	=	$——
Miscellaneous Costs Unique to Industry	$——	x	(1-t)	x	PV_a	=	$——

	Amount	x	Tax Factor	x	PV Factor	=	Total
Delivery Charges[24]	$———	x	N/A or (1-t) x N/A			=	$———
Installation Expenses[24]	$———	x	N/A or (1-t) x N/A			=	$———
Sales Tax[24]	$———	x	N/A or (1-t) x N/A			=	$———
Licenses and Permits[24]	$———	x	N/A or (1-t) x N/A			=	$———

SUB-TOTAL INDIRECT PURCHASE COSTS $———

DEDUCT INDIRECT PURCHASE BENEFITS:

Sub-Lease Income $———   x   (1-t)   x PV_a =   ($———)

NET INDIRECT COST TO
    PURCHASE (Deduct Benefits from Costs) $———

CUMULATIVE COST TO PURCHASE (Step 1 & Step 2) $———————

Following are the footnote explanations of the various components of the indirect costs associated with the lease and purchase alternatives.

Footnote Seventeen   Some leases require delivery and installation charges to be paid by the lessee in addition to deposits and advance payments at the inception of the lease. Such expenses are generally fully tax-deductible and are therefore multiplied by one minus the tax rate to convert them to after-tax expenses. However, should such expenses represent a large outlay relative to the lease payments, the IRS might force the lessee to capitalize these costs as leasehold improvements and amortize them over the life of the lease. When this situation occurs, the cost would not be multiplied by (1-t); instead it would be included in whole as an indirect cost. However, an additional indirect lease benefit would be included as a reduction of indirect leasing costs. The benefit would be equal to the tax rate multiplied by the amortized portion of the cost times a present-value factor for the period of amortization.

In net leases, executory costs such as sales tax, property tax, insurance, and maintenance are required to be paid by the lessee outside of and in addition to the lease payment. In full service leases, these expenses are hidden in the lease payments and it is preferable to isolate such and classify them as part of indirect leasing costs. Such separation of executory costs from the full-service lease payments allows direct comparison with similar executory costs incurred under the purchase alternative. Often, such executory costs are difficult if not impossible to separate from the basic lease payment.

Footnote Eighteen   In most states, sales tax or use-tax is paid as a percentage of each lease payment rather than being paid in one lump sum at the inception of the lease by the lessee. Although sales tax is then paid on a greater base, since lease payments include implicit interest. However, the present value cost of the sales tax payments is generally less than a lump sum up-front payment because such payments are spread over the future.

Footnote Nineteen   Replacement costs are incurred when temporary replacement equipment is obtained from the lessor to fill in for equipment out of service due to extraordinary breakdowns. Replacement costs might include extra rental payments to the lessor; however, if the lease has a SWAP PROVISION in it, the lessor at no cost to the lessee exchanges permanently a working piece of equipment for the nonworking one. Such a swap provision could be extremely valuable in avoiding replacement costs.

If replacements are not readily available, when purchasing an asset, additional down-time costs might be incurred in the form of lost sales or lost customer goodwill.

Footnote Twenty   Under certain full service leases for equipment that uses large amounts of fuel, cost savings can be achieved. For example, many Ryder Truck Leasing Agreements provide for the purchase of fuel from Ryder Company outlets at prices below retail. With rising energy costs these savings could become a decisive factor in favor of leasing when it is assumed that if the asset were purchased, fuel could only be purchased at retail prices.

Footnote Twenty-one   When compared to purchasing equipment, leasing equipment generally requires substantially less accounting and bookkeeping. Be careful to include only the incremental variable accounting costs that will be incurred as a result of leasing since fixed accounting costs will go on whether the asset is leased, purchased, or not acquired at all. Incremental costs are defined as the additional costs incurred solely due to the acquisition of the new equipment.

Footnote Twenty-two   At the termination of the lease, the contract might require the lessee to pay a penalty for excess use (e.g. mileage on trucks beyond a specified maximum) or for repairs and maintenance required to bring the equipment up to a specified working order and condition. The lessee should include these additional costs under the lease alternative if such costs are anticipated.

Footnote Twenty-three   Ownership of equipment frequently entails costs that would not ordinarily be incurred under a full service lease. For example, spare parts and supplies inventories must be maintained to support equipment maintenance requirements. Also, additional facilities are required to house maintenance equipment, etc. Significant added costs of ownership are represented by these incremental support costs. Should any of these support costs represent capital expenditures, they should be added to the initial cost of purchasing. These capitalized costs would subsequently result in depreciation tax savings available to the purchaser as benefits of ownership. Remember to add only those costs that are incremental; i.e., those variable costs that will be incurred only as a result of purchasing the equipment.

Footnote Twenty-four   In many cases it is more advantageous to the purchaser of equipment to capitalize costs of delivery, sales tax, installation, closing and service fees, licenses and permits. Such capitalization allows the purchaser to take investment tax credit on the capitalized costs. Moreover, these costs can be subsequently depreciated resulting in an additional tax benefit. Whether or not the ITC and depreciation will result in net savings beyond those benefits available from an immediate write-off of costs should be determined quantitatively. Compute the present values of the ITC and depreciation tax shield resulting from the capitalized costs and deduct them from the original costs. If this difference is less than the tax-adjusted costs obtained under direct write-off, then these initial costs should be capitalized. Many lessees make a standard practice of capitalizing initial start-up costs.

INDIRECT COST CONCLUSION FOR STEP TWO

Having totalled the pertinent indirect costs of both lease and purchase alternatives it can be seen through comparison how indirect costs influence the overall Lease versus Buy decision. Also, by adding the costs of Step two to those of Step one the cumulative results reveal whether there is a shift in preference from leasing to buying or vice versa. Keep in mind that the cumulative results are not yet decisive since we have five more steps to complete in the decision model.

Step Three—Capital Budgeting Decision

Before proceeding any further with the Lease versus Buy decision we must pause in order to determine whether the asset should be acquired in the first place. If the investment should not be made due to inadequate expected investment returns, the Lease versus Buy decision becomes moot.

Capital budgeting criteria provide for the acquisition of an asset if the return on the investment (internal rate of return) is equal to or greater than the firm's cost of capital. An alternative criterion, net present value, provides that an asset should be acquired if the after-tax present value of cash inflows generated by the investment exceed the cash outflows (original asset cost). Our task in this step of the decision process is to decide whether to acquire the asset. The question of whether to lease or buy a piece of equipment that has met the capital budgeting investment acquisition test of providing sufficient expected net cash returns can then be answered through completion of the remaining steps in the decision model.

To determine whether the lease or buy alternative will produce a positive net present value, it is necessary to arrive at the total present value of the after-tax cash revenues expected to be generated by the equipment. The discount rate to be used in determining the present value of the revenues will be the firm's incremental, after-tax, weighted-average cost of capital. If the project is deemed riskier than normal, a risk premium can be added to the cost of capital (check the methodology described on page 138).

If revenues are expected to grow over the period of the lease due to inflation or other causes, then the techniques described in Footnote four, Step one will be helpful. Since inflation has reached such high rates lately it is important to include its effects in any forecast of potential revenues to be obtained from an investment proposal.

Once the total after-tax present value of the revenues has been determined, compare this total to the cumulative leasing costs arrived at in Step two. If the present value of the revenues exceeds the present value of the cumulative costs, then the asset should be acquired even though the mode of acquisition (lease or buy) will still be uncertain until the completion of Step seven of the decision model.

If the present value of the revenues is in excess of only one of the alternatives, either leasing or buying, then proceed to the remaining steps of the decision model since the asset should be acquired even though its financing method is still indeterminate.

Step Four—Liquidity Preference

Liquidity preference refers to a firm's preference for cash outflows having the least adverse effect on cash. In other words, a firm may choose to acquire an asset with an installment loan in preference to an outright cash purchase in order to conserve cash needed for other working capital requirements. Then, too, the firm might prefer a lease over an installment loan if the lease provides a lower down payment and a longer payback period than the terms available in the loan.

Unfortunately, many Lease versus Buy models combine the financial decision discussed in Step one with the liquidity decision discussed here by applying the higher cost-of-capital discount rate (rather than the cost-of-debt rate) to the highly certain contractual cash flows used in Step one of this model. Combining the financial decision with the liquidity preference decision through use of a cost-of-capital discount rate creates a bias in favor of purchasing when the lease term is expected to be the same length as the loan term because "the cash flow 'benefits' of a lease tend to outweigh its cash flow 'costs' only in the later years of the asset's life. Thus, the use of a relatively high discount rate has a tendency to understate these benefits."[1]

However, when the lease repayment period extends beyond the loan installment term in a Lease versus Buy situation, the use of a relatively high discount rate results in an opposite bias in favor of the lease.

The bias resulting from the use of a relatively high cost-of-capital discount rate represents a confounding of two different decisions that should be made separately—one a financial decision, the other a liquidity preference decision. Using the cost of capital under the right circumstances and in the proper sequence shows the advantage in terms of liquidity cost savings of one alternative over the other.

When should the cost of capital be used as a discount rate? The proper timing is determined by the company's liquidity preference and underlying debt-equity struc-

---

[1] Paul F. Anderson and John D. Martin, *"Lease vs. Purchase Decisions: A Survey of Current Practice,"* Financial Management (Spring 1977), p. 43.
See also Richard S. Bower, "Issues in Lease Financing," Financial Management 2 (Winter 1973), pp. 25-34.

ture. In the first place, if the firm cannot afford to purchase the asset outright with cash nor afford the down payment required by the bank, then obviously the decision to lease has already been made on the grounds of liquidity necessity and no discount rate is needed at all. In the more common situation, the firm can afford a cash purchase or large down payment; however, it might prefer leasing simply to conserve cash and the cost-of-capital discount rate might be appropriate.

To more fully understand the concept of liquidity preference, we need to analyze the capital structure of a growing company, of a stable company, and of a contracting company. In each situation we will look at the possible debt-equity positions listed below:

Company's Capital Structure	Alternate Debt Equity Structures	Debt-Equity Ratio Position
Growing Capital Structure	1.	Increasing Debt Ratio
	2.	Constant Debt Ratio
	3.	Declining Debt Ratio
Stable Capital Structure	4.	Increasing Debt Ratio
	5.	Constant Debt Ratio
	6.	Declining Debt Ratio
Contracting Capital Structure	7.	Increasing Debt Ratio
	8.	Constant Debt Ratio
	9.	Declining Debt Ratio

In situations numbered 3, 6, 8, and 9, we have firms whose amount of debt is declining. When this situation occurs the company is systematically losing its financial leverage. It is in these four cases where the cost-of-capital discount rate should be used to discount contractual financial costs instead of using the incremental cost of debt. Use of the cost-of-capital discount rate will result in a lower present-value total of leasing costs. Leases frequently can be structured with lower down payments, longer payment periods, and larger residual values at the termination of the lease. Large residual values result in smaller lease payments. All three of these lease-structuring adjustments shift the cost of leasing to the future, and when a discount rate higher than the incremental cost of debt is used, the resulting total present value will often be less than the purchase alternative. This lowering of the present value of leasing costs results from the high discount rate applied to lease payments that have been extended far into the future. The more a payment is extended into the future and the larger the discount rate applied to the payment, the smaller the resulting present value of the payment.

Therefore, if a firm is being forced to reduce its debt structure it would be better to have the largest amount of financial leverage remain during the debt-reduction period. Leases frequently allow a higher debt-equity ratio to exist during a debt-reduction period due to the lower down payments, longer payment period, increased residuals, and smaller lease payments available in leases as compared to larger down payments and short payment periods available in bank loans. In effect, such lease-structuring permits a firm to remain more liquid and in fact more profitable (financial leverage effect) during the debt-reduction period. So, use of a discount rate that results in a smaller present-value total for leasing costs would indicate 1) a preference for liquidity and 2) that the discount rate is appropriate where debt is being reduced systematically. An example of a situation where a company is being forced to reduce its debt is the small firm which has no access to long-term debt sources such as from the bond market. These firms are frequently forced to borrow on an installment basis. Virtually all installment loans by their very nature are self-liquidating debt sources. Banks require the loans to be self-liquidating in order to minimize risk. So, if a firm is forced constantly to deal with self-liquidating sources of debt, leases offer an attractive alternative since their liquidation takes more time. As explained above, the savings result from the use of leasing as a source of equipment-financing which provides greater liquidity and a more prolonged use of financial leverage.

In the other five debt-equity positions cited above there is no need to employ the use of the cost-of-capital discount rate since the debt of the company is not being reduced. In fact, the firms are by definition either maintaining their current amount of debt or expanding the level. In these situations it is assumed that if an asset is acquired with a self-liquidating debt source, then as each dollar of debt is reduced it will be replenished from some other borrowing source. Otherwise, if the debt is not replaced, the company's debt-equity ratio would decline rather than remain constant or grow.

In other words, if a company is to maintain or increase its debt level, extended lease terms should not be considered advantageous from a financial leverage point of view. This is because the financial leverage by definition will be maintained or increased through some other source. In fact, since most leases have higher implicit interest costs hidden in the lease payments, leases should be avoided simply because it is financially more expensive than a similar term installment loan.

A company attempting to maintain or expand its debt to equity ratio, however, may prefer leasing to borrowing. Leasing's longer payback period reduces the uncertainty attached to replacing self-liquidating debt with new debt that might cost significantly more in interest charges. It would be better to prolong the repayment of debt if it is anticipated that the debt's replacement cost will be much higher. Thus, liquidity preference might be appropriate in any of the debt-equity circumstances mentioned above. When replacement debt is not expected to cost significantly more, liquidity-preference adjustments would not be appropriate.

Suppose a company has two separate divisions—one that makes financial investment decisions and one that obtains capital for investments. The investment department should choose the better investment alternative from a purely financial viewpoint (which is achieved through use of the firm's after-tax incremental cost of debt as a discount factor). Now assume that the investment department chooses to purchase the equipment and expects its use will produce investment returns of $4,000 per month. When the first $4,000 comes to the firm, the only pertinent investment consideration would be the variable costs associated with running the equipment (direct labor and supplies, etc.) and the interest cost of the borrowed funds. Once the variable costs and interest have been paid, the remainder represents profit. This profit can then be turned over to the division responsible for obtaining capital. This division might choose to use the profit to reduce debt or to invest in some new project. The only time such returns would be used to reduce debt is when the company is being forced to reduce its debt-equity ratio. Some people will contend, however, that if the funding division has obtained its debt through some sort of an installment source, then profit must then be used to reduce debt. Not necessarily so. The division certainly can borrow from some other source to replace the debt systematically lost through making installment loan payments. The point is: Why should liquidity preference make us take on more costly leases over less costly installment loans if in fact the liquidity problem is being solved through alternate debt sources (which is the assumption implicit in debt-equity positions 1, 2, 4, 5, and 7)? However, as was explained for the other positions, if the company is forced to obtain its debt from self-liquidating sources and cannot readily replace debt from other sources, then liquidity preference does require that the Lease versus Buy decision shift in favor of leasing; use of the higher cost-of-capital discount rate will achieve this.

The manner in which liquidity preference will be introduced into the lease or purchase formats described in Steps one and two is as follows:

1. Determine if the liquidity preference adjustment should be made according to the company's capital structure and debt-equity position (situations 3, 6, 8 and 9 require the liquidity preference adjustment) or because replacement debt costs are rising.

2. If the adjustment is not required go to Step five in the Lease versus Buy decision model.

3. If the company cannot afford to purchase the equipment outright with cash or cannot afford the down payment required by an installment loan, it chooses the lease alternative and the decision process is over.

4. If the adjustment is required, recompute the present value of all pertinent costs and benefits that were included in Step one of the decision model using the firm's higher discount rate—the incremental, after-tax, weighted-average cost of capital.

5. Subtract the recomputed present-value purchase and lease cost totals from the previous totals in Step one. The resulting difference will represent liquidity preference opportunity cost savings and should be subtracted from their respective cumulative cost totals (determined at the end of Step two). The resulting adjusted cumulative differences will then be carried to Step five for further processing.

Step Five—Risk Adjustment Decision

Cost components of the lease alternative or of the purchase alternative may present varying degrees of uncertainty. For example, the amount of a future guaranteed residual deficiency is much more uncertain than next year's estimate of property tax on a piece of equipment. Or, excess use warranty payments are more uncertain than insurance expenses of the leased or purchased asset. When the perceived or anticipated risk is more than what is normally expected (most decisions have greater or lesser degrees of business risk), then some adjustment to these riskier-than-average costs should be made in the Lease versus Buy decision.

To adjust present-value totals for risk we either add a *risk premium* to the firm's incremental after-tax cost of debt and to its incremental after-tax weighted-average cost of capital or we use other risk-adjustment techniques mentioned on page 138.

Once the risk premium has been decided upon we then rediscount those cost components deemed riskier-than-average using the risk-adjusted discount rates.

Indirect cost items frequently subject to risk adjustment are listed below:

1. Maintenance
2. Replacement Costs
3. Fuel Costs
4. Variable Accounting Costs
5. Down-time Losses
6. Facilities and Spare Parts Inventory Costs
7. Any cost subject to an escalation clause requiring forecasting
8. Excess Use or Warranty Payments

The more stable indirect costs such as property tax, sales tax, and insurance are seldom subjected to a risk premium.

Since indirect costs have already been discounted at the company's cost of capital, it would be appropriate to discount riskier-than-average items at the company's risk-adjusted, incremental, after-tax, weighted-average cost of capital.

Financial flows might also require risk adjustment if they exhibit above-average uncertainty, which might occur with the following costs:

1. Return of Security Deposit
2. Contingent or Percentage Rentals
3. Variable Lease or Loan Payments Tied to Prime Rate or CPI
4. Guaranteed Residual Deficiency or Surplus
5. Fair Market Value Purchase Options
6. Purchase Options in Declining Resale Market
7. Depreciation Tax Shield in a period of changing tax laws which affect tax rates
8. Estimated Salvage Values

The appropriate discount rate to be applied to the contractual financial costs depends upon whether such costs were already adjusted for liquidity preference in Step four. If so, then the company's risk-adjusted cost of capital should be used as the discount factor. Otherwise, if liquidity preference was not an issue, the firm's risk-adjusted, incremental, after-tax cost of debt should be used to discount the more uncertain contractual financial costs.

Once the riskier costs have been identified and matched with the appropriate discount rate, the costs should be rediscounted using the risk-adjusted rates. The resulting difference between the old present value of costs and the newly arrived at present value of costs should be deducted from their respective Lease or Buy cumulative present-value totals, which were calculated at the end of Step two (or Step four if liquidity preference adjustments had been made).

Step Six—Qualitative Attributes Decision

Certain qualitative attributes of either leasing or buying are difficult to quantify. For example, what is the quantitative dollar value to a lessee of a swap clause or an upgrade clause in a lease? What is the value of the maintenance hassle avoided under a full service lease compared to a net lease or an outright purchase? What value do the improved financial ratios have to the company using off balance sheet operating leases to acquire equipment?

In some cases the value of such intangible lease attributes is obvious. Some firms lease because of bad credit even though quantitatively the Lease versus Buy decision demonstrates that buying is frequently less costly. Who cares about cost savings if no financial institution is willing to loan to the firm? Yet lease companies frequently lease to high credit risks. In other cases, the value of an intangible qualitative lease or buy attribute might be difficult to quantify. What is the real value of off-balance sheet financing when FASB 13 requires footnotes to include sufficient information concerning operating leases—information that allows any analyst with a modicum of financial astuteness to determine that the company is encumbered with lease debt anyway, whether on or off the balance sheet?

No matter how difficult to quantify, intangible qualitative features of leasing often become the determining factors in the final Lease versus Buy decision. It is unfortunate, however, that frequently no attempt is made to quantify such intangibles. Although the task might be difficult and filled with uncertainty, it still should be attempted. If it still seems impossible to place a present value dollar figure on some intangible lease or buy feature perform a cost-benefit analysis before opting for a lease or buy alternative that is opposite from what the cumulative costs at the end of Step five in the decision model would indicate is preferable. In effect, the cost-benefit analysis would consist of evaluating whether the intangible value is worth the additional cost to be incurred in opting for a more costly alternative. The additional cost to be incurred would be the difference between the lease and the buy cumulative present value cost totals at the end of Step five above. For example, if the difference were $28,000 in favor of purchasing, would a swap clause included in a lease be worth incurring an additional $28,000 in expense?

Reason demands that the worth of an intangible benefit exceed the cost incurred for the benefit. Yet too often we allow intangible, difficult-to-quantify, quality attributes of leases or purchases to sway our decisions beyond reason.

Rather than the simple cost-benefit analysis explained above concerning an intangible, it is preferable to attempt to quantify the quality attribute. Probability

analysis will often assist in this endeavor. The use of a simple payoff table uses probability theory to help quantify uncertain events.

Suppose, for example, you estimate the range of possible savings from a swap
agreement in a lease to include the following values listed in the first three columns:

Event	Down-time Savings	Customer Goodwill Preserved	Sales Not Lost	Total		Probability of Event		Expected Value
1	$ 1000	$ 2000	$ 4000	$ 7000	x	.05	=	$ 350
2	3000	3000	6000	12000	x	.20	=	2400
3	4000	5000	8000	17000	x	.40	=	6800
4	5000	8000	10000	23000	x	.20	=	4600
5	7000	12000	12000	31000	x	.15	=	4650
		Expected Value				1.00		$18,800

The total of the first three columns appears in column four. Column four totals
are then multiplied by the expected probability of occurrence. The resulting products
are added together; they equal the Expected Value of the Anticipated Savings. Note
that the probability of the events must total one in order to exhaust all possibilities.
Although assessing the event probabilities and estimating the range of possible savings is a difficult and uncertain task, it is still preferable to accepting an alternative
without even questioning the underlying quantitative value of the intangible attribute that might sway the ultimate decision.

After these qualitative factors are quantified, they should be subjected to present-
value discounting just like any other benefit or cost and the resulting present-value
cost or benefit should be added or deducted from the cumulative lease or buy cost
totals arrived at in Step five. The appropriate present-value discount rate would generally be the risk-adjusted cost of capital. This is due to the uncertainty of predicting
when the savings or costs might occur, in addition to the uncertainty of the amount
of the cost or benefit. Both the expected value of the amount and the timing of
the benefit or cost require risk-adjusted discount rates.

Once these estimated discounted qualitative attributes have been calculated and
added or subtracted from their respective cumulative cost totals, we are ready for
the last step in the Lease versus Buy decision model. (The next chapter will discuss
many of the qualitative, difficult-to-quantify attributes of leasing that need to be
considered.)

Step Seven—Sensitivity Readjustment Decision

Although sensitivity analysis appears as an analytical financial tool in many different forms, it is referred to here as a final reappraisal or final challenge of the numerous costs and benefits and underlying assumptions included in the model thus far.
Also implied by sensitivity analysis is experimental adjusting of selective costs and

benefits included in the various steps to establish the final effect of the sensitivity adjustment on the final cost totals. How sensitive is the final total to changes or adjustments in selected costs or benefits? How dependent is the difference between the Lease versus Buy costs on certain components? Which component has the largest effect on the outcome? Are the assumptions underlying the most influential factors correct? Have the most sensitive and influential costs and benefits been checked for clerical and computational accuracy? These and many other questions are implied by sensitivity analysis.

Frequently we are under pressure to perform or make a decision quickly and we omit this last step in the decision-making process. Yet it is vital! If the decision to lease rather than buy is found to be almost totally dependent upon two assumptions concerning (1) maintenance costs and (2) the term of the lease, then it would be advisable to determine, should we purchase the equipment, if other maintenance arrangements might be made which would be less costly than our analysis has shown up to this point. Then, too, might a bank stretch its installment loan payback period to match that of the lease? These types of challenges must be met before we can arrive at a final answer.

It is a worthwhile practice to identify the four most influential differential costs between the purchase and the lease alternative. After identifying them, challenge their underlying assumptions and check for clerical and computational accuracy. Also, scrutinize the four most influential nondifferential costs that affect cost totals the most. Differential costs are similar-natured costs that differ in dollar amount from one alternative to the other. For example, maintenance under a lease might cost $20,000, but under a purchase situation might cost $25,000. These similar-natured costs are different because of the material $5,000 cost difference between them, whereas a nondifferential yet significant cost would be the present value of the contractual financial flows. Although the undiscounted total differences between the financial flows of a lease might not differ materially from those of the purchase, the after-tax cash flow present-value total of these costs might be significantly different. Therefore, such nondifferential costs should be scrutinized and recalculated.

Additionally, the discount rates and tax rates used should be challenged once more. Remember that tax rates should include the state income tax, too. The company's cost of capital might be recalculated using some technique other than the Gordon Growth Model, such as the Capital Asset Pricing Model. Also, the totals in each major step of the decision model should be challenged and recalculated.

Upon completion of the sensitivity analysis and resulting changes in cost and benefit amounts, and after correction of clerical and computational errors, we finally can decide whether leasing is preferable to buying a particular asset. Our conclusion is one of comprehensive preferability, *not* one of being financially less costly, or more liquid, or more profitable, or less risky, or more qualitatively advantageous. All these decision criteria have been combined into one comprehensive LEASE VERSUS BUY decision model that we have just reviewed.

To more fully understand the seven steps used in the comprehensive Lease versus Buy decision model, an illustration of the solution to a Lease versus Buy problem will be presented in case form. Also, a comprehensive Lease versus Buy format will be presented which serves to remind the reader of the many elements entering into the decision and of the sequential steps to be followed.

BETA COMPANY CASE

Beta Company is a wholesale distributor for specialized mining equipment. Beta delivers equipment in a five-state area. Until recently it has shipped equipment FOB shipping point. But now Beta has determined that shipping could be a profitable venture and, therefore, has decided to purchase six truck tractors and trailers whose retail value is $500,000. You have been engaged by Beta as a Management Consultant to determine whether Beta should purchase the trucks or lease them under a full service lease arrangement. Beta expects shipping revenue to be $40,000 per month for the next seventy-two months. Direct variable costs are expected to be $8,000 per month. Beta's debt–equity ratio is declining and, therefore, liquidity is considered very important. Following are two lists of information that Beta has assembled in regards to the two alternatives:

LEASE ALTERNATIVE INFORMATION

1. Sixty month lease with first and last two payments (three advance payments) in advance. Lease payments are $12,000 per month exclusive of executory costs. The lease contains a purchase option equal to fifteen percent of the original equipment cost (.15 x $500,000 = $75,000 which *includes* sales tax). The lease requires a $10,000 security deposit which will be refunded if the equipment is returned in satisfactory condition with all terms of the lease having been met satisfactorily. There is a one percent, $5000, nonrefundable lease service and origination fee required to be paid in advance. The lease is considered an operating lease for tax purposes; however, the lessor will pass on the investment tax credit to the lessee in the amount of $50,000 (10% of $500,000) which will be offset against taxes payable at the end of the first quarter following the lease's inception (two months hence). The lease will begin January 31 of the current year. The lease is cancelable by the lessee after the forty-eighth payment; however, the purchase option is only available at the end of the sixtieth month. The lease contains a cancellation clause which has an estimated intangible value of $5,390.

2. The lease contains an escalation clause which requires one half of each monthly lease payment ($6,000 excluding executory costs) to increase in an amount equal to 100 percent of any monthly increases in the consumer price index. The consumer price index is expected to grow at a compound rate of .8% monthly (about 9.6% annually) over the next five years. Beta's incremental, after-tax, weighted-average cost of capital is 14.4 percent (1.2% monthly) and its after-tax incremental cost of debt is 8.8378% or .7364% monthly.

3. Beta expects to pay $2,000 at the end of each year of the lease as an excess-usage charge (for extra miles driven by the fleet of trucks).

4. At the end of the lease Beta plans to exercise the purchase option and receive a full refund of the security deposit. Beta will depreciate the trucks evenly over the remaining twelve months of their expected lives.

5. Executory costs are required to be paid monthly in addition to the lease payments. Sales tax is required to be paid on the three lease payments paid in advance. Maintenance and insurance costs are not paid with the advance payments. Examples of executory costs are as follows:

   a. Sales tax, computed at five percent of each lease payment

   b. Ignore sales tax on any increases in the $12,000 monthly lease payments occasioned by an escalation clause in the lease

   c. Insurance costs, $400 per month

   d. Maintenance costs, $3,000 per month

   e. Insurance and maintenance available to the lessee at the same rate for one year beyond termination of the lease

6. Additional indirect costs incurred as a result of the lease:

   a. Replacement costs included in the lease payments for an annual two-week replacement of trucks which will be allowed the lessee without additional charge. Beta anticipates no additional replacement costs will be incurred. The leasing company will not disclose the implicit cost of the replacement clause in the lease.

   b. Fuel purchased at reduced rates through lessor outlets for an estimated $9,000 per month during the entire seventy-two-month holding period.

   c. Additional accounting costs estimated at $500 per month for the full seventy-two-month holding period.

7. Beta is in a forty-five percent incremental tax bracket.

8. Beta will use eighteen percent to discount any riskier-than-average costs.

9. Present-value factors.

					Annually = 14.4%	8.8373%	18.0%
					Monthly = 1.2%	.7364%	1.5%
P.V.	annuity	48	months	=	36.3272	40.3098	34.0426
P.V.	annuity	57	months	=	41.1122	46.4112	38.1339
P.V.	annuity	72	months	=	48.0295	55.7262	43.8447
P.V.	annuity	5	years	=	3.4003	3.9061	3.1272
P.V.	annuity	6	years	=	3.8464	4.5078	3.4976
P.V.	one	2	months	=	.9764	.9854	.9707
P.V.	one	72	months	=	.4236	.5896	.3423
P.V.	one	48	months	=	.5641	.7031	.4894
P.V.	one	60	months	=	.4888	.6439	.4093

PURCHASE ALTERNATIVE INFORMATION

1. Installment loan required to finance purchase of the equipment has the following terms:

   a. $500,000 equipment cost, $100,000 down payment required (twenty percent).

   b. Balance of $400,000 paid in forty-eight equal monthly installments of $11,350 (implicit interest rate of about 16.0678 pretax or 8.8373 after-tax).

   c. A two percent service charge of $8,000 is required to be paid in advance in addition to the down payment.

   d. Sales tax of five percent of the purchase ($25,000) is required to be paid in advance and will not be financed by the lending institution.

   e. The bank requires a permanent addition of $5,000 to the purchaser's checking account balance. This compensating balance requirement will cease at the end of the loan.

2. Beta will depreciate the asset using the new ACRs five year depreciation schedule that will be in effect from 1986 on: year 1—20%, year 2—32%, year 3—24%, year 4—16%, and year 5—8%. The two percent service fee and five percent sales tax will be capitalized for purposes of computing depreciation and determining the amount of investment tax credit available. The trucks are assumed to be worthless for tax purposes at the end of six years. The investment tax credit (10 percent of $533,000 = $53,300) is assumed to be totally available after being offset against tax liabilities at the end of the first quarter following the purchase (two months hence). The equipment will be purchased on January 31 of the current year.

3. Each installment payment consists of interest expense and a reduction of the principal balance due the bank. The interest portion of each payment is tax-deductible and, therefore, forms a tax shield to the purchaser. Interest deductions and the resulting tax shield are calculated using the company's 14.4 percent cost of capital as follows:

Year	Interest	Deduction	x	Tax Rate	x	14.4% P.V. Factor	=	Tax Benefit
1	58,730	x		.45	x	.8741		23,101
2	45,324	x		.45	x	.7641		15,584
3	29,597	x		.45	x	.6679		8,896
4	11,149	x		.45	x	.5838		2,929
				TOTAL INTEREST TAX SHIELD				$50,510

Note that the interest declines in the later years of the loan because there is less principal earning interest. Advanced financial calculators allow computation of such accumulated interest each year. The interest tax shield when using the after-tax cost of debt of 8.8373 percent is $57,516. This amount, when deducted from the present value of the installment payments, makes the total cost of purchasing equal to $500,000.

4. Executory costs required to be paid monthly in addition to the loan installment payments are as follows:

    a. Insurance costs, $500 per month (seventy-two months).

    b. Maintenance estimated at $3,500 per month beginning at the end of the first month and to increase by $30 a month thereafter (seventy-two months).

5. Additional indirect costs incurred as a result of the purchase:

    a. Replacement costs, estimated at $1,000 per year, assumed to be paid at year's end.

    b. Fuel costs, estimated at $10,000 per month.

    c. Additional accounting costs, estimated at $1,000 per month.

    d. Additional facility costs, $500 per month for rental of a maintenance shop.

6. The depreciation tax shield is computed as follows for each of the two different discount rates required in the case:

14.4% PER YEAR OR 3.6% PER QUARTER

Year	Quarter	Depreciation	Method		Tax Rate		P.V. Factor		Benefit
1	1	$ 44,416	DDB	x	.45	x	.9653	=	$ 19,294
	2	44,416	DDB	x	.45	x	.9317	=	18,622
	3	44,416	DDB	x	.45	x	.8993	=	17,974
	4	44,416	DDB	x	.45	x	.8681	=	17,351
2	1	29,611	DDB	x	.45	x	.8379	=	11,165
	2	29,611	DDB	x	.45	x	.8088	=	10,777
	3	29,611	DDB	x	.45	x	.7807	=	10,403
	4	29,611	SYD	x	.45	x	.7536	=	10,042
3	1	23,689	SYD	x	.45	x	.7274	=	7,754
	2	23,689	SYD	x	.45	x	.7021	=	7,484
	3	23,689	SYD	x	.45	x	.6777	=	7,224
	4	23,689	SYD	x	.45	x	.6542	=	6,974
4	1	17,767	SYD	x	.45	x	.6314	=	5,048
	2	17,767	SYD	x	.45	x	.6095	=	4,873
	3	17,767	SYD	x	.45	x	.5883	=	4,704
	4	17,767	SYD	x	.45	x	.5679	=	4,540
5	1	11,845	SYD	x	.45	x	.5481	=	2,922
	2	11,845	SYD	x	.45	x	.5291	=	2,820
	3	11,845	SYD	x	.45	x	.5107	=	2,722
	4	11,845	SYD	x	.45	x	.4930	=	2,628

Year	Quarter	Depreciation	Method		Tax Rate		P.V. Factor		Benefit
6	1	5,922	SYD	x	.45	x	.4758	=	1,268
	2	5,922	SYD	x	.45	x	.4593	=	1,224
	3	5,922	SYD	x	.45	x	.4433	=	1,181
	4	5,922	SYD	x	.45	x	.4279	=	1,140
		$533,000 [1]							$180,134

(For $75,000 purchase option value under lease option)

Year	Quarter	Depreciation	Method		Tax Rate		P.V. Factor		Benefit
6	1	18,750	SL	x	.45	x	.4758	=	4,015
	2	18,750	SL	x	.45	x	.4593	=	3,875
	3	18,750	SL	x	.45	x	.4433	=	3,740
	4	18,750	SL	x	.45	x	.4279	=	3,610
		$75,000							$ 15,240

8.8373% PER YEAR OR 2.2093% PER QUARTER

Year	Quarter	Depreciation	Method		Tax Rate		P.V. Factor		Benefit
1	1	$ 44,416	DDB	x	.45	x	.9784	=	$ 19,555
	2	44,416	DDB	x	.45	x	.9572	=	19,132
	3	44,416	DDB	x	.45	x	.9365	=	18,718
	4	44,416	DDB	x	.45	x	.9163	=	18,314
2	1	29,611	DDB	x	.45	x	.8965	=	11,946
	2	29,611	DDB	x	.45	x	.8771	=	11,946
	3	29,611	DDB	x	.45	x	.8582	=	11,435
	4	29,611	SYD	x	.45	x	.8396	=	11,188
3	1	23,689	SYD	x	.45	x	.8215	=	8,757
	2	23,689	SYD	x	.45	x	.8037	=	8,567
	3	23,689	SYD	x	.45	x	.7863	=	8,382
	4	23,689	SYD	x	.45	x	.7693	=	8,201
4	1	17,767	SYD	x	.45	x	.7527	=	6,018
	2	17,767	SYD	x	.45	x	.7364	=	5,888
	3	17,767	SYD	x	.45	x	.7205	=	5,761
	4	17,767	SYD	x	.45	x	.7049	=	5,636
5	1	11,845	SYD	x	.45	x	.6897	=	3,676
	2	11,845	SYD	x	.45	x	.6748	=	3,597
	3	11,845	SYD	x	.45	x	.6602	=	3,519
	4	11,845	SYD	x	.45	x	.6459	=	3,443
6	1	5,922	SYD	x	.45	x	.6320	=	1,684
	2	5,922	SYD	x	.45	x	.6183	=	1,648
	3	5,922	SYD	x	.45	x	.6049	=	1,612
	4	5,922	SYD	x	.45	x	.5919	=	1,577
		$533,000 [1]							$200,200

[1] Includes sales tax of $25,000 and service charge of $8,000.

Year	Quarter	Depreciation	Method	Tax Rate	P.V. Factor	Benefit
(For $75,000 purchase option value under lease option)						
6	1	18,750	SL x	.45 x	.6320 =	5,333
	2	18,750	SL x	.45 x	.6183 =	5,217
	3	18,750	SL x	.45 x	.6049 =	5,104
	4	18,750	SL x	.45 x	.5919 =	4,994
		$ 75,000				$ 20,648

LEASING DECISION FORMAT

Step One—Financial Decision

ADD DIRECT LEASE COSTS:

	Amount	x	Tax Factor	x	PV Factor	=	Total
Initial Costs:							
Closing, Origination, Service Fees	$—	x	(1–t)	x	N/A	=	$—
Advance Rental Payments	$—	x	(1–t)	x	N/A	=	$—
Security Deposits	$—	x	N/A	x	N/A	=	$—
Subsequent Costs:							
Remaining Base Rental Payments	$—	x	(1–t)	x	PV_a	=	$—
Renewal Option Rental Payments	$—	x	(1–t)	x	PV_a & PV_1	=	$—
Contingent or Percentage Rentals (Est.)	$—	x	(1–t)	x	PV_a	=	$—
Rental Increases Tied to CPI or Prime Rate	$—	x	(1–t)	x	Formula	=	$—
Terminal Costs:							
Residual Guarantee Deficiency	$—	x	(1–t)	x	PV_1	=	$—
Nonrenewal Penalty	$—	x	(1–t)	x	PV_1	=	$—
Purchase Option Plus Sales Tax	$—	x	N/A	x	PV_1	=	$—
SUB-TOTAL DIRECT LEASE COSTS							$—

DEDUCT DIRECT LEASE BENEFITS:

	Amount	x	Tax Factor	x	PV Factor	=	Total
Investment Tax Credit	$—	x	N/A	x	PV_1	=	($—)
Return of Security Deposit	$—	x	N/A	x	PV_1	=	($—)
Loss of Security Deposit	$—	x	(t)	x	PV_1	=	($—)

	Amount	x	Tax Factor	x	PV Factor	=	Total
Depreciation Tax Shield							
Option Exercised	$——	x	(t)	x	PV_a & PV_1	=	($——)
Residual Guarantee Rebate	$——	x	(1-t)	x	PV_1	=	($——)
SUB-TOTAL DIRECT LEASE BENEFITS							($——)
NET FINANCIAL COST TO LEASE							$——

Step Two—Indirect Cost Decision

ADD INDIRECT LEASE COSTS:

	Amount	x	Tax Factor	x	PV Factor	=	Total
Delivery & Installation Charges	$——	x	(1-t)	x	N/A	=	$——
Sales Tax in Advance	$——	x	(1-t)	x	N/A	=	$——
Sales Tax	$——	x	(1-t)	x	PV_a	=	$——
Property Tax	$——	x	(1-t)	x	PV_a	=	$——
Insurance	$——	x	(1-t)	x	PV_a	=	$——
Maintenance	$——	x	(1-t)	x	PV_a	=	$——
Replacement Costs (Est.)	$——	x	(1-t)	x	PV_a	=	$——
Fuel Costs (Est.)	$——	x	(1-t)	x	PV_a	=	$——
Variable Accounting Costs	$——	x	(1-t)	x	PV_a	=	$——
Excess Use & Maintenance Charges	$——	x	(1-t)	x	PV_1	=	$——
Miscellaneous Costs Unique to Equipment Type	$——	x	(1-t)	x	PV_a	=	$——
SUB-TOTAL INDIRECT LEASE COSTS							$——

DEDUCT INDIRECT LEASE BENEFITS:

	Amount	x	Tax Factor	x	PV Factor	=	Total
Sub-Lease Income	$——	x	(1-t)	x	PV_a	=	($——)
NET INDIRECT COST TO LEASE							$——
CUMULATIVE COST TO LEASE (Step 1 + Step 2)							$——

Step Three—Capital Budgeting Decision

ADD PROJECTED REVENUE:

	Amount	x	Tax Factor	x	PV Factor	=	Total
Gross Anticipated Revenue	$——	x	(1-t)	x	PV_a	=	$——
Inflation Increment	$——	x	(1-t)		see Formula	=	$——
SUB-TOTAL PROJECTED REVENUE							$——

	Amount	x	*Tax Factor*	x	*PV Factor*	=	*Total*

DEDUCT PROJECTED VARIABLE COSTS:

	Amount		Tax Factor		PV Factor		Total
Variable Costs of Sales	$——	x	(1-t)	x	PV_a	=	($——)
Inflation Increment	$——	x	(1-t)		see Formula	=	($——)
SUB-TOTAL PROJECTED VARIABLE COSTS							($——)
NET PROJECTED CONTRIBUTION MARGIN							$——
LESS: CUMULATIVE COST TO LEASE–Step 2							($——)

NET PRESENT VALUE (Contribution margin less cumulative cost to lease Step 2) $——

Step Four—Liquidity Preference

ADD DIRECT LEASE COSTS:

	Amount	x	*Tax Factor*	x	*PV Factor*	=	*Total*

Initial Costs:

	Amount		Tax Factor		PV Factor		Total
Closing, Origination, Service Fees	$——	x	(1-t)	x	N/A	=	$——
Advance Rental Payments	$——	x	(1-t)	x	N/A	=	$——
Security Deposits	$——	x	N/A	x	N/A	=	$——

Subsequent Costs:

Remaining Base Rental Payments	$——	x	(1-t)	x	PV_a	=	$——
Renewal Option Rental Payments	$——	x	(1-t)	x	PV_a & PV_1	=	$——
Contingent or Percentage Rentals (Est.)	$——	x	(1-t)	x	PV_a	=	$——
Rental Increases Tied to CPI or Prime Rate	$——	x	(1-t)	x	Formula	=	$——

Terminal Costs:

Residual Guarantee Deficiency	$——	x	(1-t)	x	PV_1	=	$——
Nonrenewal Penalty	$——	x	(1-t)	x	PV_1	=	$——
Purchase Option Plus Sales Tax	$——	x	N/A	x	PV_1	=	$——
SUB-TOTAL DIRECT LEASE COSTS							$——

DEDUCT DIRECT LEASE BENEFITS:

Investment Tax Credit	$——	x	N/A	x	PV_1	=	($——)
Return of Security Deposit	$——	x	N/A	x	PV_1	=	($——)
Loss of Security Deposit	$——	x	(t)	x	PV_1	=	($——)

	Amount	x Tax Factor	x PV Factor	=	Total
Depreciation Tax Shield					
Option Exercised	$—— x	(t)	x PV_a & PV_1	=	($——)
Residual Guarantee Rebate	$—— x	(1-t)	x PV_1	=	($——)
SUB-TOTAL DIRECT LEASE BENEFITS					($——)
NET ADJUSTED DIRECT COSTS & BENEFITS					$——
NET LIQUIDITY PREFERENCE ADJUSTMENT					
(Step one Total Less Step four Total)					($——)
CUMULATIVE COST TO LEASE (Steps 1 + 2 + 4)					$——

Step Five—Risk Adjustment Decision

RISK-SENSITIVE DIRECT COSTS & BENEFITS:

	Amount	x Tax Factor	x PV Factor	=	Total
Return of Security Deposit	$—— x	N/A	x PV_1	=	($——)
Guaranteed Residual Rebate	$—— x	(1-t)	x PV_1	=	($——)
Depreciation Tax Shield	$—— x	(t)	x PV_a	=	($——)
Contingent or Percentage Rentals	$—— x	(1-t)	x PV_a	=	$——
Rental Increases Tied to CPI or Prime Rate	$—— x	(1-t)	x Formula	=	$——
Guaranteed Residual Deficiency	$—— x	(1-t)	x PV_1	=	$——
Fair Market Value Purchase Option	$—— x	N/A	x PV_1	=	$——
Purchase Options in Declining Resale Market	$—— x	N/A	x PV_1	=	$——
Estimated Salvage Values	$—— x	(1-t)	x PV_1	=	$——
Miscellaneous Items Unique to Lease	$—— x	(1-t)	x PV_a or PV_1	=	$——
TOTAL RISK-ADJUSTED DIRECT COSTS & BENEFITS					$——

RISK-SENSITIVE INDIRECT COSTS & BENEFITS:

	Amount	x Tax Factor	x PV Factor	=	Total
Maintenance	$—— x	(1-t)	x PV_a	=	$——
Replacement Costs	$—— x	(1-t)	x PV_a	=	$——
Fuel Costs	$—— x	(1-t)	x PV_a	=	$——
Variable Accounting Costs	$—— x	(1-t)	x PV_a	=	$——
Excess Use or Warranty Costs	$—— x	(1-t)	x PV_a or PV_1	=	$——
Miscellaneous Items Unique to Equip.	$—— x	(1-t)	x PV_a or PV_1	=	$——
TOTAL RISK-ADJUSTED INDIRECT COSTS & BENEFITS					$——

NET RISK ADJUSTMENT (Deduct Total Risk-adjusted
Direct Costs from Step one Corresponding Costs and then deduct
the Risk-adjusted Indirect Costs from Step two Corresponding
Costs. Add these two items together)   ($———)

Direct Costs $——— Indirect Costs $———
CUMULATIVE COST TO LEASE (Steps 1 + 2 + 4 + 5)   ($———)

Step Six—Qualitative Attributes Decision

ADD: EXPECTED VALUE OF QUALITATIVE COSTS

Expected Cost$_1$ $———$(1-t)$ x PV_a or PV_1 = $———
Expected Cost$_2$ $———$(1-t)$ x PV_a or PV_1 = $———

DEDUCT: EXPECTED VALUE OF QUALITATIVE BENEFITS

Expected Benefit$_1$ $———$(1-t$ or $t)$ x PV_a or PV_1 =($———)
Expected Benefit$_2$ $———$(1-t$ or $t)$ x PV_a or PV_1 =($———)
NET EXPECTED VALUE OF COSTS AND BENEFITS   = $———

CUMULATIVE COST TO LEASE (Steps 1 + 2 + 4 + 5 + 6) $———

Step Seven—Sensitivity Analysis

IDENTIFY & SCRUTINIZE FOUR MOST INFLUENTIAL
DIFFERENTIAL COSTS:

1 ———————   Amount $———————
2 ———————   Amount $———————
3 ———————   Amount $———————
4 ———————   Amount $———————

IDENTIFY & SCRUTINIZE FOUR MOST INFLUENTIAL
NONDIFFERENTIAL COSTS:

1 ———————   Amount $———————
2 ———————   Amount $———————
3 ———————   Amount $———————
4 ———————   Amount $———————

SCRUTINIZE:

Check when Completed

Incremental Effective Tax Rate   [ ]

Discount Rates   [ ]

Six Previous Decision Steps   [ ]

Risk Premiums   ☐

Liquidity Preference Assumption   ☐

PURCHASE DECISION FORMAT

Step One—Financial Decision

ADD DIRECT PURCHASE COSTS:

	Amount	x *Tax Factor*	x	*PV Factor*	=	*Total*
Initial Costs:						
Closing, Origination, Service Fees	$——	x N/A or (1–t)	x	N/A	=	$——
Down Payment	$——	x N/A	x	N/A	=	$——
Security Deposit	$——	x N/A	x	N/A	=	$——
Compensating Bank Balance	$——	x N/A	x	N/A	=	$——
Subsequent Costs:						
Installment Loan Payments	$——	x N/A	x	PV_a	=	$——
Payment Increases, Tied to Prime Rate	$——	x N/A	x	Formula	=	$——
Terminal Costs:						
Balloon Payment	$——	x N/A	x	PV_1	=	$——
ITC Recapture for Early Salvage	$——	x N/A	x	PV_1	=	$——
SUB-TOTAL DIRECT PURCHASE COSTS						$——

DEDUCT DIRECT PURCHASE BENEFITS:

Investment Tax Credit	$——	x N/A	x	PV_1	=	($——)
Return of Security Deposit	$——	x N/A	x	PV_1	=	($——)
Loss of Security Deposit	$——	x (t)	x	PV_1	=	($——)
Depreciation Tax Shield	$——	x (t)	x	PV_a	=	($——)
Interest Tax Shield	$——	x (t)	x	PV_a	=	($——)
Tax-adjusted Salvage Value	$——	x N/A	x	PV_1	=	($——)
Return of Compensating Balance	$——	x N/A	x	PV_1	=	($——)
SUB-TOTAL DIRECT PURCHASE BENEFITS						($——)
NET FINANCIAL COST TO PURCHASE						$——

Step Two—Indirect Cost Decision

ADD INDIRECT PURCHASE COSTS:

Delivery & Installation Charges	\$——	x (1–t) or N/A x	N/A	=	\$——
Sales Tax	\$——	x (1–t) or N/A x	N/A	=	\$——
Property Tax	\$——	x	(1–t)	x	PV_a	=	\$——
Insurance	\$——	x	(1–t)	x	PV_a	=	\$——
Maintenance	\$——	x	(1–t)	x	PV_a	=	\$——
Replacement Costs (Est.)	\$——	x	(1–t)	x	PV_a	=	\$——
Fuel Costs (Est.)	\$——	x	(1–t)	x	PV_a	=	\$——
Variable Accounting Costs	\$——	x	(1–t)	x	PV_a	=	\$——
Licenses and Permits	\$——	x	(1–t)	x	PV_a	=	\$——
Down-time Losses	\$——	x	(1–t)	x	PV_a	=	\$——
Spare Parts Inventory	\$——	x	(1–t)	x	PV_a	=	\$——
Additional Maintenance Facilities Cost	\$——	x(1–t or N/A) x	PV_a	=	\$——
Misc. Costs Unique to Equipment	\$——	x	(1–t)	x PV_a or PV_1	=	\$——

SUB-TOTAL INDIRECT PURCHASE COSTS = \$——

DEDUCT INDIRECT PURCHASE BENEFITS:

Sub-Lease Income   \$—— x (1–t) x PV_a = (\$——)

NET INDIRECT COST TO PURCHASE   \$——

CUMULATIVE COST TO PURCHASE (Step 1 + 2)   \$——

Step Three—Capital Budgeting Decision

ADD PROJECTED REVENUE:

Gross Anticipated Revenue   \$—— x (1–t) x PV_a = \$——

Inflation Increment   \$—— x (1–t) see Formula = \$——

SUB-TOTAL PROJECTED REVENUE   (\$——)

DEDUCT PROJECTED VARIABLE COSTS:

Variable Costs of Sales   \$—— x (1–t) x PV_a = (\$——)

Inflation Increment   \$—— x (1–t) see Formula = (\$——)

SUB-TOTAL PROJECTED VARIABLE COSTS   \$——

NET PROJECTED CONTRIBUTION MARGIN   \$——

NET PRESENT VALUE (Contribution Margin Less Step 2 Total)   \$——

Step Four—Liquidity Preference

ADD DIRECT PURCHASE COSTS:

	Amount	x	*Tax Factor*	x	*PV Factor*	=	*Total*
Initial Costs:							
Closing, Origination, Service Fees	$——	x	N/A or (1-t)	x	N/A	=	$——
Down Payment	$——	x	N/A	x	N/A	=	$——
Security Deposit	$——	x	N/A	x	N/A	=	$——
Compensating Bank Balance	$——	x	N/A	x	N/A	=	$——
Subsequent Costs:							
Installment Loan Payments	$——	x	N/A	x	PV_a	=	$——
Payment Increases, Tied to Prime Rate	$——	x	N/A	x	Formula	=	$——
Terminal Costs:							
Balloon Payment	$——	x	N/A	x	PV_1	=	$——
ITC Recapture for Early Salvage	$——	x	N/A	x	PV_1	=	$——
SUB-TOTAL DIRECT PURCHASE COSTS							$——

DEDUCT DIRECT PURCHASE BENEFITS:

	Amount	x	*Tax Factor*	x	*PV Factor*	=	*Total*
Investment Tax Credit	$——	x	N/A	x	PV_1	=	($——)
Return of Security Deposit	$——	x	N/A	x	PV_1	=	($——)
Loss of Security Deposit	$——	x	(t)	x	PV_1	=	($——)
Depreciation Tax Shield	$——	x	(t)	x	PV_a	=	($——)
Interest Tax Shield	$——	x	(t)	x	PV_a	=	($——)
Tax-adjusted Salvage Value	$——	x	N/A	x	PV_1	=	($——)
Return of Compensating Balance	$——	x	N/A	x	PV_1	=	($——)
SUB-TOTAL DIRECT PURCHASE BENEFITS							($——)

NET ADJUSTED DIRECT COSTS & BENEFITS $——

NET LIQUIDITY PREFERENCE ADJUSTMENT $——

(Step one Total Less Step four Total) $——

CUMULATIVE COST TO PURCHASE (Steps 1 + 2 + 4) $——

Step Five—Risk Adjustment Decision

RISK-SENSITIVE DIRECT COSTS BENEFITS:

Return of Security Deposit	\$——	x	N/A	x	PV_1	=	\$——
Depreciation Tax Shield	\$——	x	(t)	x	PV_a	=	\$——
Installment Payments Tied to Prime Rate	\$——	x	N/A	x	formula	=	\$——
Estimated Salvage Value	\$——	x	(t or 1-t)	x	PV_1	=	\$——
Miscellaneous Items Unique to Loan	\$——	x	t or 1-t	x PV_a or PV_1	=	\$——

TOTAL RISK-ADJUSTED DIRECT COSTS & BENEFITS   \$——

RISK SENSITIVE INDIRECT COSTS BENEFITS:

Maintenance	\$——	x (1-t)	x	PV_a	=	\$——
Replacement Costs	\$——	x (1-t)	x	PV_a	=	\$——
Fuel Costs	\$——	x (1-t)	x	PV_a	=	\$——
Variable Accounting Costs	\$——	x (1-t)	x	PV_a	=	\$——
Down-time Losses	\$——	x (1-t)	x	PV_a	=	\$——
Spare Parts Inventory Costs	\$——	x (1-t)	x	PV_a	=	\$——
Any Cost Subject to Escalation	\$——	x (1-t)	x	PV_a	=	\$——
Excess Facilities Cost	\$——	x (1-t) or N/A x PV_a or PV_1	=	\$——

TOTAL RISK-ADJUSTED INDIRECT COSTS & BENEFITS   \$——

NET RISK ADJUSTMENT (Deduct Total Risk-adjusted Direct
Costs from Step one *Corresponding* Costs and then Deduct the
Risk-adjusted Indirect Costs from Step two *Corresponding* Costs.
Add these two items together.)   (\$——)

CUMULATIVE COST TO PURCHASE (Steps 1 + 2 + 4 + 5)   \$——

Step Six—Qualitative Attributes Decision

ADD: EXPECTED VALUE OF QUALITATIVE COSTS

Expected Cost$_1$	\$—— (1-t)	x PV_a or PV_1 =	\$——
Expected Cost$_2$	\$—— (1-t)	x PV_a or PV_1 =	\$——

DEDUCT: EXPECTED VALUE OF QUALITATIVE BENEFITS:

Expected Benefit$_1$	\$—— (1-t)	x PV_a or PV_1 =	(\$——)
Expected Benefit$_2$	\$—— (1-t)	x PV_a or PV_1 =	(\$——)

NET EXPECTED VALUE OF COSTS AND (BENEFITS)   =   \$——

CUMULATIVE COST TO PURCHASE
(Steps 1 + 2 + 4 + 5 + 6)   =   \$——

Step Seven—Sensitivity Analysis

IDENTIFY & SCRUTINIZE FOUR MOST INFLUENTIAL
DIFFERENTIAL COSTS

1 —————————————— Amount $————————————
2 —————————————— Amount $————————————
3 —————————————— Amount $————————————
4 —————————————— Amount $————————————

IDENTIFY & SCRUTINIZE FOUR MOST INFLUENTIAL
NONDIFFERENTIAL COSTS

1 —————————————— Amount $————————————
2 —————————————— Amount $————————————
3 —————————————— Amount $————————————
4 —————————————— Amount $————————————

SCRUTINIZE:

Check when Completed

Incremental Effective Tax Rate	☐
Discount Rates	☐
Six Previous Decision Steps	☐
Risk Premiums	☐
Liquidity Preference Assumption	☐

SOLUTION TO THE
LEASE VERSUS BUY CASE
LEASING DECISION FORMAT

Step One—Financial Decision

ADD DIRECT LEASE COSTS:

Initial Costs:	Amount	x	Tax Factor	x	PV Factor	=	Total
Closing, Origination, Service Fees	$ 5,000	x	(1-t)	x	N/A	=	$ 2,750
Advance Rental Payments	$36,000	x	(1-t)	x	N/A	=	$ 19,800
Security Deposits	$10,000	x	N/A	x	N/A	=	$ 10,000

	Amount	x	Tax Factor	x	PV Factor	=	Total

Subsequent Costs:

Remaining Base Rental Payments n=57	$ 6,000	x	(1-.45)	x	46.4112	=	$ 153,157
Renewal Option Rental Payments	$ N/A	x	(1-t)	x	PV_a & PV_1	=	$ -0-
Contingent or Percentage Rentals (Est.)	$ N/A	x	(1-t)	x	PV_a	=	$ -0-
Rental Increases Tied to CPI or Prime Rate	Refer to Formula & See Footnote 1					=	$ 190,065

Terminal Costs:

Residual Guarantee Deficiency	$ N/A	x	(1-t)	x	PV_1	=	$ -0-
Nonrenewal Penalty	$ N/A	x	(1-t)	x	PV_1	=	$ -0-
Purchase Option Plus Sales Tax	$75,000	x	N/A	x	.6439	=	$ 48,293

SUB-TOTAL DIRECT LEASE COSTS							$ 424,065

DEDUCT DIRECT LEASE BENEFITS:

Investment Tax Credit	$50,000	x	N/A	x	.9854	=	($ 49,270)
Return of Security Deposit n=60	$10,000	x	N/A	x	.6439	=	($ 6,439)
Loss of Security Deposit	$ N/A	x	(t)	x	PV_1	=	($ -0-)
Depreciation Tax Shield Option Exercised	$75,000	x	See Assumptions			=	($ 20,648)
Residual Guarantee Rebate	$———	x	(1-t)	x	PV_1	=	($ -0-)

SUB-TOTAL DIRECT LEASE BENEFITS							($ 76,357)

NET FINANCIAL COST TO LEASE							$ 347,708

Step Two—Indirect Cost Decision
ADD INDIRECT LEASE COSTS:

	Amount	x	Tax Factor	x	14.4% PV Factor	=	Total
Delivery & Installation Charges	$ N/A	x	(1-t)	x	N/A	=	$ -0-
Sales Tax in Advance	$ 1,800	x	(1-.45)	x	1	=	$ 990
Sales Tax	$ 600	x	(1-.45)	x	41.1122	=	$ 13,567
Property Tax	$ N/A	x	(1-t)	x	PV_a	=	$ -0-
Insurance	$ 400	x	(1-t)	x	48.0295	=	$ 10,566
Maintenance	$ 3,000	x	(1-t)	x	48.0295	=	$ 79,249
Replacement Costs (Est.)	$ N/A	x	(1-t)	x	PV_a	=	$ -0-
Fuel Costs (Est.)	$ 9,000	x	(1-t)	x	48.0295	=	$ 237,746
Variable Accounting Costs	$ 500	x	(1-t)	x	48.0295	=	$ 13,208
Excess Use & Maintenance Charges	$ 2,000	x	(1-t)	x	3.4003	=	$ 3,740
Miscellaneous Costs Unique to Equipment	$ N/A	x	(1-t)	x	PV_a	=	$ -0-

SUB-TOTAL INDIRECT LEASE COSTS $ 359,066

DEDUCT INDIRECT LEASE BENEFITS:

	Amount	x	Tax Factor	x	PV Factor	=	Total
Sub-Lease Income	$ N/A	x	(1-t)	x	PV_a	=	($ -0-)

NET INDIRECT COST TO LEASE $ 359,066

CUMULATIVE COST TO LEASE (Step 1 + Step 2) $ 706,774

Step Three—Capital Budgeting Decision
ADD PROJECTED REVENUE:

	Amount	x	Tax Factor	x	PV Factor	=	Total
Gross Anticipated Revenue n=72	$40,000	x	(1-.45)	x	48.0295	=	$1,056,649
Inflation Increment	$ N/A	x	(1-t)	x	Formula	=	$ -0-

SUB-TOTAL PROJECTED REVENUE $1,056,649

	Amount	x	*Tax Factor*	x	*PV Factor*	=	*Total*

DEDUCT PROJECTED VARIABLE COSTS:

Variable Costs of Sales

n=72	$ 8,000	x	(1–t)	x	48.0295	=	($ 211,330)
Inflation Increment	$ N/A	x	(1–t)	x	Formula	=	($ -0-)

SUB-TOTAL PROJECTED VARIABLE COSTS $ 211,330

NET PROJECTED CONTRIBUTION MARGIN $ 845,319

LESS: CUMULATIVE COST TO LEASE–Step 2   ($ 723,201)

NET PRESENT VALUE (Contribution margin less
cumulative cost to lease Step 2) $ 122,118

Step Four—Liquidity Preference

ADD DIRECT LEASE COSTS:

	Amount	x	*Tax Factor*	x	*PV Factor*	=	*Total*

Initial Costs:

Closing, Origination, Service Fees	$ 5,000	x	(1–.45)	x	N/A	=	$ 2,750
Advance Rental Payments	$36,000	x	(1–.45)	x	N/A	=	$ 19,800
Security Deposits	$10,000	x	N/A	x	N/A	=	$ 10,000

Subsequent Costs:

Remaining Base Rental Payments	$ 6,000	x	(1–t)	x	41.1122	=	$ 135,670
Renewal Option Rental Payments	$ N/A	x	(1–t)	x	PV_a & PV_1 =		$ -0-
Contingent or Percentage Rentals (Est.)	$ N/A	x	(1–t)	x	PV_a	=	$ -0-
Rental Increases Tied to CPI or Prime Rate			Refer to Formula			=	$ 166,714[2]

Terminal Costs:

Residual Guarantee Deficiency	$ N/A	x	(1–t)	x	PV_1	=	$ -0-
Nonrenewal Penalty	$ N/A	x	(1–t)	x	PV_1	=	$ -0-

	Amount x	*Tax Factor* x	*PV Factor* =	*Total*
Purchase Option Plus				
Sales Tax	$75,000 x	N/A x	.4888 =	$ 36,660
SUB-TOTAL DIRECT LEASE COSTS				$ 371,594

DEDUCT DIRECT LEASE BENEFITS:

Investment Tax Credit	$50,000 x	N/A x	.9764 =	($ 48,820)
Return of Security Deposit	$10,000 x	N/A x	.4888 =	($ 4,888)
Loss of Security Deposit	$ N/A x	(t) x	PV_1 =	($ -0-)
Depreciation Tax Shield Option Exercised	$75,000 x	See Assumptions	=	($ 15,240)
Residual Guarantee Rebate	$ N/A x	(1-t) x	PV_1 =	($ -0-)
SUB-TOTAL DIRECT LEASE BENEFITS				($ 68,948)

NET ADJUSTED DIRECT COSTS & BENEFITS $ 302,646

NET LIQUIDITY PREFERENCE ADJUSTMENT
(Step one Total Less Step four Total)   ($ 45,062)

CUMULATIVE COST TO LEASE (Steps 1 + 2 + 4) $ 661,712

Step Five—Risk Adjustment Decision

RISK-SENSITIVE DIRECT COSTS & BENEFITS:

			18%	
	Amount x	*Tax Factor* x	*PV Factor* =	*Total*
Return of Security Deposit n=60	$10,000 x	N/A x	.4093 =	($ 4,093)
Guaranteed Residual Rebate	$ N/A x	(1-t) x	PV_1 =	($ -0-)
Depreciation Tax Shield	$ N/A x	(t) x	PV_a =	($ -0-)
Contingent or Percentage Rentals	$ N/A x	(1-t) x	PV_a =	$ -0-
Rental Increases Tied to CPI or Prime Rate	$ 5,952 x	(1-.45) Refer to Formula =		$ 153,668 [3]

	Amount	x	*Tax Factor*	x	*PV Factor*	=	*Total*
Guaranteed Residual Deficiency	$ N/A	x	(1–t)	x	PV_1	=	$ -0-
Fair Market Value Purchase Option	$ N/A	x	N/A	x	PV_1	=	$ -0-
Purchase Options in Declining Resale Market	$ N/A	x	N/A	x	PV_1	=	$ -0-
Estimated Salvage Values	$ N/A	x	(1–t)	x	PV_1	=	$ -0-
Miscellaneous Items Unique to Lease	$ N/A	x	(1–t)	x	PV_a or PV_1	=	$ -0-

TOTAL RISK-ADJUSTED DIRECT COSTS & BENEFITS $ 149,575

RISK-SENSITIVE INDIRECT COSTS & BENEFITS:

	Amount	x	*Tax Factor*	x	*PV Factor*	=	*Total*
Maintenance n=72	$ 3,000	x	(1–.45)	x	43.8447	=	$ 72,344
Replacement Costs	$ N/A	x	(1–t)	x	PV_a	=	$ -0-
Fuel Costs n=72	$ N/A	x	(1–.45)	x	43.8447	=	$ 217,031
Variable Accounting Costs n=72	$ N/A	x	(1–.45)	x	43.8447	=	$ 12,057
Excess Use or Warranty Costs n=5 yrs.	$ 2,000	x	(1–.45)	x	3.1272	=	$ 3,440
Miscellaneous Items Unique to Equip.	$ N/A	x	(1–t)	x	PV_a or PV_1	=	$ -0-

TOTAL RISK-ADJUSTED INDIRECT COSTS & BENEFITS $ 304,872

NET RISK ADJUSTMENT (Deduct Total Risk-adjusted Direct
Costs from Step one Corresponding Costs and then deduct the
Risk-adjusted Indirect Costs from Step two Corresponding Costs.
Add these two items together)   ($ 41,322)

Direct Costs $ 161,826   Indirect Costs $ 333,943

CUMULATIVE COST TO LEASE (Steps 1 + 2 + 4 + 5) $ 620,390

Step Six—Qualitative Attributes Decision

ADD: EXPECTED VALUE OF QUALITATIVE COSTS

Expected Cost$_1$	$ N/A (1–t)	x PV_a or PV_1 =	$ -0-
Expected Cost$_2$	$ N/A (1–t)	x PV_a or PV_1 =	$ -0-

DEDUCT: EXPECTED VALUE OF QUALITATIVE BENEFITS

Expected Benefit$_1$
Cancelation
Clause $ _5,390_ (1-t or t) x PV$_a$ or PV$_1$ = ($ 5,390)

Expected
Benefit$_2$ $ _N/A_ (1-t or t) x PV$_a$ or PV$_1$ = ($ -0-)

NET EXPECTED VALUE OF COSTS AND BENEFITS   = $ 5,390

CUMULATIVE COST TO LEASE (Steps 1 + 2 + 4 + 5 + 6) $ 615,000

Step Seven—Sensitivity Analysis

IDENTIFY & SCRUTINIZE FOUR MOST INFLUENTIAL DIFFERENTIAL
COSTS BENEFITS

1 Maintenance   Amount ($ 45,231)[5]

2 Fuel Costs   Amount ($ 24,1.5)[6]

3 Variable Accounting   Amount ($ 12,058)[7]

4 Excess Use Charges   Amount $ 3,440

IDENTIFY & SCRUTINIZE FOUR MOST INFLUENTIAL
NONDIFFERENTIAL COSTS:

1 Net Financial Cost   Amount $ 89,337[8]

2 Liquidity Preference   Amount $ 28,931[9]

3 Rentals tied to CPI   Amount $ 17,330[10]

4 Security Deposit   Amount $ 10,000

SCRUTINIZE:

Check when Completed

Incremental Effective Tax Rate

Discount Rates

Six Previous Decision Steps

Risk Premiums

Liquidity Preference Assumption

PURCHASE DECISION FORMAT

Step One—Financial Decision

ADD DIRECT PURCHASE COSTS:

	Amount	x	*Tax Factor*	x	*PV Factor* 8.8373%	=	*Total*
Initial Costs:							
Closing, Origination, Service Fees	$ 8,000	x	N/A	x	N/A	=	$ 8,000
Down Payment	$100,000	x	N/A	x	N/A	=	$ 100,000
Security Deposit	$ N/A	x	N/A	x	N/A	=	$ -0-
Compensating Bank Balance	$ 5,000	x	N/A	x	N/A	=	$ 5,000
Subsequent Costs:							
Installment Loan Payments n=48	$ 11,350	x	N/A	x	40.3098	=	$ 457,516
Payment Increases, Tied to Prime Rate	$ N/A	x	N/A	x	Formula	=	$ -0-
Terminal Costs:							
Balloon Payment	$ N/A	x	N/A	x	PV_1	=	$ -0-
ITC Recapture for Early Salvage	$ N/A	x	N/A	x	PV_1	=	$ -0-
SUB-TOTAL DIRECT PURCHASE COSTS							$ 570,516

DEDUCT DIRECT PURCHASE BENEFITS:

Investment Tax Credit n=2	$53,300	x	N/A	x	.9854	=	($ 52,522)
Return of Security Deposit	$ N/A	x	N/A	x	PV_1	=	($ -0-)
Loss of Security Deposit	$ N/A	x	(t)	x	PV_1	=	($ -0-)
Depreciation Tax Shield	$_____		Per Assumptions			=	($ 198,591)
Interest Tax Shield	$_____		Per Assumptions			=	($ 57,516)

	Amount	x	Tax Factor	x	PV Factor	=	Total
Tax-adjusted Salvage Value	$ N/A	x	N/A	x	PV_1	=	($ -0-)
Return of Compensating Balance n=48	$ 5,000	x	N/A	x	.7031	=	($ 3,516)

SUB-TOTAL DIRECT PURCHASE BENEFITS ($ 312,145)

NET FINANCIAL COST TO PURCHASE $ 258,371

Step Two—Indirect Cost Decision

ADD INDIRECT PURCHASE COSTS:

	Amount	x	Tax Factor	x	PV Factor	=	Total
Delivery & Installation Charges	$ N/A	x	(1–t) or N/A	x	N/A	=	$ -0-
Sales Tax	$25,000	x	N/A	x	N/A	=	$ 25,000
Property Tax	$ N/A	x	(1–t)	x	PV_a	=	$ -0-
Insurance	$ 500	x	(1–.45)	x	48.0295	=	$ 13,208
Maintenance	$	x	Refer to Formula			=	$ 116,556[11]
Replacement Costs (Est.)	$ 1,000	x	(1–.45)	x	3.8464	=	$ 2,116
Fuel Costs (Est.)	$10,000	x	(1–.45)	x	48.0295	=	$ 264,162
Variable Accounting Costs	$ 1,000	x	(1–.45)	x	48.0295	=	$ 26,416
Licenses and Permits	$ N/A	x	(1–t)	x	PV_a	=	$ -0-
Down Time Losses (goodwill, etc.)	$ N/A	x	(1–t)	x	PV_a	=	$ -0-
Spare Parts Inventory	$ N/A	x	(1–t)	x	PV_a	=	$ -0-
Additional Maintenance Facilities Cost	$ 500	x	(1–.45)	x	48.0295	=	$ 13,208
Misc. Costs Unique to Equipment	$ N/A	x	(1–t)	x	PV_a or PV_1	=	$ -0-

SUB-TOTAL INDIRECT PURCHASE COSTS = $ 460,666

DEDUCT INDIRECT PURCHASE BENEFITS:

Sub-Lease Income	$ N/A	x	(1-t)	x	PV$_a$	= ($ -0-)

NET INDIRECT COST TO PURCHASE $ 460,666

CUMULATIVE COST TO PURCHASE (Step 1 + 2) $ 719,037

Step Three—Capital Budgeting Decision

ADD PROJECTED REVENUE:

Gross Anticipated Revenue n=48	$40,000	x	(1-.45)	x	48.0295	= $1,056,649
Inflation Increment	$ N/A	x	(1-t)	x	Formula	= $ -0-

SUB-TOTAL PROJECTED REVENUE $1,056,649

DEDUCT PROJECTED VARIABLE COSTS:

Variable Costs of Sales n=48	$ 8,000	x	(1-.45)	x	48.0295	= ($ 211,330)
Inflation Increment	$ N/A	x	(1-t)	x	Formula	= ($ -0-)

SUB-TOTAL PROJECTED VARIABLE COSTS $ 211,330

NET PROJECTED CONTRIBUTION MARGIN $ 845,319

NET PRESENT VALUE (Contribution Margin Less
Step 2 Total) $ 126,282

$ 110,384

Step Four—Liquidity Preference

ADD DIRECT PURCHASE COSTS:

	Amount	x	Tax Factor	x	PV Factor	=	Total
Initial Costs:							
Closing, Origination, Service Fees	$ 8,000	x	N/A	x	N/A	=	$ 8,000
Down Payment	$100,000	x	N/A	x	N/A	=	$ 100,000
Security Deposit	$ N/A	x	N/A	x	N/A	=	$ -0-
Compensating Bank Balance	$ 5,000	x	N/A	x	N/A	=	$ 5,000

	Amount x *Tax Factor*	x *PV Factor* =	*Total*

Subsequent Costs:

Installment
Loan Payments $11,350 x   N/A   x   36.3272 = $ 412,314

Payment Increases,
Tied to Prime Rate $ N/A x   N/A   see Formula = $ -0-

Terminal Costs:
Balloon Payment $ N/A x   N/A   x PV_1 = $ -0-

ITC Recapture for
Early Salvage $ N/A x   N/A   x PV_1 = $ -0-

  SUB-TOTAL DIRECT PURCHASE COSTS $ 525,314

DEDUCT DIRECT PURCHASE BENEFITS:

Investment Tax Credit $53,300 x   N/A   x   .9764   = ($ 52,042)

Return of Security
Deposit $ N/A x   N/A   x PV_1 = ($ -0-)

Loss of Security Deposit $ N/A x   (t)   x PV_1 = ($ -0-)

Depreciation Tax Shield $_____ x   Per Assumptions   = ($ 177,701)

Interest Tax Shield $ —— x   Per Assumptions   =   ($50,510)

Tax-adjusted
Salvage Value $ N/A x   N/A   x PV_1 = ($ -0-)

Return of
Compensating Balance $ 5,000 x   N/A   x   .5641   = ($ 2,821)

   SUB-TOTAL DIRECT PURCHASE BENEFITS   ($283,074)

   NET ADJUSTED DIRECT COSTS & BENEFITS $ 242,240

   NET LIQUIDITY PREFERENCE ADJUSTMENT
   (Step one Total Less Step four Total)   ($ 16,131)

   CUMULATIVE COST TO PURCHASE (Steps 1 + 2 + 4) $702,906

Step Five—Risk Adjustment Decision

RISK-SENSITIVE DIRECT COSTS BENEFITS:

18%

Return of Security Deposit	$ N/A	x	N/A	x	PV_1	=	$ -0-
Depreciation Tax Shield	$ N/A	x	(t)	x	PV_a	=	$ -0-
Installment Payments Tied to Prime Rate	$ N/A	x	N/A	x	Formula	=	$ -0-
Estimated Salvage Value	$ N/A	x	(t or 1-t)	x	PV_1	=	$ -0-
Miscellaneous Items Unique to Loan	$ N/A	x	t or 1-t	x PV_a or PV_1		=	$ -0-

TOTAL RISK ADJUSTED DIRECT COSTS & BENEFITS $ -0-

RISK-SENSITIVE INDIRECT COSTS BENEFITS:

Maintenance	$ N/A	x	(1-t)	x	PV_a	=	$ -0-
Replacement Costs	$ 1,000	x	(1-.45)	x	3.4976	=	$ 1,924
Fuel Costs	$10,000	x	(1-.45)	x	43.8447	=	$ 241,146
Variable Accounting Costs	$ 1,000	x	(1-.45)	x	43.8447	=	$ 24,115
Down-time Losses	$ N/A	x	(1-t)	x	PV_a	=	$ -0-
Spare Parts Inventory Costs	$ N/A	x	(1-t)	x	PV_a	=	$ -0-
Any Cost Subject to Escalation	$ 3,500	x	(1-t)	x	Formula	=	$ 105,518[12]
Excess Facilities Cost	$ 500	x	(1-.45)	x	43.8447	=	$ 12,057

TOTAL RISK-ADJUSTED INDIRECT COSTS & BENEFITS $ 384,760

NET RISK ADJUSTMENT (Deduct Total Risk-adjusted
Direct Cost from Step one *Corresponding* Costs and then
Deduct the Risk-adjusted Indirect Costs from Step two
Corresponding Costs. Add these two items together.)   ($ 37,698)

CUMULATIVE COST TO PURCHASE (Steps 1 + 2 + 4 + 5) $ 665,208

Step Six—Qualitative Attributes Decision

ADD: EXPECTED VALUE OF QUALITATIVE COSTS

Expected Cost$_1$ $ __N/A__   (1-t)   x PV$_a$ or PV$_1$ = $ __-0-__

Expected Cost$_2$ $ __N/A__   (1-t)   x PV$_a$ or PV$_1$ = $ __-0-__

DEDUCT: EXPECTED VALUE OF QUALITATIVE BENEFITS:

Expected Benefit$_1$ $ __N/A__   (1-t)   x PV$_a$ or PV$_1$ = $ __-0-__

Expected Benefit$_2$ $ __N/A__   (1-t)   x PV$_a$ or PV$_1$ = $ __-0-__

NET EXPECTED VALUE OF COSTS AND BENEFITS $ __-0-__

CUMULATIVE COST TO PURCHASE
(Steps 1 + 2 + 4 + 5 + 6) $ 665,208

Step Seven—Sensitivity Analysis

IDENTIFY & SCRUTINIZE FOUR MOST INFLUENTIAL
DIFFERENTIAL COSTS

1 _____   Amount $ _____

2 See Step 7 Leasing Alternative   Amount $ _____

3 _____ " _____   Amount $ _____

4 _____ " _____   Amount $ _____

IDENTIFY & SCRUTINIZE FOUR MOST INFLUENTIAL
NONDIFFERENTIAL COSTS

1 _____ " _____   Amount $ _____

2 _____ " _____   Amount $ _____

3 _____ " _____   Amount $ _____

4 _____ " _____   Amount $ _____

SCRUTINIZE:

Check when Completed

Incremental Effective Tax Rate

Discount Rates

Six Previous Decision Steps

Risk Premiums

Liquidity Preference Assumption

Conclusion

It will cost $615,000 to lease as compared to $665,208 if the equipment is purchased. Thus, leasing will save BETA Company $50,208 through leasing. Refer to the sensitivity analysis under the leasing alternative for an explanation of the primary causes for leasing's favorability.

Footnote One

$$\boxed{i} = \frac{.7364-.8}{1 + \frac{.8}{100}} = \frac{-.0636}{1.008} = -.0631$$

$$\boxed{n} = 57$$

$$\boxed{pmt} = \frac{\$6000}{1 + \frac{.8}{100}} = \frac{\$6000}{1.008} = \$5,942.38$$

$$\boxed{pv} = \$345,572.03 \times (1-.45) = \underline{\$190.065}$$

Footnote Two

$$\boxed{i} = \frac{1.2-.8}{1 + \frac{.8}{100}} = \frac{.4}{1.008} = .3968$$

$$\boxed{n} = 57$$

$$\boxed{pmt} = \frac{\$6000}{1 + \frac{.8}{100}} = \frac{\$6000}{1.008} = \$5,952.38$$

$$\boxed{pv} = \$303,117.22 \times (1-.45) = \underline{\$166.714}$$

Footnote Three

$$\boxed{i} = \frac{1.5-.8}{1 + \frac{.8}{100}} = \frac{.7}{1.008} = .6944$$

$$\boxed{n} = 57$$

$$\boxed{pmt} = \frac{\$\,6000}{1+\frac{.8}{100}} = \frac{\$\,6000}{1.008} = \$\,5,952.38$$

$$\boxed{pv} = \$\,279,397.25 \times (1-.45) = \underline{\$\,153,668}$$

Footnote Four

Maintenance	Lease	−	Buy	=	Difference
Risk-adjusted Maintenance	$ 72,344				
Maintenance (Escalation)			$ 105,518		
Excess Facilities			12,057		
	$ 72,344	−	$ 117,575	=	($ 45,231)
					Lease Benefit

Footnote Five

Fuel Costs	Lease	−	Buy	=	Difference
Individual Fuel Costs	$ 217,031	−	$ 241,146	=	($ 24,115)
					Lease Benefit

Footnote Six

	Lease	−	Buy	=	Difference
Variable Accounting	$ 12,057	−	$ 24,115	=	($ 12,048)
					Lease Benefit

Footnote Seven

	Lease	−	Buy	=	Difference
Net Financial Cost	$ 347,708	−	$258,371	=	$ 89,337
					Buy Benefit

Footnote Eight

	Lease	−	Buy	=	Difference
Liquidity Preference	$ 302,646	−	$ 242,240	=	$ 60,406
Pure Financial Cost	$ 347,708	−	$ 258,371	=	($ 89,337)
	($ 45,062)	−	$ 16,131	=	($ 28,931)
					Lease Benefit

Footnote Nine

Rentals without CPI clause		$ 153,000
Rentals with CPI clause		135,670
	$ 17,330	Buy Benefit caused by CPI escalation clause

Footnote Ten

$$\boxed{i} \quad = \quad 1.2$$

$$\boxed{n} \quad = \quad 72$$

$$\boxed{pmt} \quad = \quad \$\,3500 \left(\frac{\$\,30}{1.2/100} \right) = \$\,3500 + \$\,2500 = \$\,600$$

$$\boxed{fv} \quad = \quad -72 \left(\frac{\$\,30}{1.2/100} \right) = -72(2500) = \$\,-180{,}000$$

$$\boxed{pv} \quad = \quad \$\,211{,}920.73 \times (1-.45) = \underline{\$\,116{,}556}$$

Footnote Eleven

$$\boxed{i} \quad = \quad 1.5$$

$$\boxed{n} \quad = \quad 72$$

$$\boxed{pmt} \quad = \quad \$\,3500 \left(\frac{\$\,30}{1.5/100} \right) = \$\,3500 + \$\,2000 = \$\,5500$$

$$\boxed{fv} \quad = \quad -72 \left(\frac{\$\,30}{1.5/100} \right) = -72(2000) = \$\,-144{,}000$$

$$\boxed{pv} \quad = \quad \$\,191{,}850.15 \times (1-.45) = \underline{\$\,105{,}518}$$

Qualitative Factors
Influencing the Lease
——— Versus Buy Decision ———

A seven step quantitative method of determining whether leasing is preferable to purchasing was discussed in chapter 7. The sixth step within that model dealt with difficult-to-quantify qualitative factors that favor leasing over buying. This chapter describes many of these quality considerations that must be evaluated before a final comprehensive Lease versus Buy decision can be made. Even though many of these additional factors will be considered nonquantitative in that they are difficult to reduce to dollars and cents, they play an important role in the decision-making process.

The additional factors favoring leasing will be listed in numerical order in this chapter, side by side, with countervailing arguments against leasing. In this manner, the reader can weigh the pros and cons of leasing. Seeing both sides of an argument allows the reader to place leasing or buying into proper perspective. Perspective is essential to proper decison-making because very few of the factors affecting leasing or buying are 100 percent advantageous or disadvantageous. Thus, to avoid performing mental closure caused by black and white thinking, this chapter will present additional lease advantages in a realistic setting of gray where pros and cons have equal sway.

Leasing Advantages	Leasing Disadvantages
1. Certain types of lease financing (operating leases per FASB 13) are not shown on the balance sheet of the lessee. Therefore, these leases do not raise the debt-equity ratio nor impair the borrowing capacity of the firm. The	1. Leases are described in the footnotes to the financial statements per *FASB Statement No. 13* requirements. Therefore, the advantage of off-balance sheet financing is perhaps overstated. Only a naive analyst would ignore

193

current and acid test ratios are not affected by operating leases either.

the impact of the lease on the financial leverage or other ratios of the firm.

2. Lease-financing conserves working capital. Leases typically require a smaller down payment than do installment loans. Moreover, unlike many bank loans, no compensating balances are required. Delivery and installation charges can often be included as part of each future lease payment which also conserves working capital. The effect of conservation of working capital is included in the chapter seven Lease versus Buy model only when liquidity preference is considered.

2. Some leases do require down payments in the form of lease or rental payments in advance. The number of advance payments is partially determined by the riskiness of the lessee. If a borrower has a well established working relationship with a bank then the terms of an installment loan can be structured to match the terms of any competing lease arrangement, including no down payment and financing of delivery and installation charges as part of the equipment loan.

3. Since cash flow is a prime concern in most businesses, opting the lease route is beneficial because it does not require the initial outflow of funds for sales tax as would the purchase. Some states levy a sales tax as high as ten percent. Clearly, this has a significantly undesirable impact on cash flow. Leasing permits postponement of taxes because sales tax is charged as a percentage of each future lease payment.

3. Some states levy a sales tax on the monthly lease payment. This tax is usually included as part of the periodic payment. Since the monthly payment includes maintenance and implicit interest costs, more sales tax is being paid over the life of the lease than if the tax was levied on the purchase price only. In effect, sales tax is being paid on maintenance and interest. However, the after-tax present value of these costs in many cases is less than paying the total sales taxes due at the inception of the lease.

4. Generally, one of the criteria used by a lessor in determining the lease price is level of usage of the asset by the lessee. If the lessee expects to use the asset

4. Although it is true that lessors consider the expected usage in their profit calculations, their returns are usually sufficiently large to provide a "cushion."

more than average, leasing the asset may prove beneficial. Even if a lease contains a reimbursement clause for excessive wear and tear, the lessor will find it difficult to define exactly what is normal compared to excessive use and therefore might not be able to charge the lessee.

5. Leasing might allow the company a degree of flexibility in additional financing that might not be available when resorting to debt financing. Banks frequently impose restrictions prohibiting future financing, whereas the lease agreement will usually not impose such restrictions. The lessor's financial interest is considered secured by the equipment or property itself. Banks would require more security in the same situation.

6. Leases frequently save processing time because leases are often treated as operating rather than capital expenditures. Supervisors and managers with some discretion can complete lease transactions quickly without pursuing the lengthy capital appropriations route frequently required for capital expenditures.

7. There can be tax advantages. For example, a firm owning land and buildings can only de-

Consequently, it is unlikely that the lessee will be able to gain any real advantage from excess usage. Even if the lessor has been taken advantage of, it will probably happen only once. Furthermore, most leases contain clauses requiring reimbursement for excessive use or wear and tear.

5. Often the implicit interest rate hidden in the lease payments is higher than the rate a bank would charge for the same financing. Therefore, the flexibility obtained in increasing financial leverage must be worth more than the extra interest expense included in the lease payment. Lessees who lease from their bankers are now restricted when using leasing as a financing source. Federally chartered banks are required to include leasing along with regular loans in determining legal lending limits for a particular customer.

6. A lease should require the same capital budgeting analysis as a purchase since both are basically alternative forms of financing. If timing is so critical, then the capital budgeting department had best shorten its processing time. Such action would be preferable to transacting leases without proper analysis.

7. Tax advantages exist only if the lessee can take advantage of the additional tax shield offered by

preciate the building. If, however, the entire holding, and buildings were leased by the firm rather than purchased, then the entire lease payment becomes tax-deductible. In effect, therefore, the land cost included in each lease payment becomes tax-deductible which is not normally allowed under tax laws.

the lease arrangement. In fact, there are generally more tax advantages to buying than leasing since the buyer can use accelerated depreciation and obtain an investment tax credit and deduct the interest portion of debt installments. Note that investment tax credits are generally not available for real estate acquisitions.

8. A lease makes cash budgeting easier by permitting accurate prediction of cash expenses. Compared to the financing of equipment with short-term borrowing which requires constant refinancings at unpredictable interest rates, the fixed nature of lease payments is very helpful in forecasting cash requirements.

8. Although leasing might be more steady and predictable in terms of cash outflow than short-term financing, it is less desirable than long-term bond financing. Bonds are frequently issued at lower interest rates than the interest implicit in leases, and bonds are not required to be paid off for periods of fifteen to twenty years.

9. If the lessee is in such a low tax bracket (due to prior losses etc.) that he cannot utilize the tax advantages obtained under purchasing, such as the investment tax credit and accelerated depreciation, then these tax benefits can be transferred from the user of the asset to the supplier of the asset. If the lessor is in a high tax bracket and needs additional ITC and depreciation then part of the resulting savings to the lessor can be passed to the lessee.

9. The lessee will benefit from relinquished tax benefits only if the lessor passes on the resulting savings in the form of lower lease payments. Obviously, these benefits must be negotiated at the inception of the lease. Whether these savings have in fact been passed on to the lessee is normally determined in Step one of the Lease versus Buy decision covered in chapter seven. All too often these tax savings are not passed on to the lessee.

10. Service leases include both financing and maintenance services. IBM is one of the pioneers

10. Service leases do not necessarily imply savings to the lessee since the lessor frequently offers his

of the service lease contract. Computers and office copying machines, together with automobiles and trucks, are the primary types of equipment involved in service leases. These leases ordinarily call for the *lessor* to maintain and service the leased equipment, and such cost is built into the lease payment. Such an arrangement could save the lessee over purchasing due to the economies of scale obtained by the lessor who services leased equipment in mass. Although the direct savings from a full service lease are calculated in the second step of the Lease versus Buy model, there are nevertheless additional intangible benefits derived from avoiding the hassle inherent in managing a maintenance and service department.

maintenance services to the firms who purchase their own equipment. Thus, an owner of equipment can purchase a service-maintenance contract and avail himself of the same economies of scale obtained under a lease. However, if such services cannot be obtained at a comparable cost or if such services are not available, then a service lease would be advantageous. There are also private maintenance companies that specialize in long-term service contracts. Thus, ownership of equipment might still be preferable if such maintenance can be obtained at a low cost.

11. Many leases contain cancellation clauses giving the lessee the right to cancel the lease and return the equipment before the expiration of the basic lease agreement. This is an important consideration to the lessee, for it means that he can return the equipment if technological developments render it obsolete, or if he simply no longer needs it. This lessee benefit is difficult to quantify; nevertheless it is very valuable to the lessee.

11. Remember, the lessor also assumes the risk of obsolescence and therefore builds this into the cost of the lease payment. Obsolescence is frequently overemphasized. Many outdated computers are still doing the work they were intended for. Purchasing therefore might cost less than leasing if obsolescence is not considered a real threat or problem.

12. Leveraged leases—or three party leases—provide additional tax

12. Keep in mind that financial leverage for a purchaser can

benefits to the lessor (interest is deductible for the lessor on money borrowed to make the lease). These benefits, if passed to the lessee, could make leasing more attractive than purchasing. Many leveraged leases have effective interest costs to the lessee of between two and three percent lower than comparable nonleveraged leases.

easily be achieved with bank financing. The purchaser simply finances the equipment with an installment loan. All tax benefits inure to the benefit of the borrower even though the bank financed the majority of the purchase price.

13. Large leasing companies that purchase equipment and machinery in mass can obtain quantity discounts that small purchasers cannot obtain. Yet a lease might still be more costly than a purchase. Part of leasing's attraction lies in the intangible value of convenience. The question is generally whether the convenience is worth the additional cost and whether quantity discounts will be passed to the lessee.

13. Unless the lessor can pass on to the lessee economies derived from access to secondary markets, quantity discounts, and intensive use of maintenance facilities, such leases usually offer very little real savings. Remember, too, that just because a leasing company is large it does not necessarily follow that it is efficient.

14. In recent periods of inflation some lease companies have created leases with "floating payments" that rise and fall with changes in the prime rate. Obviously, lessees do not like such variable payment leases. Therefore, other leasing companies have introduced fixed payment variable term or variable residual leases which fix the monthly lease payment but vary the lease term instead in order to compensate the lessor for increases in underlying costs of debt.

14. Obviously a lease that contains a variable term or variable residual is preferable to a variable payment lease. Nevertheless, such leases are still expensive alternatives to buying or to leasing under a conventional fixed payment lease.

15. Leasing companies will frequently lease to poorer risks than banks since the lessor looks to the equipment value as compensation for risk. Thus, leasing might be the only available alternative to a new, small, risky corporation.

15 Nevertheless, as soon as the small company can obtain bank credit, it might save by purchasing rather than leasing. This is especially true if the lessor has built a risk factor into the lease payments to compensate for anticipated losses.

16. The lessee might have leverage in demanding adequate and prompt maintenance service on a leased asset. The lessee can refuse to make lease payments until proper service is obtained under leases where the lessor maintains the equipment.

16. The lessor will often protect himself from this situation by having the maintenance performed by a separate corporation, thus separating the legal liability. When the lessor is also the manufacturer of the equipment, maintenance will probably be done by a separate corporation. This diminishes the lessee's ability to demand proper service from the lessor.

17. Lessees can obtain "upgrade leases" where the lessor guarantees automatic exchange of superior equipment or new models for equipment that has become obsolete.

17. Obviously, the lease rate will reflect the cost of insuring against forced upgrading. Sometimes lessees are forced to wait longer than normal cash-paying customers for equipment that is overly backlogged in production and shipment.

18. Should the value of equipment drop significantly due to obsolescence, the lessee might obtain ownership of the asset at far less than the originally estimated residual value. If the equipment is still usable by the lessee, obsolescence might not be of concern.

18. Obsolescence might be so significant that even though the old asset can be acquired at a low price, it still may not be worth exercising a purchase option at any price.

19. Variable Payment Leases can aid lessees who experience wide

19. Recently, variable lease payments have been structured to

seasonal fluctuations in their revenue. Lease payments can be structured to match the lessee's revenue curve or skipped during the months where revenue is expected to be low (e.g., summer months for a toy manufacturer).

rise or fall with increases or decreases in the prime rate. Continuously rising prime rates affect the lessee adversely. Then too, some lease payments are designed to rise with increases in the consumer price index (CPI) which also makes leasing less attractive. So variable payment leases are not necessarily advantageous.

20. Performance and bid bonds for contractors are frequently based upon a company's total debt. The more debt a company has, the lower the availability and amount of the bond. Since operating leases do not create reportable debt, they can allow a contractor's bonding to remain intact.

20. Bonding companies are beginning to recognize that operating leases encumber a company financially whether or not they are considered debt from an accounting point of view. Much attention is now being paid to leasing information contained in footnote disclosures.

21. The operational efficiency of many divisions or subsidiaries of large corporations is based upon return on assets (ROA). Since operating leases are not capitalized, a larger return on assets results than if the division had purchased the asset.

21. Judging the performance of a division solely on the basis of return on assets is naive. Knowledgeable financial analysts employ multiple criteria to judge performance which include such techniques as return on equity, potential growth rate in earnings, incremental profit analysis, sensitivity models, etc.

22. A lessor will frequently offer longer terms than those offered by a financial institution. When this occurs, the present value of the after-tax lease payments may cost less than the after-tax cost of purchasing. The lower cost results from the smaller lease payments that are paid back over a longer period of time.

22. Well established clients of financial institutions can generally receive similar extended terms on loans used to finance asset acquisitions. Furthermore, the interest rates implicit in lease financing have historically been slightly higher than rates charged by banks for similar financing.

23. Swap agreements allow a lessee to exchange equipment in need of major repair with properly working replacement equipment. Immediate replacement avoids costly maintenance delays. Other methods of financing seldom permit such an exchange due to the legal complexities involved in substituting collateral.

23. Swap agreements are generally limited to manufacturer-lessors (two party lessors) who are in a position to provide replacement equipment for the swap. Some banks also offer blanket chattel mortgages which allow for permanent changes in collateral. Remember, too, the cost of expected swaps has been built into the cost of the lease.

24. In the case where a lessor is also the manufacturer of the leased equipment, a lower-than-average lease cost might be obtained by the lessee. Cost reductions occur because the lessor at the end of a lease term can rebuild and resell or lease the equipment with more ease and at a lower cost than the typical third party lessor. The manufacturer-lessor, being able to depend on higher residual values for lease yield, can pass savings on to the lessee.

24. Whether or not the lessor will in fact pass the savings on to the lessee is a question of negotiation. The growing secondary market for used equipment of all sorts has aided third-party lessors in passing savings on to lessees in the same manner that manufacturer-lessors do. When an asset is purchased, the total salvage value belongs to the owner who does not have to depend upon a lessor to pass part of the residual value savings on.

25. Depletion allowances are limited to fifty percent of pretax net income. Therefore, the higher net income shown during the early years of an operating lease would permit a larger depletion deduction.

25. Similar savings can be obtained from purchasing equipment through a subsidiary that can use all the tax benefits of ownership. The subsidiary then leases to the parent allowing it to maximize its depletion allowance.

26. Secondary markets have become widespread for equipment that has been returned at the end of a lease. Reasonable prediction of the proceeds from resale of returned equipment permits higher reliance on residual values. This reliance allows the

26. Secondary markets are also available to the purchasers of equipment. When equipment is no longer needed, it can be sold by the owner who retains the full benefit of the salvage proceeds. Such expected future salvage values should be consid-

lessor to lower lease payments in order to obtain the same expected lease yield.

27. Industrial revenue bonds have tax-exempt interest at low rates which allow a lessor to pass on savings to a lessee. Industrial revenue bonds are limited to projects equal or less than ten million dollars in cost. Larger, more expensive projects can be built by leasing some of the equipment included in the project in order to meet the government's ten million dollar borrowing limit.

28. Diversification in the sources of financing is important in times when credit is in short supply. Leasing offers additional sources of equipment financing beyond conventional bank financing. Overdependance on a single loan source whose funds may become unavailable could be disasterous (like bank financing during the 1980-81 credit crunch).

29. Leases can be paid off with inflated dollars. Although bank installment loans can be paid with inflated dollars too, they generally require greater down payments with shorter terms. Loans requiring more up-front dollars remove the opportunity for payback with inflated dollars.

30. Leasing offers certain valuable flexibilities that are not availa-

ered in the Lease versus Buy decision.

27. Activity in the industrial revenue bond area has been recently curtailed by many states. As the industrial revenue bond is paid off, the lessee may be faced with a gigantic increase in lease payments. If the increase occurs—over a short period of time—the lessee may not be able to adapt.

28. When banks are caught in a credit crunch, so too are many leasing companies. Many third-party leasing companies obtain their funding from banks. When banks stop lending, lessors stop leasing and therefore diversification might be overrated.

29. The effects of inflation can also work against a lessee. If revenue declines rather than grows, the lessee will be forced to pay off the lease with more expensive deflated dollars.

30. Some banks will allow the same sort of joint venturing arrange-

ble from lending institutions. For example, lessees can joint venture the aquisition of expensive pieces of equipment through leases. Banks are reluctant to lend on this basis. Medical equipment is frequently leased to members of a clinic where no individual doctor could afford to purchase the equipment.

ment. However, the bank appoints a trustee or escrow agent to collect funds and handle repossessions, etc.

31. Sale-leasebacks can save the lessee money by permitting the lessee to redepreciate a low basis building and to depreciate land cost in the form of tax-deductible rental payments. Purchase options can be contained in the lease to give the lessee ultimate ownership of the land.

31. Capital gains taxes will have to be paid on the sale. And the sale must qualify under IRS guidelines for a sale leaseback which includes the following:
    a. Must be a multiparty transfer (three or more).
    b. Lessor must have significant attributes of being in fact a lessor (must assume risk).
    c. Arrangement was entered into for nontax motives.
    d. Lease term must be less than 30 years.

32. Earnings per share will generally be higher during the early years of a lease. Depreciation and interest expenses associated with the purchase alternative result in a lower net income.

32. In the latter years of a lease, earnings per share will be lower than if the company had purchased the asset. Mature companies that are growing slowly might be adversely affected by leasing.

33. Operating leases are convenient in that they require less accounting attention than purchases.

33. Automated accounting systems make the accounting time requirements the same for a lease or purchase.

34. Dilution of ownership can be avoided through leasing since necessary capital for equipment

34. There are, of course, other means of obtaining capital besides equity. Bonds, notes, de-

expansion can be acquired without resorting to a stock issue.

bentures, and commercial paper
are but a few of the types of
nonequity funding available.

35. Trial use periods allow lessees
to avoid the risk involved in purchasing an asset for a new venture. If the venture fails, the
leased equipment can be
returned.

35. Lease rentals for trial periods
are usually extremely high-
priced. Sometimes manufacturers will allow a trial period
of up to six months without requiring a purchase.

36. Service leases can eliminate the
need for expensive *support facilities* and *personnel* required
to maintain and resell
equipment.

36. Sometimes support facilities
can be shared with other owners
through co-operative arrangements.

CONCLUSION

Certainly the above listing of leasing advantages and disadvantages is not all-inclusive.
New forms of leases are being created daily. The important concept is that the Lease
versus Buy decision is complex and requires many nonquantitative factors to be considered along with those quantitative items described in chapter 7.

Accounting and Reporting
_____ for Leases _____

Generally accepted accounting principles (GAAP) require that leases be accounted for according to the techniques described in *FASB Statement No. 13*. This chapter will concentrate on FASB 13 accounting for both CAPITAL and OPERATING leases from the viewpoint of the lessee as well as that of the lessor. Additionally, the reporting and disclosure requirements as promulgated by FASB 13 will be covered. First, accounting for a capital lease by a lessee will be covered followed by lessee-operating lease accounting. Then, accounting for capital leases by lessors will be followed by accounting for operating leases.

LESSEE ACCOUNTING AND REPORTING FOR CAPITAL LEASES

Capitalization of Leased Asset

Basically, a lessee is required to record a capital lease as an ASSET since equipment has been purchased at an amount equal to the present value of the minimum lease payments. Furthermore, since the lease agreement creates a legal obligation, the lessee must also record as an obligation a LIABILITY (lease payable) at the same present-value amount at which the asset was recorded. The minimum lease payments, whose present value is used in recording the lease's ASSET and LIABILITY amounts, must exclude executory costs (or at lease a reasonable estimate of them if not actually known).

What discount rate should be used in determining the present value of the minimum lease payments? It depends! The discount rate to be used is the lessee's incremental borrowing rate (rate charged currently by a bank to purchase the asset with similar terms) unless the lessee can determine the implicit rate charged by the lessor and that rate is less than the lessee's borrowing rate. When the lessor's rate is lower, a higher implicit fair market value of the asset is determined. Note, however, that the present-value amount cannot exceed the fair market value of the leased asset no matter which discount rate is used. The fair market value is viewed as a ceiling in limiting the capitalization of leased assets. Following is an example of determining the amount at which a lessee should record the leased equipment both as an asset and corresponding lease payable:

> Example – ten year, $1000 per year lease with one payment in advance. Lessee's incremental borrowing rate is twelve percent, implicit lease rate is ten percent. What should the asset be capitalized at?

> *Present-Value Factors*
> Ten percent   PV Factor – 6.759 x $1000 = $6,759 (Annuity Due)
> Twelve percent PV Factor – 6.328 x $1000 = $6,328 (Annuity Due)

> *Answer*: The asset would be capitalized at $6,759 since the lessor's implicit rate was less than the lessee's rate. Also it is assumed that neither answer exceeds the FMV of the asset. If the investment tax credit had been received by the lessee, it would *not* have affected the asset carrying amount just determined. The investment tax credit would be accounted for in the same manner as that received under a normal asset purchase; i.e. flow-through method or deferral method.

Depreciation of Capitalized Asset

The capitalized leased asset shall be amortized (depreciated) as follows:

1. If the lease transfers ownership or if a bargain purchase option exists then depreciate the capitalized equipment like any other asset; otherwise,
2. If the lease term is less than the expected life of the asset then depreciate the equipment over the term of the lease.

In other words, if the receiving of ownership during or at the end of the lease is anticipated, the asset should be depreciated over its normal expected life, even if this period exceeds the lease term. However, if the lease term is shorter than the asset's economic life and no possibility to obtain ownership exists, the asset should be depreciated over the term of the lease, even if this period is less than its economic depreciable life.

Amortization of Lease Payments

During the lease term, the effective interest method must be used to reduce the lease payable obligation and charge interest. This means each lease payment must be separated into principal and interest. Principal represents the periodic reduction in the lease payable, whereas interest represents the carrying charge assessed by the lessor (implicit interest).

Lease payments are separated into principal and interest by using the effective interest method which works in the following manner:

1. Multiply the periodic interest rate used in the capitalization of the asset (either the incremental borrowing rate or the lessor's implicit rate) by the remaining lease payable. Using the preceding example, multiplying ten percent by $5,759 = $575.90. Note the remaining lease payable was $5,759 rather than $6,759 due to the one payment made in advance. The product of $575.90 is the effective interest included in the lease payment.

2. Deduct the *product* of the *discount rate* times the *remaining lease payable* computed above from the annual lease payment: $1,000 - $575.90 = $424.10. The resulting difference of $424.10 is the principal portion of the lease payment.

3. Deduct the *principal reduction* computed in Step two above from the remaining lease payable.

4. Repeat the process next year for the next lease payment. The interest portion will be smaller since the lease payable has been reduced (Step three above) and consequently the principal portion of the lease payment will have increased.

5. Example: Separate next year's lease payment into principal and interest.

   a. .10 x ($5,759 - 424.10) = $ __533.49__ Interest

   b. $1,000 - $533.49 = $ __466.51__ Principal

   c. $5,334.90 - $466.59 = $4,868.31 Remaining lease payable

6. The principal portion of the lease payable due during any twelve-month period should be classified as a current liability and the balance due as a long-term liability.

Disclosure Requirements

The following information with respect to a capital lease shall be disclosed in the lessee's financial statements or in its footnotes:

1. Total assets recorded as capital leases (broken into functional classes, if any) should be separately identified along with separate identification of the corresponding current and long-term lease payables.

2. Future minimum lease payments broken down as follows:

   a. Rental payments for each of the next five years.

   b. Plus the amount of payments thereafter.

   c. Equals: Total remaining lease payments.

   d. Less: Executory costs including profit thereon.

   e. Less: Imputed interest in the lease.

   f. Equals: Present value of net lease payments which is the same as the remaining lease payable liability shown on the balance sheet.

3. Sublease rentals to be received in the future from noncancelable subleases.
4. Contingent rentals actually incurred by the lessee.
5. Separate identification of accumulated depreciation and current depreciation charges on any capital leases.

LESSEE ACCOUNTING AND REPORTING FOR OPERATING LEASES

Accounting for Lease Payments

A lessee accounts for an operating lease payment as a charge (debit) to lease expense and as a reduction in cash (credit). The lease payment appears on the balance sheet as a reduction in the cash account.

Although FASB 13 does not require it, it is my opinion that operating lease payments should be separated into two expenses: the first, implicit interest, and the second, lease expense representing the true cost of using the equipment. Furthermore, the lease liability should be disclosed in a separate liability class on the balance sheet. Otherwise, a significant liability that is probable and estimable has been ignored as described previously in chapter 3.

Disclosure Requirements

1. Future remaining minimum payments required, in total and for the next five years.
2. Sublease rentals expected in future from noncancelable leases.
3. Rental expense for the period separated into minimum rentals, contingent rentals, and sublease rentals.
4. General description of the lease—including basis for contingent rentals, renewal or purchase options, escalation clauses, restrictions concerning additional debt or further leasing, etc.

Note that these disclosure requirements are sufficiently comprehensive to allow any financial analyst, bank, or bonding company to fully understand the real liabilities of the lessee whether or not they appear as such on the lessee's balance sheet. These disclosure requirements were further discussed in chapter 3.

EXAMPLES OF LESSEE ACCOUNTING FOR A CAPITAL LEASE

Facts and Assumptions

1. A $1,100 per year lease payment for ten years, first and last payments in advance (eight payments left after inception of the lease).
2. Bargain purchase option of $500 at end of lease.

3. Lessee's incremental borrowing rate twelve percent.
   Lessor's implicit interest rate ten percent.
   FMV of the asset = $7,600.
4. P.V. of an annuity for eight periods, ten percent = 5.335
   P.V. of one for ten periods, ten percent = 0.386
5. Executory costs of $100 are included in the payments.
6. Current year contingent rental of $50.

Proper recording and accounting for the above lease including required reporting and disclosure would result in the following entries:

1. DETERMINATION OF CAPITALIZATION AMOUNT:

a. Minimum lease payments = $1,100 − 100 = $1,000.

b. Asset value:

two payments in advance	=	$ 2,000
eight remaining payments 5.335 x 1000	=	5,335
bargain purchase option 0.386 x 500	=	193
		$ 7,528

2. CAPITALIZATION JOURNAL ENTRIES:

a. Leased asset	$ 7,528	
Leases Payable		$ 7,528
b. Leases Payable	$ 2,000	
Cash		$ 2,000

3. DISCLOSURE REQUIREMENTS:

a. Footnotes:

1980	$ 1,100	
1981	1,100	
1982	1,100	
1983	1,100	
1984	1,100	
thereafter	3,800	(includes bargain option)
Total minimum lease payments	$ 9,300	
Executory costs	(800)	
Implicit Interest	(2,972)	
Present value of payments	$ 5,528	(equals remaining lease payable liability)

b. Current year contingent rentals of $50 were paid this year.

4. DETERMINATION OF LESSOR'S IMPLICIT INTEREST RATE

Since FASB 13 requires the lessee to use the lower of his own incremental borrowing rate or the implicit interest rate in the lease to determine the capitalization value under a capital lease, a brief review of the implicit rate is in order.

a. *Implicit Rate* is defined as the discount rate that, when applied to the minimum lease payments (excluding executory costs) together with any unguaranteed residual, causes the aggregate present value at the inception of the lease to be equal to the fair market value of the leased property (FMV must be reduced by any ITC retained by lessor). In finance we refer to this process as determining the internal rate of return.

b. *Example* - Find the implicit discount rate for the following lease:

FMV of asset	= $ 10,000
ITC retained by lessor	= 1,000
Seven lease payments (two paid in advance)	= 2,000 per year
Unguaranteed residual	= 1,500

c. *Solution* -

Time periods =	0	1	2	3	4	5	6	7
Outflow:								
FMV Asset	-$10K	0	0	0	0	0	0	0
Inflow:								
ITC Retained	$+1K							
Advance Payments	+4K							
Regular Payments		+2K	+2K	+2K	+2K	+2K	0	0
Unguaranteed Res.								+1.5
Net Cash Flows:	-5K	+2K	+2K	+2K	+2K	+2K	+0	+1.5

Implicit Interest rate or IRR = 31.06%

d. The complication in determining the lessor's implicit interest rate stems from the difficulty in obtaining certain pertinent information: (1) what value has been placed on the lessor's unguaranteed residual; (2) what ITC amount the lessor will claim since the lessor's cost of the asset might be less than FMV; (3) what the fair market value of the asset is to the lessor—it might be less than retail if the lessor can purchase the equipment wholesale.

e. The question is often asked: Since the lessor frequently uses the same discount rate to capitalize an asset as does the lessee, won't both parties to the lease record the asset at the same value? The answer is: sometimes. If the lease has an unguaranteed residual (no purchase option available to lessee) then the lessee will record only the present value of mimimum lease payments as the capitalized value which excludes the value of the unguaranteed residual. Thus, the lessee will carry the capital lease at a lower value than the lessor who must include the unguaranteed residual as part of his net lease receivable. However, if the lease contains a bargain purchase option which by definition is included as part of the minimum lease payments, the lessee will capitalize the asset at the same value as the lessor's net investment in the lease as long as lessee and lessor use the same discount rate.

Accounting for Lessee Lease Payments

Following is an example of lessee accounting for capital lease payments using the "effective interest rate method." The example makes use of the information given immediately above under determination of the implicit interest rate.

Requirements—Separate the aforementioned lease payments into principal and interest. The asset was capitalized on the lessee's books at $9,000, representing the present value of the minimum lease payments discounted at 31.06 percent. The unguaranteed residual was treated as a bargain purchase option.

SOLUTION

Time Period	Remaining Lease Payable	x	Implicit Rate	=	Interest Charge	-	Payments	=	Principal Reduction
0	$ 9,000	x	N/A	=	0	-	$ 4,000*	=	$ 4,000
1	5,000	x	.3106	=	$ 1,553	-	2,000	=	447
2	4,553	x	.3106	=	1,414	-	2,000	=	586
3	3,967	x	.3106	=	1,232	-	2,000	=	768
4	3,199	x	.3106	=	994	-	2,000	=	1,006
5	2,193	x	.3106	=	681	-	2,000	=	1,319
6	874	x	.3106	=	271	-	0	=	(271)
7	1,145	x	.3106	=	355	-	1,500	=	1,145
					$ 6,500		$ 15,500		$ 9,000

* 2 payments in advance.

LESSOR ACCOUNTING AND REPORTING
FOR CAPITAL LEASES

Initial Classification

The lessor must classify capital leases as either sales-type or direct financing. A sales-type lease gives rise to gross profit on the lease in addition to interest included in the lease payments. Sales-type leases normally result when a manufacturing company uses leasing as a means of marketing its products. A direct financing lease has interest included in its lease payments but has no gross profit. Most third party lessors direct financing leases. First a sales-type capital lease will be analyzed followed by a direct financing lease.

Initial Accounting for a Sales-type Capital Lease

Five journal entries are required to record the sale of an asset under a sales-type capital lease agreement. The required journal entries will be reviewed followed by an example of accounting for a sales-type lease.

Gross Investment Journal Entry

Debit an account titled "gross investment in lease" for an amount equal to the total of the minimum lease payments plus any unguaranteed residual value accruing to the benefit of the lessor. Executory costs and any related profit should be deducted from the minimum lease payments before establishing their total. The credit corresponding to the investment debit is an offset to sales revenue for the fair market value of the asset, and the remaining balance is credited to unearned interest income. Unearned interest income is a contra-account to the gross investment in lease account. The difference between these two accounts is known as the net investment in the lease and represents the amount shown on the balance sheet as investments in leases. The journal entry is summarized below:

Gross Investment in Lease	XXX		(Minimum Lease Payments plus unguaranteed residual)
Sales Revenue		XXX	(FMV Asset)
Unearned Interest Income		XXX	(Balance due lessor)

Cost of Sales Journal Entry—debit cost of goods sold for the assets cost and credit inventory to remove it from the balance sheet. The journal entry is summarized below:

Cost of Goods Sold	XXX		(Assets Cost)
Inventory or A/P		XXX	(Assets Cost)

Unguaranteed Residual Adjusting Entry—debit sales revenue and credit cost of goods sold in an amount equal to the present value (discounted at the implicit interest rate in the lease) of the unguaranteed residual. The theoretical justification for this adjusting entry is that since this portion of the asset was never sold (the asset reverts to the lessor at the end of the lease), it should neither be recorded as revenue nor as a cost. The entry is as follows:

Sales Revenue   XXX   (P.V. unguaranteed residual)
    Cost of Goods Sold   XXX   (P.V. unguaranteed residual)

Investment Tax Credit Journal Entry—debit income taxes payable and credit unearned interest income (from Step one) in an amount equal to the investment tax credit retained and expected to be earned by the lessor. The net effect of this journal entry is to defer the investment tax credit so that it will be taken into earnings over the life of the lease rather than being shown as immediate income. Unearned income, due to lessor's retaining of the ITC, will always increase by an amount equal to the ITC. The ITC journal entry is:

Income Taxes Payable   XXX
    Unearned Interest Income   XXX

Initial Direct Costs—debit cost of goods sold or an operating expense account and credit cash or expense payable for any initial direct costs incurred in setting up the lease. These costs are not deferred over the life of the lease. The entry for direct costs is:

Cost of Goods Sold or Direct Costs   XXX
    Cash or Accounts Payable   XXX

Sales-type Lease Example—

Assumptions:

Asset Cost———————————	$ 9,000	
Lease Payments———————	$ 2,500	per year for seven years beginning at the inception of the lease
Legal Fees—————————	$ 500	Initial direct costs
Unguaranteed Residual————	$ 1,000	end of the seventh year
Fair Market Value——————	$ 12,457	
Investment Tax Credit—————	$ 900	10% of cost and retained by lessor

Implicit Interest Rate——————18 percent
PV of annuity due, seven payments at 18%——4.4976
PV of one, seven periods, at 18%——.313

Proper accounting and recording for the above lease would result in the following entries:

1. *Gross Investment Journal Entry*—includes the minimum lease payments (excluding executory costs and any related profit) plus an unguaranteed residual value accruing to the benefit of the lessor.

Seven payments x $ 2,500 = $ 17,500
Residual Value   +   1,000
                                _____
                               $ 18,500

Gross Investment in Lease $ 18,500
    Sales Revenue $ 12,457 (Fair Market Value)
    Unearned Interest Income $ 6,043

2. *Cost of Sales Journal Entry*—represented by the assets inventory carrying value prior to the capital lease transaction in the amount of $ 9,000.

Cost of Goods Sold $ 9,000
    Inventory $ 9,000

3. *Unguaranteed Residual Adjusting Entry*—computed at its present value: .313 x $ 1,000 = $ 313.

Sales Revenue $ 313
    Cost of Goods Sold $ 313

After this adjusting entry, sales revenue and cost of sales will have the following values:

a. *Sales Revenue*—the present value of the minimum lease payments and any investment tax credit, or the assets FMV—PV of the unguaranteed residual.

4.4976 x $ 2,500 = $ 11,244
1.0   x ITC $ 900 +   900
                        _____
                       $ 12,144   or

$ 12,457 − (.313 x 1,000) = $ 12,144

b. *Cost of Sales*—the asset cost or carrying amount of the leased property less the present value of any unguaranteed residual value accruing to the benefit of the lessor.

$ 9,000 − (.313 x $ 1,000) = $ 8,687

4. *Investment Tax Credit Journal Entry*—based on ten percent of the assets cost (10% of $ 9,000 = $ 900) and is only journalized when retained by the lessor.

Taxes Payable $ 900
    Unearned Interest Income $ 900

5. *Initial Direct Costs Entry*—assuming the only initial direct costs were attorney's legal fees, the entry would be:

Costs of Goods Sold or Direct Expenses $ 500
    Cash or Accounts Payable $ 500

6. After all journal entries are complete, the unearned interest income account balance could be checked for accuracy by taking the gross investment ("a" above) less the *fair market value* of the asset reduced by any investment tax

credit. Or, the gross investment less the combined present values of the components of the gross investment.

a. $ 18,500 – (FMV of $ 12,457 – ITC or 900) = $ 6,943 or

b. $ 18,500 – PV of payments & residual
   PV Computation:
   $ 2,500 x 4.497 = $ 11,244
   $ 1,000 x .313 =   313
                             11,557

   $ 18,500 – $ 11,557 = $ 6,943

7. Also, after all journal entries have been posted the *net investment in the lease* would be determined as the gross investment less the unearned income.
   $ 18,500 – $ 6,943 = $ 11,557

8. A "T" Account summary of the above entries follows:

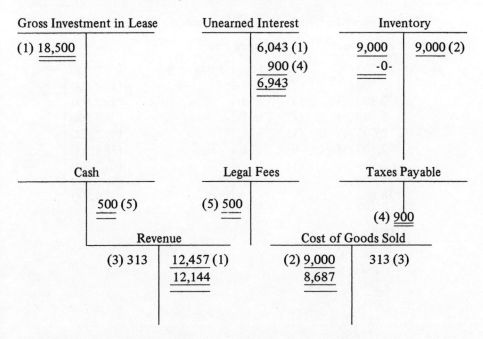

Gross Investment in Lease	Unearned Interest	Inventory
(1) 18,500	6,043 (1)	9,000 9,000 (2)
	900 (4)	-0-
	6,943	

Cash	Legal Fees	Taxes Payable
500 (5)	(5) 500	(4) 900

Revenue	Cost of Goods Sold
(3) 313 12,457 (1)	(2) 9,000 313 (3)
12,144	8,687

9. The lease payments received by the lessor would be accounted for using the "effective interest method" described under lessee capital lease accounting above. The effective interest rate method requires lease payments to be separated into principal and interest. The interest is the product of the *implicit*

interest rate multiplied by the *remaining net investment* in the lease (gross lease investment less unearned income adjusted for any previous principal reductions). Below is a summary of the computations and "T" Account results amortizing the lease payments received by the lessor.

a. Computations:

No interest charge on intial $2,500 lease payment

Lease/Rec.		Lease Pmt.		Unearned Int.		Earned Int.		Rate		Interest
1) ($ 18,500	–	$ 2,500	–	$ 6,943	+	-0-)	x	.18	=	$ 1,630
2) ($ 18,500	–	$ 5,000	–	$ 6,943	+	$ 1,630)	x	.18	=	$ 1,474
3) ($ 18,500	–	$ 7,500	–	$ 6,943	+	$ 3,104)	x	.18	=	$ 1,289
4) ($ 18,500	–	$ 10,000	–	$ 6,943	+	$ 4,393)	x	.18	=	$ 1,071
5) ($ 18,500	–	$ 12,500	–	$ 6,943	+	$ 5,464)	x	.18	=	$ 815
6) ($ 18,500	–	$ 15,000	–	$ 6,943	+	$ 6,279)	x	.18	=	$ 511
7) ($ 18,500	–	$ 17,500	–	$ 6,943	+	$ 6,790)	x	.18	=	$ 153

TOTAL $ 6,943

b. T-Account results of payment amortization.

Gross Investment in Lease		Unearned Revenue		Cash	
18,500	2,500 (0)	(1) 1,630	6,943	(0) 2,500	
	2,500 (1)	(2) 1,474		(1) 2,500	
	2,500 (2)	(3) 1,289		(2) 2,500	
	2,500 (3)	(4) 1,071		(3) 2,500	
	2,500 (4)	(5) 815		(4) 2,500	
	2,500 (5)	(6) 511		(5) 2,500	
	2,500 (6)	(7) 153		(6) 2,500	
	1,000 (7)	6,943	6,943	(7) 1,000	
	18,500		-0-	18,500	

Interest Revenue	
	1,630 (1)
	1,474 (2)
	1,289 (3)
	1,071 (4)
	815 (5)
	511 (6)
	153 (7)
	6,943

Initial Accounting For A Direct Financing Lease

Direct financing capital leases are accounted for in almost the same manner as the sales-type capital lease with the exception of one additional journal entry and the deletion of two entries. This extra journal entry deals with initial direct costs. FASB 13 requires that "initial direct cost shall be charged against income as incurred and a portion of the unearned income equal to the initial direct costs shall be recognized as income in the same period."[1] Therefore, the additional journal entry would require a debit to unearned interest income and a credit to cost of goods or sales revenue in an amount equal to the initial direct costs.

Unearned Interest Income   XXX
      Cost of Goods Sold or Sales Revenue   XXX

The two deleted entries are 1) the Cost of Sales Journal Entry, omitted since it is assumed no sale took place—rather, the leasing company has made a direct financing loan (lease), and 2) the Unguaranteed Residual Value adjusting entry which is omitted for the same reason. A slight modification is also made to the Gross Investment Journal Entry wherein the credit for the fair market value of the leased asset is credited to inventory rather than sales revenue because again a loan has transpired rather than a sale.

Direct Financing Lease Example

Assumptions:

Asset Cost———————————	$ 12,286	
Lease Payments—————————	$ 2,500	per year for seven years beginning at the inception of the lease.
Legal Fees—————————————	$ 500	
Unguaranteed Residual———————	$ 1,000	
Fair Market Value—————————	$ N/A	same as cost.
Investment Tax Credit————————	$ 1,229	10% of cost
Implicit Interest Rate———————	18 percent	

PV of an annuity due, seven payments at 18%——4.4976
PV of one, seven periods, at 18%——.313

Proper accounting for the above lease would result in the following journal entries:

1. *Gross Investment Journal Entry*—which includes the minimum lease payments (excluding executory costs and related profit) plus any unguaranteed residual value accruing to the benefit of the lessor.

---

[1] Statement of Financial Accounting Standards, No. 13. Accounting for Leases November 1976, page 20, Financial Accounting Standards Board Publications Division, High Ridge Park, Stamford, Connecticut 06905

Seven payments x $2,500 = $17,500 Unearned Interest Income
Unguaranteed Residual
Value   + $ 1,000
                                   $18,500
Gross Investment in Lease $18,500
       Inventory or A/P $12,286
       Unearned Interest Income $ 6,214 ($18,500 – $12,286)

2. *Cost of Sales Journal Entry*—Not Applicable.
3. *Unguaranteed Residual Adjusting Entry*—Not Applicable.
4. *Investment Tax Credit Journal Entry*—based on ten percent of the assets cost (10% of $12,286 = $1,229) and is only journalized when it is retained by the lessor.

    Taxes Payable $1,229
      Unearned Interest Income $1,229

5. *Initial Direct Costs Entry*—assuming the only initial direct costs were attorney's legal fees, the entry would be:

    Initial Direct Expenses $500
      Cash or Accounts Payable $500

6. *Initial Direct Costs Adjusting Entry*—requires that a portion of the unearned interest income be recognized as an offsetting revenue against the initial direct costs as follows:

    Unearned Interest Income $500
      Sales Revenue $500

7. After all journal entries are complete, the unearned interest income account balance could be checked for accuracy by taking the gross investment ("a" above) less (1) the *COST* of the asset reduced by any investment tax credit, less (2) any initial direct costs. Or, the gross investment less the combined present values of the components of the gross investment (payments and the residual).

a. $18,500 – (Cost $12,286 – ITC $1,239) –D/C $500 = $6,943

or

b. $18,500 –PV of payments and residual
    P.V. Computation:
    $2,500 x 4.4976   = $11,244
    $1,000 x .313   =   313
                 $11,557

$18,500 – $11,557 = $ 6,943

8. Also, after all journal entries have been posted the *net investment in the lease* would be determined as the gross investment in the lease less the unearned income.

$18,500 - $6,943 = $11,557

9. A "T" Account summary of the above entries follows:

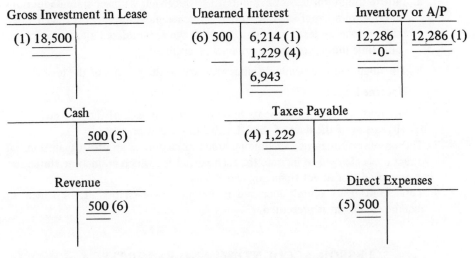

Gross Investment in Lease		Unearned Interest		Inventory or A/P	
(1) 18,500		(6) 500	6,214 (1)	12,286	12,286 (1)
			1,229 (4)	-0-	
			6,943		

Cash		Taxes Payable	
500 (5)		(4) 1,229	

Revenue		Direct Expenses	
500 (6)		(5) 500	

(Journal entries two and three were omitted since they were not applicable.)

10. Lease payments would be amortized exactly in the same manner as described for the sales-type lease.
11. Computation of the implicit interest rate in the lease which is used in separating lease payments into principal and interest and in determining the present value of the unguaranteed residual (step three above) is determined as follows:

Time	0	1	2	3	4	5	6	7
Inflows:	+2,500	+2,500	+2,500	+2,500	+2,500	+2,500	+2,500	
Unguaranteed Residual								+1,000

ITC   +1,229
Cost   −12,286
Direct Cost −500

Net
Outflow   −9,057

IRR = 18.0038%

Disclosure Requirements

Disclosure requirements for sales-type and direct financing leases:

1. The components of the net investment in sales-type and direct financing leases as of the date of each balance sheet presented:

    a. Future minimum lease payments to be received, with separate deductions for (i) amounts representing executory costs, including any profits included in the minimum lease payments, and (ii) the accumulated allowance for uncollectible minimum lease payments receivable.

    b. The unguaranteed residual values accruing to the benefit of the lessor.

    c. Unearned income.

2. Future minimum lease payments to be received for each of the five succeeding fiscal years as of the date of the latest balance sheet presented.

3. The amount of unearned income included in income as an offset against initial direct costs charged to income for each period for which an income statement is presented (for direct financing leases only).

4. Total contingent rentals included in income for each period for which an income statement is presented.

LESSOR ACCOUNTING AND REPORTING
FOR OPERATING LEASES

Leased Property Reporting and Depreciation

The leased property shall be reported in the balance sheet with or near property, plant, and equipment (fixed assets-tangible).

The property shall be depreciated following the lessor's normal depreciation policy which allows for sinking fund or annuity-type depreciation previously explained in chapter 6. The accumulated depreciation should be deducted from the investment in the leased property, the difference of which represents the net investment in the leased assets. When annuity type depreciation is used, not only is gross profit properly stated on the income statement but the resulting net investment in the lease is more indicative of the unrecouped cost of the leased asset. Use of other than annuity depreciation understates income in the early years of the lease and understates the unrecouped investment in leased equipment. In my opinion the Financial Accounting Standards Board (FASB) was remiss in not requiring this depreciation method. Note that capital lease accounting per FASB 13 in effect accomplishes the same result as annuity depreciation through the use of the "effective interest rate method" of recognizing interest.

Rental Payments

Rent shall be reported on the accrual basis which requires lease payments to be recognized as earned when they are due according to the lease provisions, whether they have been received or not. Most lease companies, however, report on a cash basis to the IRS and to management. Cash-basis accounting requires reporting lease payments as earned only when received.

If rentals vary in amount from period to period they should be recognized as income on a straight line basis unless another systematic and rational basis is more indicative of use benefits derived from the lease investment.

Initial Direct Costs

Initial direct costs when material in amount are to be deferred and allocated to income in proportion to the recognition of rental income. In my opinion, such deferral of costs is nonsense. If the FASB understood the investment nature of a lease (whether capital or operating), they would allow direct costs to be considered part of the initial cost of the lease investment. Then an internal rate of return (implicit interest rate) could be calculated similar to the FASB requirements for capital leases. Use of the implicit rate coupled with annuity type depreciation would allow initial direct costs to be considered in proper investment perspective.

Disclosure

Operating leases require the following disclosure of information:

1. The cost and carrying amount, if different, of property on lease or held for leasing by major classes of property according to nature or function, and the amount of accumulated depreciation in totals as of the date of the latest balance sheet presented.
2. Minimum future rentals on noncancelable leases as of the date of the latest balance sheet presented, in the aggregate and for each of the five succeeding fiscal years.
3. Total contingent rentals included in income for each period for which an income statement is presented.
4. A general description of the lessor's leasing agreements.

More complex accounting questions regarding capital leases could require reference to *FASB Statement No. 13* and other lease-related FASB statements and interpretations.

10

Analysis and Accounting for Leveraged Leases and ———— Real Estate Leases ————

Leveraged leases are accounted for and analyzed differently than nonleveraged leases. The purpose of this chapter is to describe the unique analytical techniques employed in leveraged-lease analysis followed with an explanation of FASB Statement No. 13 accounting requirements for leveraged leases. Real estate leases also have unique accounting rules and analytical characteristics which will be discussed at the end of the chapter.

LEVERAGED LEASE ANALYSIS

Leveraged leases are analyzed somewhat differently than nonleveraged leases primarily because of their long terms (ten to thirty years) and unique after-tax cash inflows which are usually positive in the initial years of the lease and then become negative (outflows) in the later part of the lease (due to the lessor's having used up the tax benefits of ITC, accelerated depreciation, and interest expense). At or near the end of the leveraged lease, the cash flow frequently becomes positive once again because the underlying loan has been paid off prior to the termination of the lease or a residual value becomes available to the lessor.

The unique cash flow pattern of the typical leveraged lease causes three problems that must be dealt with in leveraged-lease analysis:

1. Multiple Negative Cash Inflows
2. Debt-Equity Ratio Optimization
3. Double Financial Leverage: Recourse and Nonrecourse Debt

In order to more fully understand the problems confronting the lease analyst, an example of a leveraged lease will be presented. This example is the same one shown in FASB Statement 13, Appendix E, Schedule 1 and Schedule 2.

LEVERAGED LEASE EXAMPLE

Terms and Assumptions

Cost of leased asset (equipment)	$1,000,000
Lease term	Fifteen years, dating from January 1, 1975
Lease rental payments	$90,000 per year (payable last day of each year)
Residual value	$200,000 estimated to be realized one year after lease termination . . .
Financing: Capital investment by lessor	$400,000 (Equity $160,000, Recourse Debt $240,000 with five percent after-tax interest).[1]
Long-term nonrecourse debt	$600,000, bearing interest at nine percent and repayable in annual installments (on last day of each year) of $74,435.30
Depreciation allowable to lessor for income tax purposes	Seven-year ADR life using double-declining-balance method for the first two years (with the half-year convention election applied in the first year) and sum-of-years digits method for remaining life, depreciated to $100,000 salvage value
Lessor's income tax rate (federal and state)	50.4 percent (assumed to continue in existence throughout the term of the lease)
Investment tax credit	Ten percent of equipment cost or $100,000 (realized by the lessor on last day of first year of lease)
Initial direct costs	For simplicity, initial direct costs have not been included in the illustration.

---

[1] Information within parentheses added by authors.

CASH FLOW ANALYSIS BY YEARS

Year	Gross lease rental and residual value	Depreciation (for income tax purposes)	Loan interest payments	Income tax credits (charges)	Loan principal payments	Annual cash flow (col. 1-3 +5-6+7)
0	—	—	—	—	—	$(400,000)
1	$ 90,000	$ 142,857	$ 54,000	$153,856[2]	$ 20,435	169,421
2	90,000	244,898	52,161	104,358	22,274	119,923
3	90,000	187,075	50,156	74,204	24,279	89,769
4	90,000	153,061	47,971	55,960	26,464	71,525
5	90,000	119,048	45,589	37,617	28,846	53,182
6	90,000	53,061	42,993	3,051	31,442	18,616
7	90,000	—	40,163	(25,118)	34,272	(9,553)
8	90,000	—	37,079	(26,672)	37,357	(11,108)
9	90,000	—	33,717	(28,367)	40,719	(12,803)
10	90,000	—	30,052	(30,214)	44,383	(14,649)
11	90,000	—	26,058	(32,227)	48,378	(16,663)
12	90,000	—	21,704	(34,421)	52,732	(18,857)
13	90,000	—	16,957	(36,813)	57,478	(21,248)
14	90,000	—	11,785	(39,420)	62,651	(23,856)
15	90,000	—	6,145	(42,263)	68,290	(26,698)
16	200,000	100,000	—	(50,400)	—	149,600
Totals	$1,550,000	$1,000,000	$516,530	$(16,869)	$600,000	$166,601
				$ 83,131[2]		

[2]Includes $100,000 investment tax credit.

Multiple Negative Cash Inflows

The after-tax cash proceeds available to a lessor under a leveraged lease generally become negative (net outflows) as soon as the lessor has used up the tax shield made available early in the lease from accelerated depreciation, ITC, and interest expense. Note in the above example that cash flows were negative in the seventh through the fifteenth year. The new tax act of 1981 will exacerbate the negative inflow problem since most leased assets will now be fully depreciated in five years. Negative cash flows create several problems in lease analysis: (1) several internal rates of return might exist due to the changing signs of the cash inflows and (2) money set aside to meet cash outflow requirements probably earns less than the normal internal rate of return in the lease.

There are four basic methods for dealing with negative cash flows in leveraged-lease analysis:

1. Ignore the fact that there might be multiple solutions to the internal rate-of-return computation by choosing the closest *positive IRR* to the lessee's cost of capital. Although this method is expedient, it is nevertheless deficient because the chosen IRR might be erroneous, and the IRR improperly assumes that the funds set aside to provide for negative outflows were invested at the IRR which probably is in excess of what liquid funds could earn. Therefore, few analysts employ standard IRR analysis for leveraged leases. Computation of the IRR for the preceding example would be accomplished with a calculator using the following entries:

Amount	CHS	g	CF
$ 400,000	CHS	g	CF_0
169,421		g	CF_j
119,923		g	CF_j
89,769		g	CF_j
71,525		g	CF_j
53,182		g	CF_j
18,616		g	CF_j
9,553	CHS	g	CF_j
11,108	CHS	g	CF_j
12,803	CHS	g	CF_j
14,649	CHS	g	CF_j
16,663	CHS	g	CF_j
18,857	CHS	g	CF_j
21,248	CHS	g	CF_j
23,856	CHS	g	CF_j

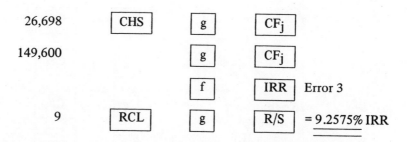

2. Use *modified IRR* where negative cash flows are discounted at a "liquid investment rate" rather than the higher IRR rate. This method was explained in chapter 5. The IRR obtained from this method will be much more conservative than the unadjusted IRR computed above in the first method. In fact, this second method may be overly conservative. It is doubtful that a lessor would set aside an amount at the inception of a long-term leveraged lease to provide for future cash outflows. It is more reasonable to assume that cash would be set aside from future positive inflows in the few months or years prior to the negative outflows. The next method to be discussed employs this more reasonable assumption. The modified IRR using an assumed three percent "liquid investment rate" which assumes a liquidity fund set aside at the inception of the lease would be calculated as follows:

a. Compute present value of negative cash flows using three percent as a discount rate:

3	$\boxed{\text{i}}$	
0	$\boxed{\text{g}}$	CF_j
6	$\boxed{\text{g}}$	N_j
9,553	$\boxed{\text{g}}$	$\boxed{\text{CF}_\text{j}}$
11,108	$\boxed{\text{g}}$	$\boxed{\text{CF}_\text{j}}$
12,803	$\boxed{\text{g}}$	$\boxed{\text{CF}_\text{j}}$
14,649	$\boxed{\text{g}}$	$\boxed{\text{CF}_\text{j}}$
16,663	$\boxed{\text{g}}$	$\boxed{\text{CF}_\text{j}}$
18,857	$\boxed{\text{g}}$	$\boxed{\text{CF}_\text{j}}$

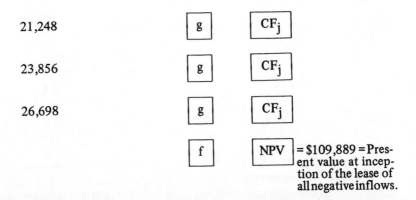

b. Add the present value of the negative cash flows, $109,889 to the initial $400,000 cost of the lease which results in a total of $509,889. Using this adjusted total at the inception of the lease we are now ready to compute the modified IRR. Note that adding the present value of the outflows to the lessor's net investment in the lease is the same as adding a sinking fund to the lessor's investment for the purpose of providing for future negative cash flows.

c. Compute the modified IRR as follows:

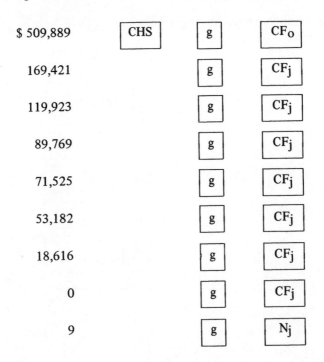

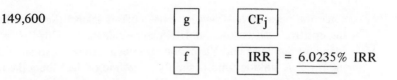

149,600   [g]   [CF$_j$]

[f]   [IRR] = <u>6.0235%</u> IRR

3. Use the *Standard Sinking Fund Method* with a zero percent reinvestment rate. This method assumes that any negative cash flows in a lease will be funded out of the immediately preceeding positive cash flows generated by the same lease. Thus, negative outflows are not added to the cost of the leased equipment as in method two above; rather, the unadjusted negative cash flows are offset with preceding positive cash flows as shown below:

Year	Positive Inflows	Negative Inflows	Offsets	Balance After Offset
1	$169,421			$169,421
2	119,923			119,923
3	89,769		# 15 (12,112) bal.	77,657
4	71,525		# 12 (11,835)# 13(21,248)	0
			# 14 (23,856)# 15(14,586)	
5	53,182		# 8 (2045)# 9 (12,803) # 10 (14,649)	0
			# 11 (16,663)# 12 (7022)	
6	18,616		# 7 (9,553) # 8 (9063)	0
7		(9,553)		0
8		(11,108)		0
9		(12,803)		0
10		(14,649)		0
11		(16,663)		0
12		(18,857)		0
13		(21,248)		0
14		(23,856)		0
15		(26,698)		0
16	149,600			149,600

Once the negative outflows have been offset against the immediately preceeding positive cash inflows, an IRR can be calculated. This IRR is known as the Standard Sinking Fund Yield, and assumes a zero reinvestment rate on the sinking fund. A sinking fund is simply a method of describing the funds set aside in the third, fourth, fifth, and sixth year of the above lease to provide for outflows in the seventh through the fifteenth year. Note that the offsetting sinking funds were not assumed to be invested and therefore no interest earnings were included in the analysis. Given the resulting positive balances as shown above, in the last column, the Standard Sinking Fund Yield can be calculated as follows:

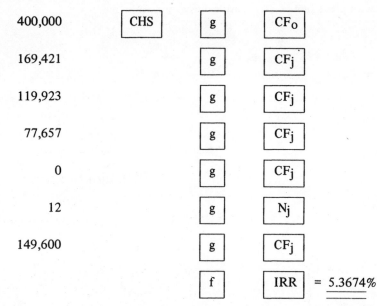

400,000	CHS	g	CF_0
169,421		g	CF_j
119,923		g	CF_j
77,657		g	CF_j
0		g	CF_j
12		g	N_j
149,600		g	CF_j
		f	IRR	= 5.3674%

This yield, of course, is the most conservative yield thus far computed since it was assumed that the sinking fund cash flows were not invested during the waiting period prior to being offset against the negative cash inflows. In general, it would be assumed that sinking funds could be invested at some minimum safe reinvestment rate. Such rates are generally assumed to be low after-tax rates that could be expected to be earned on short-term liquid investments. Three percent is often used for after-tax sinking fund analysis.

4. Use the *Standard Sinking Fund Method* with a three percent reinvestment rate. This method assumes that any negative cash flows in a lease will be funded out of the immediately preceeding positive cash flows. However, unlike method three above, this method assumes that the funds, which were set aside in the years where the lease has positive cash inflows, will earn interest at an assumed three percent reinvestment rate (other rates could be used depending upon the lessor's expectations).

The method works as follows:

a. Beginning with the first negative inflow, discount it at three percent for one period and offset the resulting present value figure against the immediately preceeding positive inflow. In the example, the first negative inflow is $9,553 which , discounted, is $9,275. This $9,275 is offset against the sixth year's positive $18,616 inflow.

b. Take the next negative inflow, discount two periods, and offset also against the first positive inflow. In the present example, the next negative outflow is $11,108 which, discounted for two periods, equals $10,470. However, only $9,341 of this amount is available to be offset against the sixth year's positive $15,616 inflow since $9,275 was used up previously. Thus, $1,129 ($10,470 - $9,341) represents excess funds that must be carried to the next period when a positive inflow is available for offset. In this case the $1,129 can be carried back to year five. However, the $1,129 must first be discounted for one additional year since it will be set aside three years prior to its use in the lease. The discounted amount is $1,096.

c. Repeat the above process with the next negative cash flow, keeping in mind the proper number of periods to discount. For example, the next negative cash flow of $12,803 occurs in the ninth period and its present value must be offset against the positive cash flow of the fifth period. Thus the negative cash flow of $12,803 must be discounted four periods (years nine through five).

d. Once all the present values of the negative outflows have been determined and offset against positive cash flows, the Standard Sinking Fund Method with a three percent reinvestment rate can be completed. The sinking fund calculations and offsets are described below.

Period	Negative Cash Inflow	X	3% PV Factor	=	PV	Discount Periods		Period Offset Against
7	$ 9,553	X	.9709	=	$ 9,275	1		6
8	11,108	X	.9426	=	10,470	2	($ 9,341 limit)	6
8	(10,470-9341)	X	.9709	=	1,096	2+1		5
9	12,803	X	.8885	=	11,375	4		5
10	14,649	X	.8626	=	12,636	5		5
11	16,663	X	.8375	=	13,955	6		5
12	18,857	X	.8131	=	15,333	7	($ 14,120 limit)	5
12	(15,333-14,120)	X	.9709	=	1,177	7+1		4
13	21,248	X	.7664	=	16,285	9		4
14	23,856	X	.7441	=	17,751	10		4
15	26,698	X	.7224	=	19,287	11		4

e. Once the above offsets have been made, the resulting net cash flows are available for futher lease analysis:

Year	Unadjusted Cash Flow	Sinking Fund Offsets	Adjusted inflow (outflow)
1	169,421		169,421
2	119,923		119,923
3	89,769		89,769
4	71,525	−1,177−16,285−17,751−19,287 ◄──	17,025
5	53,182	──► −1,096−11,375−12,636−13,955−14,120	0
6	18,616	−9,275−9,341 ◄─┐	0
7	−9,553	9,553 ───────┤	0
8	−11,108	┌─ 11,108 ─────┘	0
9	−12,803	├─ 12,803	0
10	−14,649	├─ 14,649	0
11	−16,663	├─ 16,663	0
12	−18,857	└─ 18,857 ──┐	0
13	−21,248	21,248 ──┤	0
14	−23,856	23,856 ──┤	0
15	−26,698	26,698 ──┘	0
16	149,600		0
			149,600

f. Given the adjusted cash inflows in "d" above, the IRR Standard Sinking Fund Yield can be calculated as follows:

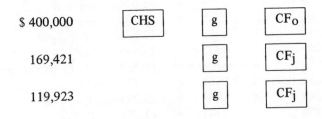

$ 400,000	CHS	g	CF₀
169,421		g	CFj
119,923		g	CFj

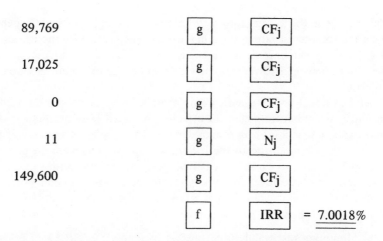

89,769	g	CF$_j$
17,025	g	CF$_j$
0	g	CF$_j$
11	g	N$_j$
149,600	g	CF$_j$
	f	IRR	= <u>7.0018%</u>

The Standard Sinking Fund Yield computed on the basis of a three percent reinvestment rate is perhaps the best yield to use in leveraged lease analysis since it is not overly conservative, like the previous methods discussed, nor unduly liberal like the multiple investment or separate phases method required by *FASB Statement No. 13* to be discussed later in this chapter.

Debt to Equity Ratio Optimization

In a leveraged lease from an accounting point of view (*FASB Statement No. 13*), earnings are booked at a level, after-tax rate of return on the net lease investment in the years in which the net investment is positive. Once the lessor has recovered his initial investment (early in a leveraged lease due to tax benefits), his investment becomes negative and therefore no book earnings will be shown until the investment once again becomes positive. This technique of reporting earnings is known as the "separate phase" or "multiple investment" method of accounting for leveraged leases and is required by *FASB Statement No. 13*. Since book earnings during the term of the lease are shown only in certain years, a firm's earnings per share will also fluctuate to reflect the omission of earnings during years when the net investment is negative. In general, it must be assumed that management would want to have a certain minimum amount of net income reported by a lease for as many years as possible during the lease. Given this, there will be an optimum amount of debt in relation to equity that will achieve this goal. Surprisingly, beyond this optimal point, as the quantity of debt increases, economic return on investment increases while book yield decreases. Book return decreases because with a fixed rental payment, as the amount of debt increases so does the proportion of the fixed rental that must be allocated to service the debt. Economic yield, however, will increase due to the increased financial leverage in the lease as long as the after-tax cost of interest on the debt is less than the after-tax interest rate implicit in the lease. Therefore, even though economic yield might not be maximized, management might choose a debt percentage less than the ninety percent IRS maximum simply to meet a minimum reported net income objective.

An additional point regarding debt structuring: Not only is the amount of debt an important structuring element affecting reported lease net income, but also the amortization schedule. For example, once the lessor's net investment has become negative then it might be to the lessor's advantage to increase the payment of debt principal in order to cause the net investment to become positive sooner. Once the net investment is positive, accounting income can once again be reported.

The most advantageous debt-equity ratio is therefore a function of many factors including the following:

1. Minimum Acceptable Reported Net Income per FASB 13
2. Length of Time Income Is Reported
3. Debt Interest Rate Cost
4. Debt Repayment Schedule
5. Overall Lease Yield
6. Tax Benefits Realizable by Lessor
7. Cash Flow Requirements of lessor

From a practical viewpoint, how does a lessor determine the optimal debt-equity ratio? Unfortunately, the FASB reporting requirements for a leveraged lease are so complex they require a computer to determine reported net income for any given year. Therefore, debt optimization is generally determined by the lessor through use of an advanced lease analysis computer program such as that offered by CLEASE. The Chase Lease Evaluation/Analysis System was developed by the Chase Manhattan Bank and has as one of its many features the "generation of 'optimal' debt structures. . . the ability to compute rentals and debt structures necessary to achieve a target rate of return."[3]

Double Financial Leverage: Recourse and Nonrecourse Debt

In general, leveraged leases have two levels of financial leverage: (1) the nonrecourse portion that cannot exceed ninety percent of the total lease per IRS requirements and (2) the full recourse debt portion of the lessors capital that has been invested in the lease. It is assumed that most leasing companies are leveraged with recourse debt to greater or lesser degrees. The existence of two levels of debt in a leveraged lease makes the computation of after-tax return on equity difficult.

---

[3]"Lease Evaluation The CLEASE Way," Leasing Digest, June 1980, pages 10-12 written by Howard K. Weber, Second Vice President, Chase Manhattan Service Corporation, 1 New York Plaza, New York, N.Y. 10051, Tel. (212) 676-5855.

The difficulty encountered with two tiers of debt is best explained by reference to the preceding lease example. At the end of the first year, the lease company will receive the following revenues:

1. Gross Lease Revenue	$ 90,000
2. Investment Tax Credit	$ 100,000
3. Income Tax Refund or Benefit	$ 53,856
Total Revenues	$ 243,856

The total revenue of $243,856 will be disbursed as follows:

1. Principal Payment on the nonrecourse debt	$ 20,435
2. Interest on the nonrecourse debt	$ 54,000
3. Return on investment at the 7.0018% (Standard Sinking Fund Rate, 3% Reinvestment)	$ 28,007
4. Return of Investment	$ 141,414

The return on assets of $28,007 was computed by multiplying the 7.0018% factor by the lessor's total investment of $400,000. The balance of the first year's net cash flow after nonrecourse loan payment and return on investment of $141,414 ($169,421 - $28,007) represents return of investment. The problem confronting the lessor is what proportion of the $141,414 return of capital is to be allocated to return of debt and how much to return of equity. Then, too, how much of the $28,007 return on capital or return on assets should be allocated to equity and how much to debt. The answers to these questions are generally given in any one of three ways:

1. Ignore the fact that the lessor's capital is composed of both debt and equity. Rely strictly on the 7.0018% return on assets (ROA) percentage as the measure of a lease's profitability. If the ROA percentage is greater than the lessor's cost of capital, it is a good lease. However, most analysts want more information than just ROA; they also want return on equity (ROE) information which directly affects evaluation of earnings per share. The next two methods fulfill this need.

2. Assume the underlying $240,000 recourse debt portion of the capital structure is amortized on a straight line, equal payment basis throughout the term of the lease. Amortized evenly over fifteen years at 10.08 percent interest (pretax), this debt requires an annual $31,698 payment. This method can seldom be used since the cash inflows in a leveraged lease are too uneven to support such a debt repayment schedule. Note that years one through four and the end of year sixteen are the only years in which the lease has net cash inflows sufficient to amortize a $31,698 debt repayment.

3. Assume the total invested capital is recouped on an actuarial basis according to the return on invested capital percentage of 7.0018 percent, computed above under the Standard Sinking Fund Method with a three percent reinvest-

ment rate. This very common method of dealing with the recourse debt works as follows:

a. Multiply the Sinking Fund Rate by the unrecouped capital investment at the end of each accounting period. The resulting product represents return on investment which is then subtracted from the period's total cash flow (after deducting the nonrecourse loan payment). The resulting difference represents return of investment. For example:

   1) Return on Investment .070018 X $400,000 = $ <u>28,007</u>

   2) Return of Investment $169,421 - $28,007 = $ <u>141,414</u>

b. Determine the amount of debt and equity that has been paid back. Generally it is assumed that the company's debt-equity ratio will remain unchanged throughout the lease term and therefore the $141,414 return of investment should be split according to the sixty percent to forty percent, debt-equity ratio of the lessor.

   i. Debt 60% of $141,414   = $ <u>84,848</u>

   ii. Equity 40% of $ 141,414 = $ <u>56,566</u>

c. Determine the amount of after-tax interest that was earned on the outstanding debt and deduct this from the total return on investment of $28,007. The amount of interest earned is determined by multiplying the after-tax interest rate, five percent in this case, by the debt outstanding during the year. In this case we assume the total debt outstanding during the entire first year was $240,000 (sixty percent of $400,000). The resulting product of these two factors (.05 X $240,000 = $12,000) represents the interest cost during the year. The interest expense is then deducted from the $28,007 total return on capital, and the resulting difference represents return on equity (ROE) in the amount of $16,007 ($28,007 - $12,000).

d. Repeat steps a, b and c during the ensuing months or years and remember to:

   i. Reduce last year's outstanding debt total by the amount amortized at the end of the year (step "b") before determining the interest expense of the current year. For example, the interest expense during the second year is calculated as follows:

     • $240,000   (1 year debt)
       $-84,848   (1st year amort step b)
       <u>$155,152</u>   (2nd year debt)

     • $155,152   (2nd year debt)
       X   .05   (Int Rate)
       $ 7,758   (2nd year interest)

ii. In years in which there is no ROA cash flow, a special adjustment must be made as follows:

- Calculate the return on investment total for the period and allocate to interest expense and return on equity as described above. However, since no return of *investment* occurred (not to be confused with return *on investment*) due to the zero cash flow, it must be assumed that an additional investment has been made to cover the return on investment just calculated.
- Split the additional investment into its proper debt-equity ratio and add back to the principal of the recourse debt outstanding and to the unrecovered equity.
- An example of this special adjustment occurs in the fifth year of the lease when the sinking fund adjusted cash flow is zero.

    1) Compute total return on investment
       Capital $66,411 X .070018 = $4,650

    2) Allocate return on investment to debt and equity.
       Debt 60% X $4650 = $2,790   Add to outstanding debt.

       Equity 40% X $4650 = $1860   Add to outstanding debt.

e. An example of the complete amortization of the investment in the *FASB Statement No. 13* example is as follows:

1	2	3	4	5	6	7	8
Year	Cash Flow	Return on Invstmt. at 7.0018%	ROE	Interest	Return on Invstmt.	Return of Equity	Return of Debt
1	169,421	28,007	16,007	12,000	141,414	56,566	84,848
2	119,923	18,106	10,348	7,758	101,817	40,727	61,090
3	89,769	10,977	6,274	4,703	78,792	31,517	47,275
4	17,025	5,460	3,121	2,339	11,565	4,626	6,939
5	0	4,650	2,658	1,992	(4,650)	(1,860)	(2,790)
6	0	4,976	2,844	2,132	(4,976)	(1,990)	(2,986)
7	0	5,324	3,043	2,281	(5,324)	(2,130)	(3,194)
8	0	5,697	3,256	2,441	(5,697)	(2,279)	(3,418)
9	0	6,096	3,484	2,612	(6,096)	(2,438)	(3,658)
10	0	6,523	3,728	2,795	(6,523)	(2,609)	(3,914)
11	0	6,979	3,989	2,990	(6,979)	(2,792)	(4,187)
12	0	7,468	4,268	3,200	(7,468)	(3,196)	(4,795)
13	0	7,991	4,567	3,424	(7,991)	(3,196)	(4,795)
14	0	8,550	4,886	3,664	(9,550)	(3,420)	(5,130)
15	0	9,149	5,229	3,920	(9,149)	(3,660)	(5,489)
16	149,600	9,785	5,590	4,195	139,815	55,925	83,890
	$545,738				$400,000	$160,000	$240,000

f. Once an amortization schedule has been made manually (or, preferably, by a computer) the analyst can determine the return on equity percentage of the lease by following these steps:

i. Add the ROE, column four, to the return of equity column seven from the above amortization schedule. The above example results in the following total equity returns:

Year	Return on Equity (4)	+	Return of Equity (7)	=	Total Returns
1	16,007	+	56,566		72,573
2	10,348	+	40,727		51,075
3	6,274	+	31,517		37,791
4	3,121	+	4,626		7,747
5	2,658	+	(1,860)		798
6	2,844	+	(1,990)		854
7	3,043	+	(2,130)		913
8	3,256	+	(2,279)		977
9	3,484	+	(2,438)		1,046
10	3,728	+	(2,609)		1,119
11	3,989	+	(2,792)		1,197
12	4,268	+	(2,987)		1,281
13	4,567	+	(3,196)		1,371
14	4,886	+	(3,420)		1,466
15	5,229	+	(3,660)		1,569
16	5,590	+	55,925		61,515
	83,292		$160,000		$243,292

ii. Compute the Return on Equity IRR Yield using the total return column from above as follows:

$160,000	CHS	g	CF₀

$$\$160,000 \quad \boxed{\text{CHS}} \quad \boxed{\text{g}} \quad \boxed{\text{CF}_0}$$

$$72,573 \quad \quad \boxed{\text{g}} \quad \boxed{\text{CF}_j}$$

$$51,075 \quad \quad \boxed{\text{g}} \quad \boxed{\text{CF}_j}$$

$$37,791 \quad \quad \boxed{\text{g}} \quad \boxed{\text{CF}_j}$$

$$7,747 \quad \quad \boxed{\text{g}} \quad \boxed{\text{CF}_j}$$

$$798 \quad \quad \boxed{\text{g}} \quad \boxed{\text{CF}_j}$$

854	g	CFj
913	g	CFj
977	g	CFj
1,046	g	CFj
1,119	g	CFj
1,197	g	CFj
1,281	g	CFj
1,371	g	CFj
1,466	g	CFj
1,569	g	CFj
61,515	g	CFj
	f	IRR = 10.0045%

A short-cut technique in converting a leveraged lease ROA to an actuarial ROE contains the following steps:

1. Determine the lessor's after-tax borrowing rate by multiplying its recourse borrowing rate times one minus the tax rate.

$$\frac{\text{Debt Cost}}{10.08\%} \times \frac{(1 - t)}{(1 - .504)} = .05$$

2. Determine the weighted average cost of debt by multiplying the after-tax borrowing rate from above, .05, by the lessor's percentage of the capital structure that is debt, 60% in this case.

$$\frac{\text{Debt\%}}{.6} \times \frac{\text{After-tax interest cost}}{.05} = .03$$

3. Deduct the weighted average after-tax cost of debt, .03, from the gross after-tax ROA yield, 7.0018% in this case.

```
  7.0018  ROA
- 3.0000  weighted debt
= 4.0018  weighted ROE
```

4. Convert the weighted ROE into its unweighted ROE counterpart by dividing the weighted ROE, 4.0018%, by the percentage of the lessor's capital structure that is equity, 40%, in this case.

4.0018 ÷ .4 = 10.0045% ROE

Note that 10.0045% ROE is the same calculated previously using the more cumbersome cash flow analysis.

LEVERAGED LEASE ANALYSIS CONCLUSION

Once the analyst has chosen his preferred method of dealing with multiple negative cash inflows, optimized his debt-equity ratio, and finally determined his return on equity under the two-tier debt structure, he will be in a position to know whether the leveraged lease is worth entering into or not. Frequently, the resulting yields from the analysts computations are converted to a pretax basis for the sake of comparison. Conversion to a pretax basis is most readily achieved by dividing the after-tax yield by one minus the tax rate.

A summary of the various after-tax yields discussed above along with their pretax equivalent is given below along with a comment on its preferability.

Analytical Method	Preferability	After-Tax Yield	Pretax Yield
1. Standard Sinking Fund 0% Reinvestment Rate	Overly Conservative Due to 0% Reinvestment Rate Assumption	5.3674%	10.8213%
2. Modified IRR 3% Safe Rate	Too conservative due to the over discounting of negative inflows	6.0235%	12.1442%
3. Standard Sinking Fund 3% Reinvestment Rate	Best overall economic indicator of yield or return on assets (ROA)	7.0018%	14.1165%
4. Multiple Investment Separate Phase	To be discussed in the next section of this chapter. Not a good indicator of ROA	8.6470%	17.4335%
5. Basic IRR (ROA) No adjustments for negative cash inflows.	Improperly overstates yield due to assumption that implicit sinking fund yield is equal to the IRR which is too high for liquid funds	9.2575%	18.6643%

Analytical Method	Preferability	After-Tax Yield	Pretax Yield
6. Basic IRR(ROE) Actuarial Recapture of debt and equity. 5% Debt Cost, with 60% Debt and 40% Equity	Best overall economic indicator of yield or return on equity (ROE)	10.0045%	20.1704%

LEVERAGED LEASE ACCOUNTING

The two primary considerations affecting leveraged lease accounting are (1) balance sheet treatment and (2) the amount of interest earned to be reported on the income statement.

Balance Sheet Treatment

The lessor shall record his investment in a leveraged lease net of the nonrecourse debt. The net of the balances of the following accounts shall represent the initial and continuing investment in leveraged leases:

1. Rentals receivable: net of that portion of the rental applicable to principal and interest on the nonrecourse debt.
2. A receivable for the amount of the investment tax credit to be realized on the transaction.
3. The estimated residual value of the leased asset which shall not exceed the amount estimated at the inception of the lease.
4. Unearned and deferred income consisting of (i) the estimated pretax lease income (or loss) after deducting initial direct costs remaining to be allocated to income over the lease term and (ii) the investment tax credit remaining to be allocated to income over the lease term.[4]

Using the *FASB Statement No. 13* Lease example cited above, the net investment would be determined as follows:

1. Rentals Receivable   15 yrs. x $90,000   = $1,350,000
   Less: Nonrecourse
   Debt Payments   15 yrs. x $74,435   = $1,116,530
                                              $ 233,470

---

[4]*FASB Statement No. 13*, Paragraph 43

Plus	2. Investment Tax Credit Receivable		+	$ 100,000
Plus	3. Estimated Residual Value of Asset		+	$ 200,000
Less	4. Unearned & Deferred Income			
	a. Pretax Lease income	$ 33,470		
	b. Less: Initial Direct Costs	$ 0		
	c. Investment Tax Credit	$100,000		
			($133,470)	
Equals	5. Net Investment in the Lease		$400,000	

The initial journal entry required to set up the lease on the books would be:

1. Rentals Receivable	$233,470	
ITC Receivable	$100,000	
Estimated Residual		
Receivable	$200,000	
Cash		$400,000
Unearned Income		$133,470

The unearned income account is a contra-account offsetting the lease receivable and should not be shown as a liability. The lease receivable net of the contra-account at the inception of the lease stands at $400,000.

Income Statement Treatment

The interest earned on the leveraged lease to be reported should be determined according to the Multiple Investment or Separate Phase Method as required by *FASB Statement No. 13*, Paragraph 44:

"Given the original investment and using the projected cash receipts and disbursements over the term of the lease, the rate of return on the net investment in the years in which it is positive shall be computed. The rate is that rate, which when applied to the net investment in the years in which the net investment is positive, will distribute the net income to those years . . . and is distinct from the *interest rate implicit in the lease*. In each year, whether positive or not, the difference between the net cash flow and the amount of income recognized, if any, shall serve to increase or reduce the net investment balance. The net income recognized shall be composed of three elements: two, pretax lease income (or loss) and investment tax credit, shall be allocated in proportionate amounts from the unearned and deferred income included in net investment, as described . . . (balance sheet treatment above) . . . ; the third element is the tax effect of the pretax lease income (or loss) recognized, which shall be reflected in tax expense for the year. The tax effect of the difference between pretax accounting income (or loss) and taxable income (or loss) for the year shall be charged or credited to deferred taxes."

Using the *FASB Statement No. 13* Lease example, allocation of annual cash flow according to the Multiple Investment Method would result in the following:

ALLOCATION OF ANNUAL CASH FLOW TO INVESTMENT AND INCOME [5]

| | 1 | 2 | 3 | 4 | 5 | 6 | 7 |
| | | | ANNUAL CASH FLOW | | COMPONENTS OF INCOME | | |
Year	Net Inv. Beg. of Yr	Cash Flow	Inv. Share	Income Share [6]	Pretax Income	Taxes	ITC
1	$400,000	$169,421	$134,833	$34,588	$9,929[7]	$(5,004)	$29,663
2	265,167	119,923	96,994	22,929	6,582	(3,317)	19,664
3	168,173	89,769	75,227	14,542	4,174	(2,104)	12,472
4	92,946	71,525	63,488	8,037	2,307	(1,163)	6,893
5	29,458	53,182	50,635	2,547	731	(368)	2,184
6	(21,177)	18,616	18,616				
7	(39,793)	(9,553)	(9,553)				
8	(30,240)	(11,108)	(11,108)				
9	(19,132)	(12,803)	(12,803)				
10	(6,329)	(14,649)	(14,649)				
11	8,320	(16,663)	(17,382)	719	206	(104)	617
12	25,702	(18,857)	(21,079)	2,222	637	(321)	1,906
13	46,781	(21,248)	(25,293)	4,045	1,161	(585)	3,469
14	72,074	(23,856)	(30,088)	6,232	1,789	(902)	5,345
15	102,162	(26,698)	(35,532)	8,834	2,536	(1,278)	7,576
16	137,694	149,600	137,694	11,906	3,418	(1,723)	10,211
Totals		$516,601	$400,000	$116,601	$33,470	$(16,869)	$100,000

[5] *FASB Statement No. 13*, Appendix E, Schedule 3

[6] Lease income is recognized as 8.64% of the unrecovered investment at the beginning of each year in which the net investment is positive. The rate is that rate which when applied to the net investment in the years in which the net investment is positive will distribute the net income (net cash flow) to those years. The rate for allocation used in this Schedule is calculated by a trial and error process. The allocation is calculated based upon an initial estimate of the rate as a starting point. If the total thus allocated to income (column 4) differs under the estimated rate from the net cash flow the estimated rate is increased or decreased, as appropriate, to derive a revised allocation. This process is repeated until a rate is selected which develops a total amount allocated to income that is precisely equal to the net cash flow. As a practical matter, a computer program is used to calculate Schedule 3 under successive iterations until the correct rate is determined.

[7] $\dfrac{34,588}{116,601}$ X 33,470 = 9,929

Given the preceding allocation of annual cash flow per the "Multiple Investment" requirement, the following additional journal entries would be made during the first year of the lease to record interest earned:

2. NET CASH RECEIVED ENTRY

Cash ($90,000 rentals – loan pmt. of $74,435)	15,565	
Rentals Receivable		15,565

To record net cash flow on difference between rental collections and non-recourse debt payment.

3. ITC ENTRY

Cash or Taxes Payable	100,000	
ITC Receivable		100,000
To record realization of ITC		

4. UNEARNED INCOME ENTRY

Unearned Income (9,929 + 29,663)	39,592	
Lease Income		9,929
ITC Recognized		29,663

To record current years earnings on lease per allocation schedule above including both lease interest earned and ITC recognized.

5. DEFERRED TAXES ENTRY

Cash	53,856	
Income Tax Expense	5,004	
Deferred Taxes		58,860

To record cash receipt of the year's tax credit from the operating loss on the lease operation ($106,857 x .504 = $53,856) and to record the income tax expense that corresponds to the current year's reported pretax income ($9,929 x .504 = $5,004). Both of these items must be deferred since the $53,856 will be reported as earnings over future years and the $5,004 of income taxes will not be paid to the IRS until years later in the lease.

The net effect of both the balance sheet and income statement journal entries is summarized as follows:

BALANCE SHEET

ASSETS

Cash				ITC Receivable	
(2) 15,565	400,000		(1)	100,000	100,000 (3)
(3) 100,000				-0-	
(5) 53,856					
169,421	400,000				
230,579					

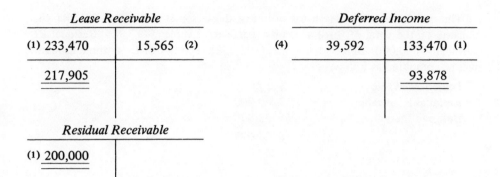

Lease Receivable			*Deferred Income*	
(1) 233,470	15,565 (2)	(4)	39,592	133,470 (1)
217,905				93,878

Residual Receivable
(1) 200,000

LIABILITIES

Deferred Tax Credits
58,860 (5)

OWNERS EQUITY

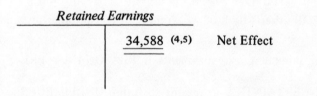

Retained Earnings	
34,588 (4,5)	Net Effect

INCOME STATEMENT

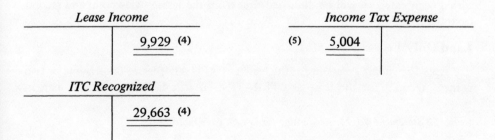

Lease Income			*Income Tax Expense*
9,929 (4)		(5)	5,004

ITC Recognized
29,663 (4)

The net lease receivable on the books of the lessor at the end of the first year consists of the total of three accounts: Lease Receivable, $217,905; Residual Receivable, $200,000; Deferred Income, ($93,878). The net of these three accounts will be computed as follows:

Lease Receivable	$217,905
Residual Receivable	$200,000
Deferred Income	($ 93,878)
	$324,027

ACCOUNTING FOR REAL ESTATE

Leases involving real estate are divided into four categories for purposes of accounting per *FASB Statement No. 13* requirements. The four categories are as follows:[8]

1. Land Only Lease.
2. Land and Building(s) Lease.
3. Land, Building(s), and Equipment Lease.
4. Part of a Building Only Lease.

In order to understand the accounting requirements for real estate leases, it is important to keep in mind the LESSEE criteria that define a capital lease:

1. Ownership Transfers
2. Bargain Purchase Option
3. Lease Term ≥ Seventy-five Percent of Economic Life
4. Present Value Min. Lease Payments ≥ 90% of FMV – ITC

The two additional LESSOR criteria both of which must be met in order for a Capital Lease to exist are:

1. COLLECTIBILITY of minimum lease payments is REASONABLY PREDICTABLE.
2. NO IMPORTANT UNCERTAINTIES in regards to future UNREIMBURSABLE COSTS yet to be incurred by the lessor.

With the CAPITAL LEASE criteria in mind we will now review the accounting requirements in each of the four real estate categories. The accounting techniques within each category will be discussed first from the lessee's viewpoint and second from the lessor's.

Land Only Leases:

Lessee Viewpoint—account for the lease as CAPITAL if lessee criteria one or two is met. Account for the lease as OPERATING if criteria three or four is met. In

---

[8]*FASB Statement No. 13,* Accounting for Leases, Paragraphs 24-28.

other words, if actual or potential actual ownership of the land is not available then the lease is treated as an operating lease.

Lessor Viewpoint—if lessee criteria one or two is met along with both lessor criteria then account for the lease as a CAPITAL LEASE; using Sales-Type or Direct Financing Accounting techniques as appropriate. If lessee criteria three or four are met and both lessor criteria, account for the lease as OPERATING since actual ownership is not available to the lessee and effective ownership is not applicable (since land generally has an indefinite economic life).

Land and Building Leases

1. Lease meeting lessee criteria one or two
   a. *Lessee Viewpoint*—
      i. The land and the building shall be separately capitalized by the lessee in proportion to their fair market values at the lease's inception.
      ii. The building would be depreciated normally.
   b. *Lessor Viewpoint*—sales-type or direct financing capital lease as one unit unless the additional two lessor criteria are not met which would require it to become an operating lease.
2. Lease meets criteria three or four and the FMV of the land is less than twenty-five percent of the total. Lessee and lessor shall consider the land and building as a single unit and the estimated economic life of the building shall determine the economic life of the single unit.
   a. *Lessee*—the land and building are capitalized as a single asset and depreciated over the *lease term.*
   b. *Lessor*—sales or direct financing type if the additional two lessor criteria are met.
3. Lease meets criteria three or four and the FMV of the land is twenty-five percent or more of the FMV of the total. Both the lessee and lessor shall consider the land and buildings separately. The minimum lease payments after deducting executory costs, including any profit applicable to the land and the building, shall be separated both by the lessee and the lessor by determining the fair value of the land and applying the lessee's incremental borrowing rate to it to determine the annual minimum lease payments applicable to the land element; the remaining minimum lease payments shall be attributed to the building element.
   a. *Lessee*—if the building element meets criteria three or four, it should be capitalized and depreciated over the life of the lease. The land portion should be treated as an operating lease. If the building portion does not meet any of the lessee criteria, it too should be considered an operating lease (combined into a single unit with the land).

b. Lessor—if the building element meets criteria three or four, treat as a sales-type or direct financing lease and treat the land portion as an operating lease. If criterion three or four is not met, treat both as a single operating lease.

Land, Building(s), and Equipment Leases

The portion of the minimum lease payments attributable to the equipment element of the lease shall be estimated and accounted for separately *according* to its own classification as any ordinary lease by both lessees and lessors.

Part of A Building Only Lease

When the leased property is part of a larger whole, its cost (or carrying amount) and fair value may not be objectively determinable, as for example, when an office or floor of a building is leased. If the cost and fair value of the leased property are objectively determinable, both the lessee and the lessor shall classify and account for the lease according to the provisions of the paragraph above describing building leases. Unless both the cost and the fair value are objectively determinable, the lease shall be classified and accounted for as follows:

1. LESSEE VIEWPOINT:
   a. If the fair value of the leased property is objectively determinable, the lessee shall classify and account for the lease according to the provisions of the paragraph describing building leases above.
   b. If the fair value of the leased property is not objectively determinable, the lessee shall classify the lease according to the criterion number three only, using the estimated economic life of the building in which the lease premises are located. If that criterion is met, the leased property shall be capitalized as a unit and depreciated over the lease term.

2. LESSOR VIEWPOINT If either the cost or the fair value of the property is not objectively determinable, the lessor shall account for the lease as an operating lease.

   FASB INTERPRETATION NO. 24 allows reasonable estimates of fair value of part of a building to be based on appraisals or estimated replacement cost data.

3. Because of special provisions normally present in leases involving terminal space and other airport facilities owned by a governmental unit or authority, the economic life of such facilities for purposes of classifying the lease is essentially indeterminate.

PROFIT RECOGNITION ON SALES-TYPE LEASES

FASB Statement No. 25 entitled "Profit Recognition on Sales-Type Leases of Real Estate" requires that in order that a lessor may recognize a profit at time of sale under a sales-type capital lease, certain criteria must be met (otherwise account for as an operating lease).

1. FASB 13 sales-type lease criteria:
    a. Sales profit at the inception.
    b. Any one of four capital lease criteria.
    c. Both of capital lease lessor criteria (*collectible* without *uncertainties*)
2. AICPA Industry Accounting Guide "Accounting for Profit on Sales of Real Estate" requires these additional criteria:
    a. Sale (closing) must be consummated.
    b. Buyer's investment must be sufficiently significant to assure buyer honoring commitment to seller.
        i. Requires down payment of five to twenty-five percent of the sales price depending on the nature of the real estate.
        ii. Must consist of cash, irrevocable letters of credit, or notes.
            - Notes must be converted to cash before being counted as part of the down payment.
            - Does not include prepayment of interest, taxes, etc.
        iii. Buyer's commitment to pay for property is evaluated annually
            - Principal and interest for land must be paid within twenty years and
            - Other real estate within terms of usual first mortgage.
    c. If buyer's investment does not meet these criteria, account for transaction with the deposit, installment, or cost recovery method as appropriate, rather than as ordinary sale.
3. A seller should not have continued involvement in the property.
    a. All or part of the sales profit should be deferred when the seller has not performed significant obligations at the time of the sale which should be recognized when the obligation is fulfilled.
    b. Sales contract is not a sale if seller's involvement carries risk of ownership, e.g., repurchase guarantees to buyer.
4. This FASB does not apply to direct financing leases or sales-type leases if there is a loss.

REAL ESTATE LEASE ANALYSIS

Basically, real estate leases are analyzed like any other leases as described in chapter 4. However, there are two very common additional factors that must be taken into consideration when analyzing a real estate lease; (1) Percentage Leases and (2) Indexed Leases.

Percentage Leases occur frequently in the leasing of commercial retail space. For example, tenants of shopping malls frequently lease on a percentage basis. Percentage leases require the lessee-tenant to pay a monthly base rental for each square foot of retail space occupied which might vary from $.50 to $1.50 per month. Beyond this fixed base amount the lessor requires the lessee to pay a percentage of his gross revenue above a certain minimum amount as additional rent. The justification for charging the additional percentage rental is to compensate the lessor for inflationary losses in the purchasing power of the dollar. Of course if the lessee never earns enough revenue to begin paying the additional percentage rent, the lessor is not compensated for inflation. In practice, however, many successful property owners have become wealthy due in a large part to their percentage rental leases which more than compensated them for the ravages of inflation.

Indexed Leases represent another technique for compensating the lessor of real estate for the loss in purchasing power of the dollar. This, too, is a contingent lease like the percentage lease. However, the indexed lease requires the lessee to pay additional rentals not as a function of increased lessee revenues, but as a function of increased lessor costs. In effect the lessor passes on to the lessee increased costs in property taxes, utilities, janitorial services, insurance, etc. Now the lessor can directly pass on his increased costs to the lessee through an escalation clause in the lease which requires adjustment in the lease payment to cover the lessor's increased costs, or he may require the lease payment to increase in relation to some external measurement of increased costs. The three most commonly used external measures or indexes of inflation are: the Consumer Price Index (CPI); the Wholesale Price Index (WPI); and the Gross National Product Deflator. When a lease has an indexed escalation clause it simply requires the lease payment to be adjusted upward periodically by a percentage amount equal to the rate of increase in the measurement index. Unfortunately, indexed leases are not as advantageous to lessees as are percentage leases even though the objective to the lessor is the same. The reason why percentage leases are preferable to indexed leases from the lessee viewpoint is that if the lessee's revenues do not keep up with inflation then the lease payment does not increase under a percentage lease; under the indexed lease the rental payments continue to grow irrespective of the lessee's lack of revenue growth.

Analyzing Contingent Rental Leases

When the lease contains a percentage or indexed escalation clause, it poses an analytical problem. How do you compute a yield, IRR or otherwise, on a lease that has a growing stream of payments? There are two basic techniques commonly used to overcome this difficulty:

1. Determine the present value of the growing stream of payments using the techniques described in chapter 7 using the company's cost of capital as the discount rate (or risk-adjusted rate due to the additional uncertainty involved in escalation payments) along with the expected growth rate in rental payments (on a constant or percentage basis). From this present-value total deduct the present value of the unadjusted (escalation ignored) rentals discounted at the cost of capital. The resulting difference should be offset against the cost of the real estate prior to computing an ordinary internal rate of return yield.

2. Estimate the anticipated rental increases over the life of the lease and include them in the determination of the internal rate of return. Although this technique is more accurate perhaps than the present-value adjusted method described above it is nevertheless cumbersome because lengthy cash forecasts must be completed. A computer is very helpful in this circumstance.

CONCLUSION

It has been shown that a leveraged lease can be analyzed according to one of several methods:

1. Standard Sinking Fund Method, Zero Percent Reinvestment Rate
2. Modified IRR, Three Percent Safe Rate
3. Standard Sinking Fund Method, Three Percent Reinvestment Rate
4. Multiple Investment or Separate Phase Method
5. Basic IRR (ROA)
6. Basic IRR (ROE) Actuarial Recapture Method.

These various methods are required because of three unique problems occurring in leveraged leases:

1. Multiple Negative Cash Inflows
2. Debt-Equity Ratio Optimization
3. Double Financial Leverage; Recourse and Nonrecourse Debt

Accounting for leveraged leases requires specialized accounting techniques for balance sheet presentation (NET INVESTMENT PRESENTATION) and income statement (INCOME COMPONENTS PRESENTATION).

Accounting for Real Estate Leases has varying requirements depending on whether the lease is for:

1. Land Only
2. Land and Building(s)
3. Land, Building(s), and Equipment
4. Part of a Building Only

Analyzing a real estate lease can be complex due to percentage and escalation clauses included in the lease which give rise to escalating contingent increased rental payments.

11

Legal Issues in
_____ Lease Transactions_____

There are enough legal issues in the leasing field to fill many books. Therefore, the purpose of this chapter is merely to acquaint the reader with the legal maze into which he enters when he assumes the role of a party to a lease agreement.

Potential Warranty Liability of Lessors

The Uniform Commercial Code (UCC) is a comprehensive network of laws governing a variety of commercial transactions, _e.g._, sales of goods, bank deposits and collections, commercial paper, and secured transactions. It has been adopted in every state except Louisiana.

Under the UCC, warranties may be created expressly (sec. 2-313) or they may be implied by law (sec. 2-314: Implied Warranty of Merchantability; sec. 2-315: Implied Warranty of Fitness for a Particular Purpose). An express warranty is a statement or representation made by a seller of goods that the character, quality, and title of goods are as he represents them to be. In other words, the seller promises that the facts are as he says they are. The UCC provides that an express warranty may be created by the seller making an express affirmation of fact or a promise, or by a description or sample made or shown to the buyer. On the other hand, _implied_ warranties arise, not by the seller's representations, but by operation of law, _i.e._, the legislature has enacted a statute providing that goods sold _shall_ be subject to these warranties unless specifically excluded by the seller. The "implied warranty of merchantability" is a warranty that the goods among other things, (1) pass without objection in the trade under the contract description, (2) are fit for the ordinary purposes for which such goods are used, (3) run of even kind, quality, and quantity within each unit and among all units involved, and (4) conform to the promises or affirmations of fact made on the container or label if any (sec. 2-314). The "implied warranty of fitness for a particular purpose" arises by operation of law "where the seller at the time of contracting has reason to know any particular purpose for which the goods are required and that the buyer is relying on the seller's skill or judgment to select or furnish" goods suitable for such purpose (sec. 2-315).

Although the UCC provisions do not explicitly apply to leases, a number of recent court decisions have extended UCC coverage to leases (whether true leases or conditional sales contracts) by analogy or otherwise. Some courts have made a distinction between a "finance" lessor and a "merchant" lessor imposing liability on the "merchant lessor" but not on the "finance lessor" ("finance lessors" being analogous to lending institutions). On the other hand, many courts have refused to extend the UCC provisions to "true lease" transactions.

In order to exclude or modify the implied warranty of merchantability, the UCC, in an oral disclaimer, requires merchantability to be mentioned, and, if the disclaimer is in writing, the term must be conspicuously displayed. With regard to the fitness warranty, there need be no mention of the phrase "warranty of fitness," but the exclusion must be by a conspicuous writing. Additionally, an implied warranty may be disclaimed by expressions like "as is," "with all faults," or other similar language which brings the buyer's attention to the warranty exclusion or disclaimer.

In light of the recent court cases which have held that leases are subject to the UCC, it would probably behoove lessors, as a precautionary measure, to explicitly and conspicuously state or disclaim the warranties as prescribed by the UCC.

Potential Tort Liability of Lessors

Recent courts have imposed strict products liability on lessors of equipment, and lessors have been subject to liability for negligence. Some courts have even discussed the possibility of subjecting lessors to vicarious liability. Products liability is a 20th-century doctrine that imposes liability on a manufacturer or person in the chain of distribution, *i.e.*, retailer, wholesaler, or lessor, if the product manufactured or distributed is defective to the point of being unreasonably dangerous to the user (or possibly even to a bystander) and causes injury to such user (or bystander). Liability for negligence may result where the manufacturer's or distributor's conduct with respect to the product creates an unreasonable risk of harm to the user. Vicarious liability involves holding one liable for the acts of another by virtue of their relationship. It is most often used in the context of the employer-employee relationship, where the employer is held responsible for the wrongful acts of the employee.

The extension of liability imposed on "merchant" lessors rather than "finance" lessors simply reinforces the necessity of securing sufficient insurance. Where the lease agreement requires the lessee to provide insurance against risk of loss of the equipment and against liability to third persons, the lessor should nonetheless maintain some form of umbrella type coverage, or better yet, specific coverage for products liability.

"True lease" or not

So far in this book, we have encountered the lease versus conditional sale controversy twice. Both the Internal Revenue Service and the Financial Accounting Standards Board are engaged in an ongoing struggle to ascertain when a lease is really a lease and when it is in fact a conditional sale. Of course, to make things more difficult, both the IRS and the FASB make this determination based on somewhat different criteria (see chapter two). Although the Economic Recovery Tax Act provides a safe harbor lease for tax purposes (see chapter two), the lease-sale uncertainty still exists in yet another context. The Uniform Commercial Code makes exceptions for "true leases" from its Article 9 filing requirements. As in the tax and accounting areas, however, the standards for determining the true status of the transaction are somewhat obscure. Section 1-201 (37) of the UCC utilizes a test based on the intent of the parties. This section states in part that "[w]hether a lease is intended as [a conditional sales contract] is to be determined by the facts of each case." Not much is clarified by this statement. The section further provides that "(a) the inclusion of an option to purchase does not of itself make the lease one intended [as a sale], and (b) an agreement that, upon compliance with the terms of the lease the lessee shall become or has the option to become the owner of the property for no additional consideration or for a nominal consideration, does make the lease one intended [as a sale]." Here again, we see a potential disparity in the rules used by the different agencies with respect to the meaning of "nominal considerations." Although the UCC provisions above do not resolve of this problem, section 9-408 of the code ameliorates the potential adverse effects of the uncertainty. This section provides that a lessor may file a financing statement and that such filing "shall not of itself be a factor in determining whether or not . . . the lease is intended as [a sale]." In addition, the section covers the situation in which the lease is not deemed a true lease: "However, if it is determined for other reasons that the . . . lease is so intended, a security interest of the . . . lessor which attaches to the . . . leased goods is perfected by such filing." For this reason, as was discussed in the lease documents section, the UCC filing requirements should be complied with whether or not the parties intend the lease to be a "true lease." Such filing is important should the lessor be required to repossess the equipment due to the lessee's breach of contract.

Bankruptcy

Bankruptcy is the state or condition existing when one cannot pay his debts as they are, or become, due. Bankruptcy proceedings may be initiated voluntarily or involuntarily in accordance with federal law in a federal bankruptcy court: voluntarily by the bankrupt person, or involuntarily by his creditors. A bankruptcy trustee is appointed by the Bankruptcy Court to administer the bankrupt person's estate. In this context, the trustee ascertains and collects the person's assets, brings suit on his claims, and defends actions against him. The bankruptcy proceedings can take the form of: (1) a liquidation which involves the collection and distribution of the bankrupt person's nonexempt property by the trustee to the creditors, or (2) a rehabilitation and reorganization of the bankrupt. In the latter case, the creditors look to the future earnings of the debtor to satisfy their claims, rather than to a current distribution of his property.

The Bankruptcy Reform Act of 1978 substantially halted the evolution of certain aspects of American bankruptcy law, particularly with regard to the certainty of and protection afforded by the law with respect to secured creditors and lessors. The Act, effective on October 1, 1979, set forth a complex labyrinth of inexact and seemingly disjointed rules and tests to be employed by the bankruptcy judge in his ascertainment and resolution of the conflicting claims of the debtor and his creditors. The complicated nature of the new statute has resulted in its being characterized as a "full-employment-for-lawyers bill."[1]

Under the new act, the trustee is granted a broad array of powers. For example, section 362(3) provides for an automatic stay of repossession of property which is subject to a lease or security interest. With some exceptions, section 365 empowers the trustee to accept or reject any executory contract or unexpired lease of the debtor. Section 364 authorizes the trustee to obtain unsecured credit and secure unsecured debt in the ordinary course of business as an administrative expense.

It should be clear that competent legal counsel is a prerequisite to a successful outcome in bankruptcy court. However, to avoid the pitfalls of noncompliance with the intricacies of the new act, legal assistance is required not only *post facto*, but more importantly, in the negotiating and drafting stages of the agreement. This allows a lawyer to practice some "preventative medicine."

The Uniform Consumer Credit Code (UCCC)

The UCCC is a uniform law adopted by many states dealing with the extension of credit to consumers. The purposes of the code are many. Among the most significant are:[2]

1. to simplify, clarify, and modernize the law governing consumer credit and usury;
2. to provide interest rate ceilings to assure an adequate credit supply to consumers;
3. to promote and further consumer understanding of credit terms and to foster competition among suppliers of consumer credit to enable consumers to obtain credit more readily;
4. to protect consumers from unfair credit practices;
5. to conform the regulation of disclosure in consumer credit transactions to the Federal Truth-in-Lending Act; and
6. to make the law uniform among the various jurisdictions.

---

[1] Aaron, *The Bankruptcy Reform Act of 1978: The Full-Employment-for-Lawyers Bill* (pts. 1-3), 1979 UTAH L. REV. 1, 175, 405 (1979).

[2] Adapted from Black's Law Dictionary 1373 (5th ed. 1979).

The Truth-in-Lending Act is a federal statute designed to assure that consumers who are in the market for credit are given adequate and meaningful information regarding the cost of that credit. "Reg Z" is the title given to a set of regulations promulgated by the Federal Reserve Board which implements the provisions of the Truth-in-Lending Act. The UCCC is the state counterpart to the federal legislation.

As the title of the UCCC indicates by implication, it is generally inapplicable to business and commercial credit. With the exception of real estate agreements, it is also inapplicable to consumer credit transactions involving amounts in excess of $40,000. Where it is applicable, *i.e.,* consumer transactions under $40,000, onerous disclosure burdens are placed on the lender. Among other things, the borrower must be informed of the dollar amount of the finance charges, the annual percentage rate of the interest charge, and his right to rescind. For failing to comply with the code's provisions, the lender may be subject to penalties.

The lender in a consumer transaction, whether he is a lessor or conventional lender, must comply with the code's requirements unless the transaction falls within an exception. Even when the transaction is of a commercial nature, a "declaration of business purpose" provision in the lease agreement is of substantial importance (see chapter 12).

In this age of consumerism, the list of proposed and enacted legislation at both the federal and state levels regarding the protection of consumer interests is almost infinite, and will probably continue to grow. Coupling this with the dramatic increase in the use of leasing as a consumer financing tool has resulted in the congressional Consumer Leasing Act of 1976. Effective in March 1977, the act basically extends the provisions of the Truth-in-Lending Act to consumer lease transactions that cover a period of more than four months and involve lease payments of less than $25,000. Leases for agricultural, business, or commercial purposes are specifically excluded. This act, among other things, mandates specific cost disclosure of a lease contract, prohibits balloon payments at least until termination, and requires accurate disclosure of lease contract items in advertisements. This legislation applies primarily to long-term consumer automobile and truck leases.

The Unconscionability Doctrine

A contract, though of full force and effect on its face, may be rendered unenforceable because of its inherent unfairness—in other words, it would be unconscionable to require performance. The unconscionability doctrine has flourished in recent years as a result of the prevalence of adhesion contracts. An adhesion contract is a standardized agreement drafted by a predominant party to cover transactions with many people rather than with an individual on a one-to-one basis. It is characterized by a lack of negotiation and is typically referred to as a "take it or leave it" contract. The ordinary lease or conditional sales contracts are adhesion contracts. Where an adhesion contract is coupled with an absence of meaningful choice on the part of one of the parties, together with contract terms which are unreasonably favorable to the other party, it is easy to see why a court may refuse to enforce the contract. Although there is no sure and simple method to protect against a contention of unconscionability, there are ways to lessen the probability of an unsuccessful courtroom battle. The purpose of the unconscionability doctrine is to prevent oppression and unfair surprise. Therefore, the contractual language should be as clear and unambiguous as possible. The lessee's attention should be brought to each and every term of the agreement. Those provisions that appear to be somewhat oppressive should be explained in detail while the others should, at the least, be briefly summed up. Doing this will eliminate the element of unfair surprise. It is just as important, however, that the substance of the provisions do not produce substantial hardship on the party (typically the lessee) having a disproportionately small amount of bargaining power. In other words, since the law views the formation of a contract as an allocation of risks between the parties and does not like to interfere with the freedom to contract, it will refuse to enforce the contract (or an unconscionable provision thereof) only if the contract (or provision) is unreasonably unfair.

Repossession

Although the law dealing with repossessions may not be strictly applicable to a lessor since the leased property is owned by the lessor and is not just representative of a security interest, the principles of repossession should nevertheless be adhered to in leasing transactions to avoid potential claims of unconscionability and denial of due process.

Normally, a lender's right to repossess collateral which is used as security for a loan accrues upon the debtor's default, *e.g.*, failure to pay as promised. The lender generally does not need to seek judicial assistance to effect the repossession so long as it is not likely to cause a breach of the peace; otherwise judicial sanction is required.

There are a variety of methods within the legal framework to obtain recovery of the property after default has occurred, *e.g.*, writ of replevin. Within the framework, however, are a number of rather exacting requirements. These specific requirements are set forth in federal and state statutes and the rules of civil procedure.

In the event that the lease is determined to be a conditional sales contract for UCC purposes, disposal of the repossessed item must be effected in compliance with a myriad of rules and requirements listed therein. The underlying theme seems to be one of fair and adequate notice to the debtor before disposal, coupled with a commercially reasonable disposition.

If the lease falls within the purview of the UCCC, a different set of rules is invoked (as is true with regard to a foreclosure on a mortgage or trust deed). The UCC, the UCCC, and foreclosure statutes are state laws, and the complexity of each requires the assistance of a competent attorney.

Sales or Use Tax

The two most frequently asked questions regarding sales tax in the context of leasing are: (1) who pays it, and (2) how is it assessed. When a *sale*, not a true lease, is the transaction at issue, the sales tax is generally paid by the buyer to the seller and then remitted by the seller to the state tax commission on a quarterly basis. With regard to leasing, such a tax is normally referred to as a "use tax." Although the manner of assessment varies from state to state, there are basically four methods currently employed. First, the lessor may have two options: (a) to charge the lessee the tax based on the purchase price (typically fair market value of the leased asset) at the time the lease is entered into, or (b) to collect the tax from the lessee based on the monthly rentals. Second, some states require that the tax be paid at the time of the lease agreement by the lessee based on the fair market value of the leased equipment. Third, the tax may be required to be paid on the monthly rentals. Fourth, and most onerous, at least one state levies the tax at the time the agreement is consummated *and* upon each monthly rental. The lessee is typically the party who bears the ultimate burden of the sales (or use) tax since the tax is included in the monthly lease payments. As with all other costs, however, where the lessee's bargaining power is substantial, some of the cost may be allocated to the lessor. In either case, the state generally looks to the lessor for payment.

Property Tax

Frequently, states will impose a tax on property owned by the record holder of the property; this tax burden, then, falls on the lessor. Again, like all other economic aspects of the lease, this item is negotiated and in part determines the lessor's return and the lessee's cost. If the lease agreement provides that the lessee should remit the tax directly, both the lessor and lessee will be safeguarded from a potential double tax situation where the lessee forwards a copy of the tax notice and a copy of the check in payment thereof to the lessor. However, in many states the record holder (lessor) remains primarily liable for payment of the tax. In other words, if the tax is not paid by the lessee, the taxing authority can require the lessor to pay it even though the lessee was contractually bound to make the payment. In such case, the lessor could sue the lessee for breach of contract to recover the amount of taxes paid.

CONCLUSION

As was mentioned at the outset of this chapter, the number of legal issues potentially involved in a leasing transaction is almost infinite. The ever-increasing complexities of day-to-day business dealings are in large part caused by the rapidly changing legal environment. Constant attention must be given to the legal ramifications of virtually all business transactions. For that reason, large leasing engagements almost mandate the assistance of experts in the field of leasing, not only from the financial viewpoint, but also from the tax and legal perspectives.

12

The Lease Agreement—
Important Provisions and
Attendant Documents

In this day and age so filled with difficulties in the current economic environment, such as rampant inflation, astounding interest rates, and staggering unemployment, business people have become increasingly more innovative in the creation of new and diverse methods of financing business operations. Where this innovation is given effect through the means of an agreement between somewhat adversarial parties, problems in construction and interpretation frequently occur. Therefore, it is imperative for the parties to make known their often conflicting demands and expectations, and to express the resulting mutuality of understanding through as clear, cogent, and unambiguous language as is feasible. One should not, however, allow the extravagant desires of lawyers to provide for every possible contingency, no matter how remote, to go unrestrained. The preferable approach is to cover the "bare bones" of the agreement with supplements where there exists a substantial likelihood of dispute or controversy. The following material illustrates the application of this approach in the context of a nonleveraged lease contract, while at the same time provides some insight into the necessity of the exemplified provisions.

I. IMPORTANT LEASE PROVISIONS

1. DATE; FULL LEGAL NAMES OF THE PARTIES; JURISDICTION IN WHICH EACH IS ORGANIZED; MAILING ADDRESS OF EACH PARTY'S PRINCIPAL PLACE OF BUSINESS.

   This LEASE AGREEMENT is made and entered into this 31st day of December, 1981, by Vestigrowth 2000, a Utah general partnership, with

261

offices at 1406 South 1100 East, Salt Lake City, Utah, 84105, telephone (801) 467-3211, as Lessor, and by Rocky Mountain Wrecker Sales, a Utah corporation with offices at 435 West 3440 South, Salt Lake City, Utah, 84115, telephone (801) 268-8850, as Lessee.

Where both the lessor and lessee are clearly designated, there is little chance for mistake as to who is bound by the contract. The date allows this lease to be easily identified, and the full mailing addresses facilitate communication between the parties.

2. DESCRIPTION OF LEASED EQUIPMENT; ADDRESS AT WHICH EQUIPMENT WILL BE LOCATED; CONSENT FOR REMOVAL.

Qty	Serial No.	Equipment Model & Description	Supplier Name and Address
1	2757	Pitney Bowes 6100 Mail Processing Sys.	Automated Business Systems 1623 So. State
1	9729	Pitney Bowes 5045 EMS-10 Electronic Scale	Salt Lake City, Utah 84115

Equipment shall be delivered and thereafter kept during the entire term of this Lease at Lessee's address as shown in paragraph 1, or at the following address:

_____

City————————————County————————————State————————————

Zip————————————————Telephone————————————————

Equipment shall not be removed therefrom without Lessor's prior written consent.

In most instances, a full description of the leased property and its location is imperative. This not only aids the lessor regarding UCC filings and identification of the equipment upon the lessee's default or bankruptcy, but it makes it easier for the lessor to periodically check on the equipment and to recover it if the lessee has sold or otherwise transferred it to a third party.

3. PAYMENT ADDRESS; AMOUNT PER MONTH (OR OTHERWISE); DATE PAYMENTS BEGIN; LEASE TERM; NUMBER AND TOTAL AMOUNT

OF ADVANCE PAYMENTS AND DATE TO BE PAID; SECURITY DE-
POSIT; LATE CHARGES; USE TAX AND/OR INSURANCE PORTION
OF RENTAL.

Lessee shall pay Lessor at the office of Lessor in Salt Lake City, Utah or at
such other place as Lessor may designate in writing, the sum of $215.25 per
month, commencing December 31, 1981 and on the last day of each consecu-
tive month thereafter, for a period of forty-eight (48) months, the Lease term
hereunder. The first and last two payments in the total amount of $645.75
are payable in advance at the time of signing this Lease. A security deposit in
the amount of $100.00 is payable at the time of signing this Lease. Lessor
may, but shall not be obligated to, apply the security deposit to cure any default of Lessee in which event Lessee shall promptly restore the security deposit to the full amount specified above. Upon termination of this Lease and
all renewals hereof, if Lessee has fulfilled all the terms and conditions of this
Agreement, Lessor shall return to Lessee the amount of the security deposit
actually made by Lessee. If Lessee fails to pay when due any rent or other
amount required herein to be paid to Lessor, Lessee shall pay to Lessor a
service charge of five per cent (5%) of each installment or part thereof for which
said rent or other amount shall be delinquent, or $10.00, whichever is greater,
plus interest on such delinquent rent or other amount from the due date thereof
until paid at the rate of 18% per annum. The monthly installment payments
referred to above include $10.25 use tax (or sales tax) and $4.30 insurance.

The location for payment remittance reduces confusion if an address other
than the lessor's principal place of business is used, *e.g.,* a post office box,
and minimizes lost interest to the lessor and the possibility of late charges to
the lessee. The amount of payment, commencement date, and lease term are
essential to avoid misconceptions by either party. The number and amount
of advance payments and the date due are necessary for the same reason. If
a security deposit is required, it should be designated as such and should not
be included as an advance payment. A security deposit is normally not taxable to the lessor unless and until the lessee fails to perform his side of the
agreement and the lessor therefore refuses to return it. This may allow the
lessor to utilize these funds free of taxes. On the other hand, a security deposit is not deductible by the lessee unless and until the lessor decides to
keep it by reason of the lessee's default. The mechanism for assessment of
late charges should be clearly delineated and enforced by the lessor so as to
put the lessee on notice beforehand. The lessor should make sure that these
late charges do not exceed the amount allowed by law, typically one to one
and one-half percent per month for interest and a one-time three to six percent service charge. The late charge is utilized to compensate the lessor for
his out-of-pocket expenses incurred as a result of the late payment, *e.g.,* tele-

phone calls and employee time, as well as lost interest. Designation of the portion of the rental payments, which is used to pay the state use or sales tax or insurance, alerts the lessee that not all of his payment goes toward the actual lease liability.

4. NO WARRANTIES BY LESSOR; SELECTION OF EQUIPMENT AND SUPPLIER; NO RELIANCE; NO AGENCY.

Lessee has selected both (a) the above equipment and (b) the supplier from whom Lessor is to purchase is based upon Lessee's own judgement. Lessee takes the property "as is," and expressly disclaims any reliance upon any statements or representations made by Lessor. Lessee agrees to execute an "Acknowledgement of Delivery and Acceptance" upon receipt of equipment in good serviceable condition, fully satisfactory to Lessee. LESSOR MAKES NO WARRANTIES EXPRESS OR IMPLIED AS TO ANY MATTER WHATSOEVER, INCLUDING THE CONDITION OF EQUIPMENT, OR ITS MERCHANTABILITY OR FITNESS FOR ANY PARTICULAR PURPOSE. Lessee understands and agrees that neither Supplier, nor any salesman or other agent of Supplier. No salesman or agent of Supplier is authorized to waive or alter any term or condition of this Lease, and no representation as to Equipment or any other matter by Supplier shall in any way affect Lessee's duty to pay the rent, and perform its other obligations as set forth in this Lease.

As was mentioned in chapter 11, exclusion of the implied warranties requires a specific, conspicuous statement to that effect. These disclaimers reduce the risk of suit by the lessee for malfunctions, etc. of the leased equipment. The warranty exclusions should effectively insulate a lessor from liability which could flow from the implied warranties. However, there seems to be a trend in favor of consumer protection away from *caveat emptor*. Evidence of this trend is the lessor's potential subjection to products liability. For that reason, insurance coverage is imperative. A statement that the lessee has selected both the equipment and the supplier, and that he takes the property "as is" and has not relied on any of lessor's statements or representations, reinforces the disclaimer. In truck and automobile leases, there is typically an additional statement to the effect that the manufacturer's warranty is the only warranty made or deemed to have been made. A copy of the warranty is given to the lessee. This, of course, informs the lessee that a warranty does exist, at least to a limited extent. The practical effect of the "acknowledgement of delivery and acceptance" is to shift the burden of any subsequent repairs to the party responsible for them as set forth in the repairs and maintenance provision of the lease contract. The fact that neither the lessor nor the supplier is an agent of the other prevents the lessee from holding the lessor liable for the supplier's representations and vice-versa.

5. REPAIRS AND MAINTENANCE; USE; ALTERATIONS.

Lessee, at its expense, shall keep Equipment in good working condition and repair and furnish all labor, parts, mechanisms and devices required therefor. Lessee shall use Equipment in a careful and lawful manner. Lessee shall not make any alterations, additions, or improvements to Equipment without Lessor's prior written consent. All additions and improvements made to Equipment shall belong to Lessor and shall not be removed without Lessor's prior written consent.

This provision defines the party obligated to keep the equipment in proper working condition, usually the lessee. That the lessee is required to use the equipment carefully and lawfully provides the lessor with a counterclaim cause of action against the lessee where a third party sues the lessor because such party has been injured as a result of the lessee's careless or unlawful operation of the equipment. The requirement of the lessor's prior written consent regarding alterations, etc. protects the equipment collateral value. For example, if the lessee proposes a modification to the equipment which would cause a reduction in fair market value, the lessor can deny the request or require additional collateral. As a practical matter, equipment subject to a long-term lease contains very few of its original components. The last sentence prohibits the lessee from returning only the skeletal frame of the leased property.

6. INSURANCE.

Lessee shall provide, maintain and pay all premiums for (a) insurance against loss, theft, destruction or damage of Equipment in an amount not less than the full replacement value thereof, with loss payable to Lessor, and (b) public liability insurance in an amount satisfactory to Lessor, in the joint names of Lessor and Lessee. All insurance shall be with companies, and in a form, satisfactory to Lessor, and Lessee shall deliver the policies of insurance to Lessor.

The objective of this provision is two-fold: (1) To protect the lessor's investment in the equipment. Full replacement value should be emphasized because without such a stipulation, the insurer would typically indemnify the lessor only to the extent of the equipment cost less accumulated depreciation, which in this age of ten percent or more inflation would be grossly inadequate. (2) To protect the lessor and lessee from liability to a third party resulting from an injury to the third party's person or property. With the lessor and the lessee named as joint beneficiaries, payment upon loss is simplified. That the insurer (s) and the policy amounts must be satisfactory to the lessor increases the probability that the coverage is adequate for the risks involved and that, in the event of loss, the insurer has the wherewithal to pay.

The lessor's right to procure insurance upon the lessee's failure to do so, and to pass the charge to the lessee through increased lease payments with an interest charge, ensures that insurance coverage will always exist with the cost borne by the lessee.

In addition to the coverages mentioned above, the lessor should carry insurance against products liability.

7. DECLARATION OF BUSINESS PURPOSE

Lessee hereby warrants and represents that Equipment will be used for business purposes, and not for personal, family, household, or agricultural purposes. Lessee acknowledges that Lessor has relied upon this representation in entering into this Lease.

This provision ensures that the lease falls outside of the purview of the extensive Reg Z and UCCC reporting and disclosure requirements mandated for consumer leases.

8. CLAIMS AGAINST SUPPLIER; ASSIGNMENT TO LESSEE OF LESSOR'S RIGHTS AGAINST SUPPLIER.

If Equipment is not properly installed, does not operate as represented or warranted by Supplier, or is or becomes unsatisfactory for any reason, Lessee shall make any and all claims arising on account thereof SOLELY AGAINST SUPPLIER and shall, nevertheless, pay Lessor without interruption, all rents payable under this Lease. Solely for the purpose of making and prosecuting any claim, Lessor assigns to Lessee, all of the rights which Lessor may have against Supplier for breach of warranty or any other representation concerning Equipment. Lessor will require Supplier to agree through Supplier's acceptance of Lessor's purchase order that all representations, agreements, and warranties which may be made by Supplier to Lessee or Lessor may be enforced by Lessee in his own name.

This provision should be read in conjunction with provision number four above (exclusion of warranties). The purpose of this provision is to direct the lessee's claims regarding the operation of the equipment, etc. solely to the supplier, and to require the lessee to continue the rental payments. The assignment by the lessor of his rights against the supplier for breach of warranty, and the inclusion by the lessor of the "enforcement by lessee" clause in the purchase order, facilitates the lessee in his effort to enforce those warranties.

9. TERMINATION BY LESSOR FOR NONDELIVERY.

Lessor shall have the exclusive option to terminate this Lease and Lessor's obligation hereunder if, within 120 days after execution hereof by Lessee, Equipment has not been delivered to Lessee. The option may be exercised by giving Lessee written notice of termination pursuant to this paragraph.

If it were not for this provision, the lessor could still be bound to the contract even though the supplier failed to provide the equipment. The provision therefore allows the lessor to escape from this potential liability. Additionally, since he may terminate the agreement *at his option*, upon notice of the supplier's nondelivery, the lessor may be able to obtain the equipment elsewhere. In such a case, he would not exercise his option to terminate.

10. SURRENDER.

At the expiration of this Lease or on Lessor's demand made pursuant to paragraph 11, Lessee, at its expense, shall return Equipment in good working condition and repair, to such place as is then specified by Lessor, carefully packed, freight prepaid, and properly insured.

Although the return of the equipment upon default or at the end of the lease is implicit in a lease arrangement, this provision reinforces the fact that the equipment is in fact owned by the lessor. This could very possibly impact the tax treatment to both the lessor and lessee. The provision also makes clear how the return is to be made and which party is to bear the cost of return including freight and insurance.

11. DEFAULT; NO WAIVER; RETURN OR REPOSSESSION OF EQUIPMENT; DAMAGES; ATTORNEYS' FEES.

Time is of the essence of this Agreement and no waiver by Lessor of any breach or default shall constitute a waiver of any other breach or default by Lessee or waiver of any of Lessor's rights.

If Lessee shall fail to pay any rental promptly when due, or if Lessee shall default in performance or fail to keep, perform or comply with any of the terms of this Agreement, such act or omission shall constitute a breach of this Agreement.

Upon any such breach, Lessee agrees, upon written demand, to immediately deliver Equipment to Lessor in the manner set forth in Paragraph 10 above; or at Lessor's option, upon written demand, to permit Lessor to enter the premises where Equipment is located and permit Lessor to obtain the possession of and remove the same; or to store Equipment in accordance with Lessor's instructions.

Lessee agrees that upon Lessee's breach of this Agreement, Lessee shall immediately pay to Lessor all damages which Lessor has sustained or will sustain by virtue of such breach, which damages are hereby agreed to be and shall be the total amount of all lease payments for the full term of this Lease, less the lease payments theretofore paid.

Lessee further agrees that upon such breach Lessee shall immediately pay to Lessor such other charges, fees, and taxes as are chargeable to Lessee by the terms of this Agreement plus reasonable attorneys' fees for legal expenses which were necessitated by repossession of Equipment or by enforcement or breach of this Agreement.

If Lessee fails to return or effect the return of Equipment in as good a condition as received, normal wear and tear excepted, within ten (10) days of written demand therefor, Lessee shall, in addition to the damages hereinabove set forth, pay Lessor the then market value of like equipment in fit and marketable condition.

Lessee further agrees that if it should appear that Lessee's ability to pay rentals promptly when due or to keep, perform or comply with the terms of this Agreement has become impaired, Lessor shall have the same rights and Lessee shall have the same duties and obligations as if Lessee had breached this Agreement.

"Time is of the essence" is a legal term indicating that the lessee should strictly adhere to the time limitations imposed on him by the lease agreement. A slight variance may give rise to a cause of action for breach.

A waiver is the voluntary and intentional relinquishment of a known right and can occur either expressly, e.g., by a written document to that effect, or implicitly, e.g., by not objecting to a default which occurs with some frequency. The inclusion of the express statement that a waiver of the lessor's rights as concerns one breach or default by the lessee does not constitute a waiver of any other, protects the lessor from an involuntary release of his rights. In other words, a course of conduct, in and of itself, cannot, in view of this provision, be the basis for the lessee's assertion that a waiver has occured. The lessor, however, may be stopped from relying on the "no waiver" provision where the lessee has justifiably relied to his detriment on the lessor's conduct.

A breach of the agreement results when one of the parties fails to perform one or more of his promises encompassed by the agreement. By expressly indicating in a broad manner those acts which constitute a breach or noncompliance with a condition, two things are accomplished: (1) the lessee is put on notice that any deviation from the contract terms may result in the lessor pursuing his "breach options" (discussed below), and (2) the lessor has expanded his possible courses of action since the lessee has agreed that virtually any breach or noncompliance invokes the lessor's right to pursue his default remedies.

Stipulation in the contract of the lessor's remedies on default does not insure that those options will be upheld in a court of law, yet it does enhance that possibility and it gives the lessee notice of what course (s) the lessor may be expected to follow.

With respect to his default remedies, the lessor is again maintaining a degree of flexibility. By providing for immediate delivery by the lessee, immediate retrieval by the lessor, or immediate storage by the lessee, the lessor can act according to the exigencies of the situation. The fourth paragraph is tantamount to a "liquidated damages" provision. Such a provision will normally be judicially enforced if (1) the damages resulting from a breach are speculative and unascertainable at the time the contract is made, and (2) the amount provided is a good faith estimate agreed upon by the parties of the damages likely to ensue as a result of a breach. However, the provision will likely be unenforceable if it is applicable to any and all breaches regardless of their magnitude. The liquidated damages clause should, therefore, be activated only by specifically enumerated acts equivalent in degree to nonpayment of the rentals.

The provision for attorneys' fees and other reasonable expenses necessitated by repossession, e.g., having to resort to judicial enforcement of the contract, etc. shifts the burden of attorneys' fees to the lessee and acts as an additional impetus for the lessee *not* to breach the contract. As a practical matter, however, aside from such causes as nonfunctional equipment, etc., a lessee will generally not breach the agreement unless he is in an unstable financial condition. In such case, the likelihood of recovery by the lessor of all contractually specified damages is small. Nevertheless, it is still advisable to provide for such damages, because if nothing else, the provision may be used to establish the lessor's claim against the lessee in a bankruptcy proceeding.

The sixth paragraph is made applicable where the lessee fails to return, store, or allow the lessor to retrieve the equipment. In such event, the lessee is required to, in effect, purchase the equipment from the lessor for its then fair market value. This could potentially have some adverse tax consequences to the lessor. Upon disposal of the asset, the lessor may have to recapture some investment tax credit (see chapter 13). Additionally, there exists the possibility that the IRS may reclassify the lease as a conditional sale. If either recapture or reclassification occurs, the lessee may be liable for the loss in tax benefits by virtue of the "tax indemnification provision" (discussed below). The remedy provided for in this (sixth) paragraph is in addition to those mentioned above. Where the lessee keeps the equipment *and* fails to make the rental payments, the lessor must be recompensed for both the loss of his equipment and the profit he would have earned but for the breach. The underlying concept here is to make the nonbreaching party "whole," that is, he should be placed as near as is possible in the position he would have been in had the breach not occurred.

The last paragraph is another safety valve for the lessor. It provides, in effect, that where the lessee's debt-paying ability is dubious, the lessor may invoke his default remedies and both parties are then to act in accordance with the provisions governing default. It is clear that this may at times be highly advantageous to the lessor. However, due to the possibility of interference with what would be an already financially unstable lessee, if he has any bargaining power whatsoever, the lessee should avoid the inclusion of such a provision in the agreement.

Because the default provisions are probably the most important in the contract, they should be drafted with utmost care. Simply using an outdated form contract or copying from a form book is likely to be inadequate.

12. TAX INDEMNIFICATION.

Due to the significance of tax benefits in leasing transactions, the loss of these benefits could turn a very profitable agreement into a seriously undesirable contract. Frequently, lessors enter into leases primarily for their tax shelter benefits: interest, depreciation, and the investment tax credit (see chapter 13). This is true now more than ever in light of the safe harbor lease election of section 168(f)8 of the Internal Revenue Code. Therefore, the loss of these advantages can be devastating. Viewed in this light, the objective of a tax indemnification provision is to place the lessor in the same *after-tax* position he would have been in had the loss not occurred. Problems emerge, however, in determining when the provision is applicable. There are normally only three ways that a tax loss will occur: (1) The lessor may cause it by his own acts or omissions, with such acts or omissions being inconsistent with the attainment or retention of the tax benefits. For example, the lessor may dispose of the asset triggering recapture of investment tax credit (ITC). (2) The lessee may be the cause as a result of his own acts or omissions. For example, he may use the new equipment before it is subject to the lease. (3) Outside of the control of the lessor or lessee is a predominant exogenous factor demanding almost constant attention: Congress, in its infinite wisdom, may elect to change the tax law. Another exogenous factor may come into play: an involuntary conversion. Because of the presumed existence of an insurance recovery and concommitant reinvestment of the proceeds, it is unlikely, however, that any tax loss would be forthcoming. For that reason, discussion will be limited to the three previously mentioned causes.

If the lessor is the cause of his own loss, the lessee should not be required to compensate him for it. If the lessor is the cause of a tax loss to the lessee, e.g., by failing to pass through the ITC in accordance with IRS requirements, then the lessor should of course indemnify the lessee. Likewise, where the lessee is the cause of the lessor's loss, the tax-loss provision should be applicable. If the lessee causes his own loss, e.g., by failing to take the ITC passthrough, the lessor should not be liable. The real problem emerges with regard to a change in the law. This will ultimately be resolved in favor of the party with the greatest bargaining power.

In determining a tax-loss formula, basically the same factors must be considered as in the computations to determine the after-tax yield to the lessor (or cost to the lessee): The tax rates of the indemnified party (both federal and state), the discount rate, the term over which the tax benefits would have been realized but for the loss, and of course the dollar amount of lost benefits. The construction of the formula will be different for each party because of the difference in their circumstances, particularly their tax and discount rates. Because of the complexity of the tax loss formula, it is suggested that each be "tailor made" by a CPA or attorney well versed in present-value concepts and tax law.

In addition to the formula itself, the parties should consider at what point liability will attach. For instance, many agreements provide that indemnification is not required unless and until (1) the indemnified party fully contests the issue with the IRS, and (2) the loss has actually occurred, either in the form of a lost deduction or credit, or in the form of a payment for deductions or credits previously taken but disallowed.

13. ASSIGNMENT; OFFSET.

Without Lessor's prior written consent, Lessee shall not (a) assign, transfer, pledge, hypothecate, or otherwise dispose of this Lease, Equipment, or any interest therein; or (b) sublet or lend Equipment or permit it to be used by anyone other than Lessee or Lessee's employees.

Lessor may assign this Lease and or mortgage Equipment, in whole or in part, without notice to Lessee. Each such assignee and or mortgagee shall have all of the rights, but none of the obligations, of Lessor under this Lease. Lessee shall not assert against assignee and or mortgagee any defense, counterclaim or offset that Lessee may have against Lessor. Notwithstanding any such assignment, Lessor warrants that Lessee shall quietly enjoy use of the Equipment subject to the terms and conditions of this Lease Agreement. Subject to the foregoing, this Lease inures to the benefit of and is binding upon the heirs, legatees, personal representatives, successors and assigns of the parties hereto.

The purpose of this provision, again, is to protect the lessor's interest in the equipment itself and in the rentals flowing from it. The "prior written consent" requirement allows the lessor to assess the transferee's credit-worthiness in terms of his ability to make the rentals and to properly care for the equipment. Even if the lessor consents to the lessee assigning his interest in the lease, the lessee is still liable to the lessor to make the lease payments unless a novation occurs. A novation in this context is an agreement whereby the lessor would relieve the lessee of liability on the lease and substitute in his place the lessee's transferee.

It is fundamental contract law that one may assign his rights but not his duties under a contract. He may delegate his duties to a third party, but this does not relieve him of those duties. In the event the third person fails to perform, the delegator is liable. With this in mind, it can be seen that an assignment by the lessor does not prejudice the rights of the lessee, and in fact, enhances the financial flexibility of the lessor. The lack of prejudice to the lessee is further illustrated by the lessor's warranty of quiet use and enjoyment of the equipment.

The last sentence of this provision is standard in every contract. It ensures, for example, that if the lessor is an individual (and not a corporation) and dies during the lease term, his estate, heirs, or legatees will be entitled to the lease payments.

14. LESSOR'S EXPENSES.

Lessee shall pay Lessor all costs and expenses including reasonable attorneys' fees, the fees of collection agencies, and other expenses such as telephone and telegraph charges, incurred by Lessor in enforcing any of the terms, conditions or provisions hereof, whether incurred before or after judgment.

This provision is an explicit reiteration of the default provision as regards the payment of attorneys' fees and other expenses resulting from the lessor's incurrence of costs associated with the enforcement of the contract. It is somewhat redundant in light of the default provision, but this is not unfavorable to either party as it merely reemphasizes that the lessee is to bear the burden of what frequently seem to be "unreasonable" attorneys' fees.

15. OWNERSHIP; PERSONAL PROPERTY.

Equipment is, and shall at all times remain, the property of Lessor; and Lessee shall have no right, title or interest therein or thereto except as expressly set forth in this Lease. Equipment is, and shall at all times be and remain, personal property notwithstanding that Equipment or any part thereof may now be, or hereafter become, in any manner affixed or attached to real property or any building thereon.

The wording of this provision substantiates the lessor's status as owner for tax and UCC purposes. The fact that the parties agree that the property will remain personal property (as opposed to real property by virtue of its potential status as a fixture) helps protect the equipment from liens or mortgages on the real property on which the equipment is located.

16. FILING OR RECORDING.

The parties hereto do not intend this Lease to be, and it is not, a conditional sales contract, chattel mortgage, or security agreement within the meaning of any statute requiring filing or recordation thereof or of any notice or statement with respect thereto. Nevertheless, this Lease may be so filed of record to give notice to interested parties. Lessee hereby gives Lessor authority to execute and complete any such notices, including financing statements filed pursuant to the Uniform Commercial Code, in behalf of and as agent for Lessee for said purposes.

A provision of this type is important for two reasons. First, it manifests the intent of the parties that the agreement is in fact a lease and not a conditional sales contract. Although not conclusive, it is a factor to be weighed in assessing the true nature of the agreement for tax and UCC purposes. Second, it protects the lessor in the event that a court finds the transaction to be a conditional sales contract which the UCC designates as a "security interest" (see "The Lease Agreement and Attendant Documents").

17. MODIFICATION.

This Lease constitutes the entire agreement between Lessor and Lessee, and supersedes all previous representations, negotiations, or conversations between the parties. This Lease Agreement can only be changed, altered, or modified, except as expressly stated herein, by a written document executed by both Lessor and Lessee.

This is another standard provision with a dual purpose: (1) To present the agreement as the entire agreement between the parties. In other words, if a term is not contained in the agreement itself, the parties are not bound by it. This has the practical effect of limiting the admissibility of parol evidence (oral testimony) of prior or contemporaneous agreements between the parties. (2) To satisfactorily document any subsequent alterations to the agreement. This, of course, minimizes the potential for misunderstanding.

18. MISCELLANEOUS; NO WAIVER; DOCUMENT REQUESTS; JOINT AND SEVERAL LIABILITY; FILING; GOVERNING LAW; LOCATION OF SUIT.

No provision of this Lease can be waived except by the written consent of Lessor. Lessee shall provide Lessor with such corporate resolutions, opinions of counsel, financial statements and other documents as Lessor shall request from time to time. If more than one Lessee is named in this Lease, the liability of each shall be joint and several. If Lessor so requests, Lessee shall execute such documents as Lessor shall require for filing or recording. The Lease shall be governed by the law of the State of Utah. If either party desires to bring an action in a court of law against the other party for any matter related to this Agreement, such action shall be brought in Salt Lake City, Utah, in the appropriate state or federal court.

The first sentence is a reiteration of a portion of the default provision. It protects the lessor from inadvertently waiving any rights. The second sentence facilitates the lessor's obtaining documents from the lessee (see "The Lease Agreement and Attendant Documents"). Joint and several liability means that each lessee (if more than one) can be sued jointly, e.g., in conjunction with the others, or severally, e.g., individually as though he owed the entire debt. The fourth sentence aids the lessor in procuring the lessee's signature as may be required to file or record documents. The fifth sentence sets forth the state law that will be controlling in the event litigation results. This could be important where the lessor is domiciled in one state and the lessee in another. The last sentence is an attempt to protect the lessor from having to defend a suit in distant places.

19. RENEWAL.

In the event Lessee fails to return Equipment in accordance with paragraph 10 hereof, at Lessor's exclusive option, this Lease may be continued on a month-to-month basis until Lessee returns Equipment to Lessor. In the event this Lease is so continued, Lessee shall pay Lessor rental in the same periodic amounts as indicated in paragraph 3 above.

A provision of this nature has its practical effect with regard to bankruptcies. Where the lessee fails to return the equipment at the end of the lease term and thereafter files for bankruptcy, this provision establishes the lessor's claim against the lessee. Otherwise, evidence of the fair rental value of the equipment would have to be gathered from past contracts, similar leases of like equipment, etc. This provision simplifies the lessor's task.

In addition, this provision could have the effect of bolstering the argument that the transaction is in fact a true lease. The month-to-month basis of the lease upon the expiration of the original term is substantially akin to a "tenancy at will." A tenancy at will is a lease agreement that typically continues on a month-to-month basis and may be terminated by either party. This has traditonally been characteristic of a lease and not of a sale. The fact that the lessor has the exclusive option to continue the lease further insulates the parties from an IRS contention that the renewal period transforms into a conditional sale what would otherwise have been a true lease. This is because the lessee has no right whatsoever, without the lessor's consent, to extend the period of the lease.

20. PURCHASE OPTION.

Few things impact the classification of a transaction as a lease or a conditional sale more than the existence and written terms of a purchase option. A nominal purchase option price will almost always result in the transaction being deemed a sale for IRS purposes and, if coupled with other indicia of a sale, for UCC purposes as well.

The IRS, and presumably state courts in their interpretation of the UCC, have no qualms about a purchase option the price of which is equal to fair market value of the equipment at time of exercise. But a different price may cause problems.

To cope with the purchase option problem, many leasing companies proceed along one or a combination of four different routes. The first and simplest is not to provide any purchase option whatsoever. This, however, may inhibit a prospective lessee from entering into the transaction. The second involves some degree of subterfuge but is nevertheless rather prevalent. Although no purchase option is provided for in the lease agreement itself, the lessor and lessee come to an oral understanding that the lessee will in fact be entitled to purchase the equipment at the expiration of the lease term. The lessor will generally approximate the option price by reference to past sales of similar equipment. This technique will normally maintain the intergrity of the lease classification since there is no documentation to provide otherwise. By the same token, though, the lessee may not be able to enforce the oral agreement.

The third method is similar to the first two in that nothing is said about a purchase option in the lease agreement itself. However, sometime after the consummation of the agreement, a letter is sent by the lessor to the lessee confirming the existence and terms of the purchase option. The terms of the option stated in the letter range from very vague and nondefinitive to extremely explicit. Generally, though, the terms will either be so vague as to make the option unenforceable, or state that the option price is the fair market value of the equipment at time of exercise. In either case, the option should withstand IRS or state court scrutiny. The letter approach really accomplishes nothing because the letter will probably be deemed a part of the contract. This method does, however, allow the leasing company to use its standard "snap out" contract without having to modify it for different lessees regarding the "terms" of a purchase option. Additionally, the unwary lessee may be somewhat comforted psychologically knowing he has a piece of paper in his possession designated "Purchase Option," even though the terms of it may be too vague to enforce.

The last method entails stipulating the purchase option price as a percentage of the fair market value *at the time the lease commenced.* The applicable percentage varies with the type and useful life of the equipment. This approach could encounter problems regarding either the tax law of the UCC or both if the stated percentage was substantially less than the fair market value at the time the option was exercised.

The four basic methods mentioned above in no way constitute an exhaustive list. To the contrary, there is an infinite array of combinations and permutations available to the parties to a lease transaction to deal with this problem. The purpose of the discussion was to alert prospective lessors and lessees of some of the alternatives used in the industry and the viability of those alternatives.

Additional Considerations.

The preceding material was fairly representative of the provisions contained in a typical lease agreement. There are a variety of items, however, that appear in the lease contract, but are generally not categorized as "provisions." For example, when the terms of a contract are contained on more than a single page, the bottom of each page will so indicate by a short phrase in large bold type, *e.g.*, "This lease also includes all terms and provisions on the reverse side thereof," or "This agreement continues on the reverse side hereof." The objective is to ensure that the lessee is aware of the contract in its entirety.

Another statement typically found at or near the bottom of each page in conspicuous bold type is: "This lease cannot be canceled by lessee." The noncancelable nature of the contract is generally implicit in the provisions. This express reiteration, however, leaves no room for question.

A third area necessitating discussion is the signature block. Most contracts require "authorized signatures and titles." For a corporation, this generally means the signatures of both the president and the secretary with their titles so designated next to their names. With regard to general partnerships, the signature and title of any partner is normally sufficient. Limited partnerships, however, require the signature of a general partner, as opposed to a limited partner. If a party is conducting business as a sole proprietorship, the word, "proprietor" should follow his signature. In addition to authorized signatures and titles, many contracts require the signatory's social security number and/or the employer's identification number. This is just an added precautionary measure to avoid any confusion with regard to who is bound to the agreement.

LEASE PROVISIONS CONCLUSION

As should be fairly evident at this point, the tone of the provisions is heavily lessor-oriented. The reason is that leasing contracts are typically drafted by lessors. The majority of leasing transactions are effectuated through the use of the lessor's standardized contracts. In contrast, there are few leases governed by "custom" lease agreements. Nevertheless, the types of issues about which the parties should be concerned have been adequately illustrated above. The authors do not suggest, however, that the example provisions are appropriate for any and all transactions. The law is constantly changing especially in the area of leasing (since leasing is in an infantile stage of development). In view of this, it is strongly recommended that before a lease contract is written or entered into, the state of the law as it affects leasing in the areas of tax, commercial law, bankruptcy, contract law, etc., be evaluated. With regard to existing standardized contracts, they should be continuously updated and revised to reflect the current legal standards by which the contracts will be judged.

II. ATTENDANT LEASE DOCUMENTS

A lease agreement is a contract, and thus is governed generally by contract law. This of course means that for the lease to be legally enforceable, the parties must have the capacity to contract; they must have a meeting-of-the-minds; consideration must be present; and the purpose of the agreement cannot be contrary to the law or public policy. Once these foundational requirements have been met, both the lessor and lessee are bound to the provisions. In the event of a breach by either party, if a lawsuit ensues, the law of contractual remedies will be invoked by the court in its resolution of the dispute.

The lease contract is the focal point for determining the rights and duties of the signatories. It should therefore contain all of the *provisions* to which the parties agreed they would be bound. Although an oral agreement may be enforceable, for safety's sake, no substantive provision of the agreement should be left to an oral understanding between the parties. Parol evidence (oral testimony) may be admissible in some circumstances in a court of law, but the agreement in its totality will be more easily enforced if it is entirely in writing. In addition to the lease contract itself and the provisions thereof, a variety of other *documents* are needed to effectuate the transaction. Some of these are only procedural in nature, but others are necessary to protect the interests of both the lessor and the lessee. Following is a list of typical documents which are necessary for, but supplemental to, an ordinary nonleveraged lease agreement.

1. *Purchase Order*—After the lessor and lessee have agreed on the equipment to be leased and the supplier from whom it will be purchased, the lessor will forward a purchase order to the supplier as the first step toward the purchase of the equipment. Although the lessee typically selects both the equipment and the supplier, it is important that the *lessor* initiate the purchase order because this may be one of the many factors used to determine whether the transaction between the lessor and lessee is a true lease or a disguised conditional sales contract. This is not necessarily true, however, in the case of a section 168(f)(8) election (see chapter 2).

   Frequently, the lessor will agree with the lessee to include certain terms in the lessor's contract with the supplier. The lessor's purchase order generally includes such terms because the purchase order is in effect an "offer" by the lessor. Upon the supplier's acceptance of the purchase order, the supplier is generally bound by the terms included in the purchase order. One such provision is that the supplier will agree that all representations, agreements, and warranties made by the supplier to either the lessee or the lessor may be enforced by the lessee in his own name (see "The Lease Agreement-Suggested Provisions" earlier in this chapter).

2. *Invoice*—After the supplier has received and accepted the purchase order, he will issue an invoice to the lessor verifying the equipment, its price, etc. Again it is mandatory that the invoice be in the lessor's name, unless a section 168(f)(8) election is in effect. After the lessor receives the invoice, it is frequently wise to contact the Secretary of State to determine whether title to the equipment is free from all liens and encumbrances.

3. *Bill of Sale from Supplier*—Typically accompanying the supplier's invoice is the bill of sale wherein the supplier should warrant title to the equipment

and agree to defend against title suits, etc. Here again, it is important that the bill of sale be in the lessor's name.

4. *Acknowledgment of Delivery and Acceptance*—The last major involvement of the supplier in the lease transaction is his delivery of the equipment to the lessee. Upon delivery, the supplier should be required to send to the lessor a document indicating that delivery has been made and that the equipment is in satisfactory condition. This should be verified in writing by the lessee.

5. *Corporate Resolution of the Secretary of the Corporation*—Assuming that the parties to the lease agreement are corporations, this requirement applies equally to both of them. The purpose is to ensure that the lease has been accepted by each corporation's Board of Directors. If either of the parties is a partnership, a document akin to a corporate resolution, indicating that the lease is within the partnership's authority, should be signed by all of the partners or by the managing partner.

6. *Guarantee Agreement*—Depending on the financial strength of the parties, either or both of them may be required to execute a personal guarantee. This is accomplished by having a principal, such as the president, sign a document whereby he becomes personally liable for the performance of the contractual obligations. For example, if the lessee corporation fails to pay the lease rentals, the officer who executed his personal guarantee would be subject to liability for payment of the rentals.

7. *Legal Opinions*—The counsel of both parties should submit opinions as to the various items that may impact the ability, both legally and factually, of a party to fulfill its contractual obligations. Four common topics are: (1) whether the entity is properly organized and in good standing, (2) whether the entity has complied with state "doing business" requirements (this usually involves nothing more than registering with the Secretary of State of each state in which the entity conducts business), (3) whether there are prohibitions in the articles of incorporation or by-laws (or partnership agreement), loan restrictions, etc., that affect a party's ability to legally enter into and perform its side of the agreement, and (4) the materiality of potential adverse lawsuits.

8. *Security Agreements*—If a lease is a conditional sales contract, and not a true lease, state law generally requires certain statements to be filed with the Secretary of State (or county recorder). These statements are "financing statements" and in most jurisdictions are referred to as either a UCC-1 or a UCC-3. The purpose of these statements is twofold: (1) to provide notice to third parties that the person filing the statement has an interest in the property, and (2) to establish a priority of claims against the property in the event the "purchaser" defaults or goes bankrupt. The UCC-1 form is filed where col-

lateral is given to secure the purchase; the equipment itself is usually collateral. The UCC-3 form is used where collateral is interchanged during the lease term.

Even where in all likelihood the lease will not be considered a conditional sales contract, it is prudent to file the financing statements anyway. The filings act as an inexpensive form of insurance that the lessor will have a priority claim in the leased equipment regardless of the transaction's classification by a court of law. In the context of a lease, however, it should be designated on the financing statements that the purpose of filing them is to provide notice, and is not an indication that the parties intend the lease agreement to be a conditional sales contract (see "The Lease Agreement-Suggested Provisions").

9. *Confirmation of Recordation*—For certain types of property, such as aircraft and ships, there are *federal* recording statutes. Additionally, in some states, the financing statements discussed earlier are not the only recording requirements. To prevent potential problems resulting from noncompliance with the recordation laws, the party responsible for recording (generally the lessor) should execute a document confirming his conformance with the applicable statutes.

10. *Consent and Waiver*—Where the leased property is to be affixed to real property, *e.g.*, a building, the lessee should obtain consent from the real property owner and landlord (and if the property is mortgaged also from the mortgagee) to affix the leased equipment to the building. The lessee should also obtain from the same parties a "waiver" of any interest in the leased property. A waiver in this context is a relinquishment of any rights the parties may have in the leased equipment by virtue of its affixation to the real property.

11. *Copy of Insurance Policies*—Irrespective of which party is to provide insurance, a copy of all pertinent policies, *e.g.*, public liability, destruction or theft, etc., should accompany the transaction. This assures the parties that the equipment is adequately protected and that public liability coverage is sufficient.

12. *Certificate of Financial Update*—Where there is an extended period between the last publication of the financial statements and the closing of the transaction, lessors often require that the lessee update its financial statements to the date of closing. This allows the lessor to ascertain whether there are any recent developments that may impair the lessee's ability to perform the contract. The same may be required of the lessor where there is any doubt as to its financial strength. In the past, of the two parties, the lessee has generally been in a less advantageous financial position. But with the significant increase in the number of equipment leasing companies, as a result of both tax shelter and high-yield potential, it is likely that many of the new companies will be far from risk-free.

13. *Assurance Against Premature Use*—Due to the importance of the investment tax credit (ITC) in leasing transactions, where a section 168(f)(8) safe harbor election is not in effect, it is paramount that the lessee does not use the equipment before the transaction is completed. If so, the ITC may be rendered unavailable. The lessee's assurance is simply a promise that the equipment will not be used until after the transaction is finalized. As a precaution against premature use, the equipment should not be delivered to the lessee until the latter stages of the transaction.

14. *Purchase Option*—If a purchase option exists (see section entitled "The Lease Agreement-Suggested Provisions") and if it does not appear as a provision in the lease agreement itself, the option should then be a supplemental document. In order for the lessee to exercise the option, he should be required to send the lessor a "notice of intent to purchase." This is simply a letter sent sometime before the exercise date, informing the lessor of the lessee's intent to exercise the option.

LEASE DOCUMENTS CONCLUSION

The preceding documents are examples of those that normally accompany a leasing transaction. Some of them protect the lessee, but most are to safeguard the lessor's interests. Depending on the magnitude and complexity of the transaction, there are of course a variety of additional documents that may be required, *e.g.,* joint venture or partnership agreements between either equity or debt participants, regulatory authorizations, trust agreements, etc. Then too, leveraged lease transactions are much more complex than the provisions and attendant nonleveraged lease documents discussed in this chapter. Whenever a leasing transaction involves a substantial sum of money, it is essential to seek the advice of legal counsel well versed in the leasing field. Generally, it is a good idea to seek advice regardless of the size of the transaction.

13

Income Tax
——Considerations in Leasing——

The Economic Recovery Tax Act of 1981 has given a major impetus to leasing primarily through the liberalization of depreciation and investment tax credit incentives.

Income taxes play a crucial role in our business and political environments. The complexities of tax law impact virtually every major business transaction. A venture which, on the surface, appears profitable can, in fact, be an undesirable pursuit when viewed in light of the massive network of tax laws. Seldom is there any doubt that tax considerations are of utmost significance in leasing arrangements.

There are many facets to consider with regard to the tax aspects of leasing. These various tax aspects are based primarily on the following distinctions: (1) whether the transaction constitutes a "true" operating lease or a capital lease, and (2) whether the taxpayer is the lessor or lessee. An analysis of the operating-capital lease distinction was made in chapter 2. The second distinction is considerably less complicated. Simply stated, the lessor is the owner of an asset who grants temporary possession and use of the leased asset to the lessee.

The following discussion will set forth a general overview of the most relevant and commonly encountered tax considerations concerning leasing. Because each taxpayer's situation is different, the tax ramifications associated with each situation cannot be comprehensively covered in a general analysis. Therefore, this chapter is not intended to be a substitute for professional tax advice, and consequently such advice should be sought prior to any major leasing decision.

The primary elements of tax analysis demanding attention are: (1) Depreciation; (2) Investment Tax Credit (ITC) Rehabilitation Tax Credit (RTC), and the Energy Tax Credit (ETC); and (3) Interest Expense. Each of these elements should be considered individually and collectively before engaging in a lease transaction.

INVESTMENT TAX CREDIT (ITC),
REHABILITATION TAX CREDIT (RTC),
AND ENERGY TAX CREDIT (ETC)

Investment Tax Credit

In 1962, the Kennedy Administration borrowed a tax concept from European countries in an effort to stimulate investment in the recessionary U.S. economy. This concept, the ITC, essentially has the effect of reducing the purchase price of the "qualified" investment. Unlike a tax deduction, the credit is applied as a direct reduction of tax liability on a dollar-for-dollar basis. For example, assuming a taxpayer is entitled to a $1,000 credit his tax liability would be reduced by $1,000. If, however, the taxpayer had been entitled to the same dollar amount as a *deduction,* his tax liability would only have been reduced by the product of his tax bracket rate and the amount of the deduction, which of course, would be less than the full $1,000. Thus, to a taxpayer in a fifty percent bracket, the ITC is worth twice as much as a tax deduction of the same amount.

Eligible Property—Generally, there are six different types of qualified investments to which the ITC, RTC, and ETC are applicable. Commonly referred to as "Section 38" property, these qualified investments must be depreciable or amortizable and must generally have a useful life of three years or more. The definition of Section 38 property is found in Section 48 of the Internal Revenue Code and includes the following:

1. Tangible personal property, *e.g.,* machinery and equipment;
2. Certain real property (excluding buildings and their structural components) if such property:

    a. Is used as an integral part of manufacturing, production, or extraction, *e.g.,* fences used in connection with raising livestock, or refrigerator and freezer structures used in the processing and storage of milk; or

    b. Is used to furnish transportation, communication, electrical energy, gas, water, or sewage disposal services, and petroleum storage facilities; or

    c. Constitutes a research or bulk storage facility used in connection with any of the activities referred to in (a) or (b) above, *e.g.,* farmer's grain storage bins and silos;

3. Certain elevators and escalators;
4. Certain rehabilitated buildings, including historic buildings;
5. Single purpose agricultural or horticultural structures; and,
6. Certain livestock and certain railroad track.

The credit is to be taken in the taxable year in which the qualified property is placed in service. Generally, an asset is "placed in service" at the point it is in a condition or state of readiness and availability for a specifically assigned function.

Ineligible Property—Keeping in mind that the congressional motive behind the enactment of the ITC was to encourage investment in domestic products, it is interesting to note the property to which the credit is inapplicable. Following are six categories of ineligible property:

1. Foreign property, *i.e.*, property which is used predominantly outside the United States government:

   a. Transportation equipment is excepted so long as it is used to and from, or within and without, the United States.

   b. An additional exception deals with aircraft operated under a contract with the United States.

2. Lodging facilities including beds, carpeting, kitchen appliances, elevators, and escalators. However, if such facilities are used predominantly by transients, *i.e.*, average length of stay is less than thirty days, and the property otherwise meets the requirements mentioned in "eligible property" discussed above, such property qualifies for the credit. This is typically the case with hotels and motels. Nursing home furnishings may also qualify for the ITC.

3. Property owned or used by tax exempt entities, *i.e.*, charitable organizations. However, the new Economic Recovery Tax Act of 1981 retroactively allows the RTC to lessors of rehabilitated buildings used by tax exempt lessees.

4. Property used by government entities, *i.e.*, the United States or any state government, or any political subdivision thereof.

   Note: Two significant exceptions to both (3) and (4) above deal with property used on a service arrangement only, e.g., vending machines and certain rehabilitated buildings leased by the government qualify for the credit.

5. Property subject to special five year amortization, *e.g.*, day care facilities, certain pollution control facilities, etc.

6. Property completed in a foreign country or predominantly of foreign origin, *i.e.*, if it enters the country in substantially operational form, or if more than fifty percent of the property is attributable to value added outside the United States.

The above list of ineligible property including exceptions is not intended to be complete. Taxpayers interested in further detail and clarification are urged to refer to Section 48 of the Internal Revenue Code and also to seek professional tax counsel.

Amount of Credit—Generally, the maximum percentage of the investment tax credit is ten percent of the Section 38 property (certain "special" equipment, however, such as energy related items, qualifies for an additional credit known as the Energy Tax Credit (ETC) see below) For ITC purposes, if a taxpayer purchases qualifying property for $10,000, he may be entitled to a credit in the amount of as much as

$1,000. However, the percentage of the credit available to the taxpayer depends on the classification of the property according to the Economic Recovery Tax Act of 1981.

Property placed in service after January 1, 1981 is classified for purposes of the Investment Tax Credit as follows:

Category	Type of Asset	ITC Percentage
3 Year ACRS Life	Automobiles, light duty trucks, special tools, R & D machinery	6 percent
5,10,15 year ACRS Life	All other qualifying Section 38 Equipment	10 percent

Based on the two categories shown above, all qualifying Section 38 property will receive an investment tax credit equal to either six percent or ten percent of the asset's cost. The ITC percentage obtainable by the owner is no longer dependent upon the depreciation life assigned to the asset, rather it is dependent upon its ACRS (Accelerated Cost Recovery System) classification. Most equipment subject to commercial leases will therefore qualify for the full ten percent ITC whether or not the lease term is five years long.

The amount of ITC is also affected by the eligible property's new or used status. With respect to new equipment, the only applicable limitation is the overall amount of ITC to be claimed in any one taxable year (see next page). With respect to qualifying used property, no more than $125,000 of its cost qualifies for the credit in any one year, until 1985 when it increases to $150,000. This however, does not mean that if a taxpayer purchases $175,000 of used property in one year that he loses the ITC with respect to the excess. Such excess may be applied to future or past years in accordance with the carryforward and carryback rules discussed later. Additionally, the taxpayer may select which property he desires to use for ITC purposes in the current taxable year.

For example, assume that of $175,000 worth of used property purchased in 1985, $75,000 of the used equipment is five year ACRS classified ten percent ITC property, $25,000 is three year ACRS six percent ITC property, and the remaining $75,000 is ten year ACRS classified ten percent ITC property. To maximize his ITC for the current year, the taxpayer would choose the $75,000 worth of five year ACRS ten percent ITC property and the $75,000 worth of ten year ACRS ten percent ITC property. The remaining $25,000 worth of used property, with a six percent ITC could be utilized in other years. For used property to be eligible for the ITC, it must be acquired through purchase; not by any other means of transfer like through a lease.

At this point, it is important to note that the dollar amount of the ITC in any one year is subject to certain limitations based on tax liability. The maximum dollar amount of the credit realizable in any one year is equal to $25,000 plus a specified percentage of tax liability for that year in excess of $25,000. For 1981, this percentage is eighty percent. In 1982, the percentage increases by ten percentage points, at which time it stabilizes at ninety percent. The following table depicts the increases:

For Taxable Year Ending In	*Maximum Dollar Amount of ITC*
1981	$25,000, plus 80% of tax liability over $25,000
1982 and thereafter	$25,000, plus 90% of tax liability over $25,000 and thereafter

Thus, if a corporate taxpayer has taxable income of $100,000 for the calendar year ending December 31, 1982, resulting in a $26,750 tax liability, the maximum amount of ITC to be claimed in that year would be $26,575: $25,000 + 90% of $1,750.

If the amount of the ITC, calculated without reference to the rules for used property and the maximum dollar amount, exceeds the limitations imposed by the above rules, the excess may be carried forward fifteen years or carried back three years. The credit is to be utilized on a first in-first out (FIFO) basis, *i.e.,* in the current taxable year amounts carried forward are to be used first, then the amount determined for the current year is to be used, and finally amounts carried back are to be used.

The last general area of investment tax credit requirements affecting the taxpayer includes the rules of "recapture." Section 47 of the Internal Revenue Code provides that in the event the qualifying property is disposed of prior to the end of the useful life on which the ITC was based, the taxpayer must recapture all or a portion of the credit previously claimed. (No interest however is paid on recaptured ITC). In the event of a recapture, the total amount of the credit to which the taxpayer is entitled is equal to the amount he would have been entitled to had he selected, in the first place, the *actual* length of time that he used the asset. For example, assume a lessor acquires $60,000 of qualifying machinery which was classified as five year ACRS ten percent ITC property. He may be entitled to a $6,000 ITC for the taxable year in which the asset was purchased. However, if the lessor sells the asset to the lessee after four years of use, he must recapture twenty percent of the credit previously claimed, or $1200. Thus, he received a total benefit of $4,800 from the ITC.

RECAPTURE RULES WORK LIKE THIS:

1. Recapture 100 percent if the equipment was disposed of during the first full year after being placed in service.
2. Beyond the first year, for five, ten and fifteen year ITC property, the 100 percentage points from the first year recapture, explained in "1." above, are reduced by twenty percentage points for each full succeeding year. In other words, ITC is earned at the rate of two percent a year or recaptured at the rate of twenty percent of ten percent a year for five, ten and fifteen year property.
3. After the first full year, on three year property ITC is recaptured at the rate of sixty-six percent for the next year, and thirty-three percent the next year.

Thus, the credit earned after a recapture in the second year is 2.04 percent (6% - (6% X .66)), and the credit earned after a recapture in the third year is 4.02% (6% - (6% - (6% X .33))).

THE FOLLOWING EXAMPLE ILLUSTRATES THE COMMONLY ENCOUNTERED PROBLEMS OF THE ITC:

On May 28, 1985, J & T Co., a construction company engaged in building telephone systems, and a calendar year taxpayer, purchased a used IBM computer for $80,000. Later in the year, J & T purchased three used light trucks for $30,000 and a new dump truck for $36,000. In September of the same year the company installed an elevator costing $68,000 in an apartment complex it had purchased a month earlier. In November, the company acquired a new twin engine Cessna for $150,000 to transport materials and employees from Costa Rica to Brazil. In that same month, J & T purchased, for $70,000, a used helicopter to facilitate the construction of a telephone system in the Andes mountains under a contract with the U.S. government. On December 15, J & T purchased and leased some new vending machines to various government institutions throughout the intermountain West. The aggregate cost of these machines was $200,000. Based on the ACRS classifications, the available investment tax credits would be:

Computer	–	10 percent
Light Trucks	–	6 percent
Dump Trucks	–	10 percent
Elevator	–	10 percent
Cessna	–	10 percent
Helicopter	–	10 percent
Vending Machines	–	10 percent

The company's tax liability, without regard to any ITC reductions, was $35,000. There was an ITC carryover from 1984 of $4,000.

FOLLOWING IS A STEP-BY-STEP ANALYSIS OF ITC COMPUTATIONS:

Step One—Section 38 property includes all of the purchases except:

1. The elevator, because although elevators and escalators are generally eligible for the credit, such is not the case when used in connection with a lodging facility, and

2. The airplane, because although it is transportation equipment and would normally qualify as an exception to the "foreign property" rule, it is used *solely* outside of the U.S. (See Ineligible Property (1)). The computer, light trucks, and dump truck fall within the first category of Section 38 property, tangible personal property. (See Eligible Property (1)). The helicopter is

tangible personal property and, although it is used wholly outside the U.S., it is so used under a contract with the U.S. government. (See Ineligible Property (1) (b)). The vending machines are tangible property and, although leased to government agencies, are used under a service arrangement only. (See Ineligible Property (4) (note)).

Step Two—The available investment tax credit percentages were supplied in accordance with the company's ACRS classification and, thus, pose no problems.

Step Three—The cost of used property totaled $180,000, thus activating the cost limitation rule on used property. To maximize the available credit, J & T may select the property to be used for ITC purposes on its 1985 tax return. To effect this maximization, J & T would choose, first, both the $70,000 helicopter and the $80,000 computer, entitling the company to the ten percent credit. The $30,000 light trucks, eligible for only the six percent tax credit, would be used either in prior or subsequent years where the "cost of used property" limitation had not been reached. Since there is no cost limitation regarding new property, the full cost of the vending machines and the dump truck can be used to generate an ITC of $20,000 and $3,600 respectively. The following tables summarize the necessary computations:

Description	Life	NEW PROPERTY Cost	ITC Percentage	$ Amount
Dump Truck	5	$ 36,000	10%	$ 3,600
Vending Machines	5	$200,000	10%	20,000
				$23,600

Description	Life	USED PROPERTY Cost	ITC Percentage	$ Amount
Computer	5	$ 80,000	10%	$ 8,000
Light Trucks	3	$ 30,000	6%	1,800
Helicopter	5	$ 70,000	10%	7,000
				$16,800

The computer and the helicopter reach the 1985 $150,000 cost limitation on used property and generate and ITC of $8,000 and $7,000 respectively. Therefore, the 1985 total dollar amount of ITC generated from the 1980 transactions is $38,600 ($3,600 + $20,000 + $8,000 + $7,000). The $1,800 for the light trucks will be carried back or forward.

Step Four—For 1985, the dollar amount limit is $25,000, plus ninety percent of the tax liability in excess of $25,000. J & T's tax liability before the ITC was $35,000. Therefore, the total dollar amount of the ITC available for the 1985 taxable year is $34,000: $25,000 + 90% ($35,000 -$25,000).

Step Five—J & T had an ITC carryover from 1984 in the amount of $4,000. When added to the amount calculated in step three, we find the total amount available to be offset against the 1985 tax liability is $42,600, ($38,600 + $4,000). The dollar amount limit computed in step four is $34,000. Therefore, applying the available ITC on a FIFO basis, the net tax liability for 1985 is $1,000 ($35,000 - $34,000)and the amount of ITC carried forward to 1986 is comprised of two elements: (1) $8,600 ($42,600 - $34,000); and (2) the $1,800 ITC for the light trucks. Both amounts can be carried forward fifteen years and back three years.

REHABILITATION TAX CREDIT (RTC)

Rehabilitation Tax Credit

A new investment credit is available for rehabilitation expenses incurred to modernize existing (1) industrial, (2) commercial, and (3) certified historic structures. The rehabilitation or renovation costs must be for buildings that have been used at least thirty years and must be expected to last at least five more years.

The rehabilitation tax credit has three percentage levels, depending on the building's age at the time of reconstruction and it applies to the qualified rehabilitation expenses as follows:

15% Tax credit for buildings thirty to thirty-nine years old.
20% Tax credit for buildings forty years old and beyond.
25% Tax credit for certified historic structures.

When the rehabilitation credit is taken, the regular ITC and energy credit are not available; otherwise, triple credits might be taken. Also, the used property ITC limitation does not apply. Additionally, the owner of the building must use the straight-line method of cost recovery over fifteen, thirty-five or forty-five years.

Such rehabilitation tax credits are only available where the building has been substantially rehabilitated i.e., renovation expenses incurred during the two-year period ending on the last day of the owner's tax year, which are the greater of $5,000 or the adjusted basis of the building (remaining undepreciated book value), as of the beginning of the renovation period.

ENERGY TAX CREDIT (ETC)

Energy Tax Credit

As previously mentioned, certain energy property qualifies for an additional credit beyond the normal ITC. The energy credit ranges from ten to fiteen percent of the cost of qualifying energy property investments which includes the following:

1. Alternative energy property (substances other than or gas),
2. Solar or wind energy property,
3. Specially defined energy property,
4. Recycling equipment,
5. Shale oil equipment,
6. Equipment for producing natural gas from geo-pressured brine.
7. Etc.

ITC LIMITATIONS ON NONCORPORATE LESSORS

Section 46(3)(e) of the Internal Revenue Code provides that an individual or any other form of noncorporate lessor (partnership, etc.) is entitled to the ITC only where: (a) the subject property was manufactured or produced by the lessor; or (b) the "50/15" rule is met where the term of the lease (including renewal options) is less than fifty percent of the asset's useful life, *and* the lease is not a "net" lease, For these purposes, a "net" lease is one where, for the first twelve months of the lease term, the sum of section 162 deductions (other than rents, depreciation, interest, and other miscellaneous reimbursed amounts) is greater than fifteen percent of the gross lease rental income. Since the code speaks in terms of Section 162 deductions, it apparently presupposes that the leasing activities occur in the course of the taxpayer's "trade or business." The determination of whether or not the leasing transactions constitute a trade or business is not specifically defined in the Internal Revenue Code or the Treasurry Regulations. Court cases in which this issue has been raised, however, have established some parameters, though they are not very definitive. The distinction between a trade or business (for purposes of Section 162 deductions) and the production of income (for purposes of section 212 deductions) seems to be based on the level of the taxpayer's activity with respect to the leasing transactions. For instance, mere investment activity is not a trade or business. But where the lessor engages in leasing as more than just a pastime, *i.e.*, he actively pursues a marketing and advertising policy, manages and administers the affairs attendant with the transactions, he repairs and maintains the equipment during the lease, and then either disposes of the equipment in the secondary market or releases it, the likelihood is substantially increased that "trade or business" status has been attained.

The purpose of the fifteen percent requirement mentioned above is to ensure that the lessor actively participates in the leasing arrangements. Thus, it restricts the ability of a noncorporate lessor to enter into a passive investment solely for tax shelter purposes. In order to satisfy this frequently rigid requirement, some commentators have suggested that an amount pegged at fifteen percent of the gross rental income be paid to an unrelated third party for management services, accounting statements, etc. Often, this may be the only legitimate way to satisfy the condition.

The fifteen percent test is generally applied on a lease-by-lease basis. Overhead expenses which are applicable to all of the leases are to be allocated on a reasonable basis, e.g., percentage of gross rentals. However, the taxpayer may elect to aggregate the leases for purposes of the fifteen percent calculation. Aggregation may be beneficial where the expenses associated with one (or more) of the leases are less than the fifteen percent requirement, but when all of the leases are combined, the expense test is met.

The 1981 Economic Recovery Tax Act describes how the "lease term" requirement for a noncorporate lessor is to be met. Recovery property leased after June 25, 1981, for purposes of the "50 percent of an asset's useful life rule" will have a "useful life" equal to its ADR class life in effect on January 1, 1981. Therefore, the noncorporate lessor must structure the lease term so that it is less than one half of the ADR class life.

AT RISK LIMITATIONS ON THE ITC

The ITC is not available for investments where the lessor is not "at risk." At risk amounts include equity contributions and recourse debt. However, the 1981 Tax Act allows a lessor to treat certain types of nonrecourse debt as "at risk" debt as long as it is obtained from qualified sources and the lessor is at risk with his own equity and recourse debt at least twenty percent in the project.

Qualified sources banks, savings and loans, thrifts, industrial loan companies, insurance companies, qualified employees pension trusts, and as certain other regularly engaged as money lenders.

The "at risk" limitations for the ITC only affect noncorporate lessors. The net effect of this limitation is that individuals and partnerships (noncorporate) cannot structure leveraged leases without being at risk at least twenty percent and that the eighty percent nonrecourse borrowings can be obtained only from qualifying sources. In contrast, a corporation under the "safe harbor" election can structure a leveraged lease with as little as ten percent at risk and the nonrecourse debt can be obtained from any source (see chapter 2).

DEPRECIATION

Generally, under pre-Economic Recovery Tax Act Law where an asset had a useful life of limited duration greater than one year, the cost of such asset must have been allocated to the periods benefited by its use. In other words, the entire cost of such an asset could not be deducted from income in the year of the asset's purchase. This is because the economic value of the asset generally decreases with time and use. This decrease in value is not caused solely by physical deterioration of the asset; it may be caused by such things as obsolescence, a loss of trade, a legal prohibition against use of the asset, etc. The concept utilized to reflect this decline in the economic value of the asset and to allocate the cost of the asset over the periods benefited by its use was known for tax purposes as depreciation. The term depreciation, now obsolete, is used for the amortization of assets purchased prior to January 1, 1981. The Economic Recovery Tax Act, however, drastically modified the whole concept of "depreciation." The term "depreciation" is no longer applicable to assets purchased after 1980; the term now used is "accelerated cost recovery." In an effort to counteract the effects of inflation, the accelerated cost recovery system (ACRS) has divorced the concept of useful life from the timing of deductions for tax purposes. For assets purchased in 1981 and later years, therefore, the period over which the assets cost will be recovered generally will be significantly shorter than the assets useful life. For example, if a copy machine is purchased in 1985 having an estimated useful life of ten years, the cost of the copier cannot be recovered in 1985, but must be allocated over the five year period of 1985 to 1989. This allocation will generally be made using either of two basic methods: straight line or the Accelerated Cost Recovery System specified percentage. The elements necessary for the computation of depreciation in accordance with the aforementioned methods, with the exceptions noted below, are: (1) cost; (2) ACRS specified percentages; and (3) alternate ACRS straight-line lives.

COST

The cost of an asset equals the dollar amount of the asset which can be recovered. Cost includes all ordinary and reasonable expenditures necessary to place the asset in a state or condition of readiness or availability for use. For example, the cost to a wood shop of a table saw includes the invoice price less any cash discount, plus freight and assembling. Any special base or foundation, power connections, or adjustments necessary to place the saw in operation, are also elements of cost.

The following chart describes both the ACRS percentages available from 1981 through 1985 and the alternate straight-line lives for various classes of assets. Straight line depreciation allows an equal percentage of an asset's cost to be recovered each year of the asset's assigned straight line life. For example, a five year life results in a constant twenty percent per annual recovery, whereas a twenty year life results in an annual five percent cost recovery.

ACRS SPECIFIED PERCENTAGES AND THE ALTERNATE STRAIGHT LINE LIVES

Recovery Period Category	Type of Assets	YR	ACRS '81-'84 %	% '85 thereafter %	%	Alternate S/L Recovery Period
3 Yr	Section 1245 class property (tangible personal property- equipment) with an ADR class life as of 1/1/81 of 4 years or less and Section 1245 property used in research and development. Effectively, this class includes only automobiles, light-duty trucks, special tools, and R & D equipment.	1 2 3	25% 38% 37%	29% 47% 24%	33% 45% 22%	3, 5 or 12 yr
5 Yr	Section 1245 class property with an ADR class life greater than 4 years, except those few items classi- fied below in the 10 & 15 yr categories. Most equipment subject to a lease would be classi- fied here, except long-lived public utility property with an ADR life of 18 years or less. Also included are petroleum storage facilities and central telephone office equipment.	1 2 3 4 5	15% 22% 21% 21% 21%	18% 33% 25% 16% 8%	20% 32% 24% 16% 8%	5, 12 or 25 yr
10 Yr	Public utility equip- ment with a 1/1/81 ADR class life of 19 to 25 years; Section 1250 prop- erty if it has on 1/1/81 an ADR class life of 12.5 years or less. Section 1250 property here includes elevators and escala- tors, railroad tank cars, mobile homes, theme park structures, and coal utilization property. Utility property includes electric, gas, telephone, and water facilities.	1 2 3 4 5 6 7 8 9 10	8% 14% 12% 10% 10% 10% 9% 9% 9% 9%	9% 19% 16% 14% 12% 10% 8% 6% 4% 2%	10% 18% 16% 14% 12% 10% 8% 6% 4% 2%	10, 25 or 35 yr

Recovery Period Category	Type of Assets	YR	ACRS % '85 thereafter			Alternate S/L Recovery Period
			'81-'84 %	%	%	
15 Yr	Section 1250 property with a 1/1/81 class life of more than 12.5 years.		175% declining balance method with straight line crossover. Tables to be published by the IRS. A 200% declining balance method for low income housing property.			15, 35 or 45 yr
15 Yr Public Utility	Public utility property with a 1/1/81 class life of more than 25 years.	1	5%	6%	7%	15, 35 or 45 yr
		2	10%	12%	12%	
		3	9%	12%	12%	
		4	8%	11%	11%	
		5	7%	10%	10%	
		6	7%	9%	9%	
		7	6%	8%	8%	
		8	6%	7%	7%	
		9	6%	6%	6%	
		10	6%	5%	5%	
		11	6%	4%	4%	
		12	6%	4%	3%	
		13	6%	3%	3%	
		14	6%	2%	2%	
		15	6%	1%	1%	
Foreign Real Estate	Real Estate (Section 1250) used primarily outside the United States.	0%	150% declining balance method with straight line crossover. Tables to be published by IRS for 35 year life.			35 or 45 yr
Foreign Equipment	Tangible personal property (Section 1245 Equipment).	0%	200% declining balance method with straight line crossover at the ADR midpoint as of 1/1/81 or 12 yrs if no ADR life was established.			5, 12, 25, 35 or 45 yr

As can be referenced to the above, the eligible property consists of Section 1245 and Section 1250 property.

"Section 1245 property" is property classified in accordance with the definitions set forth in Section 1245(a)(3) of the Internal Revenue Code. Generally speaking, it is depreciable (or amortizable) property which is either:

1. Tangible or intangible personal property;
2. Other tangible property (excluding buildings and their structural components) which is:

    a. Used as an integral part of:

        i. Manufacturing, production or extraction; or
        ii. Furnishing transportation, communications, electrical energy, gas, water, or sewage disposal services;

    b. A research or bulk storage facility used in connection with any of the activities referred to in (a)(i) or (ii);

3. An elevator or escalator;
4. Certain amortizable real property;
5. For taxable years after 1969, livestock.

Section 1250 property is defined by Section 1250(c) as "any real property (other than Section 1245 property) which is or has been property of a character subject to the allowance for depreciation provided in Section 167." This property consists primarily of buildings and their structural components.

The new Accelerated Cost Recovery System (ACRS) introduced as a major portion of the Economic Recovery Tax Act of 1981 drastically simplifies the determination of an asset's "annual cost recovery allowance," formerly known as depreciation. As the above chart indicates, all property, whether (1) new or used, (2) foreign or domestic, (3) real estate or tangible personal property (equipment) is assigned to a recovery class with a set depreciation rate or percentage. This rate is multiplied by the asset's cost to arrive at the annual cost recovery allowance. It is important to note that the following previous depreciation techniques have been eliminated:

1. *Accelerated depreciation* techniques such as declining balance or sum-of-the years digits. Note, however, that the IRS will be publishing rates for foreign assets and fifteen year property based on these depreciation techniques. Also, the ACRS designated rates already in effect are accelerated. The straight line technique is still available as an alternative to the ACRS rates.

2. *"New" versus "Used" property distinction.* Both new or used property placed in service after 1/1/1981 will be depreciated according to the ACRS guidelines. However, used property does not qualify for the Leasing "safe harbor" rules explained previously in chapter 2. Moreover, any property placed in service by a taxpayer prior to 1/1/1981 cannot be brought under the ACRS system. However, a subsequent, unrelated purchaser of the equipment can use the ACRS method unless acquired for the purpose of leasing.

3. *The concept of useful life* as a determination of the time period during which depreciation is taken. This concept has been replaced with a specific life for each category of assets over which the asset's cost is recovered.

4. *Salvage value* which formerly was deducted from cost to determine the amount of depreciation to be taken. The ACRS method wholly ignores salvage value since each asset category has set rates for each year which, if totaled, equal 100 percent. Thus, 100 percent of cost can be written off as a tax deduction or "recovery allowance."

5. *Half-year convention and modified half-year convention* methods of receiving partial or full year depreciation deductions in the years of acquisition and disposition. All personal property (tangible section 38) receives a specified percentage for the year in which the asset was purchased whether on January 1 or December 31 of the calendar taxable year. However, real estate will receive a pro-rata cost recovery allowance for the year an asset is placed in service based upon the number of months the asset is in service.

6. *Component depreciation* of real estate has been totally eliminated where separate parts of a building were assigned various depreciation lives to maximize the deduction through shortened lives.

7. *Bonus depreciation* (additional first year depreciation of twenty percent) has been eliminated. However, in its place, an election to expense $5,000 – $10,000 per year of business property has been instituted as the following chart indicates:

Year Placed in Service	Expense Allowance
1981	$ 0
1982 – 1983	5,000
1984 & 1985	7,500
1986 on	$10,000

No investment credit is allowed on amounts of property written off under this "expensing election."

8. *Self dealing or churning* of assets to maximize depreciation deductions has been limited under the 1981 Tax Act. Property placed in service prior to 1981 cannot be brought with the ACRS benefits by selling it to a related party. The effect of this rule is to limit:

a. *Sale-leasebacks* of property placed in service prior to 1/1/81, because leasing such property to a person (or related person) who owned or used the property prior to 1/1/81 causes a disallowance of the ACRS benefits, and

b. *Selling of leases* – since the purchase of leased property placed in service prior to 1/1/81 by a person unrelated to either the original lessor or lessee, with no change in lessee, causes a disallowance of the ACRS benefits.

INTEREST

Interest expense as a tax deduction must be considered primarily in the context of leveraged leases from the lessor's perspective and capital leases from the lessee's perspective. In a "true" lease, generally, the lessee is not entitled to an interest deduction under Section 163, but rather may take a Section 162(a)(3) deduction for the full amount of the lease payments. In a "tr ie" lease, the lessor is entitled to an interest deduction where he has borrowed money to purchase the leased property. Interest, like any other tax deduction, provides a tax benefit equal to the product of the taxpayer's tax bracket rate and the amound of the interest expense for the taxable year. However, a lessee, whether on the cash or accrual basis, is not entitled to deduct as interest in the current year any amount paid at the signing of a lease which is in reality a bonus or advance rental for a period beyond the current taxable year. This is congruent with the "matching" concept, that is, the expenses of one year cannot be used to reduce another year's income. Therefore, the lessee must amortize the sum paid over the entire term of the lease rather than deduct it in its entirety in the year in which it is paid. This has the effect of placing cash basis and accrual basis taxpayers on equal footing with respect to amounts of this nature paid in advance.

INCOME TAXES AND OPERATING LEASES

The lease definition guidelines set forth by the Internal Revenue Service in the Economic Recovery Tax Act of 1981 and in Revenue Procedure 75-21 concerning leveraged leases, which may be used by analogy for purposes of the operating versus capital lease distinction, were discussed in chapter 2. Generally, if the lease survives Internal Revenue Service scrutiny such that it is considered to be a "true" lease, the lessor is afforded the tax advantages of depreciation, interest, and the ITC. The rental payments received from the lessee are to be included in the lessor's revenue while at the same time are an expense deduction for the lessee.

Lessors, Lessees, and the ITC.

In the context of an operating lease, the lessor is generally entitled to the ITC. However, he has the option of passing it through to the lessee. To be eligible for the pass-through, the property must be *new* in the hands of both the lessor and lessee. For example, new property purchased by the lessor and subsequently used by him for more than three months prior to leasing it to the lessee is not eligible. In the event the property is new section 38 property, the "cost" of the property and the lessor elects to pass the ITC through to the lessee, the lessee's basis in the property for ITC purposes is generally its fair market value. The ITC percentage available, six or ten percent, is determined by the lessor without regard to the lease term. For example, if the asset has a five year ACRS classification, but the lease is for three years, the applicable percentage for purposes of the ITC pass-through is ten percent. The lessor makes the election to pass through by writing a letter to the lessee containing various information about the equipment prescribed by the Internal Revenue Service. The election is irrevocable once filed with the lessee.

The ITC pass-through is subject to a special limitation when the pass-through is in connection with a "short term lease." A "short term lease" is defined by section 48(d)(4) of the Internal Revenue Code as a lease, the property of which:

1. Is new section 38 property;
2. Has a class life in excess of fourteen years;
3. Is leased for a period which is less than eighty percent of its class life; and
4. Is not leased subject to a net lease.

A net lease is basically one where the expenses in the first year associated with the lease, less depreciation, interest, and taxes, are less than fifteen percent of the gross rental income. In the event the lease is a "short term lease" as defined above, the ITC is apportionable between the lessor and the lessee. The lessor's portion of the ITC is computed as follows:

$$\text{Cost of Property} \quad \times \quad \frac{(\text{Class Life}-\text{Lease Term})}{\text{Class Life}} \quad \times \quad \begin{array}{c}\text{Applicable}\\\text{ITC Percentage}\end{array}$$

The lessee is entitled to the remainder. This apportionment has the effect of passing through to the lessee an amount of the available ITC which is based on the lease term in relation to the useful life of the property. In light of the 1981 Economic Recovery Tax Act, it is speculative whether the IRS will discontinue this apportionment technique.

INCOME TAXES AND CAPITAL LEASES

As was mentioned in chapter 2, a capital lease is not really a lease at all; it is treated as a conditional sale of equipment by the lessor and as a purchase by the lessee. Since the "lessee" is considered the owner of the "leased" property, he obtains the tax related incidents of ownership, i.e., the ITC, and the interest and depreciation deductions. The "lessee's" basis in the property is equal to the sum of the rental payments over the term of the lease agreement less an amount for imputed interest.

For payments made on account of a sale or exchange of property entered into after July 23, 1975, the imputed interest rate is seven percent per annum compounded semi-annually. This rate is, of course, subject to change by the Internal Revenue Service. In the case of a capital lease, the "purchase" price of the property is simply the present value of the rental payments discounted at seven percent. The total amount of the interest calculated under the unstated interest rule of section 483(b) of the Internal Revenue Code is equal to the total amount of "rental" payments due under the contract less the present value of the payments. The amount of the interest allocated to each payment is equal to the product of each respective payment and total imputed interest divided by the sum of the "rental" payments.[1] For example, assume that an asset is "leased" for a five-year term at $500 per month and that for tax purposes, it is considered a capital lease. The selling price of the asset would be the present value of $500 per month for five years at seven percent (25,251). Each $500 payment would be comprised of $79.15 interest and $420.85 principal calculated as follows:

Interest

$$= \text{Payment} \times \frac{(\text{Total Imputed Interest})}{\text{Total Rental Payments}}$$

$$= \$500 \times \frac{(30,000 - 25,251)}{30,000}$$

$$= \$79.15$$

Principal

$$= \text{Payment} - \text{Interest}$$

$$= 500 - 79.15$$

$$= \$420.85$$

From the lessor's perspective, a capital lease for tax purposes can be either (1) a sales-type lease; or (2) a direct financing lease. In either case, the transaction is considered to be a sale of the property. However, a sales-type capital lease gives rise to manufacturer's or dealer's profit; a direct financing lease does not. For example, suppose M purchased and "leased" to B an asset for five years at a monthly rental charge of $500. If the transaction were deemed to be a conditional sale, taking into account the imputed interest rules, the selling price would be $25,251. Assuming M's cost of acquiring the asset was $20,000, his gain on the sale would be $5,251. This gain may be included in his income on the installment method of accounting, provided he complies with the requirements of section 453. On the other hand, a direct financing lease does not contemplate "profit" in the same sense. The "lessor's" entire return comes in the from of interest income. Therefore, in the example above, the "lessor's" cost and the selling price would be the same: $25,251. The lessor would have to include a portion of the interest income in the tax return for each year in which payments were received.

---

[1] Treas. Reg. Sec. 1.483-1(a)(2)(1980).

In summary, a capital lease is in substance a sale. Therefore, the seller-lessor must recognize gain or loss on such sale. For federal income tax purposes, he is no longer the owner (unless a section 168(f)(8) election is in effect (see chapter 2)). For this reason, he is not entitled generally to the various credits and deductions attendant to ownership. On the other hand, because the incidents of ownership have passed to the purchaser-lessee. The lessee is therefore entitled to depreciate the asset, deduct the interest expense associated with the purchase, and claim the ITC. The selling price of the asset is calculated by taking the present value of the "lease" payments discounted at seven percent compounded semi-annually. Both the seller-lessor's gain (or loss) and the purchaser-lessee's depreciation deductions are predicated on this figure.

CONCLUSION

Entering into a properly structured leasing arrangement can have highly advantageous tax consequences for both the lessor and lessee. The primary benefits and the general attributes of each have been addressed in this chapter. If the transaction is recast by the Internal Revenue Service as a conditional sale, however, the tax ramifications are grossly different and may have an adverse effect on the parties involved. Therefore, the advice of competent tax counsel should be sought prior to any major leasing decision.

Appendix A—
IRS Equipment Leasing
____ Audit Guideline Manual ____

The Internal Revenue Service Audit Manual that follows, for the examination of leasing companies and equipment leasing tax shelters, has been prepared by the IRS to educate and brief its agents prior to beginning a lease company audit. The information forms the basis of the agent's audit program. Should the IRS inform you of an impending audit you may rest assured that the agent will have read this audit guide prior to your first meeting. In any event, the Audit Manual summarizes many of the current arguments used to differentiate a true lease from a conditional sales contract. Moreover, the manual explains sales-leaseback criteria along with issues facing non-corporate lessors. Guidelines in this manual were propagated August 7, 1979.

Although the Audit Manual does not contain the provisions of the new safe harbor lease definitions (code section 168(f) 8); it nevertheless is worthwhile to read prior to an IRS audit.

819
Background

(1) The equipment leasing industry has grown spectacularly within the last decade as an alternative to the more conventional procedure of borrowing money to finance the acquisition of capital equipment and facilities that require high investments over long periods of time. Many taxpayers are now using leasing as a vehicle to acquire costly assets such as airplanes, computers, railway cars, oil tankers, etc.

(2) Traditional incentives for the lessee include the immediate deduction of rental costs and the avoidance of high outlays of working capital to acquire the property.

(3) A major incentive to the lessor is the use of equipment leasing as a sales aid when prospective buyers are unable to finance the purchase of their equipment.

(4) In many instances, equipment leasing ventures are being turned into abusive tax shelters. The cost of equip-

301

ment is being inflated by the use of non-recourse loans that would permit the lessor to claim an artificially high depreciation deduction and investment tax credit.

(5) In an abusive tax shelter, the true investor or owner of the property may be obscured among the complexities of the transactions, so that the wrong party claims the benefits of ownership and, therefore, the tax benefits of accelerated depreciation and investment credit. In this situation, the true owner might actually be the lessee who is not in need of the accelerated depreciation deduction and investment credit. The tax benefits would incorrectly accrue to the lessor, who may be in a high tax bracket and in need of a tax shelter.

(6) The Tax Reform Act of 1976 introduced IRC 465 to prevent taxpayers from deducting losses in excess of the amount at risk in equipment leasing activities for tax years beginning after 1975. Taxpayers are at risk in an activity to the extent of the money and the adjusted basis of property they contribute to the activity. Taxpayers are also at risk for loans for which they have personal liability or have pledged personal assets as security which are used to finance the activity. The "at risk" provisions of the Tax Reform Act of 1976 were applied to losses sustained by noncorporate taxpayers, electing small business corporations, and personal holding companies. Regular corporations were not affected.

For tax years beginning after 1978, the IRS applies the provisions of IRC 465 to noncorporate taxpayers and all corporations in which five or fewer individuals

own more than 50% of the stock, except for closely held corporations in which at least 50% of the gross receipts are attributable to equipment leasing.

820
Equipment Leasing Entities

821
Corporate Entities

(1) Examiners can expect to see the corporate entity used most frequently in equipment leasing shelters. Although the Revenue Act of 1978 applied the provisions of IRC 465 to closely held corporations for the first time, corporations that are not closely held continue to be excluded. Through nonrecourse financing, these corporations are still permitted to deduct losses in excess of their at risk contributions.

(2) Occasionally a corporate lessor will utilize a grantor trust as a vehicle to claim equipment leasing losses. In this situation, the corporate lessor (grantor) will create a trust and name itself the beneficiary. All income, expenses, and credits of the trust are funneled back to the grantor in the same manner as a partnership would work. A grantor trust arrangement is generally used for off balance sheet financing purposes or for other business reasons. Keep in mind that the lessor should receive the same tax benefits whether or not a grantor trust exists.

822
Noncorporate Entities

Examiners will not encounter many equipment leasing tax shelters where noncorporate lessors are involved, since IRC 48(d) of the 1971 Tax Reform Act substantially restricted the use of investment tax credits, and the Tax Reform Act of 1976 limited loss deductions to amounts at risk.

830
Economic Reality in Equipment Leases

831
General

(1) A primary purpose of any business venture should be to generate a profit. Every venture will not make a profit; however, the potential for profit realization should always exist.

(2) In a recent case, *Arnold L. Ginsburg, v. Comm.,* 35 TCM 860, 1976, the central points were whether the taxpayer could anticipate a profit, whether the amount of profit was predetermined, and if the taxpayer was covered by stop loss agreements. (In a stop loss agreement, the promoter of the venture agrees to reimburse the investor's losses in excess of a certain amount.) It was the taxpayer's burden to show that there was a reasonable expectation of a profit.

(3) A critical time in a tax shelter venture is the turnaround or crossover point when, after generating tax losses for several years, the taxpayer begins to generate taxable income. While losses are usually sustained in the formative years of the venture, a profit seeking activity must have as its goal the realization of a profit on the overall operation. The venture should eventually be expec-

ted to generate sufficient income to overcome losses in earlier years.

832
Determining Whether a Venture is Structured for Profit

(1) In examining equipment leasing shelters, one of the major considerations is whether the transaction was structured for profit or primarily for tax avoidance. Does it lack economic reality?

(2) There are several tests for determining the economic viability of a shelter, e.g. present value of future income, rate of return, and burdens and benefits of ownership. These and other tests are discussed further in text at 852 and 872 through 874.

840
Sale and Leaseback

841
General Information

(1) Normally, tax considerations are a primary reason for sale and leaseback transactions.

(2) In the typical sale and leaseback arrangement, a corporate taxpayer sells its property outright to a second party and immediately leases the property back from the new owner. The lease is generally for a term of 20 to 30 years with additional renewal periods. There may also be a repurchase option. The seller-lessee usually agrees to a net lease in which the lessee assumes the majority of the risks and burdens of ownership such as taxes, insurance, maintenance, and other expenses. Ordinarily, the rent paid allows a nominal rate of return in addition to the lessor's principal and interest payments.

842
Advantages of Sales and Leasebacks

(1) One favorable tax advantage is that the seller-lessee is entitled to a rent deduction that could be greater than the sum of the depreciation and interest expense that would have been deductible if the property had not been sold. This is true particularly if the property has been fully depreciated, or if it is being leased over a shorter term than its expected useful life.

(2) A seller-lessee may be in a tax position where he/she has no need for the interest and depreciation deductions and investment credit that are associated with the leased property. In this situation, he/she may sell the asset to a buyer who is in need of a tax shelter. An arrangement might be made whereby the seller would immediately lease the property back from the buyer at a rental fee favorable to the lessee. The rental fee would be sufficient for the buyer-lessor to make principal and interest payments on the newly acquired property and permit a nominal rate of return on the investment. Rental income received by the lessor would be offset by interest and depreciation deductions associated with the leased property.

843
Substance vs. Form

(1) Sale and leaseback transactions should be scrutinized to determine whether a legitimate business purpose exists, or if the transaction was structured only as a tax avoidance scheme. To do this, the examiner should consider what benefits, if any, the lessor is deriving from the sale and leaseback transaction other than a favorable tax write-off.

(2) If the examiner suspects that a sale and leaseback transaction is a tax avoidance scheme, reference should be made to text at 870 for suggested audit techniques that might be used.

844
Sale vs. Financing Arrangement

(1) Some tax avoidance schemes may take the form of a sale and leaseback, when in substance the arrangement is actually a loan between the "lessor" and "lessee." By using this approach, the depreciation, interest expense, and investment credit, if any, would be disallowed to the lessor and allowed to the lessee. Keep in mind that the lessee may likely be in a tax situation where he/she cannot use these additional deductions and credits. The Service's position would be that rental payments received by the lessor are in reality principal and interest payments from the lessee since a sale never took place. The lessee still owns the property for tax purposes and the lessor is acting as a conduit to make interest and principal payments on the leased property for the lessee. The downpayment made by the lessor to purchase the property would be considered a loan to the lessee. In effect, the instrument by which the seller-lessee purports to convey legal ownership to the buyer-lessor is in reality no more than security for a loan on the property.

(2) See *Helvering v. F. & R. Lazarus and Co.*, 308 U.S. 252, (1939), 1939-2 CB 208; *John Shillito Co. v. U.S.*, 39 F

. 2d 830 (6th Cir., 1942); and *John Shillito Co. v. Connor*, 42-2 USTC 9769 (D.C. Ohio, 1942). In these cases, the taxpayers' actions indicated that sales and not loans had been transacted. The courts ruled, however, that the transactions were not sales but actually loans secured by the properties in question.

(3) Recently, the Government unsuccessfully used an approach similar to the *Lazarus* case noted above in *Frank Lyon Company v. U.S.*, 98 SCt 1291, rev'g 536 F.2d, 746 (8th Cir., 1976). On April 18, 1978, the Supreme Court ruled that the transaction was a genuine sale and leaseback and not a mere financing arrangement. The Government placed great reliance on *Lazarus*, claiming that it was a precedent that should be controlling in the *Lyon* case. The Supreme Court, however, made a distinction between *Lazarus* and *Lyon*. In *Lazarus* the sale and leaseback transaction involved only two parties, and the Court acknowledged that the conclusion reached in that case was correct. In *Lyon* there wᴠre three parties involved (lessee, lessor, and an independent mortgagee) rather than a simpler two party arrangement. It was the opinion of the Court that the presence of a third party, an independent mortgagee, "significantly distinguished this case from *Lazarus*."

(4) Numerous factors were involved on both sides of the question regarding the reality of the arrangement, but of major importance appears to be the fact that *Lyon* was exclusively liable on the notes held by the independent mortgagee. A reasonable possibility exists that, if the notes were partially or fully guaranteed by the seller-lessee, the Supreme Court may have decided against

Lyon and in favor of the Government. A favorable implication derived from the unfavorable *Lyon* decision is that the Court noted "the nonfamily and nonprivate nature of the entire transaction." The Court also emphasized that the transaction was shaped by features other than tax avoidance—the diversification in the case of *Lyon* and the legal requirements of the lessee to sell and leaseback the property.

(5) Also noteworthy is the Court's mention of the fact that the Government would receive the same amount of revenue no matter how the transaction was viewed. This will not be true in many instances, especially in family trust arrangements, which are discussed in text at 860.

(6) Another consideration regarding the *Lyon* case is that even though an independent trustee (such as a family lawyer) could conceivably be regarded as the third party that was so vital to the *Lyon* decision, he/she may not be in as independent a position as the financial company in the present case. The trustee will generally have less independence and a smaller role in packaging the leaseback transaction than an unrelated financial institution.

(7) It is suggested that if an issue similar to the *Lyon* case is being considered, the examiner should consider requesting technical advice from the National Office.

845
Fair Market Value of Leased Property

(1) Consideration should be given to whether or not the lessor utilized non-

recourse financing to purchase the leased property.

(2) If nonrecourse financing is present and exceeds the fair market value of the property purchased, the leasing transaction should not be recognized for tax purposes since the taxpayer has no equity in the property as long as the unpaid balance of the purchase price exceeds the existing fair market value. By abandoning the transaction, the buyer-lessor can lose no more than a mere chance to acquire an equity in the future, should the value of the acquired property increase to an amount greater than the nonrecourse financing. It is not reasonable to expect investors to pay off a nonrecourse loan when the note exceeds the fair market value of the property. See *Franklin* v. *Commissioner*, 554 F .2d 1045 (CA 9, 1976), aff'g 64 TC 752; *Decon Corporation* v. *Comm.*, 65 TC 829 (1976); *Bolger* v. *Comm.*, 59 TC 760 (1973); *Edna Morris* v. *Comm.*, 59 TC 21 (1972).

(3) If the purchase price of the property exceeds its fair market value, and nonrecourse financing is *not* involved, the examiner should determine the cause of the discrepancy. Consideration should be given to reducing the basis of the property by the excess purchase price over the fair market value. This, of course, will result in smaller interest and depreciation deductions to the lessor. Be particularly alert for this type of situation if related parties are involved.

(4) If the fair market value of the property is materially less than the purchase price, mention of this fact should be recorded in the prospectus and/or footnotes to the certified financial statements. Comments to this effect may also be found in financial statements given to lending institutions if additional financing is needed. Comments in the minutes may disclose material facts, and there is also the possibility that an appraisal was made prior to the purchase which shows that the fair market value is less than the purchase price. Insurance policies may insure the property for an amount substantially below its purchase price. Personal property tax returns may report the smaller fair market value figure in lieu of the purchase price in order to take advantage of a lower personal property tax rate. The purchase price of the last arm's-length sale might also help in determining the current fair market value.

850
Leveraged Leasing

851
Introduction

(1) Equipment leases generally fall into two categories, leveraged leases or unleveraged leases, depending on the degree to which each is financed.

(2) A leveraged lease transaction generally involves three parties and includes:

(a) A lessor who commits a small percentage of his/her own funds (usually 20% to 30%) for the purchase of the property, borrows the remainder of the purchase price in a nonrecourse loan, then leases the property to another party on a net lease basis. (In a net lease arrangement, the lessee agrees to keep the property in good repair and is responsible for all property expenses, including taxes and insurance, during the term of the lease.)

(b) A lender who finances a substantial portion of the purchase price on a nonrecourse basis, relying solely on the leased property and the lease contract itself as security for the loan.

(c) A lessee who is obligated to make lease payments that will normally return the lessor the full purchase price of the property and perhaps a nominal profit. The lessee generally agrees to a net lease arrangement, discussed in (a) above.

(3) Unleveraged leasing requires the lessor to use his/her own funds to purchase the property. [These leases are rarely found in tax shelters due to the lack of extraordinary tax benefits that would result and the substantial cost of the assets.]

852
Criteria for Determining Whether a Transaction is a Leasing Arrangement or a Mere Financing Arrangement

(1) The lessee's right to the leased asset is derived from the lease agreement. The agreement, although cast in the form of a lease, may in substance be a conditional sales contract. This determination is made based on the intent of the parties in light of the facts existing at the time of the execution of the agreement.

(2) No one factor is controlling in determining the intent when the agreement is executed. However, if one or more of the following circumstances

exist, the examiner should consider characterizing the transaction as a sale rather than a lease:

(a) Lessee acquires equity in the property through his/her "lease" payments. For example, after 50% of the lease payments have been made, the lessee may acquire a 25% ownership interest in the asset.

(b) Lessee acquires title to the asset after a required number of lease payments.

(c) Lessee's total lease payments are due in a relatively short period of time and substantially cover the total amount required to acquire the asset.

(d) Lease payments substantially exceed the fair rental value of the property. This may indicate that the asset is actually being purchased and that the financing is for a period less than the useful life of the asset.

(e) Provision may be made for the property to be acquired by the lessee at the end of the lease term for a nominal sum.

(f) Lessee participates in the investment with the lessor by providing loan guarantees or stop loss agreements to the lessor.

(g) Lessor has little or no at risk investment in the leased asset. Note one of the requirements relating to leveraged leasing under *Rev. Proc. 75-21,* 1975-1 C.B. 715, modified by *Rev. Proc. 76-30,* 1976-2 C.B. 647, is that at all times during the lease term the lessor should have a minimum "at risk" investment of 20 percent.

(3) Consider the following example: A lessor and lessee enter into an agreement whereby the lessee agrees to lease

a computer for $31,000 per year that has an annual fair rental value of $15,000. The lease will run for 84 months (7 years) at which time the lessee will acquire title to the computer for $8,000. The lessor generally sells this type of computer for $155,000, which is equal to the present value of the seven lease payments at a 10% rate of return ($150,900) plus the present value of the $8,000 payment to the lessor at the conclusion of the lease. The life of the computer is 14 years. The lessee agrees to insure the equipment and keep it in good repair.

(a) In this example it would appear that a sale and not a lease has taken place. The lessee is paying almost double the monthly fair rental value and will take title to the computer in a relatively short period of time. The total rental payments are equal to the cost of the computer plus a 10% annual return on the unpaid balance of the cost. The lessee is accepting the burdens of ownership by insuring the property and agreeing to keep it in good repair.

(b) By handling this transaction as a lease rather than a sale, the lessee is able to deduct the rental payments, which approximate the cost of the computer, over 7 years rather than depreciating the asset over 14 years if the transaction was properly treated as a sale. If the computer is acquired and sold in a subsequent year by the lessee, any gain would not be subject to IRC 1245 recapture, since depreciation was not claimed. In this type of arrangement the lessor also generally passes the investment credit on to the lessee pursuant to IRC 48(d). It is clearly to the

benefit of the "lessee" to treat this arrangement as a lease rather than a purchase.

(4) Examiners should look to the substance of the transaction rather than the form to determine if an abusive tax shelter exists.

(a) A determination should be made as to who has the burdens and benefits of ownership.

(b) The substance of a transaction, rather than its legal form, is controlling for Federal income tax purposes. If the burdens and benefits of ownership still inure to the lessee after a sale and leaseback transaction, it is indicative that the seller is still the owner of the property. Calling a transaction a sale and leaseback does not make it one, if in fact it is something else.

(c) By using this approach the lessor would not be entitled to deductions related to the leased property since the lessee still retains ownership for Federal income tax purposes. See *Rev. Rul. 68-590,* 1968-2 C.B. 66, amplified by *Rev. Rul. 73-134,* 1973-1 C.B. 60, *Rev. Rul. 72-543,* 1972-2 C.B. 87; *Rev. Rul. 74-290,* 1974-1 C.B. 41.

860
Family Trust—Leaseback

861
General Information

(1) The family trust-leaseback offers a taxpayer the opportunity for substantial tax savings over a period of years, provided he/she is able to deduct the rent payments which he/she makes to the trust.

(2) The advantage to the taxpayer of such an arrangement is to shift income to a family member by setting up a trust and conveying income-producing property to the trust. If the trust requirements of IRC 671 through 678 are met, trust income will be taxed to the beneficiary rather than the grantor.

(3) When the taxpayer transfers property which is used in hie/her trade business to a family trust, an arrangement will be made for the grantor to lease the property back. With this type of provision, grantors have been able to shift income to lower bracket taxpayers and also to deduct the rent paid to the trust as a business expense. In a leaseback arrangement the grantor usually ends up with a rent deduction greater than the depreciation he/she would have been entitled to on the income-producing property had he/she not transferred it to a trust.

862
Example of a Family Trust-Leaseback Arrangement

(1) A typical example of a trust-leaseback arrangement involves an individual in a high tax bracket who owns equipment that is used in his/her business. Assume the equipment has a cost of $4,000 and is being depreciated over a 10-year life. By using the straight line depreciation method, the annual depreciation deduction is $400.

(2) If the equipment has a fair rental value of $800 per year, the taxpayer can get a larger deduction by transferring the equipment to a family trust, then leasing it back from the trust for $800 per year. The taxpayer now has an $800 yearly rental deduction, rather

than an annual depreciation deduction of $400.

(3) Also assume that the $800 rental income paid by the taxpayer to the trust is divided equally between the trust and the taxpayer's son. The trust will put aside $400 each year as a depreciation reserve and the balance will be paid to the son. What has happened is that the father, who is in a high tax bracket, effectively transfers $400 of his income to his son who is in a lower tax bracket. The purpose of this trust-leaseback arrangement would be tax avoidance and the transaction should be challenged as a sham. The examiner should consider disallowing the rental expense and treating the payment to the trust as a gift.

(4) The transaction should be traced to the last arm's-length sale, if possible, to aid in determining if there is an inflated purchase price.

(5) The examiner should determine if the transaction reflects economic reality. See text at 852, 872, 873, and 874 for details of the burdens and benefits test, the present value test, and the rate of return test.

(6) Determine if the transaction utilizes nonrecourse financing, stop loss agreements, or other agreements that would limit the purchaser-lessor's potential liability. If the transaction does contain nonrecourse or other financing that limits risk, see IRC 465. The examiner should also determine whether the nonrecourse financing exceeds the fair market value of the leased asset. If so, disallowance of the deductions related to the leased asset should be considered since the taxpayer has no equity in it.

See *Franklin* v. *Comm.*, supra; *Decon Corporation*, supra; *David F. Bolger*, supra; *Edna Morris*, supra.

(7) Determine if the form of the transaction reflects the substance of the transaction. The relationship between the various parties and the terms of the agreements must be carefully scrutinized to determine the true intent of the lease arrangement. The burdens and benefits test, discussed in text at 852, may also be helpful in this analysis.

863
Validity of Rental Deductions

(1) The courts consider the circumstances of each case in determining the validity of rental deductions. Three areas have been regularly explored by the courts in making this determination.

(a) Lack of equity interest—IRC 162(a)(3) specifically provides that a rental deduction is available only where the taxpayer does not hold title or have any equitable interest in the property in question. Following this concept, rent expense has not been allowed by the courts where the taxpayer retained a reversionary interest in the property.

1 *Furman* v. *Comm.*, 45 TC 360 (1966), aff'd per curiam 381 F.2d 22 (5th Cir., 1967).

2 *Van Zandt* v. *Comm.*, 341 F.2d 440 (5th Cir., 1965).

3 *Hall* v. *U.S.*, 208 FSupp. 584 (D.C.N.Y., 1962).

(b) Business purpose—economic reality. A business purpose must be served or economic viability must exist. Several courts have denied deductions where the transaction served no business purpose

and was arranged solely to permit a division of the taxpayer's income.

1 *Van Zandt* v. *Comm.*, supra.

2 *Perry* v. *U.S.*, 520 F.2d 235 (4th Cir., 1975), rev'g DC 376 FSupp 15 (1974).

3 *Mathews* v. *Comm.*, 520 F .2d 323 (5th Cir., 1975); Cert. denied, 96 SCt 1463.

4 *Penn* v. *Comm.*, 51 TC 144 (1968).

5 *Failor* v. *U.S.*, DC, Washington (1966), 66-2 USTC 9766, and 18 AFTR 2d, 6030.

(c) Independent Trustee. The independence of the trustee has been a major factor in determining if rent expense could be deducted. The courts have usually denied deductions where control has effectively remained in the hands of the grantor.

1 *Sidney W. Penn*, supra.

2 *Irvine K. Furman*, supra.

3 *Oakes* v. *Comm.*, 44 TC 524, 1966.

870
Examination Techniques

The techniques cited below provide guidance in developing equipment leasing issues.

871

GENERAL TECHNIQUES

(1) The following techniques apply to a broad range of equipment leasing transactions.

(2) The examiner should obtain and analyze the following documents:

(a) Sales contracts,

(b) Closing documents,

(c) Deeds or titles,

(d) Loan agreements,

(e) Leases,

(f) Guarantees of lease payments, and

(g) Loan guarantees.

(3) The examiner should be alert for stop loss agreements, loans of the lessor that are guaranteed by the lessee, inflated purchase prices, transfer of title from the lessor to the lessee at the conclusion of the lease, and inflated lease payments. These may indicate a sale rather than a lease.

872
Present Value Test

(1) The fair market value of a leased asset may be measured using the present value of the future income stream (rents) plus the present value of the salvage. If the present value of the future income stream does not exceed the present value of the total investment in the asset, then the examiner should question the lessor's motives for entering into the transaction.

(2) The present value of future rents at a given rate of return should approximate the fair market value of the leased asset. The examiner can use this test to help determine if the asset was acquired by the purchaser-lessor at an inflated price.

(3) The following example demonstrates the present value computation.

(a) Facts:

Purchase price of leased property	$2,500
Salvage value	$1,000
Annual rental income	$350
Annual expenses attributable to leased property	$150
Net annual income from leased property	$200
Length of lease	10 years

(b) Based on these facts, it appears that the taxpayer will have a total net profit on his/her investment of $500 since annual net income of $200 for a 10-year period plus salvage value of $1,000 equals $3,000, and the purchase price was $2,500. However, if the present value concept is applied to these same facts, the results will show that the taxpayer incurred a loss on the investment.

(c) Exhibit 800–1 shows the present value of the future income stream and the salvage at the end of 10 years assuming a 6% interest rate (the higher the assumed interest rate, the lower the present value).

(d) The $2,030 present value was obtained by multiplying the annual net income and the salvage value by the applicable factor for each period associated with the 6% rate of return. See present value table at Exhibit 800–2.

(e) The present value of the future income stream and salvage in the above example is $2,030. The investor would therefore lose $470 on his/her $2,500 investment which would indicate the transaction was not entered into for a profit.

(4) Keep in mind that the true fair market value of a leased asset can generally be measured by the present value of the future income stream.

(5) Depending on other factors involved in this type of issue, it could be argued that the taxpayer's basis should be reduced to an amount equal to the present value of the future income stream. This is especially true if a sophisticated taxpayer, such as a lending institution or insurance company is in-

volved, since many of their investment decisions are based on the present value concept.

(6) Another approach would be to disallow the entire transaction as a sham if the cost of the property is artificially inflated. This approach should be considered if other key factors are present such as the guarantee of all or part of the purchaser-lessor's loan by the seller-lessee, failure to show legitimate business purpose for the inflated purchase price, and/or the involvement of related parties.

873
Rate of Return Test

(1) Another method of determining the economic viability of an equipment leasing arrangement is to compare its market rate of return (or at least the risk free rate of return) to those for other similar investments. If the transaction was entered into for a profit, then the rate of return should at least equal the risk free rate of return. In cases where the tax shelter's rate of return is less than the risk free return, then the investor's motives for investing should be carefully studied.

(2) Inflated prices for assets are at the base of tax shelter transactions "structured for a loss." On the surface the transaction may appear to have been based on fair market value; however, upon analysis, a different conclusion may be reached. Inflated costs included in the depreciable basis of the property give inflated depreciation deductions and inflated investment tax credits.

(3) Another indication of potential tax shelter abuse is insufficient rents.

The rents charged may be less than the fair rental value, or they may appear insufficient due to the inflated price paid for the property. One may question why someone would enter into one of these transactions. The answer is not for economic gain but for tax losses. Tax losses plus investment credits are a "tax free return" that gives the participant a profit from his/her losses.

(4) The following is an example of the effect of an inflated sales price on rate of return.

		FMV	Transaction
(a)		FMV	Transaction
(b)	Cost	$300,000	$1,200,000
(c)	Rent	30,000	30,000
(d)	Return	10%	2.5

Here it can be seen that the return on the transaction is 2.5% per year, while the ordinary return on this type asset should be 10%. The low rate of return in this case reflects the inflated purchase price of the asset rather than insufficient rents.

(5) The following examination techniques can be used in conjunction with the rate of return test:

(a) Determine the going rate of return for various investments in this area by contacting bank trust departments, mortgage investment brokers, insurance companies, etc.

(b) Determine the prime lending rate by either contacting banks or obtaining publications which reflect market fluctuations in the rate.

874
Guarantee of Note by Seller-Lessee

The examiner should determine whether the seller-lessee is guaranteeing the note of the buyer-lessor. If this situation exists, the lessor would not be entitled to the deductions associated with the loan proceeds guaranteed by the lessee. See *Rev. Rul. 77-125*, 1977-1 C.B. 130 and *Rev. Rul. 78-30*, 1978-1 C.B. 133.

875
Loss Limitations Based on the Amount at Risk

The provisions of IRC 465 should be considered whenever equipment leasing transactions are examined and financing is used which involves no risk to the investor(s). See 810 of this chapter for a discussion of IRC 465.

880
Depreciation

881
Reasonable Salvage Value

(1) Generally, lessors of equipment select an accelerated method of depreciation. Examiners should determine whether the accumulated depreciation has reduced the lessor's basis in the asset below the salvage value. I.T. Reg. 1.167(a)(1)(a) provides that an asset may not be depreciated below salvage.

(2) In some cases it may be necessary to obtain engineering assistance to determine the valuations. In other cases the examiner may be able to contact equipment brokers, read industry publications, or examine taxpayer records to determine reasonable salvage value.

882
Example of Depreciation Adjustment Based on Reasonable Salvage Value

(1) An asset to be leased was purchased for $7,500,000. The lessor computes depreciation using double declining balance and a 12-year useful life. The lessor has recorded salvage value at $850,000. The taxpayer's prior asset history indicates that the salvage value at the end of 12 years should be $2,250,000.

(2) Projected depreciation over the 12-year life is shown in Exhibit 800-3.

(3) In the seventh year the lessor should only claim depreciation of $11,685, which would bring the book value to $2,500,000. No depreciation is allowable after the seventh year.

883
Date Placed in Service

Depreciation of an asset does not begin until an asset has been placed in service. See I.T. Regulations 1.167-(a)(10)(b). An asset is not considered placed in service until it has been installed and is operational. In leased asset situations there may be a great physical distance between the leased property and the lessor. Confirmation as to when the equipment was operational should be obtained.

884
Example of Adjustment Based on Date Placed in Service

The lessor, a calendar year taxpayer, purchases a computer and leases it on November 20, 1977. The lessee takes delivery of the computer December 15, 1977; however, due to the holidays, the electrical connections and software installation were not completed until January 1978. The lessor cannot claim depreciation in 1977 since the asset was not operational or placed in service before the end of the year.

885
Examination Techniques for Determining Date Placed in Service

(1) Contact lessor to establish when the asset was installed and when the asset was operational.

(2) Local regulations may require certain permits or zoning applications. These may indicate when approval was given for installation of the asset and when installation was completed.

(3) Read lease carefully. In some instances, the lessee does not begin paying rent until thirty days after the asset is accepted as installed.

890
Investment Tax Credit

891
Limitations on Certain Noncorporate Lessors

(1) I.T. Reg. 1.46-4(d) provides certain narrow criteria under which a noncorporate lessor may claim investment tax credit. These criteria are:

(a) Lessor must have manufactured or produced the leased equipment, or

(b) The lease term plus renewal options must be less than 50% of the useful life of the property, and

(c) During the first 12 months of the lease the sum of the deductions allowed to the lessor under IRC 162 must exceed fifteen percent of rental income produced by the property.

(2) Care should be taken to ensure that noncorporate lessors have not included expenses of unrelated properties in the 15% test in order to meet the requirements of I.T. Reg. 1.46-4(d)(3).

892
Pass Through of Investment Credit to Lessee

(1) The lessor can make an election pursuant to IRC 48(d) to pass the investment tax credit through to the lessee. I.T. Reg. 1.48-4 contains specific requirements for the manner and timing of the election. The Code and Regulations impose the following conditions:

(a) The property must be new IRC 38 property in the hands of the lessor.

(b) The lessee must be the original user of the property.

(c) A lessor must provide a statement to the lessee that identifies the lessee and lessor, describes the leased property, and gives the estimated useful life of the property, the date the property was transferred, and the basis of the leased property in the hands of the lessee.

(d) The lessor may not be an institution or organization described in IRC 593, IRC 851 through 858, or IRC 1381 (2).

(2) If the foregoing conditions are met, the lessee, rather than the lessor, is treated as the actual owner of the property for purposes of the credit. Moreover, if the property is disposed of or if it otherwise ceases to be IRC 38 property in the hands of the lessee, the property is subject to investment credit recapture. The terms of the lease are to determine the applicable percentage limitation for computing the investment tax credit.

(3) Example—Taxpayer B leases a new storage tank to Taxpayer C with a useful life of 10 years. The lease agreement is for a term of 6 years, and the fair market value of the leased asset is $300,000. B has elected under IRC

48(d) to pass the investment credit through to C. C is allowed to claim the credit on a qualified investment of $200,000 ($300,000 X .6667) since the useful life of the storage tank in C's hands is only 6 years.

(4) Examiners should verify that the requirements of I.T. Reg. 1.48-4 have been met. To determine whether leased equipment is new or used, obtain serial numbers and/or model numbers of the equipment. Manufacturers or equipment brokers can usually determine from these numbers the date that the equipment was manufactured.

8(10)0
Tax Preference Items

(1) For leased IRC 1245 property, accelerated depreciation that is in excess of what would be allowed under the straight line method is considered a tax preference item. See IRC 57(a)(3). The Tax Reform Act of 1976 has substantially reduced the exclusions and increased the rate in computing the minimum tax.

(2) Example—An asset costing $50,000 with a useful life of 10 years is depreciated using the double declining balance method. For the first year depreciation per the return is $10,000. The amount allowable under the straight line method would be $5,000. The excess $5,000 is a tax preference item.

(3) Whenever a lessor is claiming accelerated depreciation on leased equipment, examiners should verify that the excess over straight line depreciation is being reported as a tax preference item. The tax preference item could be a substantial amount when the leased assets are such items as airplanes, oil tankers, or computers.

8(11)0
Lease Acquisition Costs

(1) The costs of obtaining the lease, i.e. syndicators fees, travel, legal fees, filing costs, etc. should be capitalized. These costs are amortizable over the life of the lease via the straight line method and do not qualify as IRC 38 property for investment tax credit purposes.

(2) In the initial year of the lease, it is important to verify that acquisition costs are not included as part of the asset cost, and that they are not being currently deducted. The examiner may need to analyze accounts that are likely to contain these expenses; e.g., legal and professional fees, miscellaneous expenses.

Appendix B—
Lease Payment Tables

The following lease tables have been reprinted with permission by Computofacts. The complete book entitled *Monthly Lease Tables* may be ordered from:

Computofacts
209 Sheppard Avenue East
Willowdale, Ontario, Canada M2N 5W2

10% MONTHLY PAYMENTS PER $1,000

0% Residual   2% Residual

NUMBER OF ADVANCE PAYMENTS   NUMBER OF ADVANCE PAYMENTS

MOS	0	1	2	3	4	5	0	1	2	3	4	5	MOS
12	87.92	87.19	86.54	85.94	85.42	84.95	86.33	85.62	84.97	84.39	83.87	83.41	12
15	71.20	70.61	70.07	69.57	69.12	68.70	69.94	69.37	68.83	68.34	67.90	67.49	15
18	60.06	59.57	59.10	58.67	58.27	57.90	59.03	58.54	58.08	57.66	57.27	56.90	18
19	57.13	56.66	56.22	55.80	55.42	55.06	56.16	55.69	55.26	54.85	54.47	54.12	19
20	54.49	54.04	53.62	53.23	52.86	52.51	53.57	53.13	52.71	52.32	51.96	51.62	20
21	52.11	51.68	51.27	50.89	50.54	50.20	51.23	50.81	50.41	50.04	49.69	49.36	21
22	49.94	49.53	49.14	48.77	48.43	48.11	49.11	48.70	48.32	47.96	47.62	47.30	22
23	47.96	47.57	47.19	46.84	46.51	46.19	47.17	46.78	46.41	46.07	45.74	45.43	23
24	46.15	45.77	45.41	45.07	44.74	44.44	45.39	45.02	44.66	44.33	44.01	43.71	24
25	44.48	44.11	43.77	43.44	43.12	42.83	43.76	43.40	43.05	42.73	42.42	42.13	25
26	42.94	42.59	42.25	41.93	41.63	41.34	42.25	41.90	41.57	41.26	40.96	40.67	26
27	41.52	41.18	40.85	40.54	40.24	39.96	40.85	40.52	40.20	39.89	39.60	39.33	27
28	40.20	39.86	39.55	39.25	38.96	38.69	39.56	39.23	38.92	38.62	38.34	38.07	28
29	38.96	38.64	38.34	38.04	37.76	37.50	38.35	38.04	37.73	37.45	37.17	36.91	29
30	37.82	37.50	37.21	36.92	36.65	36.39	37.23	36.92	36.63	36.35	36.08	35.82	30
31	36.74	36.44	36.15	35.87	35.61	35.35	36.17	35.88	35.59	35.32	35.06	34.81	31
32	35.74	35.44	35.16	34.89	34.63	34.38	35.19	34.90	34.62	34.35	34.10	33.86	32
33	34.79	34.50	34.23	33.96	33.71	33.47	34.26	33.98	33.71	33.45	33.20	32.96	33
34	33.90	33.62	33.35	33.10	32.85	32.61	33.39	33.11	32.85	32.60	32.35	32.12	34
35	33.06	32.79	32.53	32.28	32.04	31.80	32.57	32.30	32.04	31.79	31.56	31.33	35
36	32.27	32.01	31.75	31.50	31.27	31.04	31.79	31.53	31.28	31.04	30.80	30.58	36
37	31.52	31.26	31.01	30.77	30.54	30.32	31.06	30.80	30.56	30.32	30.09	29.87	37
38	30.82	30.56	30.32	30.08	29.85	29.64	30.37	30.12	29.87	29.64	29.42	29.20	38
39	30.14	29.89	29.65	29.42	29.20	28.99	29.71	29.46	29.23	29.00	28.78	28.57	39
40	29.51	29.26	29.03	28.80	28.58	28.37	29.08	28.84	28.61	28.39	28.17	27.97	40
41	28.90	28.66	28.43	28.21	28.00	27.79	28.49	28.25	28.03	27.81	27.60	27.39	41
42	28.32	28.09	27.86	27.64	27.44	27.23	27.92	27.69	27.47	27.25	27.05	26.85	42
43	27.77	27.54	27.32	27.11	26.90	26.70	27.38	27.16	26.94	26.73	26.52	26.33	43
44	27.25	27.02	26.80	26.59	26.39	26.20	26.87	26.65	26.43	26.23	26.03	25.83	44
45	26.75	26.52	26.31	26.10	25.91	25.71	26.38	26.16	25.95	25.75	25.55	25.36	45
46	26.27	26.05	25.84	25.64	25.44	25.25	25.91	25.69	25.49	25.29	25.09	24.91	46
47	25.81	25.59	25.39	25.19	25.00	24.81	25.46	25.25	25.04	24.85	24.66	24.47	47
48	25.37	25.16	24.96	24.76	24.57	24.39	25.03	24.82	24.62	24.43	24.24	24.06	48
49	24.95	24.74	24.54	24.35	24.16	23.98	24.61	24.41	24.21	24.02	23.84	23.66	49
50	24.54	24.34	24.14	23.95	23.77	23.59	24.22	24.02	23.82	23.64	23.46	23.28	50
51	24.15	23.95	23.76	23.57	23.39	23.22	23.84	23.64	23.45	23.27	23.09	22.91	51
52	23.78	23.58	23.39	23.21	23.03	22.86	23.47	23.28	23.09	22.91	22.73	22.56	52
53	23.42	23.23	23.04	22.86	22.68	22.51	23.12	22.93	22.74	22.57	22.39	22.22	53
54	23.08	22.89	22.70	22.52	22.35	22.18	22.78	22.59	22.41	22.24	22.06	21.90	54
55	22.75	22.56	22.37	22.20	22.03	21.86	22.46	22.27	22.09	21.92	21.75	21.58	55
56	22.42	22.24	22.06	21.89	21.72	21.55	22.14	21.96	21.78	21.61	21.44	21.28	56
57	22.12	21.93	21.76	21.58	21.42	21.25	21.84	21.66	21.48	21.31	21.15	20.99	57
58	21.82	21.64	21.46	21.29	21.13	20.97	21.55	21.37	21.20	21.03	20.87	20.71	58
59	21.53	21.35	21.18	21.01	20.85	20.69	21.27	21.09	20.92	20.75	20.59	20.44	59
60	21.25	21.08	20.91	20.74	20.58	20.42	20.99	20.82	20.65	20.49	20.33	20.18	60
72	18.53	18.38	18.23	18.08	17.94	17.80	18.33	18.18	18.03	17.88	17.74	17.61	72
84	16.61	16.47	16.34	16.20	16.08	15.95	16.44	16.30	16.17	16.04	15.92	15.79	84
96	15.18	15.05	14.93	14.81	14.69	14.58	15.04	14.92	14.80	14.68	14.56	14.45	96
108	14.08	13.97	13.85	13.74	13.63	13.53	13.97	13.85	13.74	13.63	13.52	13.42	108
120	13.22	13.11	13.00	12.90	12.80	12.70	13.12	13.01	12.91	12.80	12.70	12.60	120

MONTHLY PAYMENTS PER $1,000   **10%**

5% Residual   10% Residual

MOS	NUMBER OF ADVANCE PAYMENTS						NUMBER OF ADVANCE PAYMENTS						MOS
	0	1	2	3	4	5	0	1	2	3	4	5	
12	83.94	83.25	82.62	82.05	81.55	81.10	79.96	79.30	78.70	78.16	77.68	77.26	12
15	68.06	67.50	66.98	66.50	66.07	65.67	64.92	64.38	63.88	63.43	63.01	62.64	15
18	57.48	57.00	56.56	56.15	55.76	55.41	54.89	54.44	54.01	53.62	53.25	52.92	18
19	54.69	54.24	53.82	53.42	53.05	52.71	52.25	51.82	51.42	51.04	50.69	50.36	19
20	52.19	51.76	51.35	50.97	50.62	50.29	49.88	49.47	49.08	48.72	48.38	48.06	20
21	49.92	49.51	49.12	48.76	48.41	48.09	47.73	47.34	46.97	46.62	46.29	45.99	21
22	47.86	47.47	47.09	46.74	46.41	46.10	45.78	45.40	45.05	44.71	44.39	44.10	22
23	45.98	45.60	45.24	44.90	44.58	44.28	44.00	43.64	43.29	42.97	42.66	42.38	23
24	44.26	43.89	43.55	43.22	42.91	42.62	42.37	42.02	41.69	41.37	41.08	40.80	24
25	42.67	42.32	41.99	41.67	41.37	41.09	40.87	40.53	40.21	39.91	39.62	39.35	25
26	41.21	40.87	40.55	40.24	39.95	39.68	39.48	39.16	38.85	38.55	38.27	38.01	26
27	39.86	39.53	39.22	38.92	38.64	38.37	38.20	37.88	37.58	37.30	37.03	36.77	27
28	38.60	38.28	37.98	37.69	37.42	37.15	37.01	36.70	36.41	36.14	35.87	35.62	28
29	37.43	37.12	36.83	36.55	36.28	36.03	35.90	35.61	35.32	35.05	34.80	34.55	29
30	36.34	36.04	35.76	35.48	35.22	34.97	34.87	34.58	34.31	34.04	33.79	33.55	30
31	35.32	35.03	34.75	34.48	34.23	33.99	33.90	33.62	33.35	33.10	32.85	32.62	31
32	34.37	34.08	33.81	33.55	33.30	33.06	33.00	32.72	32.46	32.21	31.97	31.75	32
33	33.47	33.19	32.93	32.67	32.43	32.20	32.15	31.88	31.63	31.38	31.15	30.93	33
34	32.62	32.35	32.10	31.85	31.61	31.38	31.35	31.09	30.84	30.60	30.37	30.15	34
35	31.83	31.56	31.31	31.07	30.84	30.62	30.59	30.34	30.10	29.86	29.64	29.43	35
36	31.08	30.82	30.57	30.34	30.11	29.89	29.88	29.63	29.39	29.17	28.95	28.74	36
37	30.36	30.11	29.87	29.64	29.42	29.20	29.21	28.96	28.73	28.51	28.30	28.09	37
38	29.69	29.45	29.21	28.98	28.77	28.56	28.57	28.33	28.10	27.89	27.68	27.48	38
39	29.05	28.81	28.58	28.36	28.15	27.94	27.96	27.73	27.51	27.30	27.09	26.89	39
40	28.45	28.21	27.99	27.77	27.56	27.36	27.39	27.16	26.94	26.73	26.53	26.34	40
41	27.87	27.64	27.42	27.21	27.00	26.80	26.84	26.62	26.41	26.20	26.00	25.81	41
42	27.32	27.10	26.88	26.67	26.47	26.27	26.32	26.11	25.90	25.69	25.50	25.31	42
43	26.80	26.58	26.36	26.16	25.96	25.77	25.83	25.61	25.41	25.21	25.02	24.83	43
44	26.30	26.08	25.87	25.67	25.48	25.29	25.36	25.15	24.94	24.75	24.56	24.38	44
45	25.82	25.61	25.41	25.21	25.01	24.83	24.90	24.70	24.50	24.31	24.12	23.94	45
46	25.37	25.16	24.96	24.76	24.57	24.39	24.47	24.27	24.08	23.89	23.70	23.53	46
47	24.93	24.73	24.53	24.34	24.15	23.97	24.06	23.86	23.67	23.48	23.30	23.13	47
48	24.52	24.31	24.12	23.93	23.75	23.57	23.66	23.47	23.28	23.10	22.92	22.75	48
49	24.12	23.92	23.72	23.54	23.36	23.18	23.29	23.09	22.91	22.73	22.55	22.38	49
50	23.73	23.54	23.35	23.16	22.98	22.81	22.92	22.73	22.55	22.37	22.20	22.03	50
51	23.36	23.17	22.98	22.80	22.63	22.46	22.57	22.39	22.21	22.03	21.86	21.70	51
52	23.01	22.82	22.63	22.46	22.28	22.12	22.24	22.05	21.88	21.70	21.54	21.37	52
53	22.67	22.48	22.30	22.12	21.95	21.79	21.91	21.73	21.56	21.39	21.22	21.06	53
54	22.34	22.16	21.98	21.80	21.64	21.47	21.60	21.42	21.25	21.08	20.92	20.76	54
55	22.02	21.84	21.67	21.50	21.33	21.17	21.30	21.13	20.96	20.79	20.63	20.48	55
56	21.72	21.54	21.37	21.20	21.03	20.88	21.02	20.84	20.67	20.51	20.35	20.20	56
57	21.43	21.25	21.08	20.91	20.75	20.59	20.74	20.57	20.40	20.24	20.08	19.93	57
58	21.14	20.97	20.80	20.64	20.48	20.32	20.47	20.30	20.14	19.98	19.82	19.67	58
59	20.87	20.70	20.53	20.37	20.21	20.06	20.21	20.04	19.88	19.72	19.57	19.42	59
60	20.61	20.44	20.27	20.11	19.95	19.80	19.96	19.80	19.64	19.48	19.33	19.18	60
72	18.02	17.87	17.73	17.59	17.45	17.31	17.51	17.37	17.23	17.09	16.96	16.83	72
84	16.19	16.06	15.93	15.80	15.68	15.56	15.78	15.65	15.52	15.40	15.28	15.16	84
96	14.84	14.71	14.59	14.48	14.36	14.25	14.50	14.38	14.26	14.14	14.03	13.92	96
108	13.80	13.68	13.57	13.46	13.36	13.25	13.51	13.40	13.29	13.18	13.08	12.97	108
120	12.98	12.87	12.76	12.66	12.56	12.46	12.73	12.63	12.52	12.42	12.32	12.23	120

10%   MONTHLY PAYMENTS PER $1,000

15% Residual   ## 20% Residual

MOS	NUMBER OF ADVANCE PAYMENTS						NUMBER OF ADVANCE PAYMENTS						MOS
	0	1	2	3	4	5	0	1	2	3	4	5	
12	75.98	75.36	74.79	74.27	73.82	73.42	72.00	71.41	70.87	70.39	69.95	69.57	12
15	61.77	61.26	60.79	60.36	59.96	59.60	58.63	58.14	57.70	57.29	56.91	56.57	15
18	52.30	51.87	51.47	51.09	50.74	50.42	49.72	49.31	48.92	48.57	48.24	47.93	18
19	49.81	49.40	49.02	48.66	48.32	48.01	47.37	46.98	46.62	46.27	45.95	45.66	19
20	47.57	47.18	46.81	46.46	46.14	45.84	45.26	44.89	44.54	44.21	43.90	43.62	20
21	45.54	45.17	44.81	44.48	44.17	43.88	43.36	43.00	42.66	42.34	42.05	41.77	21
22	43.70	43.34	43.00	42.68	42.38	42.09	41.62	41.28	40.95	40.65	40.36	40.09	22
23	42.02	41.67	41.34	41.03	40.74	40.47	40.04	39.71	39.39	39.10	38.82	38.56	23
24	40.48	40.14	39.83	39.53	39.24	38.98	38.59	38.27	37.97	37.68	37.41	37.16	24
25	39.06	38.74	38.43	38.14	37.87	37.61	37.25	36.95	36.65	36.38	36.12	35.87	25
26	37.75	37.44	37.14	36.86	36.60	36.34	36.02	35.72	35.44	35.17	34.92	34.68	26
27	36.54	36.24	35.95	35.68	35.42	35.17	34.88	34.59	34.32	34.06	33.81	33.58	27
28	35.42	35.12	34.85	34.58	34.33	34.09	33.82	33.54	33.28	33.03	32.78	32.56	28
29	34.37	34.09	33.82	33.56	33.31	33.08	32.84	32.57	32.31	32.06	31.83	31.60	29
30	33.39	33.12	32.86	32.60	32.36	32.14	31.92	31.66	31.41	31.16	30.94	30.72	30
31	32.48	32.21	31.96	31.71	31.48	31.25	31.06	30.80	30.56	30.33	30.10	29.89	31
32	31.63	31.36	31.11	30.88	30.65	30.43	30.26	30.01	29.77	29.54	29.32	29.11	32
33	30.82	30.57	30.32	30.09	29.87	29.65	29.50	29.26	29.02	28.80	28.59	28.38	33
34	30.07	29.82	29.58	29.35	29.13	28.92	28.79	28.55	28.32	28.10	27.90	27.69	34
35	29.35	29.11	28.88	28.66	28.44	28.24	28.12	27.89	27.66	27.45	27.24	27.05	35
36	28.68	28.45	28.22	28.00	27.79	27.59	27.49	27.26	27.04	26.83	26.63	26.44	36
37	28.05	27.81	27.59	27.38	27.17	26.97	26.89	26.66	26.45	26.25	26.05	25.86	37
38	27.44	27.22	27.00	26.79	26.59	26.39	26.32	26.10	25.89	25.69	25.50	25.31	38
39	26.87	26.65	26.44	26.23	26.03	25.84	25.78	25.57	25.36	25.17	24.98	24.80	39
40	26.33	26.11	25.90	25.70	25.51	25.32	25.27	25.06	24.86	24.67	24.48	24.30	40
41	25.82	25.60	25.40	25.20	25.01	24.82	24.79	24.58	24.38	24.19	24.01	23.84	41
42	25.32	25.12	24.91	24.72	24.53	24.35	24.33	24.12	23.93	23.74	23.56	23.39	42
43	24.86	24.65	24.45	24.26	24.08	23.90	23.88	23.69	23.50	23.31	23.14	22.97	43
44	24.41	24.21	24.01	23.83	23.64	23.47	23.46	23.27	23.08	22.90	22.73	22.56	44
45	23.98	23.79	23.59	23.41	23.23	23.06	23.06	22.87	22.69	22.51	22.34	22.17	45
46	23.58	23.38	23.19	23.01	22.84	22.67	22.68	22.49	22.31	22.14	21.97	21.80	46
47	23.19	23.00	22.81	22.63	22.46	22.29	22.31	22.13	21.95	21.78	21.61	21.45	47
48	22.81	22.62	22.44	22.27	22.10	21.93	21.96	21.78	21.60	21.44	21.27	21.11	48
49	22.46	22.27	22.09	21.92	21.75	21.59	21.62	21.45	21.27	21.11	20.94	20.79	49
50	22.11	21.93	21.75	21.58	21.42	21.26	21.30	21.13	20.96	20.79	20.63	20.48	50
51	21.78	21.60	21.43	21.26	21.10	20.94	20.99	20.82	20.65	20.49	20.33	20.18	51
52	21.46	21.29	21.12	20.95	20.79	20.63	20.69	20.52	20.36	20.20	20.04	19.89	52
53	21.16	20.99	20.82	20.65	20.49	20.34	20.41	20.24	20.07	19.92	19.76	19.61	53
54	20.87	20.69	20.53	20.37	20.21	20.06	20.13	19.96	19.80	19.65	19.49	19.35	54
55	20.58	20.41	20.25	20.09	19.93	19.78	19.86	19.70	19.54	19.39	19.24	19.09	55
56	20.31	20.14	19.98	19.82	19.67	19.52	19.61	19.45	19.29	19.14	18.99	18.84	56
57	20.05	19.88	19.72	19.57	19.42	19.27	19.36	19.20	19.05	18.89	18.75	18.61	57
58	19.80	19.63	19.47	19.32	19.17	19.02	19.12	18.96	18.81	18.66	18.52	18.38	58
59	19.55	19.39	19.23	19.08	18.93	18.79	18.89	18.74	18.58	18.44	18.29	18.16	59
60	19.31	19.16	19.00	18.85	18.70	18.56	18.67	18.52	18.37	18.22	18.08	17.94	60
72	17.00	16.86	16.72	16.59	16.46	16.34	16.49	16.36	16.22	16.09	15.97	15.85	72
84	15.37	15.24	15.12	14.99	14.88	14.76	14.95	14.83	14.71	14.59	14.48	14.36	84
96	14.15	14.04	13.92	13.81	13.70	13.59	13.81	13.70	13.59	13.48	13.37	13.27	96
108	13.22	13.11	13.01	12.90	12.80	12.70	12.93	12.83	12.72	12.62	12.52	12.42	108
120	12.49	12.36	12.28	12.18	12.09	11.99	12.24	12.14	12.04	11.95	11.85	11.76	120

MONTHLY PAYMENTS PER $1,000   **10%**

25% Residual | **30% Residual**

	NUMBER OF ADVANCE PAYMENTS						NUMBER OF ADVANCE PAYMENTS					
MOS	0	1	2	3	4	5	0	1	2	3	4	5 MOS
12	68.03	67.46	66.95	66.50	66.09	65.73	64.05	63.52	63.04	62.61	62.22	61.88 12
15	55.49	55.03	54.60	54.22	53.86	53.54	52.34	51.91	51.51	51.15	50.81	50.51 15
18	47.13	46.74	46.38	46.04	45.73	45.44	44.54	44.18	43.83	43.51	43.22	42.94 18
19	44.93	44.56	44.21	43.89	43.59	43.31	42.49	42.14	41.81	41.51	41.22	40.96 19
20	42.96	42.60	42.27	41.96	41.66	41.39	40.65	40.31	40.00	39.70	39.43	39.17 20
21	41.17	40.83	40.51	40.21	39.92	39.66	38.98	38.66	38.35	38.07	37.80	37.55 21
22	39.54	39.21	38.91	38.62	38.34	38.09	37.46	37.15	36.86	36.58	36.33	36.08 22
23	38.06	37.74	37.45	37.16	36.90	36.65	36.08	35.78	35.50	35.23	34.98	34.74 23
24	36.70	36.39	36.11	35.84	35.58	35.34	34.81	34.52	34.25	33.99	33.75	33.52 24
25	35.45	35.15	34.88	34.61	34.36	34.13	33.64	33.36	33.10	32.85	32.61	32.39 25
26	34.29	34.01	33.74	33.48	33.24	33.01	32.56	32.29	32.04	31.79	31.56	31.35 26
27	33.22	32.95	32.69	32.44	32.20	31.98	31.56	31.30	31.06	30.82	30.60	30.38 27
28	32.23	31.97	31.71	31.47	31.24	31.02	30.64	30.39	30.14	29.91	29.70	29.49 28
29	31.31	31.05	30.80	30.57	30.34	30.13	29.78	29.53	29.30	29.07	28.86	28.66 29
30	30.45	30.20	29.96	29.73	29.51	29.30	28.97	28.73	28.50	28.29	28.08	27.88 30
31	29.64	29.40	29.16	28.94	28.73	28.52	28.22	27.99	27.77	27.55	27.35	27.15 31
32	28.89	28.65	28.42	28.20	27.99	27.79	27.52	27.29	27.07	26.86	26.66	26.47 32
33	28.18	27.94	27.72	27.51	27.30	27.11	26.86	26.63	26.42	26.22	26.02	25.84 33
34	27.51	27.28	27.07	26.86	26.66	26.47	26.23	26.02	25.81	25.61	25.42	25.24 34
35	26.88	26.66	26.45	26.24	26.05	25.86	25.65	25.43	25.23	25.04	24.85	24.67 35
36	26.29	26.07	25.86	25.66	25.47	25.29	25.09	24.88	24.69	24.49	24.31	24.14 36
37	25.73	25.52	25.31	25.11	24.93	24.74	24.57	24.37	24.17	23.98	23.80	23.63 37
38	25.20	24.99	24.79	24.60	24.41	24.23	24.07	23.87	23.68	23.50	23.32	23.15 38
39	24.69	24.49	24.29	24.10	23.92	23.75	23.60	23.41	23.22	23.04	22.87	22.70 39
40	24.21	24.01	23.82	23.64	23.46	23.29	23.16	22.96	22.78	22.60	22.43	22.27 40
41	23.76	23.56	23.37	23.19	23.02	22.85	22.73	22.54	22.36	22.19	22.02	21.86 41
42	23.33	23.13	22.95	22.77	22.60	22.43	22.33	22.14	21.96	21.79	21.63	21.47 42
43	22.91	22.72	22.54	22.37	22.20	22.03	21.94	21.76	21.59	21.42	21.25	21.10 43
44	22.52	22.33	22.15	21.98	21.81	21.65	21.57	21.40	21.22	21.06	20.90	20.74 44
45	22.14	21.96	21.78	21.61	21.45	21.29	21.22	21.05	20.88	20.71	20.56	20.40 45
46	21.78	21.60	21.43	21.26	21.10	20.94	20.89	20.71	20.55	20.39	20.23	20.08 46
47	21.44	21.26	21.09	20.93	20.77	20.61	20.57	20.40	20.23	20.07	19.92	19.77 47
48	21.11	20.94	20.77	20.60	20.45	20.29	20.26	20.09	19.93	19.77	19.62	19.48 48
49	20.79	20.62	20.46	20.30	20.14	19.99	19.96	19.80	19.64	19.49	19.34	19.19 49
50	20.49	20.32	20.16	20.00	19.85	19.70	19.68	19.52	19.36	19.21	19.06	18.92 50
51	20.20	20.03	19.87	19.72	19.56	19.42	19.41	19.25	19.09	18.94	18.80	18.66 51
52	19.92	19.76	19.60	19.44	19.29	19.15	19.15	18.99	18.84	18.69	18.54	18.41 52
53	19.65	19.49	19.33	19.18	19.03	18.89	18.90	18.74	18.59	18.44	18.30	18.16 53
54	19.39	19.23	19.08	18.93	18.78	18.64	18.66	18.50	18.35	18.21	18.07	17.93 54
55	19.14	18.99	18.83	18.68	18.54	18.40	18.42	18.27	18.12	17.98	17.84	17.71 55
56	18.90	18.75	18.60	18.45	18.31	18.17	18.20	18.05	17.90	17.76	17.62	17.49 56
57	18.67	18.52	18.37	18.22	18.08	17.94	17.98	17.83	17.69	17.55	17.41	17.28 57
58	18.45	18.30	18.15	18.00	17.86	17.73	17.77	17.63	17.48	17.35	17.21	17.08 58
59	18.23	18.08	17.94	17.79	17.66	17.52	17.57	17.43	17.29	17.15	17.02	16.89 59
60	18.02	17.87	17.73	17.59	17.45	17.32	17.38	17.23	17.09	16.96	16.83	16.70 60
72	15.98	15.85	15.72	15.60	15.47	15.36	15.47	15.35	15.22	15.10	14.98	14.87 72
84	14.54	14.42	14.30	14.19	14.08	13.97	14.13	14.01	13.90	13.78	13.68	13.57 84
96	13.47	13.36	13.25	13.14	13.04	12.94	13.13	13.02	12.91	12.81	12.71	12.61 96
108	12.65	12.54	12.44	12.34	12.24	12.15	12.36	12.26	12.16	12.06	11.96	11.87 108
120	12.00	11.90	11.80	11.71	11.62	11.52	11.76	11.66	11.56	11.47	11.38	11.29 120

10%   MONTHLY PAYMENTS PER $1,000

35% Residual | 40% Residual

	NUMBER OF ADVANCE PAYMENTS						NUMBER OF ADVANCE PAYMENTS						
MOS	0	1	2	3	4	5	0	1	2	3	4	5	MOS
12	60.07	59.57	59.12	58.72	58.36	58.04	56.09	55.62	55.20	54.83	54.49	54.19	12
15	49.20	48.79	48.42	48.07	47.76	47.47	46.06	45.68	45.33	45.00	44.71	44.44	15
18	41.96	41.61	41.29	40.99	40.71	40.45	39.37	39.05	38.74	38.46	38.20	37.96	18
19	40.05	39.72	39.41	39.12	38.85	38.60	37.61	37.30	37.01	36.74	36.49	36.25	19
20	38.34	38.02	37.73	37.45	37.19	36.94	36.03	35.73	35.46	35.19	34.95	34.72	20
21	36.79	36.49	36.20	35.93	35.68	35.44	34.60	34.32	34.05	33.79	33.56	33.34	21
22	35.38	35.09	34.81	34.55	34.31	34.08	33.30	33.03	32.77	32.52	32.29	32.08	22
23	34.09	33.81	33.55	33.30	33.06	32.84	32.11	31.85	31.60	31.36	31.14	30.93	23
24	32.92	32.64	32.39	32.14	31.91	31.70	31.03	30.77	30.53	30.30	30.08	29.88	24
25	31.83	31.57	31.32	31.08	30.86	30.65	30.02	29.78	29.54	29.32	29.11	28.91	25
26	30.83	30.58	30.33	30.10	29.89	29.68	29.10	28.86	28.63	28.42	28.21	28.02	26
27	29.91	29.66	29.42	29.20	28.99	28.79	28.25	28.01	27.79	27.58	27.38	27.19	27
28	29.05	28.81	28.58	28.36	28.15	27.96	27.45	27.23	27.01	26.80	26.61	26.42	28
29	28.25	28.01	27.79	27.58	27.38	27.18	26.71	26.49	26.28	26.08	25.89	25.71	29
30	27.50	27.27	27.05	26.85	26.65	26.46	26.03	25.81	25.60	25.41	25.22	25.04	30
31	26.80	26.58	26.37	26.17	25.97	25.79	25.38	25.17	24.97	24.78	24.60	24.42	31
32	26.15	25.93	25.72	25.53	25.34	25.16	24.78	24.57	24.38	24.19	24.01	23.84	32
33	25.53	25.32	25.12	24.93	24.74	24.56	24.21	24.01	23.82	23.63	23.46	23.29	33
34	24.95	24.75	24.55	24.36	24.18	24.01	23.68	23.48	23.29	23.11	22.94	22.78	34
35	24.41	24.21	24.01	23.83	23.65	23.48	23.17	22.98	22.80	22.62	22.45	22.29	35
36	23.90	23.70	23.51	23.33	23.15	22.98	22.70	22.51	22.33	22.16	21.99	21.83	36
37	23.41	23.22	23.03	22.85	22.68	22.51	22.25	22.07	21.89	21.72	21.56	21.40	37
38	22.95	22.76	22.58	22.40	22.23	22.07	21.82	21.64	21.47	21.30	21.14	20.99	38
39	22.51	22.33	22.15	21.97	21.81	21.65	21.42	21.24	21.07	20.91	20.75	20.60	39
40	22.10	21.91	21.74	21.57	21.41	21.25	21.04	20.86	20.70	20.54	20.38	20.23	40
41	21.70	21.52	21.35	21.18	21.02	20.87	20.67	20.50	20.34	20.18	20.03	19.88	41
42	21.33	21.15	20.98	20.82	20.66	20.51	20.33	20.16	20.00	19.84	19.69	19.55	42
43	20.97	20.80	20.63	20.47	20.31	20.16	20.00	19.83	19.67	19.52	19.37	19.23	43
44	20.63	20.46	20.29	20.13	19.98	19.83	19.68	19.52	19.36	19.21	19.07	18.92	44
45	20.30	20.13	19.97	19.82	19.67	19.52	19.38	19.22	19.07	18.92	18.77	18.63	45
46	19.99	19.83	19.67	19.51	19.36	19.22	19.09	18.94	18.78	18.64	18.50	18.36	46
47	19.69	19.53	19.37	19.22	19.07	18.93	18.82	18.66	18.51	18.37	18.23	18.09	47
48	19.41	19.25	19.09	18.94	18.80	18.66	18.56	18.40	18.25	18.11	17.97	17.84	48
49	19.13	18.98	18.82	18.67	18.53	18.39	18.30	18.15	18.01	17.86	17.73	17.59	49
50	18.87	18.71	18.56	18.42	18.28	18.14	18.06	17.91	17.77	17.63	17.49	17.36	50
51	18.62	18.46	18.32	18.17	18.03	17.90	17.83	17.68	17.54	17.40	17.27	17.14	51
52	18.38	18.22	18.08	17.93	17.80	17.66	17.60	17.46	17.32	17.18	17.05	16.92	52
53	18.14	17.99	17.85	17.71	17.57	17.44	17.39	17.25	17.11	16.97	16.84	16.71	53
54	17.92	17.77	17.63	17.49	17.35	17.22	17.18	17.04	16.90	16.77	16.64	16.51	54
55	17.70	17.56	17.41	17.28	17.14	17.01	16.98	16.84	16.71	16.57	16.45	16.32	55
56	17.49	17.35	17.21	17.07	16.94	16.81	16.79	16.65	16.52	16.39	16.26	16.14	56
57	17.29	17.15	17.01	16.88	16.75	16.62	16.60	16.47	16.33	16.21	16.08	15.96	57
58	17.10	16.96	16.82	16.69	16.56	16.43	16.43	16.29	16.16	16.03	15.91	15.79	58
59	16.91	16.77	16.64	16.51	16.38	16.25	16.25	16.12	15.99	15.86	15.74	15.62	59
60	16.73	16.59	16.46	16.33	16.20	16.08	16.09	15.95	15.82	15.70	15.58	15.46	60
72	14.96	14.84	14.72	14.60	14.49	14.38	14.45	14.33	14.22	14.10	13.99	13.89	72
84	13.71	13.60	13.49	13.38	13.28	13.17	13.30	13.19	13.08	12.98	12.88	12.78	84
96	12.78	12.68	12.58	12.48	12.38	12.28	12.44	12.34	12.24	12.14	12.05	11.95	96
108	12.07	11.97	11.88	11.78	11.69	11.60	11.79	11.69	11.59	11.50	11.41	11.32	108
120	11.51	11.42	11.32	11.23	11.14	11.06	11.27	11.17	11.08	10.99	10.91	10.82	120

MONTHLY PAYMENTS PER $1,000   10%

	45% Residual						50% Residual						
	NUMBER OF ADVANCE PAYMENTS						NUMBER OF ADVANCE PAYMENTS						
MOS	0	1	2	3	4	5	0	1	2	3	4	5	MOS
12	52.11	51.68	51.29	50.94	50.62	50.35	48.13	47.73	47.37	47.05	46.76	46.50	12
15	42.91	42.56	42.23	41.93	41.66	41.41	39.77	39.44	39.14	38.86	38.61	38.37	15
18	36.79	36.48	36.20	35.93	35.69	35.46	34.20	33.92	33.65	33.41	33.18	32.97	18
19	35.17	34.88	34.61	34.36	34.12	33.90	32.74	32.46	32.21	31.97	31.75	31.55	19
20	33.72	33.45	33.18	32.94	32.71	32.50	31.42	31.16	30.91	30.69	30.47	30.27	20
21	32.41	32.14	31.89	31.66	31.43	31.23	30.22	29.97	29.74	29.52	29.31	29.12	21
22	31.22	30.96	30.72	30.49	30.27	30.07	29.14	28.90	28.67	28.46	28.26	28.07	22
23	30.13	29.88	29.65	29.43	29.22	29.02	28.15	27.92	27.70	27.49	27.30	27.11	23
24	29.13	28.89	28.67	28.45	28.25	28.06	27.24	27.02	26.81	26.60	26.41	26.23	24
25	28.22	27.98	27.76	27.55	27.36	27.17	26.41	26.19	25.99	25.79	25.60	25.43	25
26	27.37	27.14	26.93	26.73	26.53	26.35	25.64	25.43	25.23	25.04	24.86	24.68	26
27	26.59	26.37	26.16	25.96	25.77	25.59	24.93	24.72	24.53	24.34	24.16	24.00	27
28	25.86	25.65	25.44	25.25	25.06	24.89	24.27	24.07	23.88	23.69	23.52	23.36	28
29	25.18	24.97	24.78	24.59	24.41	24.24	23.65	23.46	23.27	23.09	22.92	22.76	29
30	24.55	24.35	24.15	23.97	23.79	23.63	23.08	22.89	22.70	22.53	22.37	22.21	30
31	23.96	23.76	23.57	23.39	23.22	23.06	22.54	22.35	22.18	22.01	21.84	21.69	31
32	23.41	23.21	23.03	22.85	22.68	22.52	22.04	21.86	21.68	21.51	21.35	21.20	32
33	22.89	22.70	22.52	22.34	22.18	22.02	21.56	21.39	21.22	21.05	20.90	20.75	33
34	22.40	22.21	22.04	21.87	21.70	21.55	21.12	20.95	20.78	20.62	20.46	20.32	34
35	21.94	21.76	21.58	21.42	21.26	21.10	20.70	20.53	20.37	20.21	20.06	19.91	35
36	21.50	21.32	21.15	20.99	20.83	20.68	20.31	20.14	19.98	19.82	19.67	19.53	36
37	21.09	20.92	20.75	20.59	20.43	20.28	19.93	19.77	19.61	19.46	19.31	19.17	37
38	20.70	20.53	20.37	20.21	20.06	19.91	19.58	19.42	19.26	19.11	18.97	18.83	38
39	20.33	20.16	20.00	19.85	19.70	19.55	19.24	19.08	18.93	18.78	18.64	18.50	39
40	19.98	19.82	19.66	19.50	19.36	19.21	18.92	18.77	18.62	18.47	18.33	18.20	40
41	19.65	19.48	19.33	19.18	19.03	18.89	18.62	18.46	18.32	18.17	18.04	17.90	41
42	19.33	19.17	19.02	18.87	18.72	18.59	18.33	18.18	18.03	17.89	17.76	17.63	42
43	19.03	18.87	18.72	18.57	18.43	18.29	18.05	17.91	17.76	17.62	17.49	17.36	43
44	18.74	18.58	18.43	18.29	18.15	18.02	17.79	17.65	17.50	17.37	17.23	17.11	44
45	18.46	18.31	18.16	18.02	17.88	17.75	17.54	17.40	17.26	17.12	16.99	16.87	45
46	18.20	18.05	17.90	17.76	17.63	17.50	17.30	17.16	17.02	16.89	16.76	16.63	46
47	17.95	17.80	17.65	17.52	17.38	17.25	17.07	16.93	16.80	16.66	16.54	16.41	47
48	17.70	17.56	17.42	17.28	17.15	17.02	16.85	16.71	16.58	16.45	16.32	16.20	48
49	17.47	17.33	17.19	17.05	16.92	16.80	16.64	16.50	16.37	16.24	16.12	16.00	49
50	17.25	17.11	16.97	16.84	16.71	16.58	16.44	16.30	16.17	16.05	15.92	15.80	50
51	17.04	16.90	16.76	16.63	16.50	16.38	16.25	16.11	15.98	15.86	15.73	15.62	51
52	16.83	16.69	16.56	16.43	16.30	16.18	16.06	15.93	15.80	15.67	15.55	15.44	52
53	16.63	16.50	16.36	16.24	16.11	15.99	15.88	15.75	15.62	15.50	15.38	15.26	53
54	16.44	16.31	16.18	16.05	15.93	15.81	15.71	15.58	15.45	15.33	15.21	15.10	54
55	16.26	16.13	16.00	15.87	15.75	15.63	15.54	15.41	15.29	15.17	15.05	14.94	55
56	16.09	15.95	15.82	15.70	15.58	15.46	15.38	15.25	15.13	15.01	14.90	14.78	56
57	15.92	15.78	15.66	15.53	15.41	15.30	15.23	15.10	14.98	14.86	14.75	14.63	57
58	15.75	15.62	15.50	15.37	15.25	15.14	15.08	14.95	14.83	14.72	14.60	14.49	58
59	15.59	15.46	15.34	15.22	15.10	14.99	14.93	14.81	14.69	14.57	14.46	14.35	59
60	15.44	15.31	15.19	15.07	14.95	14.84	14.80	14.67	14.55	14.44	14.33	14.22	60
72	13.94	13.83	13.72	13.61	13.50	13.40	13.43	13.32	13.22	13.11	13.01	12.91	72
84	12.89	12.78	12.68	12.57	12.48	12.38	12.47	12.37	12.27	12.17	12.07	11.98	84
96	12.10	12.00	11.90	11.81	11.71	11.62	11.76	11.66	11.57	11.47	11.38	11.29	96
108	11.50	11.40	11.31	11.22	11.13	11.04	11.21	11.12	11.03	10.94	10.85	10.77	108
120	11.02	10.93	10.84	10.76	10.67	10.59	10.78	10.69	10.60	10.52	10.43	10.35	120

14%   MONTHLY PAYMENTS PER $1,000

0% Residual   2% Residual

| MOS | \multicolumn{6}{c}{NUMBER OF ADVANCE PAYMENTS} | | | | | | \multicolumn{6}{c}{NUMBER OF ADVANCE PAYMENTS} | | | | | | MOS |

MOS	0	1	2	3	4	5	0	1	2	3	4	5	MOS
12	89.79	88.76	87.82	86.99	86.24	85.59	88.23	87.21	86.29	85.47	84.74	84.10	12
15	73.06	72.22	71.45	70.74	70.09	69.51	71.83	71.01	70.25	69.55	68.92	68.34	15
18	61.92	61.21	60.54	59.93	59.36	58.84	60.92	60.21	59.56	58.96	58.40	57.88	18
19	58.99	58.31	57.68	57.09	56.54	56.03	58.04	57.37	56.75	56.17	55.63	55.14	19
20	56.35	55.70	55.10	54.53	54.00	53.52	55.46	54.82	54.22	53.67	53.15	52.67	20
21	53.97	53.35	52.77	52.22	51.71	51.24	53.13	52.51	51.94	51.40	50.90	50.44	21
22	51.81	51.21	50.65	50.12	49.63	49.17	51.00	50.41	49.86	49.35	48.86	48.41	22
23	49.83	49.25	48.71	48.21	47.73	47.28	49.07	48.50	47.97	47.47	47.00	46.56	23
24	48.02	47.46	46.94	46.45	45.99	45.56	47.29	46.75	46.23	45.75	45.29	44.87	24
25	46.35	45.82	45.31	44.84	44.39	43.97	45.66	45.13	44.64	44.17	43.73	43.31	25
26	44.82	44.30	43.81	43.35	42.91	42.50	44.15	43.64	43.16	42.71	42.28	41.88	26
27	43.39	42.89	42.42	41.97	41.55	41.15	42.76	42.27	41.80	41.36	40.94	40.55	27
28	42.08	41.59	41.13	40.70	40.28	39.89	41.47	40.99	40.54	40.11	39.70	39.32	28
29	40.85	40.38	39.93	39.51	39.10	38.72	40.26	39.80	39.36	38.94	38.55	38.17	29
30	39.70	39.25	38.81	38.40	38.01	37.63	39.14	38.69	38.26	37.86	37.47	37.10	30
31	38.63	38.19	37.76	37.36	36.98	36.61	38.09	37.65	37.24	36.84	36.46	36.10	31
32	37.63	37.20	36.78	36.39	36.02	35.66	37.11	36.68	36.28	35.89	35.52	35.17	32
33	36.69	36.27	35.86	35.48	35.11	34.76	36.19	35.77	35.37	34.99	34.63	34.29	33
34	35.80	35.39	35.00	34.62	34.26	33.92	35.32	34.91	34.53	34.15	33.80	33.46	34
35	34.97	34.57	34.18	33.81	33.46	33.13	34.50	34.11	33.73	33.36	33.02	32.69	35
36	34.18	33.79	33.41	33.05	32.71	32.38	33.73	33.34	32.97	32.62	32.28	31.95	36
37	33.44	33.05	32.68	32.33	31.99	31.67	33.00	32.62	32.26	31.91	31.58	31.26	37
38	32.73	32.36	32.00	31.65	31.32	31.00	32.31	31.94	31.58	31.24	30.92	30.60	38
39	32.07	31.70	31.34	31.00	30.68	30.37	31.66	31.29	30.94	30.61	30.29	29.98	39
40	31.43	31.07	30.72	30.39	30.07	29.77	31.04	30.68	30.34	30.01	29.69	29.39	40
41	30.83	30.48	30.13	29.81	29.49	29.19	30.45	30.10	29.76	29.44	29.13	28.83	41
42	30.26	29.91	29.57	29.25	28.95	28.65	29.89	29.54	29.21	28.89	28.59	28.30	42
43	29.71	29.37	29.04	28.73	28.42	28.13	29.35	29.01	28.69	28.38	28.08	27.79	43
44	29.19	28.86	28.53	28.22	27.92	27.64	28.84	28.51	28.19	27.88	27.59	27.31	44
45	28.70	28.36	28.05	27.74	27.45	27.17	28.35	28.03	27.71	27.41	27.12	26.84	45
46	28.22	27.89	27.58	27.28	26.99	26.71	27.89	27.57	27.26	26.96	26.68	26.40	46
47	27.77	27.45	27.14	26.84	26.56	26.28	27.44	27.13	26.82	26.53	26.25	25.98	47
48	27.33	27.02	26.71	26.42	26.14	25.87	27.02	26.71	26.41	26.12	25.84	25.57	48
49	26.91	26.60	26.31	26.02	25.74	25.48	26.61	26.30	26.01	25.72	25.45	25.19	49
50	26.52	26.21	25.92	25.63	25.36	25.10	26.22	25.92	25.63	25.34	25.07	24.81	50
51	26.13	25.83	25.54	25.26	24.99	24.73	25.84	25.54	25.26	24.98	24.71	24.46	51
52	25.76	25.47	25.18	24.90	24.64	24.38	25.48	25.19	24.91	24.63	24.37	24.12	52
53	25.41	25.12	24.83	24.56	24.30	24.05	25.14	24.85	24.57	24.30	24.04	23.79	53
54	25.07	24.78	24.50	24.23	23.97	23.72	24.80	24.52	24.24	23.97	23.72	23.47	54
55	24.74	24.46	24.18	23.92	23.66	23.41	24.48	24.20	23.93	23.66	23.41	23.17	55
56	24.43	24.14	23.87	23.61	23.36	23.11	24.17	23.89	23.62	23.36	23.11	22.87	56
57	24.12	23.84	23.58	23.32	23.07	22.82	23.87	23.60	23.33	23.08	22.83	22.59	57
58	23.83	23.55	23.29	23.03	22.79	22.55	23.59	23.31	23.05	22.80	22.55	22.32	58
59	23.55	23.27	23.01	22.76	22.51	22.28	23.31	23.04	22.78	22.53	22.29	22.05	59
60	23.27	23.00	22.75	22.50	22.25	22.02	23.04	22.78	22.52	22.27	22.03	21.80	60
72	20.61	20.37	20.14	19.92	19.70	19.49	20.43	20.20	19.97	19.75	19.53	19.33	72
84	18.75	18.53	18.32	18.12	17.92	17.73	18.60	18.39	18.18	17.98	17.78	17.59	84
96	17.38	17.18	16.98	16.79	16.61	16.43	17.26	17.06	16.87	16.68	16.50	16.32	96
108	16.34	16.15	15.97	15.79	15.62	15.45	16.25	16.06	15.88	15.70	15.53	15.36	108
120	15.53	15.35	15.18	15.01	14.84	14.68	15.45	15.28	15.10	14.93	14.77	14.61	120

MONTHLY PAYMENTS PER $1,000   14%

	5% Residual						10% Residual						
	NUMBER OF ADVANCE PAYMENTS						NUMBER OF ADVANCE PAYMENTS						
MOS	0	1	2	3	4	5	0	1	2	3	4	5	MOS
12	85.89	84.90	84.00	83.20	82.49	81.87	81.98	81.03	80.18	79.42	78.74	78.14	12
15	69.99	69.19	68.44	67.77	67.15	66.59	66.92	66.15	65.44	64.80	64.21	63.67	15
18	59.41	58.72	58.09	57.50	56.95	56.45	56.90	56.24	55.63	55.07	54.54	54.06	18
19	56.62	55.97	55.36	54.80	54.27	53.79	54.26	53.63	53.05	52.51	52.01	51.54	19
20	54.12	53.50	52.91	52.37	51.86	51.39	51.89	51.29	50.73	50.21	49.72	49.27	20
21	51.86	51.26	50.70	50.17	49.69	49.23	49.74	49.17	48.63	48.13	47.66	47.22	21
22	49.80	49.22	48.69	48.18	47.71	47.27	47.79	47.24	46.72	46.24	45.79	45.36	22
23	47.92	47.37	46.85	46.36	45.90	45.47	46.01	45.48	44.98	44.51	44.08	43.66	23
24	46.20	45.67	45.17	44.69	44.25	43.83	44.38	43.87	43.39	42.94	42.51	42.11	24
25	44.62	44.10	43.62	43.16	42.73	42.32	42.88	42.39	41.92	41.48	41.07	40.68	25
26	43.16	42.66	42.19	41.75	41.33	40.93	41.50	41.02	40.57	40.14	39.74	39.36	26
27	41.81	41.33	40.87	40.44	40.03	39.64	40.22	39.76	39.32	38.90	38.51	38.14	27
28	40.56	40.09	39.64	39.22	38.83	38.45	39.04	38.59	38.16	37.75	37.37	37.01	28
29	39.39	38.94	38.50	38.10	37.71	37.34	37.93	37.49	37.08	36.68	36.31	35.96	29
30	38.30	37.86	37.44	37.04	36.66	36.30	36.90	36.47	36.07	35.69	35.32	34.98	30
31	37.28	36.86	36.45	36.06	35.69	35.34	35.94	35.52	35.13	34.75	34.40	34.06	31
32	36.33	35.91	35.51	35.13	34.77	34.43	35.03	34.63	34.25	33.88	33.53	33.20	32
33	35.44	35.03	34.64	34.27	33.92	33.58	34.19	33.79	33.42	33.06	32.72	32.39	33
34	34.60	34.20	33.82	33.45	33.11	32.78	33.39	33.01	32.64	32.29	31.95	31.64	34
35	33.80	33.42	33.04	32.69	32.35	32.03	32.64	32.26	31.90	31.56	31.23	30.92	35
36	33.06	32.68	32.31	31.96	31.63	31.31	31.93	31.56	31.21	30.88	30.55	30.25	36
37	32.35	31.98	31.62	31.28	30.95	30.64	31.26	30.90	30.56	30.23	29.91	29.61	37
38	31.68	31.32	30.97	30.63	30.31	30.01	30.63	30.28	29.94	29.61	29.30	29.01	38
39	31.05	30.69	30.35	30.02	29.70	29.40	30.03	29.68	29.35	29.03	28.73	28.44	39
40	30.45	30.09	29.76	29.44	29.13	28.83	29.46	29.12	28.79	28.48	28.18	27.90	40
41	29.87	29.53	29.20	28.88	28.58	28.29	28.92	28.58	28.26	27.96	27.66	27.38	41
42	29.33	28.99	28.67	28.36	28.06	27.77	28.40	28.07	27.76	27.46	27.17	26.89	42
43	28.81	28.48	28.16	27.85	27.56	27.28	27.91	27.59	27.28	26.98	26.70	26.42	43
44	28.32	27.99	27.68	27.37	27.09	26.81	27.44	27.12	26.82	26.53	26.25	25.98	44
45	27.84	27.52	27.21	26.92	26.63	26.36	26.99	26.68	26.38	26.10	25.82	25.55	45
46	27.39	27.08	26.77	26.48	26.20	25.93	26.57	26.26	25.96	25.68	25.41	25.15	46
47	26.96	26.65	26.35	26.06	25.79	25.52	26.16	25.86	25.57	25.29	25.02	24.76	47
48	26.55	26.24	25.95	25.66	25.39	25.13	25.77	25.47	25.18	24.91	24.64	24.39	48
49	26.15	25.85	25.56	25.28	25.01	24.75	25.39	25.10	24.82	24.54	24.28	24.03	49
50	25.77	25.48	25.19	24.91	24.65	24.39	25.03	24.74	24.46	24.20	23.94	23.69	50
51	25.41	25.12	24.83	24.56	24.30	24.05	24.69	24.40	24.13	23.86	23.61	23.36	51
52	25.06	24.77	24.49	24.22	23.97	23.72	24.35	24.07	23.80	23.54	23.29	23.05	52
53	24.72	24.44	24.16	23.90	23.64	23.40	24.04	23.76	23.49	23.23	22.99	22.75	53
54	24.40	24.12	23.85	23.59	23.33	23.09	23.73	23.46	23.19	22.94	22.69	22.46	54
55	24.09	23.81	23.54	23.28	23.04	22.79	23.44	23.16	22.90	22.65	22.41	22.18	55
56	23.79	23.51	23.25	22.99	22.75	22.51	23.15	22.88	22.63	22.38	22.14	21.91	56
57	23.50	23.23	22.97	22.72	22.47	22.24	22.88	22.61	22.36	22.11	21.88	21.65	57
58	23.22	22.95	22.70	22.45	22.20	21.97	22.61	22.35	22.10	21.86	21.62	21.40	58
59	22.95	22.69	22.43	22.19	21.95	21.72	22.36	22.10	21.85	21.61	21.38	21.15	59
60	22.69	22.43	22.18	21.93	21.70	21.47	22.11	21.86	21.61	21.37	21.14	20.92	60
72	20.16	19.93	19.71	19.49	19.28	19.07	19.72	19.49	19.27	19.06	18.85	18.65	72
84	18.39	18.18	17.97	17.77	17.58	17.39	18.04	17.83	17.63	17.43	17.24	17.06	84
96	17.09	16.89	16.70	16.52	16.34	16.16	16.81	16.61	16.42	16.24	16.06	15.89	96
108	16.11	15.92	15.74	15.56	15.39	15.23	15.87	15.69	15.51	15.34	15.17	15.01	108
120	15.34	15.16	14.99	14.82	14.66	14.50	15.15	14.97	14.80	14.64	14.47	14.32	120

14% MONTHLY PAYMENTS PER $1,000

15% Residual   20% Residual

| MOS | \multicolumn{6}{c}{NUMBER OF ADVANCE PAYMENTS} | | | | | | \multicolumn{6}{c}{NUMBER OF ADVANCE PAYMENTS} | | | | | | MOS |

MOS	0	1	2	3	4	5	0	1	2	3	4	5	MOS
12	78.07	77.17	76.36	75.63	74.99	74.42	74.17	73.31	72.54	71.85	71.24	70.70	12
15	63.85	63.12	62.44	61.82	61.26	60.75	60.78	60.08	59.44	58.85	58.32	57.83	15
18	54.38	53.76	53.17	52.63	52.13	51.68	51.87	51.27	50.72	50.20	49.73	49.29	18
19	51.89	51.29	50.74	50.22	49.74	49.29	49.53	48.96	48.42	47.93	47.47	47.05	19
20	49.65	49.08	48.55	48.05	47.58	47.15	47.42	46.87	46.36	45.88	45.44	45.03	20
21	47.63	47.08	46.56	46.08	45.63	45.21	45.51	44.99	44.50	44.04	43.61	43.21	21
22	45.79	45.26	44.76	44.30	43.86	43.46	43.78	43.27	42.80	42.36	41.94	41.55	22
23	44.11	43.60	43.12	42.67	42.25	41.85	42.20	41.71	41.25	40.82	40.42	40.04	23
24	42.57	42.08	41.61	41.18	40.77	40.38	40.75	40.28	39.84	39.42	39.03	38.66	24
25	41.15	40.68	40.23	39.81	39.41	39.03	39.42	38.96	38.53	38.13	37.75	37.39	25
26	39.84	39.39	38.95	38.54	38.15	37.79	38.19	37.75	37.33	36.94	36.57	36.22	26
27	38.64	38.19	37.77	37.37	36.99	36.64	37.05	36.62	36.22	35.84	35.47	35.13	27
28	37.52	37.08	36.67	36.28	35.92	35.57	35.99	35.58	35.19	34.81	34.46	34.13	28
29	36.47	36.05	35.65	35.27	34.91	34.57	35.01	34.61	34.23	33.86	33.52	33.19	29
30	35.50	35.09	34.70	34.33	33.98	33.65	34.10	33.70	33.33	32.98	32.64	32.32	30
31	34.59	34.19	33.81	33.45	33.11	32.78	33.24	32.86	32.49	32.15	31.82	31.50	31
32	33.74	33.35	32.98	32.62	32.29	31.97	32.44	32.06	31.71	31.37	31.05	30.74	32
33	32.94	32.56	32.19	31.85	31.52	31.21	31.69	31.32	30.97	30.64	30.32	30.02	33
34	32.18	31.81	31.46	31.12	30.80	30.49	30.98	30.62	30.28	29.95	29.64	29.35	34
35	31.48	31.11	30.77	30.43	30.12	29.82	30.31	29.96	29.63	29.31	29.00	28.71	35
36	30.81	30.45	30.11	29.79	29.48	29.18	29.68	29.34	29.01	28.70	28.40	28.12	36
37	30.17	29.83	29.49	29.17	28.87	28.58	29.09	28.75	28.43	28.12	27.83	27.55	37
38	29.58	29.23	28.91	28.60	28.30	28.01	28.52	28.19	27.88	27.58	27.29	27.01	38
39	29.01	28.67	28.35	28.05	27.75	27.47	27.99	27.67	27.36	27.06	26.78	26.51	39
40	28.47	28.14	27.83	27.53	27.24	26.96	27.48	27.16	26.86	26.57	26.29	26.02	40
41	27.96	27.63	27.33	27.03	26.75	26.47	27.00	26.69	26.39	26.10	25.83	25.57	41
42	27.47	27.15	26.85	26.56	26.28	26.01	26.54	26.23	25.94	25.66	25.39	25.13	42
43	27.01	26.69	26.40	26.11	25.83	25.57	26.10	25.80	25.51	25.24	24.97	24.72	43
44	26.56	26.26	25.96	25.68	25.41	25.15	25.69	25.39	25.11	24.83	24.57	24.32	44
45	26.14	25.84	25.55	25.27	25.00	24.75	25.29	25.00	24.72	24.45	24.19	23.94	45
46	25.74	25.44	25.16	24.88	24.62	24.36	24.91	24.62	24.35	24.08	23.83	23.58	46
47	25.35	25.06	24.78	24.51	24.25	24.00	24.55	24.26	23.99	23.73	23.48	23.24	47
48	24.98	24.69	24.42	24.15	23.89	23.65	24.20	23.92	23.65	23.39	23.15	22.91	48
49	24.63	24.34	24.07	23.81	23.55	23.31	23.87	23.59	23.33	23.07	22.83	22.59	49
50	24.29	24.01	23.74	23.48	23.23	22.99	23.55	23.28	23.01	22.76	22.52	22.29	50
51	23.96	23.69	23.42	23.16	22.92	22.68	23.24	22.97	22.71	22.47	22.23	21.99	51
52	23.65	23.38	23.11	22.86	22.62	22.38	22.95	22.68	22.43	22.18	21.94	21.72	52
53	23.35	23.08	22.82	22.57	22.33	22.10	22.66	22.40	22.15	21.91	21.67	21.45	53
54	23.06	22.79	22.54	22.29	22.05	21.82	22.39	22.13	21.88	21.64	21.41	21.19	54
55	22.78	22.52	22.27	22.02	21.79	21.56	22.13	21.87	21.63	21.39	21.16	20.94	55
56	22.51	22.25	22.00	21.76	21.53	21.30	21.88	21.62	21.38	21.15	20.92	20.70	56
57	22.25	22.00	21.75	21.51	21.28	21.06	21.63	21.38	21.14	20.91	20.69	20.47	57
58	22.01	21.75	21.51	21.27	21.04	20.82	21.40	21.15	20.91	20.68	20.46	20.25	58
59	21.77	21.51	21.27	21.04	20.81	20.59	21.17	20.93	20.69	20.46	20.24	20.03	59
60	21.53	21.28	21.04	20.81	20.59	20.37	20.95	20.71	20.48	20.25	20.03	19.82	60
72	19.27	19.05	18.83	18.62	18.42	18.23	18.82	18.61	18.40	18.19	17.99	17.80	72
84	17.68	17.48	17.28	17.09	16.90	16.72	17.33	17.13	16.94	16.75	16.57	16.39	84
96	16.52	16.33	16.15	15.97	15.79	15.62	16.24	16.05	15.87	15.69	15.52	15.35	96
108	15.64	15.46	15.28	15.11	14.95	14.78	15.41	15.23	15.05	14.89	14.72	14.56	108
120	14.95	14.78	14.61	14.45	14.29	14.13	14.76	14.59	14.42	14.26	14.11	13.95	120

MONTHLY PAYMENTS PER $1,000   14%

	25% Residual						30% Residual						
MOS	0	1	2	3	4	5	0	1	2	3	4	5	MOS
12	70.26	69.45	68.72	68.07	67.48	66.97	66.36	65.59	64.90	64.28	63.73	63.25	12
15	57.71	57.05	56.44	55.88	55.37	54.91	54.65	54.01	53.44	52.91	52.43	51.99	15
18	49.36	48.79	48.26	47.77	47.32	46.90	46.85	46.31	45.80	45.34	44.91	44.51	18
19	47.16	46.62	46.11	45.64	45.20	44.80	44.79	44.28	43.80	43.35	42.93	42.55	19
20	45.18	44.66	44.18	43.72	43.30	42.91	42.95	42.45	41.99	41.56	41.16	40.79	20
21	43.40	42.90	42.43	41.99	41.58	41.20	41.28	40.81	40.36	39.94	39.55	39.19	21
22	41.77	41.29	40.84	40.41	40.02	39.65	39.77	39.31	38.88	38.47	38.10	37.74	22
23	40.29	39.82	39.39	38.98	38.59	38.23	38.38	37.94	37.52	37.13	36.77	36.42	23
24	38.93	38.48	38.06	37.66	37.29	36.94	37.11	36.69	36.28	35.90	35.55	35.21	24
25	37.68	37.25	36.84	36.45	36.09	35.74	35.95	35.53	35.14	34.77	34.43	34.10	25
26	36.53	36.11	35.71	35.33	34.98	34.65	34.87	34.47	34.09	33.73	33.39	33.07	26
27	35.46	35.06	34.67	34.30	33.96	33.63	33.88	33.49	33.12	32.77	32.44	32.12	27
28	34.47	34.08	33.70	33.34	33.01	32.69	32.95	32.57	32.21	31.87	31.55	31.24	28
29	33.55	33.17	32.80	32.45	32.12	31.81	32.10	31.73	31.37	31.04	30.72	30.43	29
30	32.70	32.32	31.96	31.62	31.30	30.99	31.29	30.93	30.59	30.26	29.96	29.66	30
31	31.89	31.52	31.18	30.84	30.53	30.23	30.54	30.19	29.86	29.54	29.24	28.95	31
32	31.14	30.78	30.44	30.11	29.80	29.51	29.84	29.50	29.17	28.86	28.56	28.28	32
33	30.43	30.08	29.75	29.43	29.13	28.84	29.18	28.85	28.53	28.22	27.93	27.65	33
34	29.77	29.43	29.10	28.79	28.49	28.21	28.56	28.23	27.92	27.62	27.34	27.06	34
35	29.15	28.81	28.49	28.18	27.89	27.61	27.98	27.66	27.35	27.06	26.78	26.51	35
36	28.55	28.23	27.91	27.61	27.32	27.05	27.43	27.11	26.81	26.52	26.25	25.98	36
37	28.00	27.67	27.37	27.07	26.79	26.52	26.91	26.60	26.30	26.02	25.75	25.49	37
38	27.47	27.15	26.85	26.56	26.28	26.02	26.42	26.11	25.82	25.54	25.27	25.02	38
39	26.97	26.66	26.36	26.07	25.80	25.54	25.95	25.65	25.36	25.09	24.83	24.57	39
40	26.49	26.19	25.89	25.61	25.35	25.09	25.50	25.21	24.93	24.66	24.40	24.15	40
41	26.04	25.74	25.45	25.18	24.91	24.66	25.08	24.79	24.52	24.25	24.00	23.75	41
42	25.61	25.32	25.03	24.76	24.50	24.25	24.68	24.40	24.12	23.86	23.61	23.37	42
43	25.20	24.91	24.63	24.37	24.11	23.86	24.30	24.02	23.75	23.49	23.25	23.01	43
44	24.81	24.53	24.25	23.99	23.73	23.49	23.94	23.66	23.39	23.14	22.90	22.66	44
45	24.44	24.16	23.89	23.63	23.38	23.14	23.59	23.32	23.05	22.80	22.56	22.33	45
46	24.08	23.81	23.54	23.28	23.04	22.80	23.26	22.99	22.73	22.48	22.24	22.01	46
47	23.74	23.47	23.21	22.95	22.71	22.47	22.94	22.67	22.42	22.17	21.94	21.71	47
48	23.42	23.15	22.89	22.64	22.40	22.16	22.63	22.37	22.12	21.88	21.65	21.42	48
49	23.10	22.84	22.58	22.33	22.10	21.87	22.34	22.08	21.84	21.60	21.37	21.15	49
50	22.80	22.54	22.29	22.04	21.81	21.58	22.06	21.81	21.56	21.33	21.10	20.88	50
51	22.52	22.26	22.01	21.77	21.53	21.31	21.79	21.54	21.30	21.07	20.84	20.63	51
52	22.24	21.98	21.74	21.50	21.27	21.05	21.54	21.29	21.05	20.82	20.60	20.38	52
53	21.98	21.72	21.48	21.24	21.02	20.80	21.29	21.04	20.81	20.58	20.36	20.15	53
54	21.72	21.47	21.23	21.00	20.77	20.55	21.05	20.81	20.57	20.35	20.13	19.92	54
55	21.47	21.23	20.99	20.76	20.54	20.32	20.82	20.58	20.35	20.13	19.91	19.70	55
56	21.24	20.99	20.76	20.53	20.31	20.10	20.60	20.36	20.13	19.91	19.70	19.49	56
57	21.01	20.77	20.53	20.31	20.09	19.88	20.39	20.15	19.93	19.71	19.49	19.29	57
58	20.79	20.55	20.32	20.10	19.88	19.67	20.18	19.95	19.72	19.51	19.30	19.10	58
59	20.58	20.34	20.11	19.89	19.68	19.47	19.98	19.75	19.53	19.32	19.11	18.91	59
60	20.37	20.14	19.91	19.69	19.48	19.28	19.79	19.56	19.34	19.13	18.93	18.73	60
72	18.38	18.16	17.96	17.76	17.57	17.38	17.93	17.72	17.52	17.33	17.14	16.96	72
84	16.98	16.78	16.59	16.41	16.23	16.05	16.62	16.43	16.25	16.06	15.89	15.72	84
96	15.95	15.77	15.59	15.41	15.25	15.08	15.67	15.48	15.31	15.14	14.97	14.81	96
108	15.17	15.00	14.83	14.66	14.50	14.34	14.94	14.77	14.60	14.44	14.28	14.12	108
120	14.57	14.40	14.24	14.08	13.92	13.77	14.37	14.21	14.05	13.89	13.74	13.59	120

14% MONTHLY PAYMENTS PER $1,000

35% Residual | 40% Residual

| | NUMBER OF ADVANCE PAYMENTS | | | | | | NUMBER OF ADVANCE PAYMENTS | | | | | | |
MOS	0	1	2	3	4	5	0	1	2	3	4	5	MOS
12	62.45	61.73	61.08	60.50	59.98	59.53	58.54	57.87	57.26	56.71	56.23	55.80	12
15	51.58	50.98	50.43	49.94	49.48	49.07	48.51	47.95	47.43	46.96	46.54	46.15	15
18	44.33	43.82	43.35	42.91	42.50	42.13	41.82	41.34	40.89	40.48	40.09	39.74	18
19	42.43	41.94	41.48	41.06	40.67	40.30	40.06	39.60	39.17	38.77	38.40	38.06	19
20	40.72	40.25	39.81	39.40	39.02	38.66	38.48	38.04	37.62	37.24	36.88	36.54	20
21	39.17	38.71	38.29	37.90	37.53	37.18	37.05	36.62	36.22	35.85	35.50	35.18	21
22	37.76	37.32	36.91	36.53	36.17	35.84	35.75	35.34	34.95	34.59	34.25	33.93	22
23	36.47	36.05	35.66	35.29	34.94	34.61	34.57	34.17	33.79	33.44	33.11	32.80	23
24	35.30	34.89	34.51	34.15	33.81	33.49	33.48	33.09	32.73	32.39	32.07	31.76	24
25	34.21	33.82	33.45	33.10	32.77	32.45	32.48	32.11	31.75	31.42	31.11	30.81	25
26	33.22	32.83	32.47	32.13	31.81	31.50	31.56	31.19	30.85	30.53	30.22	29.93	26
27	32.29	31.92	31.57	31.23	30.92	30.62	30.71	30.35	30.02	29.70	29.40	29.12	27
28	31.43	31.07	30.73	30.40	30.09	29.80	29.91	29.57	29.24	28.93	28.64	28.36	28
29	30.64	30.28	29.95	29.63	29.33	29.04	29.18	28.84	28.52	28.22	27.93	27.66	29
30	29.89	29.55	29.22	28.91	28.61	28.33	28.49	28.16	27.85	27.55	27.27	27.01	30
31	29.20	28.86	28.54	28.24	27.95	27.67	27.85	27.53	27.22	26.93	26.66	26.39	31
32	28.54	28.22	27.90	27.60	27.32	27.05	27.25	26.93	26.63	26.35	26.08	25.82	32
33	27.93	27.61	27.30	27.01	26.73	26.47	26.68	26.37	26.08	25.80	25.54	25.28	33
34	27.36	27.04	26.74	26.45	26.18	25.92	26.15	25.85	25.56	25.29	25.03	24.78	34
35	26.82	26.51	26.21	25.93	25.66	25.40	25.65	25.35	25.07	24.80	24.55	24.30	35
36	26.30	26.00	25.71	25.43	25.17	24.92	25.18	24.89	24.61	24.35	24.09	23.85	36
37	25.82	25.52	25.24	24.97	24.71	24.46	24.73	24.45	24.17	23.91	23.66	23.43	37
38	25.36	25.07	24.79	24.52	24.27	24.02	24.31	24.03	23.76	23.50	23.26	23.02	38
39	24.93	24.64	24.37	24.10	23.85	23.61	23.91	23.63	23.37	23.12	22.87	22.64	39
40	24.52	24.23	23.96	23.70	23.46	23.22	23.53	23.26	23.00	22.75	22.51	22.28	40
41	24.13	23.85	23.58	23.32	23.08	22.84	23.17	22.90	22.64	22.40	22.16	21.94	41
42	23.75	23.48	23.22	22.96	22.72	22.49	22.82	22.56	22.31	22.07	21.83	21.61	42
43	23.40	23.13	22.87	22.62	22.38	22.15	22.50	22.24	21.99	21.75	21.52	21.30	43
44	23.06	22.79	22.54	22.29	22.06	21.83	22.18	21.93	21.68	21.45	21.22	21.00	44
45	22.74	22.47	22.22	21.98	21.75	21.52	21.89	21.63	21.39	21.16	20.93	20.72	45
46	22.43	22.17	21.92	21.68	21.45	21.23	21.60	21.35	21.11	20.88	20.66	20.45	46
47	22.13	21.88	21.63	21.40	21.17	20.95	21.33	21.08	20.85	20.62	20.40	20.19	47
48	21.85	21.60	21.36	21.12	20.90	20.68	21.07	20.82	20.59	20.37	20.15	19.94	48
49	21.58	21.33	21.09	20.86	20.64	20.43	20.82	20.58	20.35	20.12	19.91	19.70	49
50	21.32	21.07	20.84	20.61	20.39	20.18	20.58	20.34	20.11	19.89	19.68	19.48	50
51	21.07	20.83	20.59	20.37	20.15	19.94	20.35	20.11	19.89	19.67	19.46	19.26	51
52	20.83	20.59	20.36	20.14	19.92	19.71	20.13	19.89	19.67	19.46	19.25	19.05	52
53	20.60	20.36	20.14	19.91	19.70	19.50	19.91	19.69	19.46	19.25	19.04	18.85	53
54	20.38	20.15	19.92	19.70	19.49	19.29	19.71	19.48	19.26	19.05	18.85	18.65	54
55	20.17	19.93	19.71	19.49	19.29	19.08	19.51	19.29	19.07	18.86	18.66	18.47	55
56	19.96	19.73	19.51	19.30	19.09	18.89	19.32	19.10	18.89	18.68	18.48	18.29	56
57	19.76	19.54	19.32	19.10	18.90	18.70	19.14	18.92	18.71	18.50	18.30	18.11	57
58	19.57	19.35	19.13	18.92	18.72	18.52	18.97	18.75	18.54	18.33	18.14	17.95	58
59	19.39	19.17	18.95	18.74	18.54	18.35	18.80	18.58	18.37	18.17	17.97	17.78	59
60	19.21	18.99	18.78	18.57	18.37	18.18	18.63	18.42	18.21	18.01	17.82	17.63	60
72	17.48	17.28	17.09	16.90	16.71	16.54	17.04	16.84	16.65	16.46	16.29	16.11	72
84	16.27	16.08	15.90	15.72	15.55	15.39	15.92	15.73	15.55	15.38	15.21	15.05	84
96	15.38	15.20	15.03	14.86	14.70	14.54	15.09	14.92	14.75	14.59	14.43	14.27	96
108	14.71	14.54	14.37	14.21	14.05	13.90	14.47	14.31	14.14	13.98	13.83	13.68	108
120	14.18	14.02	13.86	13.70	13.55	13.41	13.99	13.83	13.67	13.52	13.37	13.22	120

MONTHLY PAYMENTS PER $1,000   **14%**

45% Residual   ### 50% Residual

	NUMBER OF ADVANCE PAYMENTS						NUMBER OF ADVANCE PAYMENTS						
MOS	0	1	2	3	4	5	0	1	2	3	4	5	MOS
12	54.64	54.01	53.44	52.93	52.48	52.08	50.73	50.15	49.62	49.15	48.73	48.36	12
15	45.44	44.91	44.43	43.99	43.59	43.23	42.37	41.88	41.43	41.02	40.65	40.31	15
18	39.31	38.86	38.43	38.04	37.68	37.35	36.80	36.37	35.98	35.61	35.28	34.96	18
19	37.70	37.26	36.86	36.48	36.13	35.81	35.33	34.92	34.54	34.19	33.86	33.56	19
20	36.25	35.83	35.44	35.07	34.74	34.42	34.01	33.62	33.25	32.91	32.60	32.30	20
21	34.94	34.53	34.16	33.80	33.47	33.17	32.82	32.44	32.09	31.76	31.45	31.16	21
22	33.75	33.36	32.99	32.65	32.33	32.03	31.74	31.37	31.03	30.71	30.41	30.12	22
23	32.66	32.28	31.93	31.59	31.28	30.99	30.75	30.40	30.06	29.75	29.46	29.18	23
24	31.66	31.30	30.95	30.63	30.32	30.04	29.84	29.50	29.18	28.87	28.58	28.31	24
25	30.75	30.39	30.06	29.74	29.44	29.16	29.01	28.68	28.36	28.06	27.78	27.52	25
26	29.90	29.56	29.23	28.92	28.63	28.36	28.24	27.92	27.61	27.32	27.05	26.79	26
27	29.12	28.78	28.47	28.17	27.88	27.61	27.53	27.22	26.92	26.63	26.36	26.11	27
28	28.39	28.07	27.76	27.46	27.18	26.92	26.87	26.56	26.27	25.99	25.73	25.48	28
29	27.72	27.40	27.10	26.81	26.54	26.28	26.26	25.96	25.67	25.40	25.14	24.89	29
30	27.09	26.78	26.48	26.20	25.93	25.68	25.69	25.39	25.11	24.84	24.59	24.35	30
31	26.50	26.19	25.90	25.63	25.37	25.12	25.15	24.86	24.59	24.32	24.07	23.84	31
32	25.95	25.65	25.36	25.09	24.84	24.59	24.65	24.37	24.10	23.84	23.59	23.36	32
33	25.43	25.14	24.86	24.59	24.34	24.10	24.18	23.90	23.64	23.38	23.14	22.91	33
34	24.94	24.66	24.38	24.12	23.87	23.63	23.74	23.46	23.20	22.95	22.72	22.49	34
35	24.49	24.20	23.93	23.68	23.43	23.20	23.32	23.05	22.80	22.55	22.32	22.09	35
36	24.05	23.78	23.51	23.26	23.02	22.78	22.93	22.66	22.41	22.17	21.94	21.72	36
37	23.64	23.37	23.11	22.86	22.62	22.39	22.56	22.30	22.05	21.81	21.58	21.36	37
38	23.26	22.99	22.73	22.49	22.25	22.03	22.20	21.95	21.70	21.47	21.24	21.03	38
39	22.89	22.63	22.37	22.13	21.90	21.68	21.87	21.62	21.38	21.14	20.92	20.71	39
40	22.54	22.28	22.03	21.79	21.56	21.35	21.55	21.30	21.07	20.84	20.62	20.41	40
41	22.21	21.95	21.71	21.47	21.25	21.03	21.25	21.01	20.77	20.55	20.33	20.12	41
42	21.89	21.64	21.40	21.17	20.94	20.73	20.96	20.72	20.49	20.27	20.06	19.85	42
43	21.59	21.35	21.11	20.88	20.66	20.45	20.69	20.45	20.22	20.00	19.79	19.59	43
44	21.31	21.06	20.83	20.60	20.38	20.17	20.43	20.20	19.97	19.75	19.54	19.34	44
45	21.03	20.79	20.56	20.34	20.12	19.91	20.18	19.95	19.73	19.51	19.31	19.11	45
46	20.77	20.53	20.30	20.08	19.87	19.66	19.95	19.72	19.49	19.28	19.08	18.88	46
47	20.52	20.29	20.06	19.84	19.63	19.43	19.72	19.49	19.27	19.06	18.86	18.67	47
48	20.28	20.05	19.83	19.61	19.40	19.20	19.50	19.28	19.06	18.85	18.65	18.46	48
49	20.06	19.82	19.60	19.39	19.18	18.98	19.29	19.07	18.86	18.65	18.45	18.26	49
50	19.84	19.61	19.39	19.17	18.97	18.77	19.09	18.87	18.66	18.46	18.26	18.07	50
51	19.62	19.40	19.18	18.97	18.77	18.57	18.90	18.68	18.47	18.27	18.08	17.89	51
52	19.42	19.20	18.98	18.77	18.57	18.38	18.72	18.50	18.29	18.09	17.90	17.71	52
53	19.23	19.01	18.79	18.59	18.39	18.20	18.54	18.33	18.12	17.92	17.73	17.55	53
54	19.04	18.82	18.61	18.41	18.21	18.02	18.37	18.16	17.95	17.76	17.57	17.38	54
55	18.86	18.64	18.43	18.23	18.04	17.85	18.21	18.00	17.79	17.60	17.41	17.23	55
56	18.69	18.47	18.26	18.06	17.87	17.68	18.05	17.84	17.64	17.45	17.26	17.08	56
57	18.52	18.31	18.10	17.90	17.71	17.52	17.90	17.69	17.49	17.30	17.11	16.93	57
58	18.36	18.15	17.94	17.75	17.55	17.37	17.75	17.55	17.35	17.16	16.97	16.80	58
59	18.20	17.99	17.79	17.59	17.41	17.22	17.61	17.41	17.21	17.02	16.84	16.66	59
60	18.05	17.84	17.64	17.45	17.26	17.08	17.47	17.27	17.08	16.89	16.71	16.53	60
72	16.59	16.40	16.21	16.03	15.86	15.69	16.14	15.96	15.77	15.60	15.43	15.27	72
84	15.56	15.38	15.21	15.04	14.88	14.72	15.21	15.03	14.86	14.70	14.54	14.38	84
96	14.81	14.64	14.47	14.31	14.15	14.00	14.52	14.36	14.19	14.04	13.88	13.73	96
108	14.24	14.07	13.91	13.76	13.61	13.46	14.01	13.84	13.69	13.53	13.39	13.24	108
120	13.79	13.64	13.48	13.33	13.18	13.04	13.60	13.44	13.29	13.14	13.00	12.86	120

18%   MONTHLY PAYMENTS PER $1,000

0% Residual   2% Residual

MOS	NUMBER OF ADVANCE PAYMENTS						NUMBER OF ADVANCE PAYMENTS						MOS
	0	1	2	3	4	5	0	1	2	3	4	5	
12	91.68	90.33	89.11	88.03	87.07	86.23	90.15	88.82	87.62	86.56	85.61	84.78	12
15	74.95	73.84	72.83	71.91	71.07	70.32	73.75	72.66	71.67	70.76	69.94	69.19	15
18	63.81	62.87	62.00	61.19	60.45	59.77	62.83	61.91	61.05	60.26	59.53	58.86	18
19	60.88	59.98	59.15	58.38	57.66	57.01	59.97	59.08	58.26	57.50	56.80	56.15	19
20	58.25	57.39	56.59	55.85	55.16	54.52	57.39	56.54	55.75	55.02	54.34	53.71	20
21	55.87	55.04	54.28	53.56	52.89	52.28	55.05	54.24	53.48	52.78	52.12	51.51	21
22	53.71	52.91	52.17	51.48	50.84	50.24	52.93	52.15	51.42	50.74	50.10	49.51	22
23	51.74	50.97	50.26	49.59	48.96	48.38	51.00	50.25	49.54	48.88	48.27	47.69	23
24	49.93	49.19	48.50	47.85	47.24	46.68	49.23	48.50	47.82	47.18	46.58	46.02	24
25	48.27	47.56	46.89	46.26	45.67	45.11	47.60	46.90	46.24	45.62	45.04	44.49	25
26	46.74	46.05	45.40	44.79	44.21	43.67	46.10	45.42	44.78	44.18	43.61	43.08	26
27	45.32	44.65	44.02	43.43	42.87	42.34	44.71	44.05	43.43	42.84	42.29	41.77	27
28	44.01	43.36	42.74	42.16	41.62	41.11	43.43	42.78	42.18	41.61	41.07	40.56	28
29	42.78	42.15	41.55	40.99	40.46	39.96	42.23	41.60	41.01	40.46	39.93	39.44	29
30	41.64	41.03	40.45	39.90	39.38	38.89	41.11	40.50	39.93	39.39	38.87	38.39	30
31	40.58	39.98	39.41	38.88	38.37	37.89	40.07	39.48	38.92	38.39	37.88	37.41	31
32	39.58	39.00	38.44	37.92	37.42	36.95	39.09	38.51	37.97	37.45	36.96	36.49	32
33	38.65	38.08	37.53	37.02	36.53	36.07	38.17	37.61	37.07	36.57	36.09	35.63	33
34	37.77	37.21	36.68	36.18	35.70	35.25	37.31	36.76	36.24	35.74	35.27	34.82	34
35	36.94	36.39	35.87	35.38	34.91	34.47	36.50	35.96	35.45	34.96	34.50	34.06	35
36	36.16	35.62	35.12	34.63	34.17	33.74	35.73	35.21	34.70	34.23	33.77	33.34	36
37	35.42	34.90	34.40	33.92	33.47	33.04	35.01	34.49	34.00	33.53	33.09	32.66	37
38	34.72	34.21	33.72	33.25	32.81	32.39	34.33	33.82	33.34	32.88	32.44	32.02	38
39	34.06	33.56	33.08	32.62	32.18	31.77	33.68	33.18	32.71	32.26	31.82	31.41	39
40	33.43	32.94	32.47	32.02	31.59	31.18	33.06	32.58	32.11	31.67	31.24	30.84	40
41	32.84	32.35	31.89	31.45	31.03	30.62	32.48	32.00	31.54	31.11	30.69	30.29	41
42	32.27	31.79	31.34	30.90	30.49	30.09	31.92	31.45	31.00	30.57	30.16	29.77	42
43	31.73	31.26	30.81	30.39	29.98	29.59	31.40	30.93	30.49	30.07	29.66	29.27	43
44	31.22	30.75	30.31	29.89	29.49	29.10	30.89	30.43	30.00	29.58	29.18	28.80	44
45	30.72	30.27	29.84	29.42	29.03	28.65	30.41	29.96	29.53	29.12	28.73	28.35	45
46	30.26	29.81	29.38	28.97	28.58	28.21	29.95	29.51	29.09	28.68	28.29	27.92	46
47	29.81	29.37	28.95	28.54	28.16	27.79	29.51	29.08	28.66	28.26	27.88	27.51	47
48	29.38	28.95	28.53	28.13	27.75	27.39	29.09	28.66	28.25	27.86	27.48	27.12	48
49	28.97	28.54	28.13	27.74	27.36	27.00	28.69	28.27	27.86	27.47	27.10	26.74	49
50	28.58	28.15	27.75	27.36	26.99	26.63	28.31	27.89	27.49	27.10	26.73	26.38	50
51	28.20	27.78	27.38	27.00	26.63	26.28	27.94	27.52	27.13	26.75	26.38	26.04	51
52	27.84	27.43	27.03	26.65	26.29	25.94	27.58	27.17	26.78	26.41	26.05	25.70	52
53	27.49	27.08	26.69	26.32	25.96	25.62	27.24	26.84	26.45	26.08	25.73	25.39	53
54	27.16	26.76	26.37	26.00	25.65	25.31	26.91	26.52	26.13	25.77	25.42	25.08	54
55	26.84	26.44	26.06	25.69	25.34	25.01	26.60	26.21	25.83	25.47	25.12	24.78	55
56	26.53	26.13	25.76	25.40	25.05	24.72	26.30	25.91	25.53	25.18	24.83	24.50	56
57	26.23	25.84	25.47	25.11	24.77	24.44	26.00	25.62	25.25	24.90	24.56	24.23	57
58	25.94	25.56	25.19	24.84	24.50	24.17	25.72	25.34	24.98	24.63	24.29	23.97	58
59	25.67	25.29	24.92	24.57	24.23	23.91	25.45	25.08	24.71	24.37	24.03	23.71	59
60	25.40	25.02	24.66	24.32	23.98	23.66	25.19	24.82	24.46	24.12	23.79	23.47	60
72	22.81	22.48	22.15	21.84	21.54	21.25	22.66	22.32	22.00	21.69	21.39	21.10	72
84	21.02	20.71	20.41	20.12	19.84	19.57	20.90	20.59	20.30	20.01	19.73	19.46	84
96	19.73	19.44	19.16	18.88	18.62	18.36	19.63	19.34	19.06	18.79	18.53	18.28	96
108	18.76	18.48	18.22	17.96	17.71	17.46	18.69	18.41	18.14	17.89	17.63	17.39	108
120	18.02	17.76	17.50	17.25	17.01	16.77	17.96	17.70	17.44	17.19	16.95	16.72	120

MONTHLY PAYMENTS PER $1,000   18%

5% Residual   10% Residual

MOS	NUMBER OF ADVANCE PAYMENTS 0	1	2	3	4	5	0	1	2	3	4	5	MOS
12	87.85	86.55	85.39	84.35	83.43	82.62	84.02	82.78	81.66	80.67	79.79	79.01	12
15	71.95	70.89	69.92	69.03	68.23	67.51	68.95	67.94	67.01	66.16	65.39	64.69	15
18	61.37	60.46	59.63	58.85	58.14	57.49	58.93	58.06	57.25	56.51	55.83	55.20	18
19	58.59	57.72	56.92	56.18	55.49	54.86	56.30	55.46	54.69	53.98	53.32	52.71	19
20	56.09	55.26	54.49	53.77	53.11	52.50	53.93	53.13	52.39	51.70	51.06	50.47	20
21	53.83	53.03	52.29	51.60	50.96	50.36	51.78	51.02	50.31	49.64	49.02	48.45	21
22	51.77	51.01	50.29	49.63	49.01	48.43	49.84	49.10	48.41	47.77	47.17	46.62	22
23	49.90	49.16	48.47	47.83	47.22	46.66	48.06	47.35	46.69	46.07	45.49	44.94	23
24	48.18	47.47	46.80	46.18	45.59	45.04	46.44	45.75	45.11	44.50	43.94	43.41	24
25	46.61	45.92	45.27	44.66	44.09	43.56	44.94	44.28	43.65	43.07	42.52	42.00	25
26	45.15	44.48	43.86	43.27	42.71	42.19	43.56	42.92	42.31	41.75	41.21	40.71	26
27	43.80	43.16	42.55	41.97	41.43	40.92	42.29	41.66	41.08	40.52	40.00	39.51	27
28	42.56	41.93	41.33	40.77	40.25	39.75	41.11	40.50	39.93	39.39	38.88	38.40	28
29	41.39	40.78	40.21	39.66	39.15	38.66	40.01	39.41	38.86	38.33	37.83	37.36	29
30	40.31	39.72	39.15	38.62	38.12	37.64	38.98	38.40	37.86	37.34	36.86	36.40	30
31	39.30	38.72	38.17	37.65	37.16	36.69	38.02	37.46	36.93	36.43	35.95	35.50	31
32	38.35	37.79	37.25	36.74	36.26	35.80	37.12	36.58	36.06	35.56	35.10	34.66	32
33	37.46	36.91	36.39	35.89	35.42	34.97	36.28	35.75	35.24	34.76	34.30	33.86	33
34	36.63	36.09	35.57	35.09	34.62	34.18	35.49	34.97	34.47	34.00	33.55	33.12	34
35	35.84	35.31	34.81	34.33	33.88	33.45	34.75	34.23	33.74	33.28	32.84	32.42	35
36	35.10	34.58	34.09	33.62	33.17	32.75	34.04	33.54	33.06	32.61	32.17	31.76	36
37	34.40	33.89	33.41	32.95	32.51	32.09	33.38	32.88	32.42	31.97	31.54	31.14	37
38	33.74	33.24	32.76	32.31	31.88	31.47	32.75	32.27	31.80	31.37	30.95	30.55	38
39	33.11	32.62	32.15	31.71	31.28	30.88	32.15	31.68	31.23	30.80	30.38	29.99	39
40	32.51	32.03	31.57	31.14	30.72	30.32	31.59	31.12	30.68	30.25	29.85	29.46	40
41	31.94	31.47	31.02	30.59	30.18	29.79	31.05	30.59	30.16	29.74	29.34	28.96	41
42	31.41	30.94	30.50	30.08	29.67	29.29	30.54	30.09	29.66	29.25	28.86	28.48	42
43	30.89	30.44	30.00	29.58	29.19	28.81	30.06	29.61	29.19	28.78	28.40	28.03	43
44	30.40	29.96	29.53	29.12	28.72	28.35	29.59	29.16	28.74	28.34	27.96	27.59	44
45	29.94	29.50	29.07	28.67	28.28	27.91	29.15	28.72	28.31	27.92	27.54	27.18	45
46	29.49	29.06	28.64	28.24	27.86	27.50	28.73	28.31	27.90	27.51	27.14	26.78	46
47	29.07	28.64	28.23	27.83	27.46	27.10	28.33	27.91	27.51	27.13	26.76	26.41	47
48	28.66	28.24	27.83	27.44	27.07	26.72	27.94	27.53	27.13	26.76	26.39	26.05	48
49	28.27	27.85	27.45	27.07	26.70	26.35	27.57	27.17	26.78	26.40	26.04	25.70	49
50	27.90	27.49	27.09	26.71	26.35	26.00	27.22	26.82	26.43	26.06	25.71	25.37	50
51	27.54	27.13	26.74	26.37	26.01	25.67	26.88	26.48	26.10	25.74	25.39	25.05	51
52	27.20	26.79	26.41	26.04	25.69	25.35	26.55	26.16	25.79	25.43	25.08	24.75	52
53	26.87	26.47	26.09	25.72	25.37	25.04	26.24	25.85	25.48	25.13	24.78	24.45	53
54	26.55	26.16	25.78	25.42	25.07	24.74	25.94	25.56	25.19	24.84	24.50	24.17	54
55	26.24	25.86	25.48	25.13	24.78	24.45	25.65	25.27	24.91	24.56	24.23	23.90	55
56	25.95	25.57	25.20	24.85	24.51	24.18	25.37	25.00	24.64	24.29	23.96	23.64	56
57	25.67	25.29	24.92	24.57	24.24	23.91	25.11	24.74	24.38	24.04	23.71	23.39	57
58	25.39	25.02	24.66	24.31	23.98	23.66	24.85	24.48	24.13	23.79	23.46	23.15	58
59	25.13	24.76	24.40	24.06	23.73	23.41	24.60	24.24	23.89	23.55	23.23	22.92	59
60	24.88	24.51	24.16	23.82	23.49	23.18	24.36	24.00	23.65	23.32	23.00	22.69	60
72	22.42	22.09	21.77	21.46	21.17	20.88	22.03	21.71	21.39	21.09	20.80	20.52	72
84	20.72	20.42	20.12	19.83	19.56	19.29	20.42	20.12	19.83	19.55	19.28	19.01	84
96	19.49	19.20	18.93	18.66	18.40	18.14	19.26	18.97	18.70	18.43	18.17	17.92	96
108	18.57	18.30	18.03	17.78	17.53	17.29	18.39	18.11	17.85	17.60	17.35	17.11	108
120	17.87	17.61	17.35	17.11	16.87	16.63	17.72	17.46	17.21	16.96	16.72	16.49	120

18%　　MONTHLY PAYMENTS PER $1,000

15% Residual　　　　　　　　　**20% Residual**

	NUMBER OF ADVANCE PAYMENTS						NUMBER OF ADVANCE PAYMENTS					
MOS	0	1	2	3	4	5	0	1	2	3	4	5	MOS
12	80.18	79.00	77.93	76.99	76.15	75.41	76.35	75.22	74.21	73.30	72.50	71.80	12
15	65.96	64.98	64.09	63.28	62.55	61.88	62.96	62.03	61.18	60.41	59.70	59.07	15
18	56.49	55.66	54.88	54.17	53.52	52.91	54.05	53.25	52.51	51.83	51.20	50.63	18
19	54.00	53.20	52.46	51.78	51.15	50.56	51.71	50.94	50.24	49.58	48.97	48.42	19
20	51.76	51.00	50.29	49.63	49.02	48.45	49.60	48.87	48.19	47.55	46.97	46.43	20
21	49.74	49.01	48.32	47.68	47.09	46.54	47.70	46.99	46.34	45.72	45.16	44.63	21
22	47.90	47.19	46.53	45.92	45.34	44.81	45.97	45.29	44.65	44.06	43.51	43.00	22
23	46.23	45.54	44.90	44.31	43.75	43.23	44.39	43.73	43.12	42.55	42.01	41.51	23
24	44.69	44.03	43.41	42.83	42.29	41.78	42.94	42.31	41.71	41.16	40.64	40.15	24
25	43.28	42.64	42.04	41.48	40.95	40.45	41.62	41.00	40.42	39.88	39.37	38.90	25
26	41.98	41.36	40.77	40.22	39.71	39.23	40.39	39.79	39.23	38.70	38.21	37.74	26
27	40.77	40.17	39.60	39.07	38.57	38.09	39.26	38.68	38.13	37.62	37.13	36.68	27
28	39.66	39.07	38.52	38.00	37.50	37.04	38.21	37.64	37.11	36.61	36.13	35.69	28
29	38.62	38.05	37.51	37.00	36.52	36.06	37.23	36.68	36.16	35.67	35.20	34.77	29
30	37.65	37.09	36.57	36.07	35.60	35.15	36.32	35.78	35.27	34.79	34.34	33.91	30
31	36.74	36.20	35.69	35.20	34.74	34.30	35.46	34.94	34.44	33.98	33.53	33.11	31
32	35.90	35.37	34.86	34.39	33.94	33.51	34.67	34.15	33.67	33.21	32.77	32.36	32
33	35.10	34.58	34.09	33.62	33.18	32.76	33.92	33.42	32.94	32.49	32.06	31.66	33
34	34.35	33.85	33.36	32.91	32.47	32.06	33.21	32.72	32.26	31.82	31.40	31.00	34
35	33.65	33.15	32.68	32.23	31.80	31.40	32.55	32.07	31.61	31.18	30.77	30.38	35
36	32.98	32.50	32.03	31.59	31.17	30.78	31.93	31.46	31.01	30.58	30.17	29.79	36
37	32.36	31.88	31.42	30.99	30.58	30.19	31.34	30.87	30.43	30.01	29.61	29.24	37
38	31.76	31.29	30.85	30.42	30.02	29.63	30.78	30.32	29.89	29.48	29.09	28.71	38
39	31.20	30.74	30.30	29.88	29.48	29.10	30.25	29.80	29.38	28.97	28.58	28.21	39
40	30.67	30.21	29.78	29.37	28.98	28.60	29.75	29.31	28.89	28.49	28.11	27.74	40
41	30.16	29.72	29.29	28.89	28.50	28.13	29.27	28.84	28.42	28.03	27.66	27.30	41
42	29.68	29.24	28.82	28.42	28.04	27.68	28.82	28.39	27.98	27.60	27.23	26.87	42
43	29.22	28.79	28.38	27.98	27.61	27.25	28.38	27.97	27.56	27.18	26.82	26.47	43
44	28.78	28.36	27.95	27.56	27.19	26.84	27.97	27.56	27.17	26.79	26.43	26.08	44
15	28.37	27.95	27.55	27.16	26.80	26.45	27.58	27.17	26.78	26.41	26.06	25.71	45
46	27.97	27.56	27.16	26.78	26.42	26.07	27.21	26.80	26.42	26.05	25.70	25.36	46
47	27.59	27.18	26.79	26.42	26.06	25.72	26.85	26.45	26.07	25.71	25.36	25.03	47
48	27.22	26.82	26.44	26.07	25.71	25.38	26.50	26.11	25.74	25.38	25.04	24.71	48
49	26.88	26.48	26.10	25.73	25.38	25.05	26.18	25.79	25.42	25.06	24.73	24.40	49
50	26.54	26.15	25.77	25.41	25.07	24.74	25.86	25.48	25.11	24.76	24.43	24.10	50
51	26.22	25.83	25.46	25.11	24.76	24.44	25.56	25.18	24.82	24.47	24.14	23.82	51
52	25.91	25.53	25.16	24.81	24.47	24.15	25.27	24.90	24.54	24.20	23.87	23.55	52
53	25.62	25.24	24.88	24.53	24.19	23.87	24.99	24.62	24.27	23.93	23.60	23.29	53
54	25.33	24.96	24.60	24.26	23.92	23.61	24.73	24.36	24.01	23.67	23.35	23.04	54
55	25.06	24.69	24.34	23.99	23.67	23.35	24.47	24.11	23.76	23.43	23.11	22.80	55
56	24.80	24.43	24.08	23.74	23.42	23.11	24.22	23.86	23.52	23.19	22.87	22.57	56
57	24.54	24.18	23.83	23.50	23.18	22.87	23.98	23.63	23.29	22.96	22.65	22.35	57
58	24.30	23.94	23.60	23.27	22.95	22.64	23.75	23.40	23.07	22.74	22.43	22.13	58
59	24.07	23.71	23.37	23.04	22.72	22.42	23.53	23.19	22.85	22.53	22.22	21.92	59
60	23.84	23.49	23.15	22.82	22.51	22.21	23.32	22.98	22.64	22.33	22.02	21.73	60
72	21.64	21.32	21.01	20.72	20.43	20.15	21.25	20.94	20.63	20.34	20.06	19.79	72
84	20.12	19.82	19.54	19.26	18.99	18.73	19.82	19.53	19.24	18.97	18.71	18.45	84
96	19.02	18.74	18.47	18.20	17.95	17.70	18.78	18.51	18.24	17.98	17.73	17.49	96
108	18.20	17.93	17.67	17.42	17.17	16.94	18.01	17.74	17.49	17.24	17.00	16.76	108
120	17.57	17.31	17.06	16.82	16.58	16.35	17.42	17.16	16.91	16.67	16.44	16.21	120

MONTHLY PAYMENTS PER $1,000   18%

25% Residual   30% Residual

	25% Residual — NUMBER OF ADVANCE PAYMENTS						30% Residual — NUMBER OF ADVANCE PAYMENTS						
MOS	0	1	2	3	4	5	0	1	2	3	4	5	MOS
12	72.51	71.44	70.48	69.62	68.86	68.20	68.68	67.67	66.76	65.94	65.22	64.59	12
15	59.96	59.08	58.27	57.53	56.86	56.26	56.97	56.12	55.36	54.65	54.02	53.45	15
18	51.61	50.85	50.14	49.49	48.89	48.34	49.17	48.44	47.77	47.15	46.58	46.06	18
19	49.41	48.68	48.01	47.38	46.80	46.27	47.12	46.42	45.78	45.18	44.63	44.12	19
20	47.44	46.74	46.09	45.48	44.92	44.40	45.28	44.61	43.99	43.41	42.87	42.38	20
21	45.65	44.98	44.35	43.77	43.22	42.72	43.61	42.97	42.37	41.81	41.29	40.80	21
22	44.03	43.38	42.77	42.21	41.68	41.19	42.10	41.48	40.89	40.35	39.85	39.38	22
23	42.55	41.92	41.34	40.79	40.27	39.79	40.72	40.11	39.55	39.03	38.53	38.07	23
24	41.20	40.59	40.02	39.48	38.98	38.51	39.45	38.87	38.32	37.81	37.33	36.88	24
25	39.95	39.36	38.81	38.29	37.80	37.34	38.29	37.72	37.19	36.69	36.23	35.79	25
26	38.80	38.23	37.69	37.18	36.71	36.26	37.22	36.67	36.15	35.66	35.21	34.78	26
27	37.74	37.18	36.66	36.16	35.70	35.26	36.23	35.69	35.19	34.71	34.26	33.84	27
28	36.76	36.21	35.70	35.22	34.76	34.33	35.31	34.78	34.29	33.83	33.39	32.98	28
29	35.84	35.31	34.81	34.34	33.89	33.47	34.45	33.94	33.46	33.01	32.58	32.17	29
30	34.98	34.47	33.98	33.52	33.08	32.67	33.65	33.16	32.69	32.24	31.82	31.42	30
31	34.19	33.68	33.20	32.75	32.32	31.92	32.91	32.42	31.96	31.53	31.11	30.72	31
32	33.44	32.94	32.48	32.03	31.61	31.21	32.21	31.73	31.28	30.86	30.45	30.07	32
33	32.74	32.25	31.79	31.36	30.95	30.55	31.55	31.09	30.65	30.23	29.83	29.45	33
34	32.08	31.60	31.15	30.73	30.32	29.94	30.94	30.48	30.05	29.64	29.24	28.87	34
35	31.46	30.99	30.55	30.13	29.73	29.35	30.36	29.91	29.48	29.08	28.69	28.33	35
36	30.87	30.41	29.98	29.57	29.18	28.80	29.81	29.37	28.95	28.55	28.18	27.82	36
37	30.32	29.87	29.44	29.04	28.65	28.28	29.30	28.86	28.45	28.06	27.69	27.33	37
38	29.79	29.35	28.93	28.53	28.15	27.79	28.81	28.38	27.98	27.59	27.22	26.87	38
39	29.30	28.86	28.45	28.06	27.68	27.33	28.34	27.92	27.53	27.15	26.78	26.44	39
40	28.83	28.40	27.99	27.61	27.24	26.88	27.90	27.49	27.10	26.72	26.37	26.03	40
41	28.38	27.96	27.56	27.18	26.81	26.47	27.49	27.08	26.69	26.32	25.97	25.63	41
42	27.95	27.54	27.15	26.77	26.41	26.07	27.09	26.69	26.31	25.94	25.59	25.26	42
43	27.55	27.14	26.75	26.38	26.03	25.69	26.71	26.32	25.94	25.58	25.24	24.91	43
44	27.16	26.76	26.38	26.01	25.66	25.33	26.35	25.96	25.59	25.24	24.90	24.57	44
45	26.79	26.40	26.02	25.66	25.31	24.98	26.01	25.62	25.26	24.91	24.57	24.25	45
46	26.44	26.05	25.68	25.32	24.98	24.65	25.68	25.30	24.94	24.59	24.26	23.94	46
47	26.11	25.72	25.35	25.00	24.66	24.34	25.37	24.99	24.63	24.29	23.96	23.65	47
48	25.79	25.41	25.04	24.69	24.36	24.04	25.07	24.70	24.34	24.00	23.68	23.37	48
49	25.48	25.10	24.74	24.40	24.07	23.75	24.78	24.41	24.06	23.73	23.41	23.10	49
50	25.18	24.81	24.46	24.11	23.79	23.47	24.51	24.14	23.80	23.46	23.15	22.84	50
51	24.90	24.53	24.18	23.84	23.52	23.21	24.24	23.88	23.54	23.21	22.90	22.59	51
52	24.63	24.27	23.92	23.58	23.26	22.95	23.99	23.63	23.29	22.97	22.66	22.36	52
53	24.37	24.01	23.66	23.33	23.01	22.71	23.74	23.39	23.06	22.73	22.43	22.13	53
54	24.12	23.76	23.42	23.09	22.78	22.47	23.51	23.16	22.83	22.51	22.20	21.91	54
55	23.88	23.52	23.19	22.86	22.55	22.25	23.29	22.94	22.61	22.29	21.99	21.70	55
56	23.65	23.30	22.96	22.64	22.33	22.03	23.07	22.73	22.40	22.09	21.79	21.50	56
57	23.42	23.08	22.74	22.43	22.12	21.82	22.86	22.52	22.20	21.89	21.59	21.30	57
58	23.21	22.86	22.54	22.22	21.91	21.62	22.66	22.33	22.00	21.70	21.40	21.11	58
59	23.00	22.66	22.33	22.02	21.72	21.43	22.47	22.14	21.82	21.51	21.22	20.93	59
60	22.80	22.46	22.14	21.83	21.53	21.24	22.28	21.95	21.63	21.33	21.04	20.76	60
72	20.86	20.55	20.26	19.97	19.69	19.43	20.47	20.17	19.88	19.60	19.32	19.06	72
84	19.52	19.23	18.95	18.68	18.42	18.17	19.22	18.93	18.66	18.39	18.14	17.89	84
96	18.55	18.27	18.01	17.75	17.50	17.27	18.31	18.04	17.78	17.53	17.28	17.05	96
108	17.82	17.56	17.30	17.06	16.82	16.59	17.63	17.37	17.12	16.88	16.64	16.41	108
120	17.27	17.01	16.77	16.53	16.30	16.07	17.12	16.87	16.62	16.38	16.15	15.93	120

18% MONTHLY PAYMENTS PER $1,000

35% Residual   ## 40% Residual

| | NUMBER OF ADVANCE PAYMENTS | | | | | | NUMBER OF ADVANCE PAYMENTS | | | | | | |
MOS	0	1	2	3	4	5	0	1	2	3	4	5	MOS
12	64.85	63.89	63.03	62.26	61.58	60.99	61.01	60.11	59.30	58.58	57.94	57.38	12
15	53.97	53.17	52.44	51.78	51.18	50.63	50.97	50.22	49.53	48.90	48.34	47.82	15
18	46.73	46.04	45.40	44.81	44.27	43.77	44.29	43.63	43.03	42.47	41.96	41.49	18
19	44.83	44.16	43.55	42.98	42.46	41.97	42.53	41.90	41.32	40.78	40.28	39.82	19
20	43.11	42.48	41.89	41.34	40.83	40.35	40.95	40.35	39.78	39.26	38.78	38.33	20
21	41.57	40.95	40.38	39.85	39.35	38.89	39.52	38.94	38.40	37.89	37.42	36.98	21
22	40.16	39.57	39.01	38.50	38.02	37.57	38.23	37.66	37.13	36.64	36.18	35.76	22
23	38.88	38.31	37.77	37.27	36.80	36.36	37.04	36.50	35.98	35.50	35.06	34.64	23
24	37.71	37.15	36.63	36.14	35.68	35.25	35.96	35.43	34.93	34.46	34.03	33.62	24
25	36.63	36.09	35.58	35.10	34.65	34.23	34.96	34.45	33.96	33.51	33.08	32.68	25
26	35.63	35.10	34.61	34.14	33.71	33.29	34.04	33.54	33.07	32.62	32.21	31.81	26
27	34.71	34.20	33.71	33.26	32.83	32.43	33.19	32.70	32.24	31.81	31.40	31.01	27
28	33.86	33.36	32.88	32.44	32.02	31.62	32.41	31.93	31.48	31.05	30.65	30.27	28
29	33.06	32.57	32.11	31.68	31.26	30.88	31.67	31.20	30.76	30.35	29.95	29.58	29
30	32.32	31.84	31.39	30.96	30.56	30.18	30.99	30.53	30.10	29.69	29.30	28.94	30
31	31.63	31.16	30.72	30.30	29.90	29.53	30.35	29.90	29.48	29.08	28.69	28.34	31
32	30.98	30.52	30.09	29.68	29.29	28.92	29.75	29.31	28.90	28.50	28.13	27.77	32
33	30.37	29.92	29.50	29.09	28.71	28.35	29.19	28.76	28.35	27.96	27.59	27.24	33
34	29.80	29.36	28.94	28.55	28.17	27.81	28.66	28.24	27.84	27.46	27.09	26.75	34
35	29.26	28.83	28.42	28.03	27.66	27.31	28.17	27.75	27.35	26.98	26.62	26.28	35
36	28.75	28.33	27.93	27.54	27.18	26.83	27.70	27.29	26.90	26.53	26.18	25.84	36
37	28.27	27.86	27.46	27.08	26.72	26.38	27.25	26.85	26.47	26.10	25.76	25.43	37
38	27.82	27.41	27.02	26.65	26.29	25.95	26.83	26.44	26.06	25.70	25.36	25.03	38
39	27.39	26.99	26.60	26.23	25.88	25.55	26.44	26.05	25.68	25.32	24.98	24.66	39
40	26.98	26.58	26.20	25.84	25.50	25.17	26.06	25.68	25.31	24.96	24.63	24.31	40
41	26.60	26.20	25.83	25.47	25.13	24.80	25.70	25.32	24.96	24.62	24.29	23.97	41
42	26.23	25.84	25.47	25.12	24.78	24.46	25.36	24.99	24.63	24.29	23.96	23.65	42
43	25.88	25.49	25.13	24.78	24.45	24.13	25.04	24.67	24.32	23.98	23.66	23.35	43
44	25.54	25.16	24.80	24.46	24.13	23.81	24.73	24.37	24.02	23.68	23.36	23.06	44
45	25.22	24.85	24.49	24.15	23.83	23.52	24.44	24.08	23.73	23.40	23.09	22.78	45
46	24.92	24.55	24.20	23.86	23.54	23.23	24.16	23.80	23.46	23.13	22.82	22.52	46
47	24.63	24.26	23.92	23.58	23.26	22.96	23.89	23.53	23.20	22.87	22.56	22.27	47
48	24.35	23.99	23.64	23.31	23.00	22.70	23.63	23.28	22.95	22.63	22.32	22.03	48
49	24.08	23.73	23.39	23.06	22.75	22.45	23.38	23.04	22.71	22.39	22.09	21.80	49
50	23.83	23.47	23.14	22.81	22.50	22.21	23.15	22.81	22.48	22.16	21.86	21.57	50
51	23.58	23.23	22.90	22.58	22.27	21.98	22.92	22.58	22.26	21.95	21.65	21.36	51
52	23.35	23.00	22.67	22.35	22.05	21.76	22.70	22.37	22.05	21.74	21.44	21.16	52
53	23.12	22.78	22.45	22.14	21.84	21.55	22.50	22.16	21.85	21.54	21.25	20.96	53
54	22.90	22.56	22.24	21.93	21.63	21.34	22.30	21.97	21.65	21.35	21.06	20.78	54
55	22.69	22.36	22.04	21.73	21.43	21.15	22.10	21.78	21.46	21.16	20.87	20.60	55
56	22.49	22.16	21.84	21.54	21.24	20.96	21.92	21.59	21.28	20.98	20.70	20.42	56
57	22.30	21.97	21.65	21.35	21.06	20.78	21.74	21.42	21.11	20.81	20.53	20.25	57
58	22.11	21.79	21.47	21.17	20.88	20.60	21.57	21.25	20.94	20.65	20.37	20.09	58
59	21.93	21.61	21.30	21.00	20.71	20.43	21.40	21.08	20.78	20.49	20.21	19.94	59
60	21.76	21.44	21.13	20.83	20.55	20.27	21.24	20.93	20.63	20.34	20.06	19.79	60
72	20.08	19.78	19.50	19.22	18.96	18.70	19.69	19.40	19.12	18.85	18.59	18.34	72
84	18.92	18.64	18.37	18.11	17.86	17.61	18.62	18.34	18.08	17.82	17.57	17.33	84
96	18.08	17.81	17.55	17.30	17.06	16.83	17.84	17.58	17.32	17.07	16.84	16.61	96
108	17.45	17.19	16.94	16.70	16.46	16.24	17.26	17.00	16.76	16.52	16.29	16.06	108
120	16.97	16.72	16.47	16.24	16.01	15.79	16.82	16.57	16.33	16.09	15.87	15.65	120

MONTHLY PAYMENTS PER $1,000   18%

45% Residual | 50% Residual

MOS	| NUMBER OF ADVANCE PAYMENTS						| NUMBER OF ADVANCE PAYMENTS						MOS
	0	1	2	3	4	5	0	1	2	3	4	5	
12	57.18	56.33	55.58	54.90	54.30	53.77	53.34	52.56	51.85	51.22	50.66	50.17	12
15	47.97	47.27	46.62	46.03	45.49	45.01	44.98	44.31	43.71	43.15	42.65	42.20	15
18	41.85	41.23	40.66	40.13	39.65	39.20	39.41	38.83	38.29	37.79	37.33	36.91	18
19	40.24	39.64	39.09	38.58	38.11	37.68	37.94	37.38	36.86	36.38	35.94	35.53	19
20	38.79	38.22	37.68	37.19	36.73	36.31	36.63	36.09	35.58	35.12	34.68	34.28	20
21	37.48	36.93	36.41	35.93	35.48	35.07	35.44	34.91	34.43	33.97	33.55	33.16	21
22	36.29	35.76	35.25	34.79	34.35	33.95	34.36	33.85	33.37	32.93	32.52	32.14	22
23	35.21	34.69	34.20	33.74	33.32	32.92	33.37	32.88	32.42	31.98	31.58	31.20	23
24	34.21	33.71	33.23	32.79	32.37	31.98	32.47	31.99	31.54	31.12	30.72	30.35	24
25	33.30	32.81	32.35	31.91	31.51	31.12	31.64	31.17	30.73	30.32	29.93	29.57	25
26	32.46	31.98	31.53	31.10	30.70	30.33	30.87	30.41	29.99	29.58	29.20	28.85	26
27	31.68	31.21	30.77	30.35	29.96	29.60	30.16	29.72	29.30	28.90	28.53	28.18	27
28	30.96	30.50	30.07	29.66	29.28	28.92	29.51	29.07	28.66	28.27	27.91	27.56	28
29	30.28	29.84	29.41	29.01	28.64	28.28	28.89	28.47	28.06	27.68	27.32	26.99	29
30	29.66	29.22	28.80	28.41	28.04	27.69	28.32	27.91	27.51	27.14	26.78	26.45	30
31	29.07	28.64	28.23	27.85	27.49	27.14	27.79	27.38	26.99	26.63	26.28	25.95	31
32	28.52	28.10	27.70	27.32	26.97	26.63	27.29	26.89	26.51	26.15	25.80	25.48	32
33	28.01	27.59	27.20	26.83	26.48	26.14	26.83	26.43	26.05	25.70	25.36	25.04	33
34	27.52	27.12	26.73	26.36	26.02	25.69	26.39	26.00	25.63	25.27	24.94	24.62	34
35	27.07	26.67	26.29	25.93	25.58	25.26	25.97	25.59	25.22	24.88	24.55	24.24	35
36	26.64	26.25	25.87	25.52	25.18	24.86	25.58	25.20	24.84	24.50	24.18	23.87	36
37	26.23	25.85	25.48	25.13	24.79	24.47	25.21	24.84	24.49	24.15	23.83	23.52	37
38	25.85	25.47	25.10	24.76	24.43	24.11	24.86	24.50	24.15	23.81	23.50	23.19	38
39	25.49	25.11	24.75	24.41	24.08	23.77	24.53	24.17	23.82	23.50	23.18	22.88	39
40	25.14	24.77	24.41	24.08	23.75	23.45	24.22	23.86	23.52	23.19	22.88	22.59	40
41	24.81	24.45	24.10	23.76	23.44	23.14	23.92	23.57	23.23	22.91	22.60	22.31	41
42	24.50	24.14	23.79	23.46	23.15	22.85	23.64	23.29	22.95	22.64	22.33	22.04	42
43	24.20	23.85	23.50	23.18	22.87	22.57	23.37	23.02	22.69	22.38	22.08	21.79	43
44	23.92	23.57	23.23	22.91	22.60	22.30	23.11	22.77	22.44	22.13	21.83	21.55	44
45	23.65	23.30	22.97	22.65	22.34	22.05	22.86	22.53	22.20	21.90	21.60	21.32	45
46	23.39	23.05	22.72	22.40	22.10	21.81	22.63	22.30	21.98	21.67	21.38	21.10	46
47	23.15	22.80	22.48	22.16	21.86	21.58	22.41	22.08	21.76	21.46	21.17	20.89	47
48	22.91	22.57	22.25	21.94	21.64	21.36	22.19	21.86	21.55	21.25	20.96	20.69	48
49	22.69	22.35	22.03	21.72	21.43	21.15	21.99	21.66	21.35	21.05	20.77	20.49	49
50	22.47	22.14	21.82	21.51	21.22	20.94	21.79	21.47	21.16	20.86	20.58	20.31	50
51	22.26	21.93	21.62	21.32	21.03	20.75	21.60	21.28	20.98	20.68	20.40	20.13	51
52	22.06	21.74	21.42	21.12	20.84	20.56	21.42	21.10	20.80	20.51	20.23	19.96	52
53	21.87	21.55	21.24	20.94	20.66	20.38	21.25	20.93	20.63	20.34	20.07	19.80	53
54	21.69	21.37	21.06	20.77	20.48	20.21	21.08	20.77	20.47	20.18	19.91	19.64	54
55	21.51	21.19	20.89	20.60	20.31	20.04	20.92	20.61	20.31	20.03	19.76	19.49	55
56	21.34	21.03	20.72	20.43	20.15	19.89	20.77	20.46	20.16	19.88	19.61	19.35	56
57	21.18	20.86	20.56	20.28	20.00	19.73	20.62	20.31	20.02	19.74	19.47	19.21	57
58	21.02	20.71	20.41	20.12	19.85	19.58	20.47	20.17	19.88	19.60	19.33	19.07	58
59	20.87	20.56	20.26	19.98	19.71	19.44	20.34	20.03	19.75	19.47	19.20	18.95	59
60	20.72	20.42	20.12	19.84	19.57	19.30	20.20	19.90	19.62	19.34	19.08	18.82	60
72	19.30	19.01	18.74	18.47	18.22	17.97	18.91	18.63	18.36	18.10	17.85	17.61	72
84	18.31	18.04	17.78	17.53	17.29	17.05	18.01	17.75	17.49	17.24	17.00	16.77	84
96	17.60	17.34	17.09	16.85	16.61	16.39	17.37	17.11	16.86	16.62	16.39	16.17	96
108	17.07	16.82	16.58	16.34	16.11	15.89	16.88	16.63	16.39	16.16	15.93	15.71	108
120	16.67	16.42	16.18	15.95	15.73	15.51	16.51	16.27	16.03	15.81	15.58	15.37	120

22%   MONTHLY PAYMENTS PER $1,000

0% Residual   ## 2% Residual

	NUMBER OF ADVANCE PAYMENTS						NUMBER OF ADVANCE PAYMENTS					
MOS	0	1	2	3	4	5	0	1	2	3	4	5	MOS
12	93.60	91.91	90.41	89.07	87.89	86.86	92.09	90.44	88.96	87.64	86.48	85.46	12
15	76.86	75.48	74.22	73.08	72.05	71.12	75.69	74.33	73.09	71.97	70.95	70.04	15
18	65.73	64.55	63.46	62.46	61.55	60.71	64.79	63.62	62.55	61.56	60.66	59.83	18
19	62.81	61.68	60.64	59.68	58.79	57.98	61.92	60.81	59.78	58.83	57.96	57.16	19
20	60.18	59.10	58.10	57.17	56.32	55.53	59.35	58.28	57.29	56.38	55.53	54.75	20
21	57.81	56.77	55.80	54.91	54.08	53.31	57.02	55.99	55.04	54.16	53.34	52.59	21
22	55.65	54.65	53.72	52.85	52.05	51.31	54.90	53.92	53.00	52.14	51.35	50.62	22
23	53.68	52.72	51.82	50.98	50.20	49.48	52.98	52.02	51.14	50.31	49.54	48.82	23
24	51.88	50.95	50.08	49.27	48.51	47.80	51.21	50.29	49.43	48.63	47.88	47.18	24
25	50.23	49.32	48.48	47.69	46.95	46.26	49.59	48.70	47.86	47.08	46.36	45.68	25
26	48.70	47.83	47.01	46.24	45.52	44.85	48.10	47.23	46.42	45.66	44.95	44.29	26
27	47.29	46.44	45.64	44.90	44.20	43.54	46.71	45.87	45.09	44.35	43.65	43.01	27
28	45.99	45.16	44.38	43.65	42.97	42.33	45.43	44.62	43.85	43.13	42.45	41.82	28
29	44.77	43.96	43.21	42.50	41.83	41.20	44.24	43.45	42.70	41.99	41.33	40.71	29
30	43.64	42.85	42.11	41.42	40.76	40.15	43.13	42.36	41.63	40.94	40.29	39.68	30
31	42.58	41.81	41.09	40.41	39.77	39.17	42.10	41.34	40.62	39.95	39.32	38.72	31
32	41.59	40.84	40.14	39.47	38.84	38.25	41.13	40.39	39.69	39.03	38.41	37.82	32
33	40.66	39.93	39.24	38.59	37.97	37.39	40.22	39.49	38.81	38.16	37.56	36.98	33
34	39.79	39.07	38.40	37.76	37.15	36.58	39.36	38.65	37.98	37.35	36.75	36.19	34
35	38.97	38.27	37.60	36.98	36.38	35.82	38.56	37.86	37.21	36.59	36.00	35.44	35
36	38.20	37.51	36.86	36.24	35.66	35.11	37.80	37.12	36.47	35.87	35.29	34.74	36
37	37.46	36.79	36.15	35.55	34.98	34.43	37.08	36.41	35.78	35.18	34.62	34.08	37
38	36.77	36.11	35.49	34.89	34.33	33.79	36.41	35.75	35.13	34.54	33.98	33.45	38
39	36.12	35.47	34.85	34.27	33.72	33.19	35.76	35.12	34.51	33.93	33.38	32.86	39
40	35.50	34.86	34.26	33.68	33.13	32.62	35.16	34.52	33.92	33.35	32.81	32.30	40
41	34.91	34.28	33.69	33.12	32.58	32.07	34.58	33.96	33.37	32.81	32.27	31.77	41
42	34.35	33.73	33.15	32.59	32.06	31.56	34.03	33.42	32.84	32.29	31.76	31.26	42
43	33.82	33.21	32.63	32.08	31.56	31.06	33.51	32.91	32.34	31.79	31.27	30.78	43
44	33.32	32.72	32.15	31.60	31.09	30.60	33.02	32.42	31.86	31.32	30.81	30.32	44
45	32.83	32.24	31.68	31.14	30.64	30.15	32.54	31.96	31.40	30.87	30.37	29.88	45
46	32.37	31.79	31.23	30.71	30.20	29.73	32.09	31.51	30.96	30.44	29.94	29.47	46
47	31.93	31.36	30.81	30.29	29.79	29.32	31.66	31.09	30.55	30.03	29.54	29.07	47
48	31.51	30.94	30.40	29.89	29.40	28.93	31.25	30.69	30.15	29.64	29.15	28.69	48
49	31.11	30.55	30.02	29.51	29.02	28.56	30.85	30.30	29.77	29.26	28.78	28.32	49
50	30.72	30.17	29.64	29.14	28.66	28.20	30.48	29.93	29.40	28.91	28.43	27.98	50
51	30.35	29.81	29.29	28.79	28.32	27.86	30.11	29.57	29.06	28.56	28.09	27.64	51
52	30.00	29.46	28.95	28.45	27.98	27.54	29.77	29.23	28.72	28.23	27.77	27.32	52
53	29.66	29.13	28.62	28.13	27.67	27.22	29.43	28.90	28.40	27.92	27.46	27.02	53
54	29.33	28.81	28.30	27.82	27.36	26.92	29.11	28.59	28.09	27.61	27.16	26.72	54
55	29.02	28.50	28.00	27.52	27.07	26.63	28.81	28.29	27.79	27.32	26.87	26.44	55
56	28.72	28.20	27.71	27.24	26.79	26.36	28.51	28.00	27.51	27.04	26.59	26.17	56
57	28.43	27.92	27.43	26.96	26.52	26.09	28.23	27.72	27.24	26.77	26.33	25.90	57
58	28.15	27.64	27.16	26.70	26.26	25.83	27.96	27.45	26.97	26.51	26.07	25.65	58
59	27.88	27.38	26.90	26.44	26.00	25.58	27.69	27.19	26.72	26.26	25.83	25.41	59
60	27.62	27.13	26.65	26.20	25.76	25.35	27.44	26.94	26.47	26.02	25.59	25.17	60
72	25.13	24.68	24.25	23.83	23.43	23.05	25.00	24.55	24.11	23.70	23.30	22.92	72
84	23.43	23.01	22.60	22.22	21.84	21.48	23.33	22.91	22.51	22.12	21.75	21.39	84
96	22.22	21.82	21.44	21.07	20.71	20.37	22.14	21.75	21.36	20.99	20.64	20.30	96
108	21.34	20.95	20.58	20.23	19.89	19.56	21.28	20.89	20.53	20.17	19.83	19.50	108
120	20.67	20.30	19.94	19.60	19.27	18.95	20.63	20.26	19.90	19.56	19.22	18.90	120

MONTHLY PAYMENTS PER $1,000   22%

5% Residual

NUMBER OF ADVANCE PAYMENTS

MOS	0	1	2	3	4	5
12	89.84	88.22	86.77	85.49	84.36	83.37
15	73.94	72.61	71.40	70.30	69.31	68.41
18	63.36	62.22	61.17	60.21	59.33	58.52
19	60.59	59.50	58.49	57.56	56.71	55.93
20	58.09	57.04	56.08	55.18	54.36	53.60
21	55.83	54.83	53.90	53.03	52.23	51.49
22	53.79	52.82	51.92	51.08	50.31	49.59
23	51.92	50.98	50.11	49.30	48.55	47.85
24	50.21	49.30	48.46	47.67	46.94	46.26
25	48.63	47.76	46.94	46.18	45.46	44.80
26	47.19	46.34	45.54	44.80	44.10	43.45
27	45.85	45.02	44.25	43.52	42.84	42.21
28	44.60	43.80	43.05	42.34	41.68	41.05
29	43.45	42.67	41.93	41.24	40.59	39.98
30	42.37	41.61	40.89	40.22	39.58	38.98
31	41.37	40.62	39.92	39.26	38.64	38.05
32	40.43	39.70	39.01	38.37	37.76	37.18
33	39.55	38.83	38.16	37.53	36.93	36.36
34	38.72	38.02	37.36	36.74	36.15	35.60
35	37.94	37.25	36.61	36.00	35.42	34.88
36	37.20	36.53	35.90	35.30	34.73	34.20
37	36.51	35.85	35.23	34.64	34.08	33.55
38	35.85	35.21	34.60	34.02	33.47	32.95
39	35.23	34.60	34.00	33.43	32.89	32.37
40	34.64	34.02	33.43	32.87	32.33	31.83
41	34.08	33.47	32.89	32.34	31.81	31.31
42	33.55	32.95	32.38	31.83	31.31	30.82
43	33.05	32.45	31.89	31.35	30.84	30.35
44	32.57	31.98	31.42	30.89	30.39	29.91
45	32.11	31.53	30.98	30.46	29.96	29.49
46	31.67	31.10	30.56	30.04	29.55	29.08
47	31.25	30.69	30.15	29.64	29.16	28.69
48	30.85	30.30	29.77	29.26	28.78	28.33
49	30.47	29.92	29.40	28.90	28.43	27.97
50	30.10	29.56	29.05	28.55	28.08	27.64
51	29.75	29.22	28.71	28.22	27.76	27.31
52	29.42	28.89	28.38	27.90	27.44	27.00
53	29.09	28.57	28.07	27.59	27.14	26.70
54	28.78	28.27	27.77	27.30	26.85	26.42
55	28.49	27.97	27.49	27.02	26.57	26.14
56	28.20	27.69	27.21	26.75	26.30	25.88
57	27.93	27.42	26.94	26.48	26.05	25.63
58	27.66	27.16	26.69	26.23	25.80	25.38
59	27.41	26.91	26.44	25.99	25.56	25.15
60	27.16	26.67	26.20	25.76	25.33	24.92
72	24.79	24.35	23.92	23.51	23.11	22.74
84	23.18	22.76	22.36	21.97	21.60	21.25
96	22.03	21.63	21.25	20.88	20.53	20.19
108	21.19	20.81	20.44	20.09	19.75	19.42
120	20.56	20.19	19.83	19.49	19.16	18.84

10% Residual

NUMBER OF ADVANCE PAYMENTS

0	1	2	3	4	5	MOS
86.07	84.52	83.14	81.91	80.82	79.87	12
71.01	69.73	68.57	67.52	66.56	65.71	15
60.99	59.90	58.89	57.96	57.11	56.33	18
58.36	57.31	56.34	55.45	54.63	53.87	19
56.00	54.99	54.06	53.20	52.40	51.67	20
53.86	52.89	51.99	51.16	50.39	49.67	21
51.92	50.98	50.12	49.31	48.56	47.87	22
50.15	49.25	48.41	47.62	46.90	46.22	23
48.53	47.66	46.84	46.08	45.37	44.71	24
47.04	46.19	45.40	44.66	43.97	43.33	25
45.67	44.85	44.08	43.36	42.68	42.05	26
44.40	43.60	42.85	42.15	41.49	40.87	27
43.22	42.44	41.71	41.03	40.38	39.78	28
42.13	41.37	40.66	39.99	39.36	38.77	29
41.11	40.37	39.67	39.02	38.40	37.82	30
40.16	39.43	38.75	38.11	37.51	36.94	31
39.27	38.56	37.89	37.26	36.67	36.11	32
38.43	37.74	37.09	36.47	35.89	35.34	33
37.64	36.97	36.33	35.72	35.15	34.61	34
36.91	36.24	35.61	35.02	34.46	33.93	35
36.21	35.56	34.94	34.36	33.81	33.28	36
35.55	34.91	34.31	33.73	33.19	32.67	37
34.93	34.30	33.71	33.14	32.61	32.10	38
34.34	33.72	33.14	32.58	32.06	31.55	39
33.78	33.18	32.60	32.05	31.53	31.04	40
33.25	32.66	32.09	31.55	31.04	30.55	41
32.75	32.16	31.60	31.07	30.57	30.08	42
32.27	31.69	31.14	30.62	30.12	29.64	43
31.82	31.24	30.70	30.18	29.69	29.22	44
31.38	30.82	30.28	29.77	29.28	28.82	45
30.97	30.41	29.88	29.38	28.89	28.44	46
30.57	30.02	29.50	29.00	28.52	28.07	47
30.19	29.65	29.13	28.64	28.17	27.72	48
29.83	29.29	28.78	28.30	27.83	27.39	49
29.48	28.95	28.45	27.97	27.51	27.07	50
29.15	28.63	28.13	27.65	27.20	26.76	51
28.83	28.32	27.82	27.35	26.90	26.47	52
28.53	28.02	27.53	27.06	26.61	26.18	53
28.24	27.73	27.24	26.78	26.34	25.91	54
27.95	27.45	26.97	26.51	26.07	25.65	55
27.68	27.18	26.71	26.25	25.82	25.40	56
27.42	26.93	26.46	26.01	25.57	25.16	57
27.17	26.68	26.21	25.77	25.34	24.93	58
26.93	26.44	25.98	25.54	25.11	24.71	59
26.70	26.21	25.76	25.32	24.90	24.49	60
24.45	24.01	23.59	23.19	22.80	22.43	72
22.92	22.51	22.11	21.73	21.37	21.02	84
21.83	21.44	21.06	20.70	20.35	20.01	96
21.04	20.66	20.29	19.94	19.61	19.28	108
20.44	20.07	19.72	19.38	19.05	18.73	120

22%   MONTHLY PAYMENTS PER $1,000

	15% Residual						20% Residual						

NUMBER OF ADVANCE PAYMENTS

MOS	0	1	2	3	4	5	0	1	2	3	4	5	MOS
12	82.31	80.83	79.50	78.33	77.29	76.38	78.55	77.13	75.87	74.75	73.76	72.89	12
15	68.08	66.86	65.74	64.73	63.82	63.00	65.16	63.99	62.92	61.95	61.08	60.29	15
18	58.62	57.57	56.60	55.71	54.89	54.14	56.25	55.24	54.31	53.46	52.67	51.95	18
19	56.14	55.13	54.20	53.34	52.55	51.82	53.92	52.95	52.05	51.23	50.47	49.77	19
20	53.91	52.94	52.04	51.21	50.44	49.74	51.81	50.88	50.02	49.22	48.48	47.81	20
21	51.89	50.95	50.09	49.28	48.54	47.85	49.91	49.02	48.18	47.41	46.69	46.03	21
22	50.05	49.15	48.32	47.54	46.82	46.15	48.19	47.32	46.51	45.77	45.07	44.43	22
23	48.38	47.51	46.70	45.95	45.24	44.59	46.61	45.78	44.99	44.27	43.59	42.96	23
24	46.85	46.01	45.22	44.49	43.80	43.17	45.17	44.36	43.60	42.89	42.24	41.62	24
25	45.45	44.63	43.86	43.15	42.48	41.86	43.85	43.06	42.32	41.63	40.99	40.39	25
26	44.15	43.35	42.61	41.91	41.26	40.65	42.63	41.86	41.15	40.47	39.84	39.26	26
27	42.95	42.18	41.45	40.77	40.14	39.54	41.50	40.76	40.06	39.40	38.78	38.21	27
28	41.84	41.09	40.38	39.72	39.09	38.51	40.46	39.73	39.04	38.40	37.80	37.24	28
29	40.81	40.07	39.38	38.73	38.12	37.55	39.48	38.77	38.11	37.48	36.89	36.33	29
30	39.84	39.13	38.45	37.82	37.22	36.66	38.58	37.88	37.23	36.62	36.04	35.49	30
31	38.94	38.24	37.58	36.96	36.38	35.82	37.73	37.05	36.41	35.81	35.24	34.71	31
32	38.10	37.42	36.77	36.16	35.59	35.04	36.94	36.28	35.65	35.06	34.50	33.97	32
33	37.31	36.64	36.01	35.41	34.85	34.31	36.20	35.55	34.93	34.35	33.80	33.29	33
34	36.57	35.91	35.29	34.70	34.15	33.63	35.50	34.86	34.26	33.69	33.15	32.64	34
35	35.87	35.23	34.62	34.04	33.50	32.98	34.84	34.22	33.62	33.06	32.53	32.03	35
36	35.22	34.58	33.98	33.42	32.88	32.37	34.22	33.61	33.03	32.47	31.95	31.46	36
37	34.60	33.97	33.38	32.83	32.30	31.80	33.64	33.03	32.46	31.92	31.40	30.92	37
38	34.01	33.40	32.82	32.27	31.75	31.25	33.09	32.49	31.93	31.39	30.89	30.41	38
39	33.45	32.85	32.28	31.74	31.23	30.74	32.56	31.98	31.42	30.90	30.40	29.92	39
40	32.93	32.33	31.77	31.24	30.73	30.25	32.07	31.49	30.94	30.42	29.93	29.46	40
41	32.43	31.84	31.29	30.76	30.26	29.79	31.60	31.03	30.49	29.98	29.49	29.03	41
42	31.95	31.38	30.83	30.31	29.82	29.35	31.15	30.59	30.06	29.55	29.07	28.61	42
43	31.50	30.93	30.39	29.88	29.39	28.93	30.72	30.17	29.65	29.15	28.67	28.22	43
44	31.07	30.51	29.98	29.47	28.99	28.53	30.32	29.77	29.26	28.76	28.29	27.85	44
45	30.66	30.11	29.58	29.08	28.61	28.15	29.93	29.39	28.88	28.39	27.93	27.49	45
46	30.27	29.72	29.20	28.71	28.24	27.79	29.56	29.03	28.53	28.04	27.59	27.15	46
47	29.89	29.35	28.84	28.35	27.89	27.45	29.21	28.69	28.19	27.71	27.26	26.82	47
48	29.54	29.00	28.50	28.02	27.56	27.12	28.88	28.36	27.86	27.39	26.94	26.51	48
49	29.19	28.67	28.17	27.69	27.24	26.80	28.55	28.04	27.55	27.08	26.64	26.21	49
50	28.87	28.35	27.85	27.38	26.93	26.50	28.25	27.74	27.25	26.79	26.35	25.93	50
51	28.55	28.04	27.55	27.08	26.63	26.21	27.95	27.45	26.97	26.51	26.07	25.66	51
52	28.25	27.74	27.26	26.79	26.35	25.93	27.67	27.17	26.70	26.24	25.81	25.40	52
53	27.96	27.46	26.98	26.52	26.08	25.66	27.40	26.90	26.43	25.98	25.55	25.14	53
54	27.69	27.19	26.71	26.26	25.82	25.41	27.14	26.65	26.18	25.74	25.31	24.90	54
55	27.42	26.93	26.45	26.00	25.57	25.16	26.88	26.40	25.94	25.50	25.08	24.67	55
56	27.16	26.67	26.21	25.76	25.33	24.93	26.64	26.16	25.71	25.27	24.85	24.45	56
57	26.92	26.43	25.97	25.53	25.10	24.70	26.41	25.94	25.48	25.05	24.63	24.24	57
58	26.68	26.20	25.74	25.30	24.88	24.48	26.19	25.72	25.27	24.84	24.42	24.03	58
59	26.45	25.97	25.52	25.08	24.67	24.27	25.97	25.51	25.06	24.63	24.22	23.83	59
60	26.23	25.76	25.31	24.88	24.46	24.07	25.77	25.30	24.86	24.44	24.03	23.64	60
72	24.11	23.68	23.26	22.86	22.48	22.11	23.77	23.34	22.93	22.54	22.16	21.80	72
84	22.67	22.26	21.87	21.49	21.13	20.78	22.41	22.01	21.62	21.25	20.89	20.55	84
96	21.64	21.25	20.88	20.52	20.17	19.84	21.45	21.06	20.69	20.33	19.99	19.66	96
108	20.89	20.51	20.15	19.80	19.47	19.14	20.74	20.36	20.00	19.66	19.33	19.01	108
120	20.32	19.96	19.61	19.27	18.94	18.63	20.21	19.84	19.49	19.16	18.83	18.52	120

MONTHLY PAYMENTS PER $1,000   22%

	25% Residual						30% Residual						
	NUMBER OF ADVANCE PAYMENTS						NUMBER OF ADVANCE PAYMENTS						
MOS	0	1	2	3	4	5	0	1	2	3	4	5	MOS
12	74.78	73.44	72.24	71.17	70.22	69.40	71.02	69.74	68.60	67.59	66.69	65.91	12
15	62.23	61.11	60.09	59.17	58.33	57.58	59.31	58.24	57.27	56.39	55.59	54.88	15
18	53.88	52.91	52.02	51.20	50.45	49.76	51.52	50.59	49.73	48.95	48.23	47.58	18
19	51.69	50.76	49.90	49.11	48.38	47.72	49.47	48.58	47.76	47.00	46.30	45.66	19
20	49.72	48.83	48.00	47.23	46.53	45.88	47.63	46.77	45.98	45.25	44.57	43.94	20
21	47.94	47.08	46.28	45.54	44.85	44.21	45.97	45.14	44.37	43.66	43.00	42.39	21
22	46.32	45.49	44.71	43.99	43.33	42.71	44.46	43.66	42.91	42.22	41.58	40.99	22
23	44.85	44.04	43.29	42.59	41.94	41.33	43.08	42.30	41.58	40.91	40.28	39.70	23
24	43.50	42.71	41.98	41.30	40.67	40.07	41.82	41.07	40.36	39.71	39.10	38.53	24
25	42.26	41.50	40.78	40.12	39.50	38.92	40.66	39.93	39.25	38.61	38.01	37.45	25
26	41.11	40.37	39.68	39.03	38.42	37.86	39.59	38.88	38.21	37.59	37.01	36.46	26
27	40.05	39.33	38.66	38.02	37.43	36.87	38.61	37.91	37.26	36.65	36.08	35.54	27
28	39.07	38.37	37.71	37.09	36.51	35.96	37.69	37.01	36.38	35.78	35.22	34.69	28
29	38.16	37.48	36.83	36.22	35.65	35.12	36.84	36.18	35.55	34.97	34.42	33.90	29
30	37.31	36.64	36.01	35.42	34.86	34.33	36.05	35.40	34.79	34.21	33.67	33.17	30
31	36.52	35.86	35.24	34.66	34.11	33.59	35.31	34.67	34.07	33.51	32.98	32.48	31
32	35.78	35.13	34.53	33.95	33.41	32.90	34.61	33.99	33.40	32.85	32.33	31.84	32
33	35.08	34.45	33.85	33.29	32.76	32.26	33.96	33.35	32.78	32.23	31.72	31.23	33
34	34.43	33.81	33.22	32.67	32.15	31.65	33.35	32.75	32.19	31.65	31.15	30.67	34
35	33.81	33.20	32.63	32.08	31.57	31.08	32.78	32.19	31.63	31.10	30.61	30.13	35
36	33.23	32.63	32.07	31.53	31.02	30.54	32.24	31.66	31.11	30.59	30.10	29.63	36
37	32.68	32.10	31.54	31.01	30.51	30.04	31.73	31.16	30.62	30.10	29.62	29.16	37
38	32.17	31.59	31.04	30.52	30.03	29.56	31.24	30.68	30.15	29.64	29.17	28.71	38
39	31.67	31.10	30.56	30.05	29.57	29.10	30.79	30.23	29.71	29.21	28.74	28.29	39
40	31.21	30.65	30.12	29.61	29.13	28.67	30.35	29.81	29.29	28.80	28.33	27.89	40
41	30.77	30.22	29.69	29.19	28.72	28.27	29.94	29.40	28.89	28.40	27.94	27.50	41
42	30.35	29.80	29.28	28.79	28.32	27.88	29.55	29.02	28.51	28.03	27.58	27.14	42
43	29.95	29.41	28.90	28.41	27.95	27.51	29.18	28.65	28.15	27.68	27.23	26.80	43
44	29.57	29.04	28.53	28.05	27.59	27.16	28.82	28.30	27.81	27.34	26.89	26.47	44
45	29.21	28.68	28.18	27.71	27.25	26.82	28.48	27.97	27.48	27.02	26.58	26.16	45
46	28.86	28.34	27.85	27.38	26.93	26.50	28.16	27.65	27.17	26.71	26.28	25.86	46
47	28.53	28.02	27.53	27.07	26.62	26.20	27.85	27.35	26.88	26.42	25.99	25.57	47
48	28.22	27.71	27.23	26.77	26.33	25.91	27.56	27.06	26.59	26.14	25.71	25.30	48
49	27.92	27.41	26.94	26.48	26.04	25.63	27.28	26.79	26.32	25.87	25.45	25.04	49
50	27.63	27.13	26.66	26.20	25.77	25.36	27.01	26.52	26.06	25.62	25.20	24.79	50
51	27.35	26.86	26.39	25.94	25.51	25.11	26.75	26.27	25.81	25.37	24.95	24.55	51
52	27.08	26.60	26.13	25.69	25.27	24.86	26.50	26.02	25.57	25.14	24.72	24.33	52
53	26.83	26.35	25.89	25.45	25.03	24.63	26.26	25.79	25.34	24.91	24.50	24.11	53
54	26.59	26.11	25.65	25.21	24.80	24.40	26.04	25.57	25.12	24.69	24.29	23.89	54
55	26.35	25.88	25.42	24.99	24.58	24.18	25.82	25.35	24.91	24.48	24.08	23.69	55
56	26.12	25.65	25.21	24.78	24.37	23.97	25.61	25.14	24.70	24.28	23.88	23.50	56
57	25.91	25.44	25.00	24.57	24.16	23.77	25.40	24.95	24.51	24.09	23.69	23.31	57
58	25.70	25.24	24.79	24.37	23.97	23.58	25.21	24.75	24.32	23.91	23.51	23.13	58
59	25.50	25.04	24.60	24.18	23.78	23.39	25.02	24.57	24.14	23.73	23.33	22.96	59
60	25.30	24.85	24.41	24.00	23.60	23.22	24.84	24.39	23.96	23.56	23.16	22.79	60
72	23.43	23.01	22.61	22.22	21.85	21.49	23.09	22.68	22.28	21.90	21.53	21.18	72
84	22.16	21.76	21.38	21.01	20.66	20.32	21.90	21.51	21.13	20.77	20.42	20.08	84
96	21.25	20.87	20.50	20.15	19.81	19.48	21.06	20.68	20.31	19.96	19.63	19.30	96
108	20.59	20.22	19.86	19.52	19.19	18.87	20.44	20.07	19.72	19.38	19.05	18.73	108
120	20.09	19.73	19.38	19.05	18.72	18.41	19.97	19.61	19.27	18.94	18.61	18.30	120

22%   MONTHLY PAYMENTS PER $1,000

35% Residual   ## 40% Residual

MOS	\multicolumn{6}{c}{NUMBER OF ADVANCE PAYMENTS}	\multicolumn{6}{c}{NUMBER OF ADVANCE PAYMENTS}	MOS
	0	1	2	3	4	5	0	1	2	3	4	5	
12	67.26	66.05	64.97	64.00	63.16	62.41	63.49	62.35	61.33	60.42	59.62	58.92	12
15	56.38	55.36	54.44	53.61	52.85	52.17	53.45	52.49	51.62	50.82	50.11	49.46	15
18	49.15	48.26	47.45	46.70	46.01	45.39	46.78	45.93	45.16	44.45	43.80	43.20	18
19	47.25	46.39	45.61	44.89	44.22	43.61	45.02	44.21	43.46	42.77	42.14	41.56	19
20	45.54	44.72	43.96	43.26	42.61	42.01	43.44	42.66	41.94	41.27	40.65	40.08	20
21	43.99	43.20	42.47	41.79	41.16	40.57	42.02	41.26	40.56	39.91	39.31	38.75	21
22	42.59	41.82	41.11	40.45	39.84	39.27	40.73	39.99	39.31	38.68	38.09	37.55	22
23	41.31	40.57	39.88	39.23	38.63	38.07	39.55	38.83	38.17	37.55	36.98	36.45	23
24	40.14	39.42	38.75	38.12	37.53	36.98	38.47	37.77	37.13	36.52	35.96	35.44	24
25	39.07	38.36	37.71	37.09	36.52	35.98	37.47	36.80	36.17	35.58	35.03	34.51	25
26	38.08	37.39	36.75	36.15	35.59	35.06	36.56	35.90	35.28	34.71	34.17	33.66	26
27	37.16	36.49	35.86	35.28	34.73	34.21	35.71	35.07	34.47	33.90	33.37	32.88	27
28	36.31	35.66	35.04	34.47	33.93	33.42	34.93	34.30	33.71	33.15	32.63	32.15	28
29	35.52	34.88	34.28	33.71	33.18	32.69	34.20	33.58	33.00	32.46	31.95	31.47	29
30	34.78	34.16	33.57	33.01	32.49	32.00	33.52	32.91	32.35	31.81	31.31	30.84	30
31	34.10	33.48	32.90	32.36	31.85	31.36	32.88	32.29	31.73	31.21	30.71	30.25	31
32	33.45	32.85	32.28	31.75	31.24	30.77	32.29	31.71	31.16	30.64	30.16	29.70	32
33	32.85	32.26	31.70	31.17	30.68	30.21	31.73	31.16	30.62	30.11	29.63	29.18	33
34	32.28	31.70	31.15	30.63	30.14	29.68	31.21	30.65	30.12	29.62	29.14	28.69	34
35	31.75	31.18	30.64	30.13	29.64	29.19	30.72	30.16	29.64	29.15	28.68	28.24	35
36	31.25	30.68	30.15	29.65	29.17	28.72	30.25	29.71	29.19	28.71	28.24	27.81	36
37	30.77	30.22	29.69	29.20	28.73	28.28	29.81	29.28	28.77	28.29	27.83	27.40	37
38	30.32	29.78	29.26	28.77	28.30	27.86	29.40	28.87	28.37	27.89	27.44	27.02	38
39	29.90	29.36	28.85	28.36	27.91	27.47	29.01	28.49	27.99	27.52	27.08	26.65	39
40	29.49	28.96	28.46	27.98	27.53	27.10	28.64	28.12	27.63	27.17	26.73	26.31	40
41	29.11	28.59	28.09	27.62	27.17	26.74	28.28	27.77	27.29	26.83	26.40	25.98	41
42	28.75	28.23	27.74	27.27	26.83	26.41	27.95	27.44	26.97	26.51	26.08	25.67	42
43	28.40	27.89	27.41	26.94	26.50	26.09	27.63	27.13	26.66	26.21	25.78	25.38	43
44	28.07	27.57	27.09	26.63	26.20	25.78	27.32	26.83	26.37	25.92	25.50	25.09	44
45	27.76	27.26	26.78	26.33	25.90	25.49	27.03	26.55	26.09	25.65	25.23	24.83	45
46	27.46	26.97	26.50	26.05	25.62	25.22	26.76	26.28	25.82	25.38	24.97	24.57	46
47	27.17	26.68	26.22	25.78	25.35	24.95	26.49	26.02	25.56	25.13	24.72	24.33	47
48	26.90	26.42	25.96	25.52	25.10	24.70	26.24	25.77	25.32	24.89	24.48	24.09	48
49	26.64	26.16	25.70	25.27	24.85	24.46	26.00	25.53	25.09	24.66	24.26	23.87	49
50	26.39	25.91	25.46	25.03	24.62	24.22	25.77	25.31	24.86	24.44	24.04	23.66	50
51	26.15	25.68	25.23	24.80	24.39	24.00	25.55	25.09	24.65	24.23	23.83	23.45	51
52	25.92	25.45	25.01	24.58	24.18	23.79	25.34	24.88	24.44	24.03	23.63	23.25	52
53	25.70	25.24	24.79	24.37	23.97	23.59	25.13	24.68	24.25	23.84	23.44	23.07	53
54	25.49	25.03	24.59	24.17	23.77	23.39	24.94	24.49	24.06	23.65	23.26	22.89	54
55	25.28	24.83	24.39	23.98	23.58	23.20	24.75	24.30	23.88	23.47	23.08	22.71	55
56	25.09	24.63	24.20	23.79	23.40	23.02	24.57	24.13	23.70	23.30	22.91	22.54	56
57	24.90	24.45	24.02	23.61	23.22	22.85	24.39	23.95	23.54	23.13	22.75	22.38	57
58	24.72	24.27	23.85	23.44	23.05	22.68	24.23	23.79	23.37	22.98	22.59	22.23	58
59	24.54	24.10	23.68	23.27	22.89	22.52	24.06	23.63	23.22	22.82	22.44	22.08	59
60	24.37	23.94	23.52	23.11	22.73	22.36	23.91	23.48	23.07	22.67	22.30	21.94	60
72	22.75	22.34	21.95	21.58	21.21	20.87	22.41	22.01	21.62	21.25	20.90	20.56	72
84	21.65	21.26	20.88	20.53	20.18	19.85	21.39	21.01	20.64	20.28	19.94	19.61	84
96	20.86	20.49	20.13	19.78	19.45	19.12	20.67	20.30	19.94	19.60	19.26	18.95	96
108	20.29	19.92	19.57	19.23	18.91	18.59	20.14	19.78	19.43	19.09	18.77	18.46	108
120	19.86	19.50	19.16	18.82	18.51	18.20	19.74	19.38	19.04	18.71	18.40	18.09	120

MONTHLY PAYMENTS PER $1,000   22%

45% Residual   ## 50% Residual

		NUMBER OF ADVANCE PAYMENTS					NUMBER OF ADVANCE PAYMENTS					
MOS	0	1	2	3	4	5	0	1	2	3	4	5	MOS
12	59.73	58.66	57.70	56.84	56.09	55.43	55.97	54.96	54.06	53.26	52.56	51.94	12
15	50.53	49.62	48.79	48.04	47.36	46.75	47.60	46.74	45.96	45.26	44.62	44.05	15
18	44.41	43.61	42.87	42.20	41.58	41.01	42.04	41.28	40.58	39.94	39.36	38.82	18
19	42.80	42.03	41.32	40.66	40.06	39.51	40.57	39.84	39.17	38.55	37.98	37.45	19
20	41.35	40.61	39.92	39.28	38.70	38.15	39.26	38.55	37.90	37.30	36.74	36.22	20
21	40.05	39.33	38.66	38.04	37.46	36.93	38.07	37.39	36.75	36.16	35.62	35.11	21
22	38.86	38.16	37.51	36.91	36.35	35.83	36.99	36.33	35.71	35.13	34.60	34.11	22
23	37.78	37.10	36.47	35.88	35.33	34.82	36.01	35.36	34.76	34.20	33.67	33.19	23
24	36.79	36.13	35.51	34.93	34.39	33.89	35.11	34.48	33.89	33.34	32.83	32.35	24
25	35.88	35.23	34.63	34.06	33.54	33.05	34.28	33.67	33.09	32.55	32.05	31.58	25
26	35.04	34.41	33.82	33.27	32.75	32.27	33.52	32.92	32.35	31.82	31.33	30.87	26
27	34.26	33.65	33.07	32.53	32.02	31.54	32.82	32.23	31.67	31.15	30.67	30.21	27
28	33.54	32.94	32.37	31.84	31.34	30.87	32.16	31.58	31.04	30.53	30.05	29.60	28
29	32.88	32.28	31.73	31.21	30.71	30.25	31.55	30.99	30.45	29.95	29.48	29.04	29
30	32.25	31.67	31.13	30.61	30.13	29.67	30.99	30.43	29.91	29.41	28.95	28.51	30
31	31.67	31.10	30.56	30.06	29.58	29.13	30.46	29.91	29.39	28.91	28.45	28.02	31
32	31.13	30.57	30.04	29.54	29.07	28.63	29.96	29.43	28.92	28.44	27.98	27.56	32
33	30.62	30.07	29.55	29.05	28.59	28.15	29.50	28.97	28.47	28.00	27.55	27.13	33
34	30.14	29.59	29.08	28.60	28.14	27.71	29.06	28.54	28.05	27.58	27.14	26.72	34
35	29.69	29.15	28.65	28.17	27.72	27.29	28.65	28.14	27.65	27.19	26.75	26.34	35
36	29.26	28.73	28.23	27.76	27.32	26.89	28.27	27.76	27.28	26.82	26.39	25.98	36
37	28.86	28.34	27.85	27.38	26.94	26.52	27.90	27.40	26.92	26.47	26.05	25.64	37
38	28.48	27.97	27.48	27.02	26.58	26.17	27.56	27.06	26.59	26.15	25.72	25.32	38
39	28.12	27.61	27.13	26.68	26.25	25.84	27.23	26.74	26.27	25.83	25.42	25.02	39
40	27.78	27.28	26.80	26.35	25.93	25.52	26.92	26.43	25.98	25.54	25.13	24.73	40
41	27.45	26.96	26.49	26.05	25.62	25.22	26.63	26.15	25.69	25.26	24.85	24.46	41
42	27.15	26.66	26.19	25.75	25.33	24.94	26.35	25.87	25.42	24.99	24.59	24.20	42
43	26.85	26.37	25.91	25.48	25.06	24.66	26.08	25.61	25.16	24.74	24.34	23.95	43
44	26.58	26.10	25.64	25.21	24.80	24.41	25.83	25.36	24.92	24.50	24.10	23.72	44
45	26.31	25.84	25.39	24.96	24.55	24.16	25.59	25.12	24.69	24.27	23.87	23.50	45
46	26.06	25.59	25.14	24.72	24.31	23.93	25.35	24.90	24.46	24.05	23.66	23.28	46
47	25.81	25.35	24.91	24.49	24.09	23.70	25.13	24.68	24.25	23.84	23.45	23.08	47
48	25.58	25.12	24.68	24.27	23.87	23.49	24.92	24.48	24.05	23.64	23.25	22.88	48
49	25.36	24.91	24.47	24.06	23.66	23.28	24.72	24.28	23.85	23.45	23.07	22.70	49
50	25.15	24.70	24.27	23.85	23.46	23.09	24.53	24.09	23.67	23.27	22.88	22.52	50
51	24.95	24.50	24.07	23.66	23.27	22.90	24.35	23.91	23.49	23.09	22.71	22.35	51
52	24.75	24.31	23.88	23.48	23.09	22.72	24.17	23.73	23.32	22.92	22.55	22.18	52
53	24.57	24.12	23.70	23.30	22.91	22.55	24.00	23.57	23.16	22.76	22.39	22.03	53
54	24.39	23.95	23.53	23.13	22.75	22.38	23.84	23.41	23.00	22.61	22.23	21.88	54
55	24.21	23.78	23.36	22.96	22.59	22.22	23.68	23.25	22.85	22.46	22.09	21.73	55
56	24.05	23.62	23.20	22.81	22.43	22.07	23.53	23.11	22.70	22.32	21.95	21.59	56
57	23.89	23.46	23.05	22.66	22.28	21.92	23.38	22.96	22.56	22.18	21.81	21.46	57
58	23.74	23.31	22.90	22.51	22.14	21.78	23.24	22.83	22.43	22.04	21.68	21.33	58
59	23.59	23.16	22.76	22.37	22.00	21.64	23.11	22.69	22.30	21.92	21.55	21.21	59
60	23.45	23.02	22.62	22.23	21.86	21.51	22.98	22.57	22.17	21.79	21.43	21.09	60
72	22.07	21.68	21.30	20.93	20.58	20.24	21.73	21.34	20.97	20.61	20.26	19.93	72
84	21.14	20.76	20.39	20.04	19.71	19.38	20.88	20.51	20.15	19.80	19.47	19.15	84
96	20.47	20.11	19.75	19.41	19.08	18.77	20.28	19.92	19.56	19.23	18.90	18.59	96
108	19.99	19.63	19.28	18.95	18.63	18.32	19.84	19.48	19.14	18.81	18.49	18.18	108
120	19.62	19.27	18.93	18.60	18.29	17.98	19.51	19.16	18.82	18.49	18.18	17.88	120

26% MONTHLY PAYMENTS PER $1,000

0% Residual　　　　　　　　　　　2% Residual

MOS	0	1	2	3	4	5	0	1	2	3	4	5	MOS
	NUMBER OF ADVANCE PAYMENTS						NUMBER OF ADVANCE PAYMENTS						
12	95.54	93.51	91.71	90.11	88.71	87.49	94.06	92.06	90.29	88.72	87.34	86.14	12
15	78.80	77.13	75.62	74.26	73.03	71.92	77.66	76.01	74.52	73.18	71.97	70.88	15
18	67.69	66.25	64.94	63.74	62.64	61.64	66.77	65.35	64.06	62.87	61.79	60.80	18
19	64.77	63.40	62.14	60.98	59.92	58.95	63.91	62.55	61.31	60.17	59.12	58.16	19
20	62.15	60.83	59.62	58.50	57.48	56.53	61.34	60.04	58.84	57.74	56.73	55.80	20
21	59.78	58.51	57.34	56.26	55.27	54.35	59.02	57.77	56.61	55.55	54.56	53.66	21
22	57.63	56.41	55.28	54.23	53.27	52.38	56.91	55.71	54.59	53.56	52.60	51.72	22
23	55.67	54.49	53.40	52.38	51.45	50.57	54.99	53.83	52.75	51.74	50.82	49.96	23
24	53.88	52.74	51.68	50.69	49.78	48.93	53.24	52.11	51.06	50.09	49.18	48.34	24
25	52.23	51.13	50.10	49.14	48.25	47.42	51.62	50.53	49.51	48.56	47.68	46.86	25
26	50.72	49.64	48.64	47.71	46.84	46.03	50.14	49.07	48.08	47.16	46.30	45.50	26
27	49.31	48.27	47.29	46.38	45.53	44.74	48.76	47.73	46.76	45.86	45.02	44.24	27
28	48.02	47.00	46.05	45.16	44.33	43.55	47.49	46.48	45.54	44.66	43.84	43.07	28
29	46.81	45.82	44.89	44.02	43.21	42.45	46.31	45.32	44.41	43.55	42.74	41.99	29
30	45.68	44.72	43.81	42.96	42.16	41.42	45.20	44.25	43.35	42.51	41.72	40.98	30
31	44.64	43.69	42.80	41.97	41.19	40.46	44.18	43.24	42.36	41.54	40.77	40.04	31
32	43.65	42.73	41.86	41.05	40.28	39.56	43.21	42.30	41.44	40.63	39.88	39.16	32
33	42.74	41.83	40.98	40.18	39.43	38.72	42.31	41.42	40.57	39.78	39.04	38.34	33
34	41.87	40.98	40.15	39.37	38.63	37.93	41.47	40.59	39.76	38.99	38.25	37.57	34
35	41.06	40.19	39.37	38.60	37.88	37.19	40.67	39.81	39.00	38.24	37.52	36.84	35
36	40.30	39.44	38.64	37.88	37.17	36.49	39.92	39.08	38.28	37.53	36.82	36.16	36
37	39.57	38.74	37.94	37.20	36.50	35.83	39.22	38.38	37.60	36.86	36.17	35.51	37
38	38.89	38.07	37.29	36.56	35.87	35.21	38.55	37.73	36.96	36.23	35.55	34.90	38
39	38.25	37.44	36.67	35.95	35.27	34.62	37.92	37.11	36.35	35.64	34.96	34.32	39
40	37.64	36.84	36.09	35.38	34.70	34.07	37.32	36.53	35.78	35.08	34.41	33.78	40
41	37.06	36.27	35.53	34.83	34.17	33.54	36.75	35.97	35.24	34.54	33.88	33.26	41
42	36.51	35.73	35.00	34.31	33.66	33.04	36.21	35.44	34.72	34.03	33.38	32.77	42
43	35.99	35.22	34.50	33.82	33.17	32.56	35.70	34.94	34.23	33.55	32.91	32.30	43
44	35.49	34.74	34.03	33.35	32.71	32.11	35.21	34.47	33.76	33.09	32.46	31.86	44
45	35.02	34.27	33.57	32.91	32.28	31.68	34.75	34.01	33.31	32.66	32.03	31.44	45
46	34.56	33.83	33.14	32.48	31.86	31.27	34.31	33.58	32.89	32.24	31.62	31.03	46
47	34.13	33.41	32.72	32.08	31.46	30.87	33.88	33.17	32.49	31.84	31.23	30.65	47
48	33.72	33.01	32.33	31.69	31.08	30.50	33.48	32.77	32.10	31.46	30.86	30.28	48
49	33.33	32.62	31.95	31.32	30.71	30.14	33.10	32.39	31.73	31.10	30.50	29.93	49
50	32.95	32.25	31.59	30.96	30.37	29.80	32.73	32.03	31.38	30.75	30.16	29.60	50
51	32.59	31.90	31.25	30.63	30.03	29.47	32.38	31.69	31.04	30.42	29.83	29.27	51
52	32.25	31.56	30.92	30.30	29.72	29.16	32.04	31.36	30.71	30.10	29.52	28.97	52
53	31.92	31.24	30.60	29.99	29.41	28.86	31.71	31.04	30.40	29.80	29.22	28.67	53
54	31.60	30.93	30.30	29.69	29.12	28.57	31.40	30.74	30.11	29.50	28.93	28.39	54
55	31.30	30.63	30.00	29.40	28.84	28.29	31.10	30.45	29.82	29.22	28.66	28.12	55
56	31.01	30.35	29.72	29.13	28.57	28.03	30.82	30.17	29.54	28.95	28.39	27.86	56
57	30.72	30.07	29.45	28.87	28.31	27.77	30.54	29.90	29.28	28.70	28.14	27.61	57
58	30.45	29.81	29.20	28.61	28.06	27.53	30.28	29.64	29.03	28.45	27.89	27.37	58
59	30.20	29.56	28.95	28.37	27.82	27.29	30.02	29.39	28.78	28.21	27.66	27.14	59
60	29.95	29.31	28.71	28.13	27.59	27.06	29.78	29.15	28.55	27.98	27.43	26.91	60
72	27.56	26.97	26.42	25.89	25.38	24.90	27.44	26.86	26.30	25.78	25.27	24.79	72
84	25.96	25.41	24.88	24.38	23.90	23.44	25.87	25.33	24.80	24.30	23.82	23.37	84
96	24.84	24.32	23.81	23.33	22.87	22.43	24.78	24.26	23.75	23.27	22.81	22.37	96
108	24.05	23.54	23.05	22.58	22.14	21.71	24.00	23.49	23.00	22.54	22.09	21.66	108
120	23.46	22.97	22.49	22.03	21.60	21.18	23.43	22.93	22.46	22.00	21.56	21.15	120

MONTHLY PAYMENTS PER $1,000   26%

	5% Residual						10% Residual					
	NUMBER OF ADVANCE PAYMENTS						NUMBER OF ADVANCE PAYMENTS					
MOS	0	1	2	3	4	5	0	1	2	3	4	5	MOS
12	91.84	89.89	88.16	86.63	85.28	84.11	88.15	86.28	84.62	83.15	81.85	80.72	12
15	75.95	74.34	72.88	71.56	70.38	69.32	73.09	71.54	70.14	68.87	67.73	66.71	15
18	65.39	64.00	62.73	61.57	60.51	59.54	63.09	61.75	60.52	59.40	58.38	57.45	18
19	62.62	61.29	60.07	58.95	57.93	56.99	60.46	59.18	58.00	56.92	55.93	55.03	19
20	60.13	58.85	57.68	56.60	55.60	54.69	58.10	56.87	55.74	54.69	53.73	52.85	20
21	57.88	56.65	55.52	54.47	53.51	52.62	55.97	54.78	53.69	52.68	51.75	50.89	21
22	55.83	54.65	53.56	52.54	51.61	50.74	54.04	52.89	51.83	50.85	49.94	49.11	22
23	53.97	52.83	51.77	50.78	49.87	49.03	52.27	51.16	50.14	49.19	48.30	47.49	23
24	52.27	51.16	50.13	49.18	48.29	47.47	50.66	49.58	48.59	47.66	46.80	46.00	24
25	50.71	49.63	48.63	47.70	46.84	46.03	49.18	48.13	47.16	46.26	45.42	44.64	25
26	49.26	48.22	47.25	46.34	45.50	44.71	47.81	46.80	45.85	44.97	44.15	43.39	26
27	47.93	46.92	45.97	45.08	44.26	43.49	46.55	45.56	44.64	43.78	42.98	42.23	27
28	46.70	45.71	44.78	43.92	43.11	42.36	45.38	44.42	43.52	42.68	41.90	41.16	28
29	45.55	44.59	43.68	42.84	42.05	41.31	44.29	43.36	42.48	41.66	40.89	40.17	29
30	44.48	43.54	42.66	41.83	41.06	40.33	43.28	42.37	41.51	40.70	39.95	39.24	30
31	43.49	42.57	41.70	40.89	40.13	39.42	42.34	41.44	40.60	39.81	39.07	38.38	31
32	42.56	41.65	40.81	40.01	39.27	38.57	41.46	40.58	39.75	38.98	38.25	37.57	32
33	41.68	40.80	39.97	39.19	38.46	37.77	40.63	39.77	38.96	38.20	37.48	36.81	33
34	40.86	40.00	39.18	38.42	37.70	37.02	39.85	39.01	38.21	37.47	36.76	36.10	34
35	40.09	39.24	38.44	37.69	36.98	36.31	39.12	38.29	37.51	36.78	36.09	35.44	35
36	39.36	38.53	37.74	37.00	36.31	35.65	38.43	37.62	36.85	36.13	35.45	34.81	36
37	38.68	37.86	37.09	36.36	35.67	35.02	37.78	36.98	36.23	35.52	34.85	34.21	37
38	38.03	37.23	36.47	35.75	35.07	34.43	37.17	36.38	35.64	34.94	34.28	33.65	38
39	37.42	36.63	35.88	35.17	34.50	33.87	36.59	35.81	35.08	34.39	33.74	33.12	39
40	36.84	36.06	35.32	34.63	33.97	33.35	36.04	35.28	34.56	33.87	33.23	32.62	40
41	36.29	35.52	34.79	34.11	33.46	32.84	35.52	34.77	34.06	33.38	32.75	32.15	41
42	35.77	35.01	34.29	33.61	32.97	32.37	35.03	34.28	33.58	32.92	32.29	31.70	42
43	35.27	34.52	33.82	33.15	32.51	31.91	34.55	33.82	33.13	32.47	31.85	31.27	43
44	34.80	34.06	33.36	32.70	32.08	31.48	34.11	33.38	32.70	32.05	31.44	30.86	44
45	34.35	33.62	32.93	32.28	31.66	31.07	33.68	32.97	32.29	31.65	31.05	30.47	45
46	33.92	33.20	32.52	31.87	31.26	30.68	33.27	32.57	31.90	31.27	30.67	30.10	46
47	33.51	32.80	32.13	31.49	30.88	30.31	32.89	32.19	31.53	30.90	30.31	29.75	47
48	33.12	32.42	31.75	31.12	30.52	29.96	32.52	31.83	31.17	30.56	29.97	29.41	48
49	32.75	32.05	31.39	30.77	30.18	29.62	32.16	31.48	30.84	30.22	29.64	29.09	49
50	32.39	31.70	31.05	30.43	29.85	29.29	31.83	31.15	30.51	29.90	29.33	28.78	50
51	32.05	31.37	30.72	30.11	29.53	28.98	31.50	30.83	30.20	29.60	29.03	28.48	51
52	31.72	31.05	30.41	29.80	29.23	28.68	31.19	30.53	29.90	29.31	28.74	28.20	52
53	31.41	30.74	30.11	29.51	28.94	28.39	30.89	30.24	29.62	29.03	28.47	27.93	53
54	31.10	30.45	29.82	29.22	28.66	28.12	30.61	29.96	29.34	28.76	28.20	27.67	54
55	30.82	30.16	29.54	28.95	28.39	27.86	30.33	29.69	29.08	28.50	27.95	27.42	55
56	30.54	29.89	29.28	28.69	28.14	27.61	30.07	29.43	28.83	28.25	27.71	27.18	56
57	30.27	29.63	29.02	28.44	27.89	27.36	29.82	29.19	28.59	28.02	27.47	26.95	57
58	30.02	29.38	28.77	28.20	27.65	27.13	29.58	28.95	28.35	27.79	27.25	26.73	58
59	29.77	29.14	28.54	27.97	27.42	26.91	29.34	28.72	28.13	27.57	27.03	26.52	59
60	29.53	28.91	28.31	27.74	27.20	26.69	29.12	28.50	27.91	27.36	26.82	26.32	60
72	27.26	26.69	26.14	25.61	25.11	24.63	26.97	26.40	25.85	25.33	24.84	24.36	72
84	25.75	25.20	24.68	24.18	23.70	23.25	25.53	24.99	24.47	23.98	23.51	23.06	84
96	24.69	24.16	23.66	23.18	22.73	22.29	24.53	24.01	23.51	23.04	22.58	22.14	96
108	23.93	23.42	22.93	22.47	22.03	21.60	23.81	23.30	22.82	22.36	21.92	21.49	108
120	23.37	22.88	22.40	21.95	21.51	21.10	23.28	22.79	22.32	21.87	21.43	21.02	120

26%   MONTHLY PAYMENTS PER $1,000

15% Residual   ### 20% Residual

MOS	NUMBER OF ADVANCE PAYMENTS						NUMBER OF ADVANCE PAYMENTS						MOS
	0	1	2	3	4	5	0	1	2	3	4	5	
12	84.46	82.66	81.07	79.66	78.42	77.34	80.76	79.05	77.53	76.18	74.99	73.96	12
15	70.23	68.74	67.40	66.18	65.08	64.10	67.38	65.95	64.66	63.49	62.44	61.49	15
18	60.79	59.50	58.32	57.24	56.25	55.35	58.49	57.24	56.11	55.07	54.12	53.26	18
19	58.31	57.07	55.94	54.89	53.94	53.06	56.15	54.96	53.87	52.86	51.95	51.10	19
20	56.08	54.89	53.79	52.79	51.86	51.01	54.05	52.91	51.85	50.88	49.99	49.17	20
21	54.06	52.92	51.86	50.88	49.98	49.16	52.16	51.05	50.03	49.09	48.22	47.42	21
22	52.24	51.13	50.11	49.16	48.28	47.47	50.44	49.37	48.38	47.47	46.62	45.84	22
23	50.57	49.50	48.51	47.59	46.73	45.94	48.87	47.84	46.88	45.99	45.16	44.40	23
24	49.05	48.01	47.04	46.15	45.31	44.54	47.44	46.43	45.50	44.63	43.83	43.08	24
25	47.65	46.64	45.70	44.83	44.01	43.26	46.12	45.14	44.23	43.39	42.60	41.87	25
26	46.36	45.38	44.46	43.61	42.81	42.07	44.91	43.96	43.07	42.24	41.47	40.75	26
27	45.17	44.21	43.32	42.48	41.71	40.98	43.79	42.86	41.99	41.18	40.43	39.73	27
28	44.06	43.13	42.26	41.44	40.68	39.97	42.75	41.84	40.99	40.20	39.46	38.77	28
29	43.04	42.13	41.27	40.47	39.73	39.03	41.78	40.90	40.07	39.29	38.57	37.89	29
30	42.08	41.19	40.36	39.57	38.84	38.15	40.88	40.02	39.20	38.44	37.73	37.06	30
31	41.19	40.32	39.50	38.73	38.01	37.34	40.04	39.19	38.40	37.65	36.95	36.30	31
32	40.36	39.50	38.70	37.95	37.24	36.57	39.26	38.43	37.64	36.91	36.22	35.58	32
33	39.58	38.74	37.95	37.21	36.51	35.86	38.52	37.71	36.94	36.22	35.54	34.90	33
34	38.84	38.02	37.24	36.52	35.83	35.19	37.83	37.03	36.28	35.57	34.90	34.27	34
35	38.15	37.34	36.58	35.87	35.19	34.56	37.18	36.39	35.65	34.96	34.30	33.68	35
36	37.50	36.71	35.96	35.25	34.59	33.96	36.57	35.80	35.07	34.38	33.73	33.12	36
37	36.89	36.11	35.37	34.68	34.02	33.40	35.99	35.23	34.51	33.83	33.20	32.59	37
38	36.31	35.54	34.81	34.13	33.48	32.87	35.45	34.70	33.99	33.32	32.69	32.09	38
39	35.76	35.00	34.29	33.61	32.98	32.37	34.93	34.19	33.49	32.83	32.21	31.62	39
40	35.24	34.50	33.79	33.12	32.50	31.90	34.44	33.71	33.03	32.37	31.76	31.18	40
41	34.75	34.01	33.32	32.66	32.04	31.45	33.98	33.26	32.58	31.94	31.33	30.75	41
42	34.28	33.56	32.87	32.21	31.61	31.02	33.54	32.83	32.16	31.52	30.92	30.35	42
43	33.84	33.12	32.44	31.80	31.19	30.62	33.12	32.42	31.76	31.13	30.54	29.97	43
44	33.42	32.71	32.04	31.40	30.80	30.23	32.73	32.03	31.38	30.75	30.17	29.61	44
45	33.01	32.31	31.65	31.02	30.43	29.87	32.35	31.66	31.01	30.40	29.82	29.26	45
46	32.63	31.94	31.28	30.66	30.08	29.52	31.99	31.31	30.67	30.06	29.48	28.93	46
47	32.26	31.58	30.93	30.32	29.74	29.18	31.64	30.97	30.34	29.73	29.16	28.62	47
48	31.91	31.24	30.60	29.99	29.41	28.87	31.31	30.65	30.02	29.42	28.86	28.32	48
49	31.58	30.91	30.28	29.67	29.10	28.56	31.00	30.34	29.72	29.13	28.57	28.03	49
50	31.26	30.60	29.97	29.37	28.81	28.27	30.70	30.05	29.43	28.84	28.29	27.76	50
51	30.96	30.30	29.68	29.09	28.52	27.99	30.41	29.76	29.15	28.57	28.02	27.50	51
52	30.66	30.01	29.40	28.81	28.25	27.72	30.13	29.49	28.89	28.31	27.77	27.25	52
53	30.38	29.74	29.13	28.55	27.99	27.47	29.87	29.24	28.63	28.06	27.52	27.01	53
54	30.11	29.47	28.87	28.29	27.74	27.22	29.62	28.99	28.39	27.83	27.29	26.77	54
55	29.85	29.22	28.62	28.05	27.51	26.99	29.37	28.75	28.16	27.60	27.06	26.55	55
56	29.61	28.98	28.38	27.81	27.28	26.76	29.14	28.52	27.93	27.38	26.85	26.34	56
57	29.37	28.74	28.15	27.59	27.05	26.54	28.91	28.30	27.72	27.16	26.64	26.14	57
58	29.14	28.52	27.93	27.37	26.84	26.34	28.70	28.09	27.51	26.96	26.44	25.94	58
59	28.92	28.30	27.72	27.17	26.64	26.14	28.49	27.89	27.31	26.77	26.25	25.75	59
60	28.70	28.10	27.52	26.97	26.44	25.94	28.29	27.69	27.12	26.58	26.06	25.57	60
72	26.68	26.11	25.57	25.06	24.57	24.10	26.38	25.82	25.29	24.78	24.30	23.83	72
84	25.32	24.78	24.27	23.78	23.31	22.86	25.10	24.57	24.06	23.58	23.11	22.67	84
96	24.37	23.85	23.36	22.89	22.43	22.00	24.21	23.70	23.21	22.74	22.29	21.86	96
108	23.69	23.19	22.71	22.25	21.81	21.38	23.57	23.07	22.59	22.14	21.70	21.28	108
120	23.19	22.70	22.23	21.78	21.35	20.94	23.10	22.61	22.15	21.70	21.27	20.85	120

MONTHLY PAYMENTS PER $1,000   26%

	25% Residual						30% Residual						
	NUMBER OF ADVANCE PAYMENTS						NUMBER OF ADVANCE PAYMENTS						
MOS	0	1	2	3	4	5	0	1	2	3	4	5	MOS
12	77.07	75.43	73.98	72.70	71.56	70.58	73.38	71.82	70.44	69.21	68.14	67.20	12
15	64.52	63.15	61.91	60.80	59.79	58.89	61.66	60.36	59.17	58.11	57.14	56.28	15
18	56.18	54.99	53.90	52.91	51.99	51.16	53.88	52.74	51.70	50.74	49.86	49.07	18
19	54.00	52.85	51.80	50.84	49.95	49.14	51.84	50.74	49.73	48.81	47.96	47.18	19
20	52.03	50.93	49.91	48.98	48.12	47.33	50.01	48.95	47.97	47.07	46.25	45.49	20
21	50.25	49.19	48.21	47.30	46.46	45.69	48.35	47.32	46.38	45.50	44.70	43.96	21
22	48.64	47.61	46.66	45.77	44.96	44.21	46.84	45.85	44.93	44.08	43.30	42.57	22
23	47.17	46.17	45.25	44.39	43.59	42.85	45.47	44.51	43.61	42.79	42.02	41.31	23
24	45.83	44.86	43.95	43.12	42.34	41.62	44.22	43.28	42.41	41.60	40.85	40.15	24
25	44.59	43.65	42.77	41.95	41.19	40.48	43.06	42.15	41.30	40.51	39.78	39.09	25
26	43.46	42.53	41.68	40.88	40.13	39.44	42.00	41.11	40.28	39.51	38.79	38.12	26
27	42.40	41.50	40.67	39.88	39.15	38.47	41.02	40.15	39.34	38.58	37.88	37.22	27
28	41.43	40.55	39.73	38.96	38.25	37.58	40.11	39.26	38.47	37.73	37.03	36.38	28
29	40.52	39.67	38.86	38.11	37.41	36.75	39.27	38.43	37.66	36.93	36.25	35.61	29
30	39.68	38.84	38.05	37.31	36.62	35.98	38.48	37.66	36.90	36.19	35.52	34.89	30
31	38.89	38.07	37.30	36.57	35.89	35.26	37.75	36.95	36.20	35.49	34.83	34.21	31
32	38.16	37.35	36.59	35.88	35.21	34.58	37.06	36.27	35.54	34.85	34.20	33.59	32
33	37.47	36.67	35.93	35.23	34.57	33.95	36.42	35.64	34.92	34.24	33.60	33.00	33
34	36.82	36.04	35.31	34.62	33.97	33.36	35.81	35.05	34.34	33.67	33.04	32.44	34
35	36.21	35.45	34.72	34.04	33.40	32.80	35.24	34.50	33.79	33.13	32.51	31.92	35
36	35.64	34.88	34.17	33.50	32.87	32.28	34.71	33.97	33.28	32.63	32.01	31.43	36
37	35.10	34.35	33.65	32.99	32.37	31.78	34.20	33.48	32.80	32.15	31.54	30.97	37
38	34.59	33.85	33.16	32.51	31.90	31.32	33.73	33.01	32.34	31.70	31.10	30.54	38
39	34.10	33.38	32.70	32.06	31.45	30.87	33.28	32.57	31.90	31.28	30.68	30.12	39
40	33.65	32.93	32.26	31.62	31.02	30.46	32.85	32.15	31.49	30.87	30.29	29.73	40
41	33.21	32.51	31.84	31.21	30.62	30.06	32.44	31.75	31.11	30.49	29.91	29.36	41
42	32.80	32.10	31.45	30.83	30.24	29.68	32.06	31.38	30.74	30.13	29.55	29.01	42
43	32.41	31.72	31.07	30.46	29.88	29.32	31.69	31.02	30.38	29.78	29.22	28.68	43
44	32.03	31.36	30.71	30.11	29.53	28.98	31.34	30.68	30.05	29.46	28.89	28.36	44
45	31.68	31.01	30.37	29.77	29.20	28.66	31.01	30.35	29.73	29.14	28.59	28.06	45
46	31.34	30.68	30.05	29.45	28.89	28.35	30.70	30.05	29.43	28.85	28.29	27.77	46
47	31.02	30.36	29.74	29.15	28.59	28.06	30.40	29.75	29.14	28.56	28.01	27.49	47
48	30.71	30.06	29.44	28.86	28.30	27.78	30.11	29.47	28.86	28.29	27.75	27.23	48
49	30.41	29.77	29.16	28.58	28.03	27.51	29.83	29.20	28.60	28.03	27.49	26.98	49
50	30.13	29.49	28.89	28.31	27.77	27.25	29.57	28.94	28.35	27.78	27.25	26.74	50
51	29.86	29.23	28.63	28.06	27.52	27.00	29.32	28.70	28.11	27.55	27.01	26.51	51
52	29.60	28.98	28.38	27.82	27.28	26.77	29.08	28.46	27.87	27.32	26.79	26.29	52
53	29.36	28.73	28.14	27.58	27.05	26.54	28.84	28.23	27.65	27.10	26.58	26.08	53
54	29.12	28.50	27.92	27.36	26.83	26.33	28.62	28.02	27.44	26.89	26.37	25.88	54
55	28.89	28.28	27.70	27.14	26.62	26.12	28.41	27.81	27.24	26.69	26.17	25.68	55
56	28.67	28.06	27.49	26.94	26.42	25.92	28.21	27.61	27.04	26.50	25.99	25.50	56
57	28.46	27.86	27.28	26.74	26.22	25.73	28.01	27.41	26.85	26.31	25.80	25.32	57
58	28.26	27.66	27.09	26.55	26.03	25.54	27.82	27.23	26.67	26.14	25.63	25.15	58
59	28.06	27.47	26.90	26.37	25.85	25.36	27.64	27.05	26.50	25.97	25.46	24.98	59
60	27.88	27.29	26.72	26.19	25.68	25.19	27.46	26.88	26.33	25.80	25.30	24.82	60
72	26.09	25.53	25.01	24.50	24.02	23.57	25.79	25.25	24.72	24.23	23.75	23.30	72
84	24.89	24.36	23.86	23.38	22.91	22.47	24.67	24.15	23.65	23.17	22.72	22.28	84
96	24.05	23.54	23.05	22.59	22.14	21.71	23.89	23.39	22.90	22.44	22.00	21.57	96
108	23.45	22.96	22.48	22.02	21.59	21.17	23.33	22.84	22.37	21.91	21.48	21.06	108
120	23.02	22.53	22.06	21.61	21.18	20.77	22.93	22.44	21.97	21.53	21.10	20.69	120

26%   MONTHLY PAYMENTS PER $1,000

35% Residual   ## 40% Residual

MOS	NUMBER OF ADVANCE PAYMENTS						NUMBER OF ADVANCE PAYMENTS						MOS
	0	1	2	3	4	5	0	1	2	3	4	5	
12	69.68	68.21	66.89	65.73	64.71	63.81	65.99	64.59	63.35	62.25	61.28	60.43	12
15	58.81	57.56	56.43	55.41	54.50	53.67	55.95	54.76	53.69	52.72	51.85	51.07	15
18	51.58	50.49	49.49	48.57	47.74	46.97	49.28	48.24	47.28	46.41	45.61	44.88	18
19	49.69	48.63	47.67	46.78	45.96	45.22	47.53	46.52	45.60	44.75	43.97	43.26	19
20	47.98	46.96	46.03	45.17	44.37	43.65	45.96	44.98	44.09	43.26	42.50	41.80	20
21	46.44	45.46	44.55	43.71	42.94	42.23	44.54	43.59	42.72	41.92	41.18	40.49	21
22	45.05	44.09	43.21	42.39	41.64	40.94	43.25	42.33	41.48	40.70	39.97	39.30	22
23	43.77	42.84	41.98	41.19	40.45	39.76	42.07	41.18	40.35	39.59	38.88	38.22	23
24	42.61	41.70	40.86	40.09	39.36	38.69	41.00	40.13	39.32	38.57	37.88	37.23	24
25	41.54	40.66	39.84	39.08	38.37	37.71	40.01	39.16	38.37	37.64	36.96	36.32	25
26	40.55	39.69	38.89	38.14	37.45	36.80	39.10	38.27	37.50	36.78	36.11	35.48	26
27	39.64	38.80	38.02	37.28	36.60	35.96	38.26	37.45	36.69	35.98	35.32	34.71	27
28	38.80	37.97	37.20	36.49	35.82	35.19	37.48	36.68	35.94	35.25	34.60	33.99	28
29	38.01	37.20	36.45	35.75	35.09	34.47	36.75	35.97	35.25	34.56	33.93	33.33	29
30	37.28	36.49	35.75	35.06	34.41	33.80	36.08	35.31	34.60	33.93	33.30	32.71	30
31	36.60	35.82	35.10	34.41	33.77	33.17	35.45	34.70	33.99	33.33	32.71	32.13	31
32	35.96	35.20	34.48	33.81	33.18	32.59	34.86	34.12	33.43	32.78	32.17	31.59	32
33	35.36	34.61	33.91	33.25	32.63	32.04	34.31	33.58	32.90	32.26	31.65	31.09	33
34	34.80	34.06	33.37	32.72	32.11	31.53	33.79	33.08	32.40	31.77	31.17	30.61	34
35	34.27	33.55	32.86	32.22	31.62	31.04	33.30	32.60	31.93	31.31	30.72	30.17	35
36	33.78	33.06	32.39	31.75	31.15	30.59	32.85	32.15	31.49	30.88	30.30	29.75	36
37	33.31	32.60	31.94	31.31	30.72	30.16	32.41	31.73	31.08	30.47	29.89	29.35	37
38	32.87	32.17	31.51	30.89	30.31	29.76	32.00	31.33	30.69	30.08	29.51	28.98	38
39	32.45	31.76	31.11	30.50	29.92	29.37	31.62	30.95	30.32	29.72	29.16	28.62	39
40	32.05	31.37	30.73	30.12	29.55	29.01	31.25	30.59	29.96	29.37	28.82	28.29	40
41	31.67	31.00	30.37	29.77	29.20	28.67	30.90	30.25	29.63	29.05	28.49	27.97	41
42	31.32	30.65	30.02	29.43	28.87	28.34	30.57	29.93	29.31	28.73	28.19	27.67	42
43	30.98	30.32	29.70	29.11	28.56	28.03	30.26	29.62	29.01	28.44	27.90	27.38	43
44	30.65	30.00	29.39	28.81	28.26	27.73	29.96	29.33	28.73	28.16	27.62	27.11	44
45	30.35	29.70	29.09	28.52	27.97	27.45	29.68	29.05	28.45	27.89	27.36	26.85	45
46	30.05	29.41	28.81	28.24	27.70	27.18	29.41	28.78	28.19	27.63	27.10	26.60	46
47	29.77	29.14	28.54	27.98	27.44	26.93	29.15	28.53	27.95	27.39	26.87	26.37	47
48	29.50	28.88	28.29	27.72	27.19	26.69	28.90	28.29	27.71	27.16	26.64	26.14	48
49	29.25	28.63	28.04	27.48	26.95	26.45	28.67	28.06	27.48	26.94	26.42	25.93	49
50	29.00	28.39	27.81	27.25	26.73	26.23	28.44	27.84	27.27	26.72	26.21	25.72	50
51	28.77	28.16	27.58	27.03	26.51	26.02	28.22	27.63	27.06	26.52	26.01	25.52	51
52	28.55	27.94	27.37	26.82	26.30	25.81	28.02	27.42	26.86	26.33	25.82	25.33	52
53	28.33	27.73	27.16	26.62	26.11	25.62	27.82	27.23	26.67	26.14	25.63	25.15	53
54	28.13	27.53	26.96	26.43	25.91	25.43	27.63	27.04	26.49	25.96	25.46	24.98	54
55	27.93	27.34	26.77	26.24	25.73	25.25	27.45	26.87	26.31	25.79	25.29	24.81	55
56	27.74	27.15	26.59	26.06	25.56	25.07	27.27	26.69	26.14	25.62	25.13	24.65	56
57	27.56	26.97	26.42	25.89	25.39	24.91	27.10	26.53	25.98	25.46	24.97	24.50	57
58	27.38	26.80	26.25	25.72	25.22	24.75	26.94	26.37	25.83	25.31	24.82	24.35	58
59	27.21	26.64	26.09	25.56	25.07	24.59	26.79	26.22	25.68	25.16	24.68	24.21	59
60	27.05	26.48	25.93	25.41	24.92	24.45	26.64	26.07	25.53	25.02	24.54	24.07	60
72	25.50	24.96	24.44	23.95	23.48	23.03	25.20	24.67	24.16	23.67	23.21	22.77	72
84	24.46	23.94	23.45	22.97	22.52	22.09	24.24	23.73	23.24	22.77	22.32	21.89	84
96	23.73	23.23	22.75	22.29	21.85	21.43	23.58	23.08	22.60	22.14	21.70	21.29	96
108	23.22	22.72	22.25	21.80	21.37	20.96	23.10	22.61	22.14	21.69	21.26	20.85	108
120	22.84	22.35	21.89	21.44	21.02	20.61	22.75	22.26	21.80	21.36	20.94	20.53	120

MONTHLY PAYMENTS PER $1,000   26%

45% Residual   50% Residual

MOS	0	1	2	3	4	5	0	1	2	3	4	5	MOS
	NUMBER OF ADVANCE PAYMENTS						NUMBER OF ADVANCE PAYMENTS						
12	62.30	60.98	59.80	58.76	57.85	57.05	58.60	57.36	56.26	55.28	54.42	53.67	12
15	53.09	51.97	50.95	50.03	49.20	48.46	50.24	49.17	48.21	47.34	46.55	45.85	15
18	46.98	45.98	45.07	44.24	43.48	42.78	44.68	43.73	42.87	42.07	41.35	40.69	18
19	45.38	44.41	43.53	42.72	41.98	41.30	43.22	42.31	41.46	40.69	39.98	39.34	19
20	43.93	43.00	42.15	41.36	40.63	39.96	41.91	41.02	40.20	39.45	38.76	38.12	20
21	42.63	41.73	40.89	40.12	39.41	38.76	40.73	39.86	39.07	38.33	37.65	37.03	21
22	41.45	40.57	39.76	39.01	38.31	37.67	39.65	38.81	38.03	37.31	36.65	36.04	22
23	40.37	39.52	38.72	37.99	37.31	36.68	38.67	37.85	37.09	36.39	35.74	35.13	23
24	39.39	38.55	37.78	37.06	36.39	35.77	37.78	36.97	36.23	35.54	34.90	34.30	24
25	38.48	37.66	36.91	36.20	35.54	34.93	36.95	36.17	35.44	34.76	34.13	33.55	25
26	37.65	36.85	36.10	35.41	34.77	34.17	36.19	35.43	34.71	34.05	33.43	32.85	26
27	36.88	36.09	35.36	34.68	34.05	33.46	35.49	34.74	34.04	33.38	32.77	32.20	27
28	36.16	35.39	34.68	34.01	33.38	32.80	34.84	34.10	33.41	32.77	32.17	31.60	28
29	35.50	34.74	34.04	33.38	32.77	32.19	34.24	33.51	32.84	32.20	31.61	31.05	29
30	34.88	34.14	33.45	32.80	32.19	31.62	33.68	32.96	32.30	31.67	31.08	30.53	30
31	34.30	33.57	32.89	32.25	31.65	31.09	33.15	32.45	31.79	31.17	30.60	30.05	31
32	33.76	33.05	32.37	31.74	31.15	30.60	32.66	31.97	31.32	30.71	30.14	29.60	32
33	33.26	32.55	31.89	31.27	30.68	30.13	32.20	31.52	30.88	30.28	29.71	29.18	33
34	32.78	32.09	31.43	30.82	30.24	29.70	31.77	31.10	30.47	29.87	29.31	28.78	34
35	32.34	31.65	31.01	30.40	29.83	29.29	31.37	30.70	30.08	29.49	28.93	28.41	35
36	31.91	31.24	30.60	30.00	29.44	28.90	30.98	30.33	29.71	29.13	28.58	28.06	36
37	31.52	30.85	30.22	29.63	29.07	28.54	30.62	29.97	29.36	28.79	28.24	27.73	37
38	31.14	30.48	29.86	29.27	28.72	28.20	30.28	29.64	29.04	28.46	27.93	27.42	38
39	30.79	30.14	29.52	28.94	28.39	27.87	29.96	29.32	28.73	28.16	27.63	27.12	39
40	30.45	29.81	29.20	28.62	28.08	27.56	29.65	29.03	28.43	27.87	27.34	26.84	40
41	30.13	29.50	28.89	28.32	27.78	27.27	29.37	28.74	28.15	27.60	27.07	26.58	41
42	29.83	29.20	28.60	28.04	27.50	27.00	29.09	28.47	27.89	27.34	26.82	26.33	42
43	29.54	28.92	28.33	27.77	27.24	26.73	28.83	28.22	27.64	27.09	26.58	26.09	43
44	29.27	28.65	28.06	27.51	26.98	26.48	28.58	27.97	27.40	26.86	26.35	25.86	44
45	29.01	28.40	27.81	27.26	26.74	26.25	28.34	27.74	27.17	26.64	26.13	25.64	45
46	28.76	28.15	27.58	27.03	26.51	26.02	28.12	27.52	26.96	26.42	25.92	25.44	46
47	28.53	27.92	27.35	26.81	26.29	25.80	27.90	27.31	26.75	26.22	25.72	25.24	47
48	28.30	27.70	27.13	26.59	26.08	25.60	27.70	27.11	26.55	26.03	25.53	25.05	48
49	28.08	27.49	26.92	26.39	25.88	25.40	27.50	26.92	26.36	25.84	25.34	24.87	49
50	27.88	27.29	26.73	26.19	25.69	25.21	27.31	26.73	26.18	25.66	25.17	24.70	50
51	27.68	27.09	26.54	26.01	25.51	25.03	27.13	26.56	26.01	25.49	25.00	24.53	51
52	27.49	26.91	26.35	25.83	25.33	24.86	26.96	26.39	25.85	25.33	24.84	24.38	52
53	27.31	26.73	26.18	25.66	25.16	24.69	26.80	26.23	25.69	25.18	24.69	24.23	53
54	27.13	26.56	26.01	25.49	25.00	24.53	26.64	26.07	25.54	25.03	24.54	24.08	54
55	26.97	26.39	25.85	25.34	24.84	24.38	26.48	25.92	25.39	24.88	24.40	23.94	55
56	26.81	26.24	25.70	25.18	24.70	24.23	26.34	25.78	25.25	24.75	24.27	23.81	56
57	26.65	26.09	25.55	25.04	24.55	24.09	26.20	25.64	25.11	24.61	24.14	23.68	57
58	26.50	25.94	25.41	24.90	24.42	23.95	26.06	25.51	24.99	24.49	24.01	23.56	58
59	26.36	25.80	25.27	24.76	24.28	23.82	25.93	25.38	24.86	24.36	23.89	23.44	59
60	26.22	25.67	25.14	24.63	24.16	23.70	25.81	25.26	24.74	24.25	23.77	23.32	60
72	24.91	24.38	23.88	23.40	22.94	22.50	24.62	24.09	23.60	23.12	22.67	22.24	72
84	24.03	23.52	23.03	22.57	22.13	21.70	23.82	23.31	22.83	22.37	21.93	21.51	84
96	23.42	22.92	22.45	21.99	21.56	21.14	23.26	22.76	22.29	21.84	21.41	21.00	96
108	22.98	22.49	22.02	21.58	21.15	20.74	22.86	22.37	21.91	21.47	21.04	20.63	108
120	22.66	22.18	21.72	21.28	20.85	20.45	22.57	22.09	21.63	21.19	20.77	20.37	120

_____ Appendix C _____

SPECIAL RULES FOR LEASES UNDER CODE SEC. 168 (f) (8)

TEXT OF TEMPORARY REGULATIONS
PROVIDING GUIDANCE FOR
LEASE ARRANGEMENTS

T.D. 7791
FILED OCTOBER 20, 1981

AGENCY: Internal Revenue Service, Treasury.

ACTION: Temporary regulations.

SUMMARY: This document contains temporary regulations relating to the special rules for leases under the Economic Recovery Tax Act of 1981. These regulations provide guidance to persons executing lease agreements under section 168(f)(8) of the Internal Revenue Code of 1954.

DATE: The regulations apply with respect to certain property placed in service after December 31, 1980.

FOR FURTHER INFORMATION CONTACT: John A. Tolleris, of the Legislation and Regulations Division, Office of Chief Counsel, Internal Revenue Service, 1111 Constitution Ave., N.W., Washington, D.C. 20224 (202) 566-3294.

SUPPLEMENTARY INFORMATION:

BACKGROUND

This document contains temporary regulations relating to the special rules for leases under section 168(f)(8) of the Internal Revenue Code of 1954, as enacted by section 201(a) of the Economic Recovery Tax Act of 1981 (95 Stat. 214). These regulations are included in Part 5c, Temporary Income Tax Regulations Under the Economic Recovery Tax Act of 1981. The temporary regulations provided by this document will remain in effect until superseded by later final regulations with respect to section 168 concerning the accelerated cost recovery system (ACRS). These temporary regulations are expected to be revised and proposed in the forthcoming notice of proposed rulemaking with respect to section 168 concerning ACRS.

EXPLANATION

In addition to normal regulating authority granted to the Secretary by section 7805 of the Code, section 168(f)(8)(G) of the Code provides that the Secretary shall prescribe such regulations as may be necessary to carry out the purposes of section 168(f)(8), including (but not limited to) regulations which limit the lessor to the aggregate amount of (and timing of) deductions and credits in respect of the qualified leased property that would have been allowable to the lessee without regard to section 168(f)(8). These regulations contain certain rules promulgated under the authority of section 168(f)(8)(G). For example, these rules include a requirement that the lease term cannot be shorter than the ACRS life of the property in the hands of the lessee and requirements regarding the reporting of interest under purchase money obligations and rent under the lease agreement.

Section 5c.168(f)(8)-9 reserves the issue of whether section 168(f)(8) leases may be used to transfer only the investment tax credit. The Treasury Department does not imply by such reservation that section 168(f)(8) applies in the case of transactions that transfer only the investment tax credit to a party other than the ultimate user of the property.

INAPPLICABILITY OF EXECUTIVE ORDER 12291

These regulations are not major legislative regulations for purposes of Executive Order 12291 because the economic effect of these regulations flows principally from the statutory provisions upon which these regulations are based.

DRAFTING INFORMATION

The principal author of this regulation is John A. Tolleris of the Legislation and Regulations Division of the Office of Chief Counsel, Internal Revenue Service. However, personnel from other offices of the Internal Revenue Service and Treasury Department participated in developing the regulation, both on matters of substance and style.

Adoption of amendments to the regulations

Accordingly, the following temporary regulations are adopted:

Paragraph 1. Part 5c is amended as follows:

PART 5c–TEMPORARY INCOME TAX REGULATIONS UNDER THE ECONOMIC RECOVERY TAX ACT OF 1981

§ 5c.44F-1 Leases and qualified research expenses.
§ 5c.103-1 Leases and capital expenditures.

* * * * *

§ 5c.168(f)(8)-1 Special rules for leases.
§ 5c.168(f)(8)-2 Election to characterize transaction as a section 168(f)(8) lease.
§ 5c.168(f)(8)-3 Requirements for lessor.
§ 5c.168(f)(8)-4 Minimum investment of lessor.
§ 5c.168(f)(8)-5 Term of lease.
§ 5c.168(f)(8)-6 Qualified leased property.
§ 5c.168(f)(8)-7 Reporting of income and deductions; at risk rules.
§ 5c.168(f)(8)-8 Loss of section 168(f)(8) protection; recapture.
§ 5c.168(f)(8)-9 Pass-through leases–transfer of investment tax credit only.
§ 5c.168(f)(8)-10 Leases between related parties.
§ 5c.168(f)(8)-11 Consolidated returns.

Paragraph 2. New §§ 5c.44F-1, 5c. 103-1, and 5c.168(f)(8)-1 through 5c.168(f)(8)-11 are added. The new sections read as follows:

Temporary Regulations

§ 5c.44F-1. Leases and qualified research expenses.–For purposes of section 44 F(b)(2)(A)(iii), the determination of whether any amount is paid or incurred to another person for the right to use personal property in the conduct of qualified research shall be made without regard to the characterization of the transaction as a lease under section 168(f)(8). See § 5c.168(f)(8)-1(b). [Temporary Reg. § 5c.44F-1.]

Temporary Regulations

§ 5c.103-1. Leases and capital expenditures.–For purposes of section 103(b)(6) (D) and § 1.103-10(b)(2)(iv)(*b*), the determination of whether property is leased and whether property is of a type that is ordinarily subject to a lease shall be made without regard to the characterization of the transaction as a lease under section 168 (f)(8). [Temporary Reg. § 5c.103-1.]

Temporary Regulations

§ 5c.168(f)(8)-1. Special rules for leases.–(a) *In general.* Section 168(f)(8) of the Internal Revenue Code of 1954 provides special rules for characterizing certain agreements as leases and characterizing the parties to the agreement as lessors and lessees for Federal tax law purposes. These rules apply only with respect to qualified leased property. If all the requirements of section 168(f)(8) and §§ 5c.168(f)(8)-2 through 5c.168(f)(8)-11 are met, then the agreement shall be treated as a lease, and the party characterized as the lessor shall be treated as the owner of the property. In such case, the lessor shall be deemed to have entered into the lease in the course of carrying on a trade or business and shall be allowed accelerated cost recovery system (ACRS) deductions under section 168 and the investment tax credit under section 38 with respect to the leased property.

(b) *Exception for qualified research expenditures.* For purposes of section 44F (b)(2)(A)(iii), the determination of whether any amount is paid or incurred to another person for the right to use personal property in the conduct of qualified research shall be made without regard to the characterization of the transaction as a lease under section 168(f)(8). Thus, if a lessee would be considered the owner of the property without regard to section 168(f)(8), any amounts paid by the lessee under the lease shall not be considered amounts paid or incurred for the right to use the property.

(c) *Other factors disregarded.* If an agreement meets the requirements of section 168(f)(8) and §§ 5c.168(f)(8)-2 through 5c.168(f)(8)-11, the following factors will not be taken into account in determining whether the transaction is a lease:

(1) Whether the lessor or lessee must take the tax benefits into account in order to determine that a profit is made from the transaction;

(2) The fact that the lessee is the nominal owner of the property for State or local law purposes (e.g., has legal title to the property) and retains the burdens, benefits, and incidents of ownership (such as payment of taxes and maintenance charges with respect to the property);

(3) Whether or not a person other than the lessee may be able to use the property after the lease term;

(4) The fact that the property may (or must) be bought or sold at the end of the lease term at a fixed or determinable price that is more or less than its fair market value at that time;

(5) The fact that the lessee or related party has provided financing or has guaranteed financing for the transaction (other than for the lessor's minimum ten percent investment); and

(6) The fact that the obligation of any person is subject to any contingency or offset agreement. See, for example, the rent and debt service offset in Example (2) of paragraph (e).

An agreement that meets the requirements of section 168(f)(8) and §§ 5c.168 (f) (8)-2 through §§ 5c.168(f)(8)-11 may be treated by the parties as a lease for Federal tax law purposes only. Similarly, a sale by the lessee of the leased property to the lessor in a transaction where the property is leased back under an agreement that meets the requirements of section 168(f)(8) may be treated by the parties as a sale for Federal tax law purposes only. The agreements need not comply with State law requirements concerning transfer of title, recording, etc.

(d) *Ownership in one of the parties.* Notwithstanding any other section, if neither the lessor nor the lessee would be the owner of the property without regard to section 168(f)(8), or, if any party with an economic interest in the property (other than the lessor or lessee) claims ACRS deductions or an investment tax credit with respect to the leased property, an election under section 168(f)(8) with respect to such property shall be void as of the date of the execution of the lease agreement.

(e) *Examples.* The application of section 168(f)(8) and § § 5c.168(f)(8)-2 through 5c.168(f)(8)-11 may be illustrated by the following examples:

Example (1). X Corp. wishes to acquire a $1 million piece of equipment which is "qualified leased property" as defined in section 168(f)(8)(D). The equipment has a ten-year economic life and falls within the five-year ACRS class. Y Corp. is a person meeting the qualifications set forth in section 168(f)(8)(B)(i) and § 5c.168 (f)(8)-3 and wishes to be the owner of the property for Federal tax law purposes. Y therefore purchases the equipment from the manufacturer for $1 million, paying $200,000 in cash and borrowing $800,000 from a bank (payable over nine years and requiring nine equal annual payments of principal and interest of $168,000). Y then leases the equipment to X under an agreement providing for nine annual rental payments of $168,000, and the parties elect in accordance with the provisions of § 5c.168(f)(8)-2 to have the provisions of section 168(f)(8) apply. The timing and amount of the rental payments required to be made by X (the "lessee-user") under the lease will be exactly equal to the timing and amount of the principal and interest payments that Y (the "lessor") will be required to make to the bank under its purchase money note. Under these circumstances, Y is treated as the owner and lessor of the property for Federal tax law purposes; it therefore is entitled to the investment tax credit and the ACRS deductions with respect to the property. Y's basis in the property is $1 million. Y must report the rent as income and will be entitled to deduct the interest on the purchase money note. The aggregate payments required to be made by X under the lease are treated as rent in accordance with § 5c.168(f) (8)-7 and are deductible as such.

Example (2). The facts are the same as in example (1) except that X purchases the equipment for $1 million and wishes to transfer ownership of the property for Federal tax law purposes to Y under a sale and leaseback arrangement. Accordingly, X sells the property to Y for $200,000 in cash (which represents the agreed upon compensation for the tax benefits to be enjoyed by Y as lessor) plus a nine-year, $800,000 note calling for nine $168,000 annual payments of principal and interest. Y then leases the property back to X under an agreement providing for nine annual rental payments of $168,000. The parties elect in accordance with the provisions of § 5c.168(f)(8)-2 to have the provisions of section 168(f)(8) apply. The timing and amount of the rental payments required to be made by X (as the lessee-user) under the lease will be exactly equal to the timing and amount of the principal and interest payments that Y will be required to make to X under Y's purchase money note, so that the only cash transferred between X and Y is the $200,000 down payment. Y's obligation to make debt service payments on the note is contingent on X's obligation to make rental payments under the lease. Under these circumstances, Y is treated as the owner and lessor of the property for Federal tax law purposes; it therefore is entitled to the investment tax credit and ACRS deductions with respect to the property. Y's basis in the property is $1 million. Y must report the rent as income and will be entitled to deduct the interest on the purchase money note. No gain or loss will be recognized by X on the sale of the property since the sale price equals X's basis in the property. X must report as income the interest paid by Y on the note and will be entitled to a deduction for the rental payments it makes under the lease in accordance with § 5c.168(f)(8)-7.

Example (3). Assume that in both examples (1) and (2) X has an option to purchase the equipment at the end of the lease term for $1.00. The fact that the property may (or must) be bought or sold at the end of the lease term at a fixed or determinable price that is more or less than its fair market value is not taken into account in determining the status of the transactions as leases under section 168(f)(8). [Temporary Reg. § 5c.168(f)(8)-1.]

Temporary Regulations

§ 5c.168(f)(8)-2. Election to characterize transaction as a section 168(f)(8) lease.–(a) *Election*–(1) *In general.* The election to characterize a transaction as a lease qualifying under section 168(f)(8) shall be made within the time and manner as set forth in this section without regard to section 168(f)(4).

(2) *Lease agreement.* For an agreement to be treated as a lease under section 168 (f)(8) and this section, the lease agreement must be executed not later than three months after the property was first placed in service, as defined in § 5c.168(f)(8)-6 (b)(2)(i) (or prior to November 14, 1981, if the property was first placed in service by the lessee after December 31, 1980, and before August 14, 1981). The agreement must be in writing and must state that all of the parties to the agreement agree to characterize it as a lease for purposes of Federal tax law and elect to have the provisions of section 168(f)(8) apply to the transaction. The agreement must also name the party who will be treated as the lessor and the party who will be treated as the lessee.

(3) *Information return concerning the election.* (i) The lessor and lessee shall file information returns concerning their election under section 168(f)(8) with respect to a particular property (or properties) with their income tax returns by the date set forth in subdivision (ii) of this subparagraph (3). Each information return shall be signed by both the lessor and the lessee. The failure by the lessor to file the information return shall be a disqualifying event which shall cause an agreement to cease to be treated as a lease under section 168(f)(8). For the Federal income tax

consequences of a disqualifying event, see § 5c.168(f)(8)-8. The information return shall include the following items:

(A) The name, address, and taxpayer identifying number of the lessor and the lessee;

(B) The district director's office with which the income tax returns of the lessor and lessee are filed;

(C) A description of each property with respect to which the election is made;

(D) The date on which the lessee places the property in service (determined as defined in § 5c.168(f)(8)-6(b)(2)(i)), the date on which the lease begins and the term of the lease;

(E) The recovery property class of the leased property under section 168(c) (2) (for example, five years);

(F) For the lessor only: the unadjusted basis of the property as defined in section 168(d)(1);

(G) For the lessor only: if the lessor is a partnership or a grantor trust, the name, address, and taxpayer identifying number of the partners or the beneficiaries, and the district director's office with which the income tax return of each partner or beneficiary is filed; and

(H) Such other information as required by the return or its instructions.

(ii) The information return described in subdivision (i) of this subparagraph (3) shall be filed by each party with its income tax return for its taxable year during which the lease term begins. However, for taxable years ending in 1981 with respect to lease agreements executed during calendar year 1981, such statement shall be filed by the later of (A) the due date (taking extensions into account) of the party's 1981 income tax return, or (B) where the filing of an amended income tax return is required, with the amended return within three months following the execution of the lease agreement. For the requirement to file an amended return within three months and the consequences of the failure to so file, see § 5c.168(f)(8)-6(b)(2)(ii). A taxpayer that is required to file the information return before an information return form is available shall file, in lieu of the required information return, a statement signed by the lessor and the lessee which contains the information set forth in subdivisions (A) through (G) of subdivision (i) of this subparagraph (3).

(4) *Election is irrevocable.* An agreement made pursuant to paragraph (a)(2) of this section shall be irrevocable as of the later of the date such agreement was executed or [THIRTY DAYS AFTER DATE OF PUBLICATION OF THIS TREASURY DECISION IN THE FEDERAL REGISTER].

(5) *Disposition by lessee.* If the lessee (or any subsequent transferee of the lessee's interest) sells or assigns its interest in the lease or the property, whether volun-

tarily (such as, for example, in a foreclosure proceeding), the agreement will cease to be characterized as a lease under section 168(f)(8) as of the time of the sale or assignment unless (i) the transferee furnishes to the lessor within sixty days following the transfer the transferee's written consent to take the property subject to the lease, and (ii) the transferee and lessor file a statement with their income tax return for the taxable year in which the transfer occurs containing the following information:

(A) The name, address, and taxpayer identifying number of the lessor and the transferee;

(B) The district director's office with which the income tax returns of the lessor and transferee are filed;

(C) A description of the property.

See § 5c.168(f)(8)-8 for the Federal income tax consequences where an agreement ceases to be characterized as a lease under section 168(f)(8).

(b) *Examples.* The application of the provisions of this section may be illustrated by the following examples:

Example (1). X Corp. maintains its books and records for Federal tax law purposes on a calendar year basis. On February 1, 1981, X acquires certain equipment for use in its business, and the equipment is deemed to be placed in service on that date within the meaning of § 5c.163(f)(8)-6(b)(2)(i). On November 1, 1981, X sells the equipment to Y and leases it back under a lease in which the parties elect to have the provisions of section 168(f)(8) apply. The election is considered timely for purposes of making Y the owner of the property under section 168(f)(8) since the lease agreement was executed before November 14, 1981.

Example (2). The facts are the same as in example (1) except that X Corp.'s taxable year ends on February 28, 1981. X claimed the investment tax credit and depreciation deductions with respect to the property in its return filed April 1, 1981. The lease will qualify for safe harbor treatment under section 168(f)(8) provided X, within three months after the lease agreement was executed, files an amended return pursuant to § 5c.168(f)(8)-6(b)(2)(ii) for its taxable year ending February 28, 1981, in which X foregoes its right to claim any investment tax credit or ACRS deductions with respect to the property subject to the lease. [Temporary Reg. § 5c.168(f)(8)-2.]

Temporary Regulations

§ 5c.168(f)(8)-3. Requirements for lessor.—(a) *Qualified lessor.* In order for an agreement to be treated as a lease under section 168(f)(8), the party characterized in the agreement as the lessor must be a qualified lessor. The term "qualified lessor" means—

(1) A corporation which is neither an electing small business corporation under section 1371(b) nor a personal holding company under section 542(a), or

(2) A partnership all of whose partners are corporations described in subparagraph (1), or

(3) A grantor trust whose grantor and beneficiaries are all corporations described in subparagraph (1) or partnerships described in subparagraph (2).

(b) *Effect of disqualification of lessor.* If at any time during the term of the agreement the lessor ceases to be a qualified lessor, the agreement will lose its characterization as a lease under section 168(f)(8) as of the date of the event causing such disqualification. If any partner of a partnership described in paragraph (a)(2) ceases to be a corporation described in paragraph (a)(1), the partnership entity shall cease to be a qualified lessor. Similarly, if any beneficiary of a trust described in paragraph (a)(3) ceases to be a corporation described in paragraph (a)(1), the trust shall cease to be a qualified lessor. See § 5c.168(f)(8)-8 for the Federal income tax consequences of such a disqualification.

(c) *One tax owner per property.* Only one person may be a qualified lessor under section 168(f)(8) with respect to leased property. Thus, property that is subject to a lease under section 168(f)(8) may not be subleased under a lease for which a section 168(f)(8) election is made. In addition, if a lessor sells or assigns in a taxable transaction its interest in a section 168(f)(8) lease or in the underlying property, the lease shall cease to qualify under section 168(f)(8), and no other lease may be executed under section 168(f)(8) with respect to the property. See § 5c.168(f)(8)-8 for the Federal income tax consequences where a lease ceases to qualify under section 168(f)(8). However, lease brokers, agents, etc., may, for example, prepare executory contracts with the lessee whereby the broker's assignee may execute a lease as lessor, and, if the requirements of section 168(f)(8) and §§ 5c.168(f)(8)-1 through 5c.168(f)(8)-11 are met, the lease will qualify under section 168(f)(8).

(d) *Examples.* The application of paragraph (c) may be illustrated by the following examples:

Example (1). X Corp. (as lessee) sells certain new equipment to Y Corp. (as lessor) and leases it back under a section 168(f)(8) lease. Within three months after the property was placed in service, Y assigns its interest in the lease to Z. Upon the transfer to Z, the lease will no longer qualify for treatment under section 168(f). The property may not thereafter be the subject of a section 168(f)(8) lease. property may not thereafter be the subject of a section 168(f)(8) lease.

Example (2). X Corp. wishes to acquire certain equipment for use in its business and also wishes to transfer ownership of the property for Federal tax law purposes. LB, a lease broker, purchases the equipment and enters into a contract with X under which X agrees to execute a section 168(f)(8) lease (as lessee) with a third party assignee of LB's interest in the property. LB assigns the equipment and contract to T Corp. (which wishes to secure Federal tax law ownership), and at a later date (but within the prescribed three-month period) X and T execute a lease agreement in accordance with § 5c.168(f)(8)-2. The lease will qualify for treatment under section 168(f)(8). [Temporary Reg. § 5c.168(f)(8)-3.]

Temporary Regulations

§ 5c.168(f)(8)-4. Minimum investment of lessor.–(a) *Minimum investment.* Under section 168(f)(8)(B)(ii), an agreement will not be characterized as a lease for purposes of section 168(f)(8) unless the qualified lessor has a minimum at risk investment which, at the time the property is placed in service under the lease and at all times during the term of the lease, is not less than ten percent of the adjusted basis of the leased property. As the adjusted basis of the leased property is reduced by capital cost recovery deductions, the minimum investment required will also be reduced to ten percent of the revised adjusted basis, until the adjusted basis has been completely recovered, at which time no minimum investment will be required. Financing provided by the lessee or a party related to the lessee, such as a recourse note given by the lessor to the lessee, will not be taken into account in determining the lessor's minimum investment.

(b) *At risk amount.* The minimum investment which the lessor has at risk with respect to the leased property for purposes of paragraph (a) of this section includes only consideration paid and recourse indebtedness incurred by the lessor to purchase the property. The lessor must have sufficient net worth (without regard to the value of any leases which qualify under section 168(f)(8)) to satisfy any personal liability incurred. Any tax benefits which the lessor derives from the leased property shall not be taken into account to reduce the amount the lessor has at risk. An agreement between the lessor and the lessee requiring either or both parties to purchase or sell the qualified leased property at some price (whether or not fixed in the agreement) at the end of the lease term shall not affect the amount the lessor has at risk with respect to the property. However, an option held by the lessor to sell the property that is exercisable before the end of the period prescribed under section 168(c)(2) for the recovery property class of the leased property (taking into account any election by the lessor or lessee under section 168(b)(3)) shall reduce the amount the lessor is considered to have at risk by the amount of the option price at the time the option becomes exercisable. [Temporary Reg. § 5c.168(f)(8)-4.]

Temporary Regulations

§ 5c.168(f)(8)-5. Term of lease.–(a) *Term of lease–*(1) *Basic rules.* To qualify as a lease under section 168(f)(8) and § 5c.168(f)(8)-1 (a), the lease agreement must provide for a term that does not exceed the maximum term described in paragraph (b) of this section; such term must also at least equal the minimum term described in paragraph (c).

(b) *Maximum term.* For purposes of section 168(f)(8)(B)(iii) and this section, the term of the lease may not exceed the greater of–

(i) Ninety percent of the useful life of the property under section 167, or

(ii) 150 percent of the asset depreciation range (ADR) present class life ("midpoint") of such property, applicable as of January 1, 1981 (without regard to section 167(m)(4)), published in Rev. Proc. 77-10, 1977-1 C.B. 548, and revisions thereto.

Solely for purposes of this paragraph (b), "useful life" means the period when the leased asset can reasonably be expected to be economically useful in anyone's trade or business; such term does not mean the period during which the lessor expects to lease the property. Any option to extend the term of the lease, whether or not at fair market value rent, must be included in the term of the lease for purposes of this paragraph. If several different pieces of property are the subject of a single lease, the maximum allowable term for such lease will be measured with respect to the property with the shortest life. In no case, however, will the lease term qualify under this section if such term with respect to any piece of property is less than the minimum term described in paragraph (c).

(c) *Minimum term.* For purposes of this section, the term of the lease must at least equal the period prescribed under section 168(c)(2) for the recovery property class of the leased property. For example, if a piece of leased equipment is in the five-year recovery property class, the lease agreement must have a minimum term of five years. In general, the determination of whether property is three-year recovery property, five-year recovery property, etc., in the hands of the lessor will be based on the characterization of the property in the hands of the owner as determined without regard to the section 168(f)(8) lease. Thus, for example, property which is public utility property or RRB replacement property absent the section 168(f)(8) lease will be characterized as such in the hands of the lessor for purposes of section 168 (f)(8). However, with respect to RRB replacement property, the transitional rule of section 168(f)(3) shall be inapplicable to the lessor. In addition, any election under section 168(b)(3) by the lessor with respect to the class of recovery property to which the qualified leased property is assigned shall apply to the leased property in determining the term of the lease. A lease term that does not exceed the term required to satisfy the minimum lease term of this paragraph will be deemed to comply with the maximum lease term described in paragraph (b) if such minimum lease term exceeds such maximum lease term.

(d) *Examples.* The application of this section may be illustrated by the following examples:

Example (1). X Corp. (as lessee) and Y Corp. (as lessor) enter into a lease which they elect to be treated under section 168(f)(8) with respect to a chemical manufacturing facility that will also generate steam for use in the production of electricity. The assets comprising the chemical plant are described in ADR guideline class 28.0 (midpoint life of 9.5 years), and the assets comprising the steam plant are described in ADR class 00.4 (midpoint life of twenty-two years). To satisfy the maximum lease term requirement of section 168(f)(8)(B)(iii)(II) and § 5c.168(f)(8)-5(b), the lease term may not exceed 14. 25 years (150 percent of the 9.5 year midpoint life of the chemical plant).

Example (2). The facts are the same as in example (1) except that the chemical plant and the steam plant are the subject of separate leases. For purposes of section 168(f)(8)(B)(iii)(II) and § 5c.168(f)(8)-5(b), the maximum term of the lease with respect to the chemical plant is 14.25 years (150 percent of 9.5 years) and the maximum term of the lease with respect to the steam plant is thirty-three years (150 percent of twenty-two years). [Temporary Reg. § 5c.168(f)(8)-5.]

Temporary Regulations

§ 5c.168(f)(8)-6. Qualified leased property.—(a) *Basic rules*—(1) *In general.* An agreement shall be treated as a section 168(f)(8) lease only if the property which is leased is qualified leased property. Qualified leased property is recovery property as defined in section 168(c) and is either—

(i) Except as provided in subparagraph (2), new section 38 property of the lessor which is leased no later than three months after the date the property was placed in service (or prior to November 14, 1981, if the property was placed in service after December 31, 1980, and before August 14, 1981) and which, if acquired by the lessee, would have been new section 38 property of the lessee, or

(ii) Property which is a qualified mass commuting vehicle (as defined in section 103(b)(9)) and which is financed in whole or in part by proceeds from an issue of obligations the interest on which is excludable from income under section 103(a).

(2) *Sale and leaseback arrangement.* (i) Where the leased property is purchased, directly or indirectly, by the lessor from the lessee (or a party related to the lessee), the property will not be qualified leased property unless the property was (or would have been) new section 38 property of the lessee and was purchased and leased no later than three months after the date the property was placed in service by the lessee (or prior to November 14, 1981, if the property was placed in service by the lessee after December 31, 1980 and before August 14, 1981) and with respect to which the lessor's adjusted basis does not exceed the adjusted basis of the lessee (or a party related to the lessee) at the time of the lease. If the lessor's adjusted basis in the property exceeds the seller's adjusted basis with respect to the property at the beginning of the lease, the property will not be qualified leased property.

(ii) For purposes of this subparagraph (2), transactional costs with respect to a sale and leaseback arrangement that are not currently deductible shall be allocated to the lease agreement (and not included in the lessor's adjusted basis with respect to the property) and amortized over the term of the lease. These costs include legal and investment banking fees and printing costs.

(iii) [*Examples.*] The application of this subparagraph (2) may be illustrated by the following examples:

Example (1). X, an airline, contracts to have an airplane constructed for a fixed price of $10 million. Prior to completion of construction of the airplane, the value of the airplane increases to $11 million. X buys the airplane at the contract price of $10 million and, before it is placed in service, sells the airplane at its fair market value of $11 million to Y and then leases it back. The lease will not qualify for safe harbor protection under section 168(f)(8) because the lessor's adjusted basis in the airplane exceeds the lessee's adjusted basis. This result obtains even though the airplane qualifies as new section 38 property of X airline.

Example (2). Assume the same facts as in example (1) except that, prior to completion of the construction of the airplane, X assigns its contract to Y for $1 million, and Y thereafter buys the airplane at the contract price of $10 million. The acquisition by Y is treated as an indirect purchase from the lessee. Because Y's adjusted basis in the airplane would exceed the lessee's adjusted basis, the lease will not qualify under section 168(f)(8).

(b) *Special rules*–(1) *New section 38 property.* (i) New section 38 property is section 38 property described in subsection (b) of section 48 and the regulations thereunder other than a qualified rehabilitated building (within the meaning of section 48(g)(1)). Qualified leased property must be new section 38 property at the beginning of the lease and must continue to be section 38 property in the hands of the lessor and the lessee throughout the lease term. The fact that the lessee used the property within the three-month period prior to the lease will not disqualify the property as new section 38 property of the lessee.

(ii) *[Examples.]* The application of this subparagraph (1) may be illustrated by the following examples:

Example (1). N is a hospital exempt from Federal income tax and wishes to purchase certain equipment for use in furtherance of its exempt functions (*i.e.,* other than for use in an unrelated trade or business). O, a qualified lessor as defined in § 5c.168(f)(8)-3(a), acquires the property and leases it to N. Since the equipment would not be new section 38 property of N if N had acquired it by virtue of section 48(a)(4) (relating to exception from definition of section 38 property for certain property used by certain tax-exempt organizations), the equipment is not qualified leased property and the lease does not qualify under section 168(f)(8). Whether O is considered the owner of the property for Federal tax law purposes will be determined without regard to the provisions of section 168(f)(8).

Example (2). P Corp. is constructing progress expenditure property as defined in section 46(d)(2) for R Corp. Progress expenditure property is property which it is reasonable to believe will be section 38 property in the hands of the taxpayer when it is placed in service. Before the date that the property is placed in service (as defined in § 5c.168(f)(8)-6(b)(2)(i)), the property is not new section 38 property. Accordingly, progress expenditure property cannot be qualified leased property.

Example (3). R Corp., a foreign railroad, acquires new rolling stock and enters into a sale and leaseback transaction with B Corp., a domestic corporation. R uses the rolling stock within and without the United States, but predominantly outside the United States within the meaning of section 48(a)(2)(A). Section 48(a)(2)(B)(ii) is inapplicable to R because R is neither a domestic railroad corporation nor a United States person; therefore, the rolling stock cannot be section 38 property to R. The property is not qualified leased property.

(2) *Placed in service.* (i) Property shall be considered as placed in service at the time the property is placed in a condition or state of readiness and availability for a specifically assigned function. If an entire facility is leased under one lease, property which is part of the facility will not be considered placed in service under this rule until the entire facility is placed in service. If the lessee claims any investment tax credit or ACRS deductions with respect to any component which is part of an entire facility that is subsequently leased, the lessee must file an amended return within the time prescribed in paragraph (b)(2)(ii) of this section in which it foregoes its claim to the investment tax credit and ACRS deductions. If such amended return may not be filed because the time for filing a claim for refund with respect to any component under section 6511 has expired, each component of the facility will be considered as placed in service at the time the individual component is placed in a condition or state of readiness and availability for a specifically assigned function and not when the entire facility is placed in service.

(ii) For purposes other than determining whether property is qualified leased property, property subject to a lease under section 168(f)(8) will be deemed to have been placed in service not earlier than the date such property is used under the lease. If the lessee claims any investment tax credit or ACRS deductions with respect to property placed in service under a lease, the lessee must file an amended return within three months following the execution of the lease agreement in which the lessee foregoes its claim to the investment tax credit and ACRS deductions with respect to the leased property or the election under section 168(f)(8) will be void.

(iii) The application of this subparagraph (2) may be illustrated by the following examples:

Example (1). X Corp. acquires equipment on December 31, 1982, and places the equipment in service. X's taxable year ends December 31. On March 20, 1983, X sells the equipment to Y Corp. and leases it back in a transaction that qualifies under section 168(f)(8). The property is considered to be new section 38 property to X under paragraph (b)(1). X is not allowed any investment tax credit or ACRS deductions with respect to the property in 1982 because the property is not considered to have been placed in service for purposes other than determining whether it is qualified leased property until it is used under the lease subdivision (ii) of this subparagraph (2). If X has claimed credits or deductions on its 1982 return, it must file an amended return for 1982 within three months following the execution of the lease agreement or the election will be void.

Example (2). In March 1985, K Corp. completes reconditioning of a machine, which it constructed and placed in service in 1982 and which has an adjusted basis in 1985 of $10,000. The cost of reconditioning amounts to an additional $20,000.

K would be entitled to a basis of $20,000 in computing its qualified investment in new section 38 property for 1985. In May 1985, K enters into a sale and leaseback transaction with L Corp. with respect to the reconditioned parts of the machine that are new section 38 property to K. K and L elect to have section 168(f)(8) apply. Assuming that the adjusted basis of the leased property is the same to L as it is to K, the property qualifies as qualified leased property under section 168(f)(8)(D) (ii) and L is considered the tax owner of the property. Since, for purposes other than determining whether property is qualified leased property, the property is deemed originally placed in service not earlier than the date the property is used under the lease, the property is new section 38 property to L and L may claim the investment tax credit (and ACRS deductions) with respect to the leased property.

(3) *Qualified mass commuting vehicle.* [Reserved].

(4) *Foreign lessees.* In addition to the other provisions of this section, property which is leased to a foreign person shall not be qualified leased property unless the gross income attributable to the property from all sources (determined without regard to sections 872(a) or 882(b)) is effectively connected with a trade or business within the United States, and the taxable income, if any, attributable to the property is subject to tax under section 871(b)(1) or 882(a)(1). For this purpose, if income attributable to the property is not included in gross income of a foreign lessee, and is exempt from taxation, under sections 872 or 883, or if the income is otherwise exempt from taxation under any income tax convention to which the United States is a party, then the property shall not be qualified leased property.

(5) *Other rules.* (i) Qualified leased property may include undivided interests in property or property regardless of whether or not it is considered separate property under State or local law. If property subject to a section 168(f)(8) lease is later determined not to be qualified leased property, disqualification of the lease under section 168(f)(8) will apply only as to that property.

(ii) The application of this subparagraph (5) may be illustrated by the following examples:

Example (1). On July 1, 1981, X Corp. contracts to have a manufacturing facility constructed for use in its business. Construction of the facility is completed on July 1, 1982, and the facility is deemed to be placed in service as of that date under § 5c.168(f)(8)-6(b)(2)(i). The facility is comprised of a mixture of new section 38 property and buildings that do not qualify as section 38 property. On August 1, 1982, X sells the new section 38 property in the facility to Y and leases it back under an agreement in which the parties elect to be treated as a lease described in section 168(f)(8). Assuming that the other requirements of this paragraph are met, the new section 38 property contained in the facility will be qualified leased property. If it is later determined that property subject to the section 168(f)(8) lease is not new section 38 property (and thus not qualified leased property), the safe harbor protection will be lost only as to that property.

Example (2). X Corp. acquires a certain piece of equipment (which is new section 38 property) for use in its business. Within three months, X sells a seventy percent undivided interest in the property to lessor A and a ten percent undivided interest in the property to lessor B and leases both portions back under separate section 168(f)(8) leases. The investment tax credit and ACRS deductions associated with the property will be divided among X, lessor A, and lessor B, on a basis of twenty percent, seventy percent, and ten percent, respectively. [Temporary Reg. § 5c.168(f)(8)-6.]

Temporary Regulations

§ 5c.168(f)(8)-7. Reporting of income, deductions and investment tax credit; at risk rules.–(a) *In general.* The fact that the lessor's payments of interest and principal and the lessee's rental payments under the lease are not equal in amount will not prevent the lease from qualifying under section 168(f)(8). However, see paragraph (b) for special requirements in sale and leaseback transactions. In determining the parties' income, deductions, and investment tax credit under the lease, the rules in paragraphs (c) through (g) of this section shall apply regardless of the overall method of accounting otherwise used by the parties.

(b) *Requirements for sale and leaseback transaction.* If the property leased is financed by the lessee (or a related party of the lessee) in a sale and leaseback transaction, the lease will not qualify under section 168(f)(8) unless (1) the term of the lessor's purchase money obligation is coterminous with the term of the lease, and (2) the lessor's obligation bears a reasonable rate of interest within the meaning of § 1.385-6(e) or an arm's-length rate of interest as defined in § 1.482-2.

(c) *Interest deductions and income*–(1) *Deductibility from income.* In determining the amount of interest that a lessor may deduct in a taxable year with respect to its purchase money obligation given to the lessee or to a third party creditor, the lessor may not claim a deduction that would be–

(A) Greater than a deduction that would be allowed under a level-payment mortgage, amortized over a period equal to the term of the lessor's obligation, or

(B) Less than a deduction that would be allowed to an accrual basis taxpayer under a straight line amortization of the principal over the term of the lessor's obligation.

In cases in which the property is not financed by the lessee or a party related to the lessee, the computation of the interest deduction may take into account fluctuations in the interest rate which are dependent on adjustments in the prime rate or events outside the control of the lessor and the third party creditor.

(2) *Includibility in income.* The lessee shall include interest on the lessor's purchase money obligation in income at the same time and in the same amount as the lessor's interest deductions, as determined under paragraph (c)(1).

(d) *Rental income and deductions—*(1) *Deductibility from income.* The amount of the lessee's annual rent deduction with respect to the rent under a section 168 (f)(8) lease shall be a pro rata portion of the aggregate amount required to be paid by the lessee to the lessor under the terms of the lease agreement. If the lessee is required to purchase the leased property at the end of the lease term, or if the lessor has an option to sell the property to the lessee, rent shall not include the lesser of—

(A) The amount of the lessee's purchase obligation, whether fixed by the terms of the lease agreement or conditioned on the exercise of the lessor's option to sell the property to the lessee, or

(B) The fair market value of the property at the end of the lease term determined at the beginning of the lease term.

For this purpose, fair market value shall be determined without taking into account any increase or decrease for inflation or deflation during the lease term. Rent deductions may be adjusted pursuant to the terms of the lease agreement to account for fluctuations which are dependent on events outside the control of the lessor and lessee, such as a change in the interest rate charged by a third party creditor of the lessor on the debt incurred to finance the purchase of the leased property.

(2) *Includibility in income.* The lessor shall include rent in income as follows:

(A) In the case of prepayments of rent, the earlier of when such rent is paid by the lessee or accrued under the lease, and

(B) In the case of other rent, at the same time and in the same amount as the lessee's rent deductions, as determined under paragraph (d)(1).

(e) *ACRS deductions.* The deductions that the lessor is allowed under section 168(a) with respect to property subject to a section 168(f)(8) lease shall be determined without regard to the limitation in section 168(f)(10)(B)(iii). The recovery class of qualified leased property in the hands of the lessor shall be determined by the character of the property in the hands of the owner of the property without regard to section 168(f)(8). Any elections under section 168(b)(3) by the lessor with respect to the class of recovery property to which the qualified leased property is assigned shall apply to the leased property. However, with respect to RRB replacement property, the transitional rule of section 168(f)(3) shall be inapplicable to the lessor.

(f) *At risk requirements.* The amount of the investment credit and ACRS deductions that a lessor shall be allowed with respect to the leased property shall be limited to the extent the at risk rules under the investment tax credit provisions and section 465 apply to the lessee or to the lessor. In determining the amount the lessee would be at risk, the at risk rules will be applied as if the lessee had not elected to have section 168(f)(8) apply. Thus, for example, if, without regard to section 168(f)(8), an individual lessee would be treated as the owner of the leased property for Federal tax law purposes, the lessor under a section 168(f)(8) lease would be allowed ACRS deductions or investment tax credits with respect to the property only to the extent that the lessee may have claimed them had the parties not elected treatment under section 168(f)(8). In addition, the ACRS deductions and investment tax credits that a lessor is allowed with respect to the property are further limited to the extent that the at risk rules apply to the lessor as owner of the property under the section 168 (f)(8) lease. If the lessor and the lessee are subject to the at risk rules, the lessor is allowed only the lesser of the ACRS deductions and investment tax credits allowable to the lessor and the lessee.

(g) *Limitations on section 48(d) amount.* If in a sale and leaseback transaction the lessor elects pursuant to section 48(d) to treat the lessee (which is the user of the property) as having acquired the property for purposes of claiming the investment tax credit, the lessee shall be treated as acquiring the property for an amount equal to the basis of the property to the lessor (and not for an amount equal to its fair market value). The investment tax credit allowable to the lessee is further limited to the extent the at risk rules apply to either the lessor or to the lessee. See paragraph (f) of this section.

(h) *Examples.* The application of the provisions of this section may be illustrated by the following examples.

Example (1). Y, a qualified lessor, acquires a piece of equipment which is qualified leased property for $1 million and leases it to X under a lease which the parties properly elect to have characterized as a lease described in section 168(f)(8). The equipment has a ten-year economic life and falls within the five-year ACRS class. Under the terms of the lease, X, the lessee-user, is obligated to pay Y nine annual payments of $10,000 and, at the end of the lease term, Y has the option to sell the property to X for $2,160,000. Under § 5c.168(f)(8)-7(d), the aggregate payments required to be made by X under the lease are $2,250,000 ($90,000 rent plus $2,160,000 option price) and are treated as rent to Y (less a reasonable estimate for the residual value of the property) and taxable as such. Assuming a reasonable estimate of the residual value is zero, the full $2,250,000 will be treated as rent, and under § 5c.168(f)(8)-7(d), such amount is deductible by X and includible in Y's income ratably over the term of the lease, *i.e.*, at a rate of $250,000 per year ($2,250,000 divided by nine).

Example (2). The facts are the same as in example (1) except that under the terms of the lease X is obligated to make rental payments of $100,000 for each of the first five years of the lease and $300,000 for each of the four remaining years under the lease. Further, X has an option to purchase the equipment for $1.00 at the end of the lease term. Pursuant to § 5c.168(f)(8)-7(d), X's aggregate rental payments are deductible by X and are includible in Y's income ratably over the term of the lease. Thus, the annual rental payments are deemed to be $188,000 per year ($1,700,000 divided by nine). [Temporary Reg. § 5c.168(f)(8)-7.]

Temporary Regulations

§ 5c.168(f)(8)-8. Loss of section 168(f)(8) protection; recapture.—(a) *In general.* Upon the occurence of an event that causes an agreement to cease to be characterized as a lease under section 168(f)(8), the characterization of the lessor and lessee shall be determined without regard to section 168(f)(8).

(b) *Events which cause an agreement to cease to be characterized as a lease.* A disqualifying event shall cause an agreement to cease to be treated as a lease under section 168(f)(8) as of the date of the disqualifying event. A disqualifying event shall include the following:

(1) The lessor sells or assigns its interest in the lease or in the qualified leased property in a taxable transaction.

(2) The failure by the lessor to file the required information return described in § 5c.168(f)(8)-2(a)(3).

(3) The lessee (or any subsequent transferee of the lessee's interest) sells or assigns its interest in the lease or in the qualified leased property, whether voluntarily or involuntarily (such as, for example, in a foreclosure proceeding), and the transferee fails to execute, within the prescribed time, the consent described in § 5c.168(f)(8)-2(a)(5).

(4) The property ceases to be section 38 property as defined in § 1.48-1 in the hands of the lessor or lessee, for example, due to its conversion to personal use or to use predominantly outside the United States, or to use by a lessee exempt from Federal income taxation.

(5) The lessor ceases to be a qualified lessor by becoming an electing small business corporation or a personal holding company (within the meaning of section 542(a)).

(6) The minimum investment of the lessor becomes less than ten percent of the adjusted basis of the qualified leased property as described in section 168(f)(8)(B)(ii) and § 5c.168(f)(8)-4.

(7) The lease terminates.

(8) The property becomes subject to more than one lease for which an election is made under section 168(f)(8).

(9) Retirements and casualties. [Reserved]

(c) *Recapture.* The required amount of recapture of the investment tax credit and of accelerated cost recovery deductions after a disqualifying event shall be determined under section 47 and 1245, respectively.

(d) *Consequences of loss of safe harbor protection.* The tax consequences of a disqualifying event depend upon the characterization of the parties without regard to section 168(f)(8), the disqualifying event will be deemed to be a sale of the qualified leased property by the lessor to the lessee. The amount realized by the lessor on the sale will include the outstanding amount (if any) of the lessor's debt on the property plus the sum of any other consideration received by the lessor.

(e) *Examples.* The application of the provisions of this section may be illustrated by the following examples:

Example (1). M Corp. and N Corp. enter into a sale and leaseback transaction in which the leaseback agreement is characterized as a lease under section 168 (f)(8) and M is treated as the lessor. In the second year of the lease, M becomes an electing small business corporation under subchapter (0). The agreement ceases to be treated as a lease under section 168(f)(8) as of the date of the subchapter S election. Without respect to section 168(f)(8), N would be considered the owner of the property. The disqualification will be treated as a sale of the qualified leased property from M to N for the amount of the purchase money debt on the property then outstanding. M will realize gain or loss, depending upon its basis, with applicable investment tax credit and section 1245 recapture. N will acquire the property with a base equal to the amount of the outstanding obligation. The property will not be used section 38 property to N under § 1.48-3(a)(2).

Example (2). Q Corp. (as lessor) and P Corp. (as lessee) enter into a lease that is characterized as a lease under section 168(f)(8). The lease has a six-year term. P has no option to renew the lease or to purchase the property. At the end of six years, if P would be considered the owner of the property without regard to section 168 (f)(8), upon the termination of the lease the property will be deemed to be sold by Q to P for the amount of the purchase money debt outstanding with respect to the property. [Temporary Reg. § 5c.168(f)(8)-8.]

§ 5c.168(f)(8)-9. Pass-through leases—transfer of only the investment tax credit to a party other than the ultimate user of the property. [Reserved]

§ 5c.168(f)(8)-10. Leases between related parties. [Reserved]

§ 5c.168(f)(8)-11. Consolidated returns. [Reserved]

Bibliography

BOOKS

Clark, T.M. *Leasing*. Maidenhead Berkshire England: McGraw–Hill Book Company (UK) Limited, 1978.

Contino, Richard M. *Legal and Financial Aspects of Equipment Leasing Transactions*. Englewood Cliffs, N.J.: Prentice-Hall, Inc., 1979.

Elgers, P.T., and Clark, J.J. *The Lease/Buy Decision*. New York, N.Y.: The Free Press, A Division of MacMillian Publishing Co., Inc., 1980.

Financial Accounting Standards Board. *FASB Statement No. 13 as amended and interpreted through May 1980: Accounting for Leases*. High Ridge Park, Stamford, Conn., May 1980.

Green, Jack L. *Leasing Principles & Methods*. New York, N.Y.: Sound Publishing Company, Inc., 1978.

Pritchard, R.E. and Hindelang, T.J. *The Lease/Buy Decision*. New York, N.Y.: AMACOM, A Division of the American Management Associations, 1980.

Reisman, Albert F. *Equipment Leasing*. New York, N.Y., Practicing Law Institute, 1980, Course Handbook Series Number 236.

ARTICLES

Aaron. (1979) *The Bankruptcy Reform Act of 1978;* The Full-Employment-for Lawyers Bill. *1979 Utah Law Review 1:* 175, 405.

Anderson, Paul F., and Martin D. (Spring 1977) Lease versus purchase decision: A survey of current practice. *Financial Management*.

Basi, Bart A. (Jul 1975) Tax aspects of leasing: Lessee's viewpoint. *Tax Executive* 365-78.

369

Benjamin, James J., and Strawser, R.H. (1976) Developments in lease accounting. *CPA Journal* 33-36.

Bierman, Harold, Jr. (April 1973) Accounting for capitalized leases: Tax considerations. *Accounting Review* 421-24.

Bower, Richard S. (Winter 1973) Issues in lease financing. *Financial Management* 25-34.

Bower, Richard S., Herringer, Frank C. and Williamson, Peter J. (April 1966) Lease evaluation. *Accounting Review* 257-65.

Brown, Norman M. (August 1972) Return on investment and book accounting for leveraged lease investments. *The Journal of Commercial Bank Lending* 24-33.

Carlson, C. Rober, and Wort Donald H. (Spring 1974) A new look at the lease-vs.-purchase decision. *Journal Economics and Business* 199-202.

Chasteen, Lanny G. (Oct 1973) Implicit factors in the evaluation of lease vs. but alternatives *Accounting Review* 764-67.

Clark, Robert A., Jantorni Joan M. and Gann Robert R. (Sep 1973) Analysis of the lease-or-buy decision: Comment. *Journal of Finance* 1015-16.

Davidson, Sidney, and Weil Roman L. (Nov-Dec 1975) Lease capitalization and inflation accounting *Financial Analysts Journal* 22-29, 57.

Elam, Rick. (Jan 1975) The effect of lease data on the predictive ability of financial ratios. *The Accounting Review* 25-43.

Equipment Leasing & Rental Industries: Trends and Prospects, U.S. Department of Commerce, December 1976, Document No. 003-003-00175-1, U.S. Government Printing Office.

Ferrara, William L. (May 1974) Lease vs. purchase: A quasi-financing approach. *Management Accounting* 37-41.

Finn, F.J. (Apr 1970) Lease or purchase: A financing decision. *Management Accounting* (British) 145-150.

Fishback, J. Karl. (Apr 1974) A look at lease disclosure requirements. *Financial Executive* 24-37.

Harris, Milton M. (Sep 1975) Leveraged leasing: Profits or illusions? *Bank Administration* 56-63.

Henry, James B. (May 1974) Leasing: Cost measurement and disclosure. *Management Accounting* 42-47.

Honig, Lawrence E., and Coley, Stephen C. (Winter 1975) An after-tax equivalent payment approach to conventional lease analysis. *Financial Management* 18-27.

IRS Audit Guidelines. (1979) *Equipment Leasing* 8:8.

Johnson, Robert W., and Lewellen Wilbur G. (Sep 1972) Analysis of the lease or buy decision. *Journal of Finance* 815-23.

Keller, Thomas F., and Peterson Russell J. (Autumn 1974) Optimal financial structure, cost of capital, and the lease-or-buy decision. *Journal of Business, Finance and Accounting* 405-14.

Korn, Barry P. (Sep 1974) Leveraged leasing: A new way to manage credit. *Credit and Financial Management* 34-40.

LeWellen, Wilbur G., Long, Michael S. and McConnell, John J. (Jun 1976) Asset leasing in competitive capital markets. *Journal of Finance* 787-98.

Marcus, Robert P. (Dec 1976) The buy vs. lease decision revisited. *Financial Executive* 34-38.

Miller, Merton H., and Upton, Charles W. (Jun 1976) Leasing, buying, and the cost of capital services. *Journal of Finance* 761-86.

Mitchell, G.B. (Apr 1979) After-tax cost of leasing. *Accounting Review* 308-14.

Moyer, Charles R. (Summer 1975) Lease evaluation and the investment tax credit: A framework for analysis. *Financial Management* 39-44.

Sartoris, William L., and Paul, Ronda, S. (Summer 1973) Lease evaluation—Another capital budgeting decision. *Financial Management* 46-52.

Schmidt, Henry W., and Larsen, Richard G. (Oct 1974) Leveraged lease arrangements: Tax factors that contribute to their attractiveness. *The Journal of Taxation*

Smith, Pierce R. (Jul 1973) A straightforward approach to leveraged leasing. *The Journal of Commercial Bank Lending*

Straus, Lee E. (Jun 1974) Leveraged lease analysis: Some additional considerations. *The Journal of Commercial Bank Lending*

Vanderwicken, Peter (Nov 1973) The powerful logic of the leasing boom. *Fortune* *88* 132-36.

Weiss, Steven J., and McGugan, Vincent John (Nov-Dec 1973) The equipment leasing industry and emerging role of banking organizations. *New England Economic Review of the Federal Reserve Bank of Boston* 3-30.

Weston, J.F., and Craig, R. (Winter 1960) Understanding lease financing. *California Management Review* 67-75.

Wilson, C.J. (Dec 1973) The operating lease and the risk of obsolescence. *Management Accounting* 41-44.

Wyatt, Arthur R. (Apr 1974) Accounting for leveraged leases. *The Arthur Anderson Chronicle* 38-49.

Wyman, H.E. (Jul 1973) Financial lease evaluation under conditions of uncertainty. *Accounting Review* 489-93.

Index

Please send updated income Tax information as it is available, through June 1983.

Fill-in, detach, and mail this postpaid card today.

NAME_____

ADDRESS_____

CITY_____STATE _____ ZIP_____

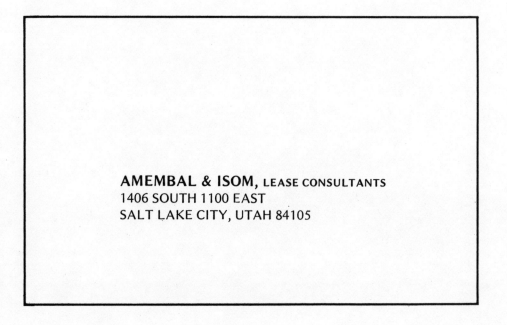

AMEMBAL & ISOM, LEASE CONSULTANTS
1406 SOUTH 1100 EAST
SALT LAKE CITY, UTAH 84105